TRAVEL WISE

GERMAN

Susanne Easterbrook

BARRON'S

Photo sources

M. Brick, Stuttgart: 20, 25; with kind permission of Deutsche Bahn AG: 41; S. Easterbrook, Sindelfingen: 22, 28, 63, 99, 191; G. Eichele-Malina, Steinheim: 152; IfA, Stuttgart: 11, 121, 124, 141, 159, 174; R. Kämpf, Stuttgart: 153, 156; J. Keute, Frankfurt: 126, 131, 133, 209; based on ALEXANDER Schulatlas, KLETT PERTHES, Stuttgart and Gotha 1993: inside front cover; Mairs Geographischer Verlag, Ostfildern: 49, 64/65, 81; Österreich Werbung, Frankfurt: 129, 147 (Markowitsch: 77; DeW/Lammerhuber: 92); A. Proctor, Stuttgart: 83; G. Reinboth, Stuttgart: 127, 134, 135, 149; Schweiz Tourismus, Frankfurt: 45, 68

© Ernst Klett Verlag GmbH,
Stuttgart, Federal Republic of Germany, 1997
The title of the German book is *Reiseworterbuch*

English version translated and edited by Kathleen Luft
Pronunciation by Paul Kingsbury

All inquiries should be addressed to:
Barron's Educational Series, Inc.
250 Wireless Boulevard
Hauppauge, NY 11788
http://www.barronseduc.com

Library of Congress Catalog Card No. 97-48408

International Standard Book No. 0-7641-0391-1 (book)
0-7641-7115-1 (package)

Library of Congress Cataloging-in-Publication Data

Easterbrook, Susanne.
[Reisewörterbuch. English & German]
Travelwise German / by Susanne Easterbrook ; [English version translated and edited by Kathleen Luft].
p.   cm.
ISBN 0-7641-0391-1 (bk.). — ISBN 0-7641-7115-1
(bk./cassette pkg.)
1. German language—Conversation and phrase books—English.
I. Title.
PF3121.E1613   1998   97-48408
438.3'421—dc21   CIP

Printed in Hong Kong
9 8 7 6 5 4 3 2 1

Contents

9   **Services** 191

10   **Health** 205

11   **A Business Trip** 223

Preface

Barron's *TravelWise German* is an invaluable aid when traveling in German-speaking countries. It will help you understand not only individual words, but whole phrases and set expressions. Useful tips and background information on lifestyles and customs will make your stay more enjoyable. Short dialogues not only show you what to say yourself, but enable you to understand better.

Barron's *TravelWise German* contains 11 practical chapters covering dozens of everyday situations during your travels abroad: from arriving at your destination to checking out of a hotel; from sampling the local cuisine to conversing with a new acquaintance. Each section lists the most important words and expressions and includes thematic word lists with additional useful terms. The mini-dictionary (German/English, English/German) contains additional words that you might encounter.

Also at the back of the book is a grammar section to help you understand the basic structure of the German language.

The color photos will give you an idea of some of the places to see and things to do in Germany, Austria, and Switzerland.

Pronunciation

Vowels			
Sound	**like**	**in**	**Word**
[ii]	ee	see	Vieh
[ih]	i	hit	mit
[ey]	ey	they	Weh
[eh]	e	bed	Zähne
[ə]	a	ago	zahle
[oo]	oo	boot	gut
[uh]	u	bull	Bulle
[oh]	o	ago	Boot
[o]	o	got	Gott
[ah]	a	father	Base
Special German vowels			
[œ]	e	net (but with rounded "kissing" lips)	können
[ew]	ee	feel (with "kissing" lips)	fühlen
If you have trouble pronouncing those sounds, NEVER replace them by [o/u]!! Don't say [Svool] for "schwül" [Svewl] (hot/humid), for example, because "schwul" means "gay."			
Diphthongs			
[ay]	y	by	bei
[au]	ou	house	Haus
[oy]	oy	boy	neu

Consonants			
Sound	**like**	**in**	**Word**
[b]	b	ball	Ball
[ç]	ti	almost as in "nation" but farther back (but not as far back as [x] below)	mich
[d]	d	down	danke
[f]	f	fine	fein Vater
[g]	g	give (never as in "George")	geben
[h]	h	house	Haus
[y]	y	yeah	ja
[k]	k	kindly	Kind
[l]	l	love	Liebe
[m]	m	mister	Mädchen
[n]	n	no	nein
[ŋ]	ng	longing	lang
[p]	p	pair	Paar
[r]	r	uvular or trilled r	warum
[s]	ss	missing	missen, Maß
[S]	sh	show	schon, Stein
[t]	t	table	Tisch
[v]	v	very	wo
[x]	ch	guttural, "clearing of the throat" sound as in Scottish Loch Ness	Loch
[z]	z	zero	sehr
[Z]	su	treasure	Garage
[ts]	ts	Patsy, its	Zeit, Blitz
[tS]	ch	check	deutsch

Other symbols:	
boldface	main stress

German stress is fairly predictable. For the most part, stress falls on the first syllable. Exceptions to this rule include many foreign words, verbs ending in -ieren, verbs with inseparable prefixes and words derived from them, as well as nouns and adjectives with the prefixes **be-** and **ge-**. Schwa [ə] is never stressed. In this guide, stress will only be marked when there is more than one stressable syllable in the word (i.e., more than one syllable containing a non-schwa vowel).

The Alphabet

A a	ah	J j	yot	S s	ehs
B b	bey	K k	kah	T t	tey
C c	tsey	L l	ehl	U u	oo
D d	dey	M m	ehm	V v	fau
E e	ey	N n	ehn	W w	vey
F f	ehf	O o	oh	X x	ihks
G g	gey	P p	pey	Y y	**ew**psihlon
H h	hah	Q q	koo	Z z	tseht
I i	ii	R r	ehr	ß	**ess**-tseht

Abbreviations

adj	Adjektiv, Eigenschaftswort	adjective
adv	Adverb, Umstandswort	adverb
conj	Konjunktion, Bindewort	conjunction
el	Elektrotechnik, Elektrizität	electricity
f	Femininum, weiblich	feminine gender
fam	Umgangssprache, familiär	familiar, colloquial
fig	bildlich, übertragen	figurative
m	Maskulinum, männlich	masculine gender
n	Neutrum, sächlich	neuter gender
pl	Plural, Mehrzahl	plural
poss prn	Possessivpronomen, besitzanzeigendes Fürwort	possessive pronoun
prp	Präposition, Verhältniswort	preposition
rel	kirchlich, geistlich	religious
sing	Singular, Einzahl	singular
s.o.	jemand	someone
s.th.	etwas	something
tele	Telekommunikation	telecommunications
v	Verb, Zeitwort	verb

Some Notes on Pronunciation

For the most part, German spelling is much more closely reflective of actual pronunciation than is English spelling. The pronunciation table in the Introduction will give you a good indication of the correspondences. There are, however, a few details that are not immediately obvious, dealing with the letters v, s, and r.

V is usually pronounced as [f], as in Vater [fahtər]. However, in many words recently imported into German (from English, usually) v is pronounced as [v]. For example, "Kurve," from English "curve" is pronounced [kuhrvə], not [kuhrfə].

S has some complex pronunciation issues. At the beginning of a word, when "s" stands before a vowel, it is pronounced as [z], as in "sein" [zayn] "to be." If it stands before a consonant, it is pronounced as [S], as in "Stein" [Stayn] "stone." The cluster "sch" is always pronounced as [S], as in "Schein" [Sayn] "light." A double "ss" or "ß" is always pronounced as [s]. The biggest complexities arise when an "s" comes in the middle of a word. If the "s" lies at an obvious compound boundary, the same rules as above apply; the difficulty lies in deciding whether the "s" is at the end of the first compound element or at the beginning of the second. Otherwise, "s" is usually pronounced as [s]. As you grow more familiar with German you will be able to decide how "s" is to be properly pronounced. This guide shows the syllabification and pronunciation of s's.

R is even more complex. When it occurs before a vowel, it is pronounced as either an apical or uvular trill. The former means the tip of the tongue is trilled against the roof of the mouth, as in saying "d-d-d-d-d-d-d-d" very quickly (or exactly like a Spanish trilled "r"). The latter, a "uvular" trill, takes place at the very back of the mouth. That little blob of flesh hanging down at the back of the mouth is the uvula, and it is trilled by bringing the back of the tongue close to but not touching the uvula. It can take some practice, and must be differentiated from the velar fricative [x]. The uvular trill for [r] is the same as is used in France. There is a slow movement in central Europe away from the apical trill towards the uvular; Germany exhibits both. Thus neither pronunciation is incorrect, but the apical trill is less common.

When R occurs after a vowel, however, the situation changes dramatically. As in many parts of England and the Northeastern US, post-vocalic "r"s are not pronounced at all. The best approximation of what happens to the "r"s is that they are replaced by a schwa [ə]. Thus "sehr" "very" is transcribed as [zehr] but is more properly pronounced as [zehə]. Rs have been left in the pronunciation guide in post-vocalic position to aid the readability of the transcriptions.

Some confusion can arise when an R occurs both before and after a vowel. Should it be dropped, or trilled? In general, any time an R occurs before a vowel it will be pronounced as an [r]. The exception lies at word compound boundaries, where an R is not resyllabified into the pre-vocalic position but rather remains post-vocalic. For example, "veraltet" "antiquated" is composed of the preverb "ver" followed by the adjective "altet." The two are pronounced basically as if they were independent words, not a single word, so the R at the end of "ver" is dropped. These types of boundaries are noted in the pronunciations with syllable breaks: [fehr-ahltət]. If an R is followed by a consonant or a hyphen (indicating a syllable boundary) it should be dropped.

Common Abbreviations

A	Österreich	Austria
Abi	Abitur	school-leaving exam (=graduation from secondary school)
ADAC	Allgemeiner deutscher Automobilclub	German automobile association
AG	Aktiengesellschaft	(stock) corporation
ATS	Österreichischer Schilling	Austrian shilling
b. w.	bitte wenden	p.t.o.
BRD	Bundesrepublik Deutschland	German Federal Republic
bzw.	beziehungsweise	or, respectively
°C	(Grad) Celsius	(degrees) Celsius/Centigrade
CH	Schweiz (Helvetia)	Switzerland
CHF	Schweizer Franken	Swiss francs
D	Deutschland	Germany
d. h.	das heißt	i.e.
DB	Deutsche Bahn	German railroad
DJH	Deutsches Jugendherbergswerk	German Youth Hostel Association
DM	Deutsche Mark	German mark
Dr. med.	Doktor der Medizin	M.D.
Dr. phil.	Doktor der Philosophie	Ph.D.
DRK	Deutsches Rotes Kreuz	German Red Cross
etw.	etwas	something
EU	Europäische Union	European Union
GmbH	Gesellschaft mit beschränkter Haftung	limited liability company
H	Haltestelle	bus or streetcar stop
jdm.	jemandem	for, to someone
jdn.	jemanden	someone
Jh.	Jahrhundert	century
JH	Jugendherberge	youth hostel
Kfz	Kraftfahrzeug	motor vehicle
LKW	Lastkraftwagen	truck
n. Chr.	nach Christi Geburt	AD
Nr.	Nummer	number
ÖBB	Österreichische Bundesbahn	Austrian railroad
Pf.	Pfennig	pfennig
PKW	Personenkraftwagen	car/auto
PS	Pferdestärke	horsepower
Rel.	Religion	religion
s.	siehe	viz.
S.	Seite	page
SB	Selbstbedienung	self-service
SBB	Schweizer Bundesbahnen	Swiss railroad
Std.	Stunde	hour
Str.	Straße	street
StVO	Straßenverkehrsordnung	traffic regulations
Tel.	Telefon	telephone
tgl.	täglich	daily
TÜV	Technischer Überwachungsverein	Technical Control Board, organization that checks the safety of motor vehicles
u.A.w.g.	um Antwort wird gebeten	r.s.v.p.
usw.	und so weiter	etc.
v. Chr.	vor Christi Geburt	BC
z. B.	zum Beispiel	e.g.
z. Hd. v.	zu Händen von	attn.

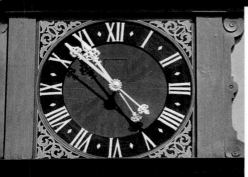

Frequently Used Expressions

Oft gesagt und oft gehört

Yes.	Ja. [yah]
No.	Nein. [nayn]
Please.	Bitte. [bihtə]

> *On its own, "bitte" expresses a request or is said in response to somebody saying "thank you." "Bitte schön" translates as "here you are" or "you're welcome," whereas "wie bitte?" expresses lack of understanding or embarrassment ("pardon?").*
> *"Danke" on its own means "thank you." But be careful: if someone offers you something and you reply with "danke," this will be interpreted as meaning "no, thank you." To avoid misunderstandings, say "ja bitte" (for "yes, please"/"thanks") and "nein danke" or "danke" (for "no, thanks").*

Thank you.	Danke. [dahŋkə]
You're welcome.	Bitte schön. [bihtə Sœn]
(I beg your) Pardon?	Wie bitte? [vii bihtə]
Of course.	Selbstverständlich. [zehlpst-fehr-**Stehnt**-liç]
Agreed!/All right!	Einverstanden! [**ayn**-fehr-Stahn-dən]
OK!	In Ordnung! [ihn **ord**-nuhŋ]
Excuse me.	Verzeihung! [fehr-**tsay**-uhŋ]
Just a minute, please.	Einen Augenblick, bitte. [aynən **augən**-blihk, bitə]
That's enough!	Genug! [gənuhk]
Help!	Hilfe! [hihlfə]
How?	Wie? [vii]
How long?	Wie lange? [vii lahŋgə]
How many?	Wie viele? [vii fiilə]
How much?	Wie viel? [vii fiil]
What?	Was? [vahs]
What ... for?	Wofür?/ Wozu? [voh-**fewr**, voh-**tsoo**]
When?	Wann? [vahn]
Where?	Wo? [voh]

Where's / Where are …?	Wo ist / Wo sind …? [voh ihst, voh zihnt]
Where … from?	Woher? [voh-**hehr**]
Where … to?	Wohin? [voh-**hihn**]
Which?	Welcher/Welche/Welches? [vehlçər, vehlçə, vehlçəs]
Who?	Wer? [vehr]
Whom?	Wen? [veyn]
Who … to?/To whom?	Wem? [veym]
Why?	Warum?, Weshalb? [vah-**ruhm**, vehs-**hahlp**]
I'd like …	Ich möchte … [ihç mœçtə]
Is there …?/Are there …?	Gibt es …? [gihpt ehs]

Numbers/Measures/Weights

Zahlen/Maße/Gewichte

0	null [nuhl]
1	eins [ayns]
2	zwei [tsvay]

> "Zwo" [tsvoh] *is sometimes used when speaking to distinguish "zwei" from "drei."*

3	drei [dray]
4	vier [fiir]
5	fünf [fewnf]
6	sechs [zehks]
7	sieben [ziibən]
8	acht [ahxt]
9	neun [noyn]
10	zehn [tseyn]
11	elf [ehlf]
12	zwölf [tsvœlf]

13	dreizehn [**dray**-tseyn]
14	vierzehn [**fiir**-tseyn]
15	fünfzehn [**fewnf**-tseyn]
16	sechzehn [**zehx**-tseyn]
17	siebzehn [**ziip**-tseyn]
18	achtzehn [**ax**-tseyn]
19	neunzehn [**noyn**-tseyn]
20	zwanzig [**tsvahn**-tsihç]
21	einundzwanzig [**ayn**-uhnt-tsvahn-tsihç]
22	zweiundzwanzig [**tsvay**-uhnt-tsvahn-tsihç]
23	dreiundzwanzig [**dray**-uhnt-tsvahn-tsihç]
24	vierundzwanzig [**fiir**-uhnt-tsvahn-tsihç]
30	dreißig [**drey**-sihç]
40	vierzig [**fiir**-tsihç]
50	fünfzig [**fewnf**-tsihç]
60	sechzig [**zehx**-tsihç]
70	siebzig [**ziip**-tsihç]
80	achtzig [**ax**-tsihç]
90	neunzig [**noyn**-tsihç]
100	(ein)hundert [(**ayn**)-**huhn**-dərt]
101	hundert(und)eins [huhn-dərt-(uhnt)-**ayns**]
200	zweihundert [**tsvay**-huhn-dərt]
300	dreihundert [**dray**-huhn-dərt]
1,000	(ein)tausend [(**ayn**)-**tau**-zənt]
2,000	zweitausend [**tsvay**-tau-zənt]
3,000	dreitausend [**dray**-tau-zənt]
10,000	zehntausend [**tseyn**-tau-zənt]
100,000	hunderttausend [**huhn**-dərt-**tau**-zənt]
1,000,000	Million [mihl-**yohn**]
1st	erste(r, s) [ehr-stə, ehr-stər, ehr-stəs]
2nd	zweite(r, s) [tsvay-tə, -tər, -təs]

3rd	dritte(r, s) [drih-tə, -tər, -təs]
4th	vierte(r, s) [fiir-tə, -tər, -təs]
5th	fünfte(r, s) [fewnf-tə, -tər, -tes]
6th	sechste(r, s) [zehks-tə, -tər, -təs]
7th	siebte(r, s) [ziip-tə, -tər, -təs]
8th	achte(r, s) [ahx-tə, -tər, -təs]
9th	neunte(r, s) [noyn-tə, -tər, -təs]
10th	zehnte(r, s) [tsehn-tə, -tər, -təs]
1/2	halb [hahlp]
1/3	drittel [drih-təl]
1/4	viertel [fiir-təl]
3/4	dreiviertel [**dray**-fiir-təl]
3.5%	3,5 % (dreikommafünf Prozent) [**dray**-kom-ə-fewnf proh-**tsehnt**]
27°C	27 °C [**ziib**-ən-uhnt-tsvahn-siç tsehl-zyuhs]
−5°C	minus 5 Grad [**mii**-nuhs fewnf graht]
1998	neunzehnhundertachtundneunzig [**noyn**-tseyn-huhn-dərt-axt-uhnt-**noyn**-tsiç]
millimeter	der Millimeter [dehr mihl-ih-**mey**-tər]
centimeter	der Zentimeter [dehr tsehn-tih-**mey**-tər]
meter	der Meter [dehr **mey**-tər]
kilometer	der Kilometer [dehr kii-loh-**mey**-tər]
mile	die Meile [dii maylə]
square meter	der Quadratmeter [dehr kvah-**draht**-mey-tər]
square kilometer	der Quadratkilometer [dehr kvah-**draht**-kii-loh-mey-tər]
are (100 m^2)	das/der Ar [dahs/dehr ahr]
hectare (10,000 m^2)	das/der Hektar [dahs/dehr hehk-tahr]
liter	der Liter [dehr lii-tər]
gram	das Gramm [dahs grahm]
kilogram	das Kilo [dahs kii-loh]
pound	das Pfund [dahs pfuhnt]
a dozen	ein Dutzend [ayn **duh**-tsehnt]

Weights and Measures

German-speaking countries use the metric system when referring to distances, weights, and quantities. The decimal point is represented by a comma.

1 Zentimeter (cm)	≅ 0.39 inches
1 Meter (m) = 100 cm	≅ 1.09 yards / 3.28 feet / 39.3 inches
1 Kilometer (km) = 1000 m	≅ 0.62 miles / 1,090 yards
1 Liter (l)	≅ 2.11 pints/1.05 quarts/0.26 gallons
1 Gramm (g)	≅ 0.035 ounces
1 Kilogramm (kg) = 1000 g	≅ 35 ounces/2.205 pounds
1 Zentner = 50 kg	≅ 112 pounds (metric hundredweight)

Rule of thumb for converting miles and kilometers:

$$\frac{miles \times 8}{5} = kilometers \qquad \frac{kilometers \times 5}{8} = miles$$

Expressions of Time

Zeitangaben

Telling Time	Uhrzeit
What time is it?	Wie viel Uhr ist es? [vii fiil oor ihst ehs]
Can you tell me the time, please?	Können Sie mir bitte sagen, wie spät es ist? [kœnən zii miir bihtə zahgən, vii Speht ehs ihst]
It's (exactly/about) …	Es ist (genau/ungefähr) … [ehs ihst (gənau / uhŋ-gə-fehr)]
three o'clock.	3 Uhr. [dray oor]
five past three.	5 nach 3. [fewnf nahx dray]
ten past three.	3 Uhr 10. [dray oor tseyn]
quarter past three.	Viertel nach 3. [fiirtəl nahx dray]
half past three.	halb 4. [hahlp fiir]

quarter to four.	Viertel vor 4. [fiirtəl fohr fiir]
five to four.	5 vor 4. [fewnf fohr fiir]
one o'clock.	1 Uhr. [ayns oor]
noon.	12 Uhr mittag. [tsvœlf oor **mih**-tahk]
midnight.	Mitternacht. [**mih**-tər-nahxt]
Is this clock right?	Geht diese Uhr richtig? [geyt diizəs oor **rihx**-tiç]
It's fast/slow.	Sie geht vor/nach. [zii geyt fohr / nahx]
It's late.	Es ist spät. [ehs ihst Speht]
It's too early.	Es ist zu früh. [ehs ihst tsoo frew]
What time?/ When?	Um wie viel Uhr? [uhm vii fiil oor]/ Wann? [vahn]
At one o'clock.	Um 1 Uhr. [uhm ayns oor]
At two o'clock.	Um 2 Uhr. [uhm tsvay oor]
At about four o'clock.	Gegen 4 Uhr. [geygən fiir oor]
In an hour.	In einer Stunde. [ihn aynər Stuhndə]
In two hours.	In zwei Stunden. [ihn tsvay Stuhn-dən]
Not before nine A.M.	Nicht vor 9 Uhr morgens. [nihxt fohr noyn oor **mor**-gəns]
After eight P.M.	Nach 8 Uhr abends. [nahx axt oor **ah**-behnts]
Between three and four.	Zwischen 3 und 4. [**tsvih**-Sən dray uhnt fiir]
How long?	Wie lange? [vii lahŋgə]
For two hours.	Zwei Stunden (lang). [tsvay Stuhn-dən (lahŋ)]
From ten to eleven.	Von 10 bis 11. [fohn tseyn bihs ehlf]
Till five o'clock.	Bis 5 Uhr. [bihs fewnf oor]
Since when?	Seit wann? [zayt vahn]
Since eight A.M.	Seit 8 Uhr morgens.[zayt ahxt oor **mor**-gəns]
For half an hour.	Seit einer halben Stunde.[zayt aynər halbən Stuhndə]
For a week.	Seit acht Tagen. [zayt ahxt tahgən]

Other Statements of Time	**Andere Zeitangaben**
in the evening	abends [**ah**-bənts]
every half hour	alle halbe Stunde [ahlə hahlbə **Stuhn**də]
every other day	alle zwei Tage [ahlə tsvay tahgə]
on Sunday	am Sonntag [ahm **zohn**-tahk]
on the weekend	am Wochenende [ahm **voh**-ən-ehndə]
soon	bald [bahlt]
this week	diese Woche [diizə vohxə]
about noon/midday/ lunchtime	gegen Mittag [geygən **miht**-tahk]
yesterday	gestern [**gehs**-tehrn]
today	heute [hoytə]
this morning	heute Morgen [hoytə **mor**-gən]
this evening	heute Abend [hoytə **ah**-bənt]
last night	gestern Abend [**gehs**-tehrn **ah**-bənt]
in two weeks	in 14 Tagen [ihn fiir-tseyn **tahg**ən]
within a week	innerhalb einer Woche [**ihn**ərhahlp aynər vohxə]
every day	jeden Tag [yeydən tahk]
now	jetzt [yehtst]
recently	kürzlich [**kewrts**-lihç]
last Monday	letzten Montag [lehts-tən **mohn**-tahk]
sometimes	manchmal [**mahnx**-mahl]
at noon, at lunchtime	mittags [**miht**-tahks]
tomorrow	morgen [**mor**-gən]
tomorrow morning	morgen früh [**mor**-gən frew]
tomorrow evening	morgen Abend [**mor**-gən ah-bənt]
in the morning	morgens [**mor**-gəns]
in the afternoon	nachmittags [**nahç**-miht-tahks]
next year	nächstes Jahr [nehkstəs yahr]
at night	nachts [nahxts]
every hour, hourly	stündlich [**stewnd**-lihç]
every day, daily	täglich [**tehk**-lihç]

during the day	tagsüber [**tahks**-ewbər]
the day after tomorrow	übermorgen [**ewb**ər-mor-gən]
about this time	um diese Zeit [uhm diizə tsayt]
from time to time	von Zeit zu Zeit [fohn tsayt tsoo tsayt]
ten minutes ago	vor zehn Minuten [fohr tseyn mih-**noo**-tən]
the day before yesterday	vorgestern [**fohr**-gehs-tehrn]
in the morning, every morning	vormittags [**fohr**-miht-tahks]

Days of the Week	**Wochentage**
Monday	Montag [**mon**-tahk]
Tuesday	Dienstag [**diins**-tahk]
Wednesday	Mittwoch [**miht**-vohx]
Thursday	Donnerstag [**don**ərstahk]
Friday	Freitag [**fray**-tahk]
Saturday	Samstag [**zahms**-tahk], Sonnabend [**zon**-ah-bənt]
Sunday	Sonntag [**zon**-tahk]

Months of the Year	**Monate**
January	Januar [**yahn**-oo-ahr], (Austria) Jänner [**yehn**ər]
February	Februar [**Feh**-broo-ahr]
March	März [mehrts]
April	April [ahp-rihl]
May	Mai [may]
June	Juni [**yoo**-nii], Juno [**yoo**-noh]

"Juno" is sometimes used when speaking instead of "Juni" to distinguish it from "Juli."

July	Juli [**yoo**-lii]
August	August [au-**goost**]

September	September [zehp-**tehm**-bər]
October	Oktober [ok-**toh**-bər]
November	November [noh-**vehm**-bər]
December	Dezember [dey-**tsehm**-bər]

Seasons	**Jahreszeiten**
spring	der Frühling [dehr **frew**-lihŋ]
summer	der Sommer [dehr zohmər]
autumn/fall	der Herbst [dehr hehrpst]
winter	der Winter [dehr **vihnt**ər]

| **Holidays** | **Feiertage** |

In addition to the holidays mentioned below, there are various local religious holidays.

New Year's Day	Neujahr [**noy**-yahr]
Swiss Holiday	Berchtoldstag [**behrç**-tolts-tahk] (2. Januar)
Epiphany	Erscheinungsfest (6. Januar) [ehr-**Say**-nuhŋs-fehst]
carnival, Shrovetide	Fasching [**fah**-Sihŋ], Fasnacht [**fahs**-nahxt]
Good Friday	Karfreitag [kahr-fray-tahk]
Easter	Ostern [**oh**-stehrn]
Easter Monday	Ostermontag [oh-stehrn **mon**-tahk]
Labor Day *(celebrated on May 1st in Germany)*	Tag der Arbeit [tahk dehr **ahr**-bayt] (1. Mai)
Whitsun(tide), Pentecost	Pfingsten [**pfihŋ**-stən]
Ascension Day	Christi Himmelfahrt [krihstii **hihm**əlfahrt]
Corpus Christi	Fronleichnam [fron-**layç**-nahm]
German Unification Day	Tag der Einheit [tahk dehr **ayn**-hayt] 3. Oktober

Austrian National Day	26. Oktober
Swiss National Day	1. August
All Saints' Day	Allerheiligen [ahlər-hay-lih-gən]
Christmas Eve	Heiliger Abend [hay-lih-gər **ah**-bənt]
Christmas	Weihnachten [**vay**-nahx-tən]
Christmas Day	1. Weihnachtsfeiertag [ehrstər **vay**-nahxts-fay(ə)r-tahk]
Day after Christmas (26th December)	2. Weihnachtsfeiertag [tsvaytər **vay**-nahts-fay(ə)r-tahk]
New Year's Eve	Silvesterabend [zihl-**vehs**-tər-ah-bənt]

The Date — Datum

What's the date (today)?	Welches Datum ist heute? [vehlçəs **dah**-tuhm ist hoytə]
Today's the first of May (May the first).	Heute ist der 1. Mai. [hoytə ist dehr ehrstə may]

The Weather

Wetter

What's the weather going to be like today?	Wie wird das Wetter heute? [vii vihrt dahs vehtər hoytə]
It's going to be fine/bad/changeable.	Es wird schönes/schlechtes/unbeständiges Wetter geben. [ehs vihrt Sœnəs / Slehxtəs / **uhn**-bə-Stehn-dih-gəs vehtər gey-bən]
It's going to stay fine.	Es bleibt schön. [ehs blaypt Sœn]
It's going to get warmer/colder.	Es wird wärmer/kälter. [ehs vihrt vehr-mər / kehl-tər]
It's going to rain.	Es wird regnen. [ehs vihrt rehg-nən]
It's going to snow.	Es wird schneien. [ehs vihrt Sney-ən]
It's cold/hot/humid.	Es ist kalt/heiß/schwül. [ehs ihst kahlt / hays / Svewl]
There's going to be a thunderstorm.	Es zieht ein Gewitter auf. [ehs tsiit ayn gə-vihtər auf]
It's foggy.	Es ist neblig. [ehs ist **neyb**-liç]
It's windy.	Es ist windig. [ehs ihst **vihn**-dihç]

The sun's shining.	Die Sonne scheint. [dii zonə Saynt]
The sky's clear/overcast.	Der Himmel ist wolkenlos/bedeckt. [dehr hihməl ihst **vol**-kən-lohs / bə-dehkt]
What's the temperature today?	Wie viel Grad haben wir heute? [vii fiil graht hah-bən vihr hoytə]
It's twenty degrees (Centigrade).	Es ist 20 Grad (Celsius). [ehs ihst **tsvahn**-tsihç graht (**tsehl**-zyuhs)]
What are the roads like in …?	Wie ist der Straßenzustand in …? [vii ihst dehr **Strah**-sən-tsoo-Stahnt ihn]
The roads are icy.	Die Straßen sind glatt. [dii Strah-sən zihnt glaht]
Visibility is only 20 m/less than 50 m.	Die Sicht beträgt nur 20 Meter/weniger als 50 Meter. [dii zihxt bə-treykt nuhr **tsvahn**-zihç **mey**-tər / **vey**-nih-gər ahlz **fewnf**-tsihç **mey**-tər]
You need snow chains.	Schneeketten sind erforderlich. [**Sney**-keht-ən zihnt ehr-**fohr**-dər-lihç]

Word List: Weather

air	die Luft [dii luhft]
air pressure	der Luftdruck [dehr **luhft**-druhk]
anticyclone	das Hoch [dahs hohx]
atmospheric pressure	der Luftdruck [dehr **luhft**-druhk]
barometer	das Barometer [dahs ba-roh-**mey**-tər]
black ice	das Glatteis [dahs **glaht**-ays]
bright	heiter [haytər]
calm	windstill [**vihnt**-Stihl]
changeable	wechselhaft [**vehk**-səl-hahft]
clear	sonnig [**zon**-ihç]
clear (night)	sternenklar [**Stehr**-nən-klahr]
climate	das Klima [dahs kliimə]
cloud	die Wolke [dii volkə]
cloudburst	der Wolkenbruch [dehr **volk**ənbruhx]

cloudy	bewölkt [bəvœlkt]
cold	kalt [kahlt]
damp	feucht [foyçt]
dawn	die Morgendämmerung [dii **mor**-gən-deh-mə-ruhŋ]
depression	das Tief [dahs tiif]
drizzle	der Nieselregen [dehr **nii**-zəl-rey-gən]
dry	trocken [trok-ən]
dusk	die Abenddämmerung [dii **ah**-bənt-deh-mə-ruhŋ]
flooding, floods	die Überschwemmung [dii ewbər-**Sveh**-muhŋ]
fog	der Nebel [dehr ney-bəl]
frost	der Frost [dehr frost]
glare ice	das Glatteis [dahs **glaht**-ays]
gust of wind	die Bö [dii bœ]
gusty	böig [**bœ**-ihç]
hail	der Hagel [dehr hahgəl]
hailstone	der Graupel [dehr grau-pəl]
hazy	diesig [**dii**-zihç]
heat	die Hitze [dii hihtsə]
heatwave	die Hitzewelle [dii **hihts**əvehlə]
high	das Hoch [dahs hohx]
high tide	die Flut [dii floot]
hot	heiß [hays]
humid	schwül [Svewl]
ice	das Eis [dahs ays]
lightning	der Blitz [dehr blihts]
low	das Tief [dahs tiif]
low tide	die Ebbe [dii ehbə]
powder snow	der Pulverschnee [dehr **puhl**-fər-Sney]
rain	der Regen [dehr rey-gən]
rain(fall)	der Niederschlag [dehr **niid**ər-Slahk]
rainy	regnerisch [**rehg**-nə-rihS]
shower	der Regenschauer [dehr **rey**-gən-Sau-ər]

snow	der Schnee [dehr Sney]
snowstorm	der Schneesturm [dehr **Sney**-Stoorm]
sun	die Sonne [dii zonə]
sunny	sonnig [**zon**-ihç]
sunrise	der Sonnenaufgang [dehr **zon**-ən-auf-gahŋ]
sunset	der Sonnenuntergang [dehr **zon**-ən-uhn-tər-gahŋ]
temperature	die Temperatur [dii tehm-pehr-ə-**toor**]
thaw	das Tauwetter [dahs **tau**-vehtər]
thunder	der Donner [dehr donər]
variable	wechselhaft [**vehks**əlhahft]
velocity	die Windstärke [dii **vihnt**-Stehrkə]
warm	warm [wahrm]
weather forecast	die Wettervorhersage [dii **vehtə**r-fohr-hehr-zahgə]
weather report	der Wetterbericht [dehr **vehtə**r-bərihçt]
wet	nass [nahs]
wind	der Wind [dehr vihnt]
wind-force	die Windstärke [dii **vihnt**-Stehrkə]
windy	windig [**vihn**-diç]

Word List: Colors

beige	beige [beyZ]
black	schwarz [Svahrts]
blue	blau [blau]
brown	braun [braun]
colored	farbig [**fahr**-bihç]
plain	einfarbig [**ayn**-fahr-bihç]
multicolored	mehrfarbig [**mehr**-fahr-bihç]
dark ...	dunkel... [**duhŋ**-kəl]
gold(en)	golden [gohl-dən]
green	grün [grewn]
gray	grau [grau]

light …	hell… [hehl]
lilac	lila [liilə]
orange	orange [oh-**rahnZ**]
pink	rosa [rohzə]
purple	lila [liilə]
red	rot [roht]
silver	silbern [**zihl**-behrn]
violet	violett [vii-oh-**leht**]
white	weiß [vays]
yellow	gelb [gehlp]

In German there are two ways of saying "you." In formal situations (and when in doubt) you should use "Sie" [zii] (both singular and plural). In informal situations (or with family, friends, and children) or when you are on first-name terms with someone you can use "du" [doo] (singular) and "ihr" [iir] (plural). In general, adults use first names only with someone they know well.

Saying Hello/Introductions/Getting Acquainted

Begrüßung/Vorstellung/Bekanntschaft

Good morning/afternoon!	Guten Morgen/Tag! [gootən **mor**-gən / tahk]
Good evening.	Guten Abend! [gootən ah-bənt]
Hello/Hi!	Hallo!/Grüß dich! [**hah**-loh / grews dihç]
What's your name?	Wie ist Ihr Name? / Wie heißt du? [vii ihst iir nahmə / vii hayst doo]
My name's …	Mein Name ist …/Ich heiße … [mayn nahmə ihst / ihç haysə]
How do you do.	Angenehm. [**ahn**-gə-neym]
Pleased to meet you.	Es freut mich, Sie kennenzulernen. [ehs froyt mihç zii **kehn**ən-zuh-lehrnən]
May I introduce you?	Darf ich bekannt machen? [dahrf ihç bə**kahnt** mahxən]
This is …	Das ist … [dahs ihst]
Mrs./Ms. X.	Frau X. [frau]
Miss X.	Fräulein X. [**froy**-layn]
Mr. X.	Herr X. [hehr]
my husband.	mein Mann. [mayn mahn]
my wife.	meine Frau. [maynə frau]
my son.	mein Sohn. [mayn zohn]
my daughter.	meine Tochter. [maynə toxtər]
my brother/sister.	mein Bruder/meine Schwester. [mayn broodər / maynə **Sveh**stər]
my boyfriend/girlfriend.	mein Freund/meine Freundin. [mayn froynt / maynə **froyn**-dihn]
my colleague.	mein Kollege/meine Kollegin. [mayn koh-**leh**gə / maynə koh-**leh**-gihn]

How are you?	Wie geht es Ihnen?/Wie geht's? [vii geyt ehs iinən / vii geyts]
Fine, thanks. And you?	Danke. Und Ihnen/dir? [dahŋkə. uhnt iinən / diir]
Where are you from?	Woher kommen Sie/kommst du? [**voh**-hehr komən zii / komst doo]
I'm from …	Ich bin aus … [ihç bihn aus]
Have you been here long?	Sind Sie/Bist du schon lange hier? [zihnt zii / bihst doo Sohn lahŋgə hiir]
I've been here since …	Ich bin seit … hier. [ihç bihn zayt … hiir]
How long are you staying?	Wie lange bleiben Sie/bleibst du? [vii lahŋgə blaybən zii / blaypst doo]
Is this your first time here?	Sind Sie/Bist du zum ersten Mal hier? [zihnt zii / bihst doo zuhm ehrstən mahl hiir]
Are you on your own?	Sind Sie/Bist du allein? [zihnt zii / bihst doo əlayn]
No, I'm …	Nein, ich bin … [nayn ihç bihn]
with my family.	mit meiner Familie hier. [miht maynər fah-**mihl**-yə hiir]
with friends.	mit Freunden unterwegs. [miht froyndən uhntər**vehks**]
Are you staying at the Astoria Hotel/at the campground, too?	Sind Sie/Bist du auch im Hotel Astoria/auf dem Campingplatz …? [zihnt zii / bihst doo aux ihm hoh-**tehl** ah-**stor**-yə / auf dehm **kehm**-pihŋ-plahts]

Traveling Alone/Making a Date

Alleine unterwegs / Verabredung

Are you waiting for someone?	Warten Sie/Wartest du auf jemanden? [vahrtən zii / **vahr**-tehst doo auf **yey**mahndən]
Do you have any plans for tomorrow?	Haben Sie/Hast du für morgen schon etwas vor? [hahbən zii / hahst doo fewr mor-gən Sohn **eht**vahs fohr]

Shall we go together?	Wollen wir zusammen hingehen? [volən viir tsuh-**zahm**ən **hihn**geyən]
Shall we go out together this evening?	Wollen wir heute Abend miteinander ausgehen? [volən viir hoytə ah-bənt miht-ayn-**ahn**dər **aus**-gey-ən]
May I invite you for a meal?	Darf ich Sie/dich zum Essen einladen? [dahrf ihç zii / dihç tsuhm ehsən **ayn**-lahdən]
When/Where shall we meet?	Wann/Wo treffen wir uns? [vahn / voh trehfən viir uhns]
May I pick you up?	Darf ich Sie/dich abholen? [dahrf ihç zii / dihç **ahp**-hohlən]
When shall I come (by)?	Wann soll ich (vorbei-) kommen? [vahn zol ihç (fohr-**bay**) komən]
Let's meet at 9 o'clock …	Treffen wir uns um 9 Uhr … [trehfən viir uhns uhm noyn oor]
in front of the movie theater.	vor dem Kino. [fohr deym **kii**-noh]
at … Square.	auf dem … Platz. [auf dehm … plahts]
in the café/coffee shop.	im Café. [ihm kah-fey]

Are you married?	Sind Sie / Bist du verheiratet? [zihnt zii / bihst doo fehr-**hay**-rah-tət]

Do you have a boyfriend/girlfriend?	Hast du einen Freund/eine Freundin? [hahst doo aynən froynt / aynə **froyn**-dihn]
Can I take you home?	Darf ich Sie/dich nach Hause bringen? [dahrf ihç zii / dihç nahx hauzə brihŋən]
I'll take you as far as the …	Ich bringe Sie/dich noch zum/zur … [ihç brihŋə zii / dihç nox tsuhm / tsuhr]
Would you like to come in for a (cup of) coffee?	Möchten Sie/Möchtest du auf einen Kaffee hereinkommen? [mœçtən zii / **mœç**-tehst doo auf (aynən) **kah**-fey heh-**rayn**-komən]
Can I see you again?	Kann ich Sie/dich wieder sehen? [kahn ihç zii / dihç viidər zey-ən]
I hope I'll see you again soon.	Ich hoffe, Sie/dich bald wieder zu sehen. [ihç hohfə zii / dihç bahlt viidər tsuh zey-ən]
Thank you very much for a pleasant evening.	Vielen Dank für den netten Abend. [fiilən dahŋk fewr deyn nehtən ah-bənt]
Please leave me alone.	Lassen Sie / Lass mich bitte in Ruhe! [lahsən zii / lahs mihç bihtə ihn roo-ə]
Go away!/Get lost!	Hau ab! [hau ahp]

A Visit

Besuch

Excuse me, does Mr./Mrs./Ms. X live here?	Entschuldigen Sie, wohnt hier Herr/Frau X? [ehnt-**Suhl**-dih-gən zii, vohnt hiir hehr / frau]
No, he's/she's moved.	Nein, er/sie ist umgezogen. [nayn, ehr/zii ihst **uhm**-gətsohgən]
Do you know where he's/she's living now?	Wissen Sie, wo er/sie jetzt wohnt? [vihsən zii, voh ehr/zii yehtst vohnt]
Can I speak to Mr./Mrs./Ms. X, please?	Kann ich mit Herrn/Frau X sprechen? [kahn ihç miht hehrn / frau iks Sprehçən]
When will he/she be home?	Wann ist er/sie zu Hause? [vahn ihst ehr/zii tsoo hauzə]

Can I leave a message?	Kann ich eine Nachricht hinterlassen? [kahn ihç aynə **nahx**-rihxt hihntərlahsən]
I'll come back later.	Ich komme später noch einmal vorbei. [ihç komə Speytər nox **ayn**-mahl fohr-**bay**]
Come in.	Kommen Sie/Komm herein. [komən zii / kom heh-**rayn**]
Please sit down.	Nehmen Sie/Nimm bitte Platz. [neymən zii / nihm bihtə plahts]
Paul asked me to give you his regards.	Ich soll Sie/dich von Paul grüßen. [ihç zol zii / dihç fohn pol grewsən]
What can I offer you to drink?	Was darf ich Ihnen/dir zu trinken anbieten? [vahs dahrf ihç iinən / diir tsuh trihŋkən **ahn**-biitən]
Please help yourself!	Bitte greifen Sie zu! / Bitte greif zu! [bihtə grayfən zii tsuh / bihtə grayf tsuh]
Cheers!/Here's to you!	Zum Wohl!/Prosit!/ Prost! [tsuhm vohl / **proh**-siht / prohst]
Can't you stay for lunch/dinner?	Können Sie/Kannst du nicht zum Mittagessen/Abendessen bleiben? [kœnən zii / kahnst doo nihçt tsuhm **mih**-tahkehsən **ah**-bəntehsən blaybən]
Thank you. I'd like to stay, if I'm not causing you any bother.	Vielen Dank. Ich bleibe gern, wenn ich nicht störe. [fiilən dahŋk. ihç blaybə gehrn, vehn ihç nihçt Stœrə]
I'm sorry, but I have to go now.	Es tut mir Leid, aber ich muss jetzt gehen. [ehs toot miir layt, ahbər ihç muhs yehtst gey-ən]

Saying Goodbye

Abschied

Goodbye/Bye-bye!	Auf Wiedersehen! [auf **viid**-ərzey-ən]
See you soon!	Bis bald! [bihs bahlt]
See you later!	Bis später! [bihs Speytər]
See you tomorrow!	Bis morgen! [bihs mor-gən]

Everyone knows "Auf Wiedersehen" is a German way of saying "goodbye." But you will often hear it shortened to "Wiederseh'n." Regional variations—and also less formal—are "Ade" (South German), "Ciao" (from Italian), or simply "Tschüs." "See you later" equals "Also bis dann," with the time of the next meeting being left open. To say goodbye on the phone, you would say "Auf Wiederhören" or just "Wiederhör'n."

Good night!	Gute Nacht! [gootə nahxt]
Bye!/So long!	Tschüs! [tSews]
All the best!	Alles Gute! [ahləs gootə]
Have fun!	Viel Vergnügen/Viel Spaß! [fiil vehrg-**new**gən / fiil Spahs]
Have a good trip.	Gute Reise! [gootə rayzə]
I'll be in touch.	Ich lasse von mir hören. [ihç lahsə fon miir hœrən]
Give … my regards.	Grüßen Sie/Grüß … von mir. [grewsən zii / grews … fon miir]

Making Requests and Expressing Thanks

Bitte und Dank

Yes, please.	Ja, bitte. [yah bihtə]
No, thank you.	Nein, danke. [nayn dahŋkə]
Could you do me a favor?	Darf ich Sie um einen Gefallen bitten? [dahrf ihç zii uhm aynən gəfahlən bihtən]
May I?	Gestatten Sie? *(formal)*/ Darf ich? *(informal)* [gəSthtən zii / dahrf ihç]
Can you help me, please?	Können Sie/Kannst du mir bitte helfen? [kœnən zii / kahnst doo miir bihtə helfən]
Thank you.	Danke. [dahŋkə]
Thank you very much.	Vielen Dank. [fiilən dahŋk]
Yes, thank you.	Danke, sehr gern. [dahŋkə zehr gehrn]
Thank you. The same to you.	Danke, gleichfalls! [dahŋkə **glayç**fahls]

That's very kind, thank you.	Das ist nett, danke. [dahs ihst neht dahŋkə]
Thank you very much for your help/trouble.	Vielen Dank für Ihre/Deine Hilfe/Mühe. [fiilən dahŋk fyr iirə / daynə hihlfə / mew-ə]
Don't mention it./You're welcome.	Bitte sehr./Gern geschehen. [bihtə zehr / gehrn gəSey-ən]

Apologies/Regrets

Entschuldigung / Bedauern

I'm sorry!/Excuse me!	Entschuldigung! [ehnt-**Sool**-dih-guhŋ]
I must apologize.	Ich muss mich entschuldigen. [ihç muhs mihç ehnt-**Sool**-dih-gən]
I'm so sorry!	Das tut mir Leid. [dahs toot miir layt]
I didn't mean it.	Es war nicht so gemeint. [ehs vahr nihçt zoh gəmaynt]
What a pity!/That's too bad!	Schade! [Sahdə]
I'm afraid that's impossible.	Es ist leider nicht möglich. [ehs ihst laydər nihçt **mœg**-lihç]
Perhaps another time.	Vielleicht ein andermal. [vih-**layçt** ayn **ahn**dərmahl]

Congratulations/Best Wishes

Glückwunsch

Congratulations!	Herzlichen Glückwunsch! [**hehrts**-lihçən **glewk**-vewnS]
All the best!	Alles Gute! [ahləs gootə]
Happy birthday!	Alles Gute zum Geburtstag! [ahləs gootə tsuhm gəbuhrts-tahk]
I wish you every success!	Viel Erfolg! [fiil ehr-folg]
Good luck!	Viel Glück!, Hals- und Beinbruch! [fiil glewk, hahls uhnt **bayn**-bruhx]

Get well soon!	Gute Besserung! [gootə **beh**-sə-ruhŋ]
Have a nice weekend!	Schönes Wochenende! [Sœnəs **voh**-xən-ehndə]

"Good luck" meaning "viel Glück" or "viel Erfolg" expresses a general wish for luck and success in an anticipated difficult situation (such as an examination). The (ironic) meaning "Hals- und Beinbruch" is used for physically dangerous circumstances (before an expedition, a mountain climb, a sporting event, and the like).

Language Difficulties

Verständigungsschwierigkeiten

(I beg your) Pardon?	Wie bitte? [vii bihtə]
I don't understand. Would you repeat that, please?	Ich verstehe Sie/dich nicht. Bitte, wiederholen Sie/wiederhole es. [ihç fehr-**Steh**-ə zii / dihç nihçt. Bihtə viidər**hohl**ən zii / viidər**hohl**ə ehs]
Would you speak a bit more slowly/a bit louder, please?	Bitte sprechen Sie/sprich etwas langsamer/lauter. [bihtə Sprehçən zii / Sprihç **eht**-vahs **lahŋ**-zahmər / lautər]
I understand.	Ich verstehe/habe verstanden. [ihç fehr-**Stey**-ə / hahbə fehr-**Stahn**-dən]
Do you speak …	Sprechen Sie/Sprichst du … [Sprehçən zii / Sprihçst doo]
English?	Englisch? [**Ehŋ**-liS]
French?	Französisch? [frahnt-**sœ**-zihS]
I only speak a little …	Ich spreche nur wenig … [ihç Sprehçə noor **vey**-nihç]
What's … in German?	Was heißt … auf Deutsch? [vahs hayst … auf doytS]
What does that mean?	Was bedeutet das? [vahs bədoytət dahs]
How do you pronounce this word?	Wie spricht man dieses Wort aus? [vii Sprihçt mahn diizəs vort aus]
Would you write it down for me, please?	Schreiben Sie/Schreibe es mir bitte auf! [Sraybən zii / Sraybə ehs miir bihtə auf]

Could you spell it, please?	Buchstabieren Sie/Buchstabiere es bitte! [buhx-Stah-**biir**ə zii / buhx-Stah-**biir**ə ehs bihtə]

Expressing Opinions

Meinungsäußerung

I (don't) like it.	Das gefällt mir (nicht). [dahs gəfehlt miir (nihçt)]
I'd prefer ...	Ich möchte lieber ... [ihç mœçtə liibər]
I'd really like ...	Am liebsten wäre mir ... [ahm liipstən vehrə miir]
That would be nice.	Das wäre nett. [dahs vehrə neht]
With pleasure.	Mit Vergnügen. [miht fehrg-**newg**ən]
Fine!	Prima! [priimə]
I don't feel like it.	Ich habe keine Lust dazu. [ihç hahbə kaynə luhst dah-**tsoo**]
I don't want to.	Ich will nicht. [ihç vihl nihçt]
That's out of the question.	Das kommt nicht in Frage. [dahs komt nihçt in frahgə]
Certainly not!	Auf gar keinen Fall. [auf gahr kaynən fahl]
I don't know yet.	Ich weiß noch nicht. [ihç vays nox nihçt]
Perhaps./Maybe.	Vielleicht. [fih-**layçt**]
Probably.	Wahrscheinlich. [vahr-**Sayn**-lihç]

Personal Information

Angaben zur Person

Age	Alter
How old are you?	Wie alt sind Sie/bist du? [vii ahlt zihnt zii / bihst doo]

I'm thirty-nine.	Ich bin 39. [ihç bihn noyn-uhnt-**dray**-sihç]
When's your birthday?	Wann haben Sie/hast du Geburtstag? [vahn hahbən zii / hahst doo gə**buhrts**-tahk]
I was born on April the twelfth, 1954.	Ich bin am zwölften April neunzehnhundertvierundfünfzig geboren. [ihç bihn ahm tsvœlftən ah-**prihl** noyn-tseyn-huhn-dehrt-fiir-uhnt-**fewnf**-tsihç]

Work/Education/ Training	**Beruf/Studium/Ausbildung**
What do you do for a living?	Was machen Sie/machst du beruflich? [vahs mahxən zii / mahkst doo bə**roof**-lihç]
I work in a factory.	Ich bin Fabrikarbeiter/in. [ihç bihn fah-brihk-ahr-baytər]
I work in an office.	Ich bin Büroangestellte/r. [ihç bihn bew-roh-ahngə-Stehlər]
I'm a civil servant.	Ich bin Beamter/Beamtin. [ihç bihn beh-**ahmt**ər / beh-**ahm**-tihn]
I do freelance work.	Ich bin Freiberufler. [ihç bihn **fray**-bəruhflər]
I'm retired.	Ich bin Rentner/in. [ihç bihn rehnt-nər / **rehnt**-nər-ihn]
I'm unemployed.	Ich bin arbeitslos. [ihç bihn **ahr**-bayts-lohs]
I work for …	Ich arbeite bei … [ihç **ahr**-baytə bay]
I'm still in school.	Ich gehe noch zur Schule. [ihç geyə nox tsuhr Soolə]
I go to high school/to a comprehensive.	Ich gehe ins Gymnasium/in eine Gesamtschule. [ihç geyə ihns gihm-**nahz**-yuhm / ihn aynə gə**zahmt**-Soolə]
I'm a (college) student.	Ich bin Student/in. [ihç bihn Stoo-**dənt** / Stoo-**dənt**-ihn]
Where/What are you studying?	Wo/Was studieren Sie/studierst du? [voh / vahs Stoo-**diir**ən zii / Stoo-**di-irst** doo]

| I'm studying … at Yale. | Ich studiere … an Yale. [ihç Stood-yiirə … ahn yeyl] |
| What are your hobbies? | Was für Hobbys haben Sie/hast du? [vahs fewr **hoh**-biiz hahbən zii / hahst doo] |

Most names of professions have two forms–masculine and feminine–with the corresponding articles "der" and "die." Feminine forms are obtained either by adding "-in" to the masculine forms (der Lehrer/die Lehrerin) or by replacing "-mann" with "-frau" (der Geschäftsmann/die Geschäftsfrau).
If the masculine form only is listed below, the job is still predominantly carried out by men.

accountant	Buchhalter/in [**buhx**-hahltər / -ihn]
actor/actress	Schauspieler/in [**Sau**-Spii-lər / -ihn]
apprentice	der Lehrling [dehr **lehr**-lihŋ]
archaeology	die Archäologie [dii ahr-çeh-oh-loh-**gii**]
architect	Architekt/in [**ahr**-çih-tehkt / -ihn]
architecture	die Architektur [dii ahr-çih-tehk-**toor**]
artist	Künstler/in [**kewnst**-lehr / -ihn]
auditor	Wirtschaftsprüfer/in [**vihrt**-Sahfts-prew-fehr / -ihn]
author/ess	Schriftsteller/in [**Srihft**-Steh-lər / -ihn]
baker	Bäcker/in [**beh**-kər / -ihn]
barber, hairdresser	Friseur, Friseuse [frih-**zœr** / frih-**zœzə**]
biologist	Biologe/Biologin [bii-oh-**logə** / bii-oh-**loh**-gihn]
biology	die Biologie [dii bii-oh-loh-**gii**]
blue-collar worker	Arbeiter/in [**ahr**-baytər / -ihn]
bookkeeper	Buchhalter/in [**buhx**-hahl-tər / -ihn]
bookseller	Buchhändler/in [**buhx**-hehnd-lər / -ihn]
bricklayer	der Maurer [dehr **mau**-rər]

business management	die Betriebswirtschaft [dii bətriips-vihrt-Sahft]
businessman/-woman	Geschäftsmann/-frau [gəSahfts-mahn / -frau]
butcher	Metzger/in, Fleischer/in [mehts-gər / -ihn, flaySər / -ihn]
car/auto mechanic	Automechaniker/in [au-toh-meh-çah-nihkər / -ihn]; Kraftfahrzeug-mechaniker/in [krahft-fahr-tsoyg-meh-çah-nihkər / -ihn]
caretaker	Hausmeister/in [haus-maystər / -ihn]
carpenter	Schreiner/in [Sraynər / -ihn], Zimmermann [tsihmərmahn]
cashier	Kassierer/in [kahs-iir-ər / -ihn]
chemist	Chemiker/in [keh-mih-kər/ -ihn (çeh-mih-kər / -ihn)]
chemistry	die Chemie [dii keh-mii, çeh-mii]
civil servant	Beamter/Beamtin [beh-ahmtər / beh-ahm-tihn]
college	die Hochschule [dii hohx-Soolə]
college of art	die Kunstakademie [dii kuhnst-ah-kah-də-mii]
commercial school/ business college	die Handelsschule [dii hahn-dəlz-Soolə]
computer operator	Operator/in [opəreytor / -ihn]
(computer) programmer	Programmierer/in [proh-grahm-yiir-ər / -ihn]
computer science	die Informatik [dii ihn-for-mah-tihk]
computer specialist	EDV-Fachmann/-Fachfrau [ey-dey-fau-fahx-mahn / fahx-frau]
confectioner	Konditor/in [kon-dih-tor / -ihn]
cook	Koch/Köchin [kox / kœ-çihn]
craftsman/-woman	Kunsthandwerker/in [kuhnst-hahnt-vehr-kər / -ihn]
decorator	Dekorateur/in [deh-ko-rah-toor / -ihn]
dental technician	Zahntechniker/in [tsahn-tehç-nihkər / -ihn]

dentist	Zahnarzt/-ärztin [**tsahn**-ahrtst / ehrts-tihn]
designer	Designer/in [deh-**zay**-nər / -ihn]
doctor	Arzt/Ärztin [ahrtst / **ehrts**-tihn]
doctor's assistant	die Arzthelferin [dii **ahrtst**-hehlfərihn]
draftsman/-woman	Technische(r) Zeichner/in [tehç-nihSə(r) **tsayç**-nehr / -ihn]
dressmaker	Schneider/in [Snaydər / -ihn]
driver	Kraftfahrer/in [**krahft**-fahrər / -ihn]
driving instructor	Fahrlehrer/in [**fahr**-lehrər / -ihn]
druggist	Drogist/in [droh-**gihst** / -ihn]
economist	Wirtschaftswissenschaftler/in [**vihrt**-Sahfts-vihsən-Saft-lər / -ihn]
editor	Redakteur/in [reh-dahk-**tœr** / -ihn]
electrician	Elektriker/in [eh-**lehk**-trihkər / -ihn] (Elektro)Installateur/in [(eh-lehk-troh)-ihn-Stah-lə-**tœr** / -ihn]
engineer	Ingenieur/in [ihn-zehn-**yœr** / -ihn]
English studies	die Anglistik [dii ahŋ-**glih**-stihk]
environmental officer	Umweltbeauftragter/-beauftragte [**uhm**-vehlt-beh-auf-trahk-tər / beh-auf-trahk-tə]
farmer	Landwirt/in [**lahnt**-vihrt / -ihn]
fashion model	das Mannequin [dahs **mahn**-ih-keh]
fisherman	der Fischer [dehr fihSər]
flight attendant	Steward/ess [styoo-ərt / styoo-ərdehs]
florist	Florist/in [**flo**-rihst / -ihn]
forester	Förster/in [fœrs-tər / -ihn]
gardener	Gärtner/in [gehrt-nər / -ihn]
gas fitter	(Gas-)Installateur/in [(gahs-)ihn-Stah-lə-**tœr** / -ihn]
geography	die Geografie [dii gey-oh-grah-**fii**]
geology	die Geologie [dii gey-oh-loh-**gii**]
geriatric nurse	Altenpfleger/in [**ahl**tən-pfleygər / -ihn]
German studies	die Germanistik [dii gehr-mah-**nih**-stihk]

glazier	der Glaser [dehr glahzər]
history	die Geschichte [die gəSihçtə]
history of art	die Kunstgeschichte [die **kuhnst**-gəSihçtə]
househusband	der Hausmann [dehr **haus**-mahn]
housewife	die Hausfrau [dehr **haus**-frau]
institute	das Institut [dahs ihn-Stih-**toot**]
interpreter	Dolmetscher/in [**dol**-meht-Sər / -ihn]
jeweler	der Juwelier [dehr yoo-veh-**liir**]
journalist	Journalist/in [Zuhr-nə-**lihst** / -ihn]
judge	Richter/in [riçtər / -ihn]
keyboarder	Datentypist/in [**daht**ən-tew-pihst / -ihn]
laboratory technician	Laborant/in [lah-bo-**rahnt** / -ihn]
landlord/landlady	Gastwirt/in [**gahst**-vihrt / -ihn]
law	Jura [yoorə]
lawyer	Rechtsanwalt/-anwältin [**rehçts**-ahn-vahlt / ahn-vehltihn]
lecturer	Dozent/in [doh-**tsehnt** / -ihn]
lectures	die Vorlesungen *(pl)* [dii **fohr**-leh-zuhŋən]
librarian	Bibliothekar/in [bihb-lii-oh-teh-**kahr** / -ihn]
locksmith	Schlosser/in [Slosər / -ihn]
mail carrier	Briefträger/in [**briif**-treygər / -ihn]
male nurse	der Krankenpfleger [dehr **krahŋ**kən-pfleygər]
management expert, M.B.A.	Betriebswirt/in [bə**triips**-viirt / -ihn]
manager	Geschäftsführer/in [gə**Sehfts**-fewrər / -ihn]
manual worker	Handwerker/in [**hant**-vehrkər / -ihn]
masseur/masseuse	Masseur/in [mah-**sœr** / -ihn]
mathematics	die Mathematik [dii mah-tə-mah-**tihk**]
mechanic	Mechaniker/in [meh-**çah**-nih-kər / -ihn]

mechanical engineering	der Maschinenbau [dehr mah-**Siin**ən-bau]
medicine	die Medizin [dii meh-diht-**sihn**]
metalworker	Schlosser/in [**Slohs**ər / -ihn]
meteorologist	Meteorologe/-login [meh-teh-o-ro-**loh**-gə/ -**loh**-gihn]
midwife	die Hebamme [dii **hey**-bahmə]
minister *(rel)*	Pfarrer/in [**pfahr**ər / -ihn]
music	die Musik [dii muh-**ziik**]
musician	Musiker/in [**mooh**-zihkər / -ihn]
nonmedical practitioner	Heilpraktiker/in [**hayl**-prahk-tihkər / -ihn]
notary public	Notar/in [noh-**tahr** / -ihn]
nurse	die Krankenschwester [dii **krahŋ**kənSvehstər]
nursery-school teacher	Erzieher/in [ehr-**tsii**ər / ihn]
optician	Optiker/in [**ohp**-tihkər / -ihn]
painter	Maler/in [**mahl**ər / -ihn]
parish priest	Pfarrer/in [**pfahr**ər / -ihn]
pensioner	Rentner/in [**rehnt**-nər / -ihn]
pharmacist	Apotheker/in [ah-poh-**teyk**ər / -ihn]
pharmacy	die Pharmazie [dii fahr-mah-**tsii**]
philosophy	die Philosophie [dii fih-loh-zoh-**fii**]
photographer	Fotograf/in [foh-toh-**grahf** / -ihn]
physicist	Physiker/in [**few**-zihkər / -ihn]
physics	die Physik [die few-**zihk**]
physiotherapist	Krankengymnast/in [**krahŋ**kəngewm-nahst / -ihn]
pilot	Pilot/in [pih-**loht** / -ihn]
plumber	Installateur/in [ihn-Stah-lətœr / -ihn]
policeman/-woman	Polizist/in [poh-liht-**sihst** / -ihn]
political science	die Politikwissenschaft [dii poh-lih-**tihk**-vihsən-Sahft]
postman/-woman	Briefträger/in [**briif**-trey-gər / -ihn]
post-office worker	Postbeamter/-beamtin [**post**-beh-ahmtər / -beh-ahm-tihn]

professor	Professor/in [proh-**feh**-sohr / -ihn]
psychologist	Psychologe/-login [psew-çoh-**loh**-gə / -**loh**-gihn]
psychology	die Psychologie [dii psew-çoh-loh-**gii**]
railroader, railroad worker	Eisenbahner/in [**ayz**ən-bahnər / -ihn]
real estate agent, realtor	Makler/in [**mahk**lər / -ihn]
representative, rep	Vertreter/in [fehr-**treht**ər / -ihn]
restorer	Restaurator/in [reh-stau-**rah**-tohr / -ihn]
Romance languages	die Romanistik [dii roh-mah-**nih**-stihk]
roofer	Dachdecker/in [**dahx**-dehkər / -ihn]
sailor	der Matrose [dehr mah-**troh**zə]
salesperson	Verkäufer/in [fehr-**koyf**ər / -ihn]
school	die Schule [dii Soolə]
comprehensive ~	die Gesamtschule [dii gə**zahmt**-Soolə]
elementary ~	die Grundschule [dii **gruhnt**-Soolə]
high ~	das Gymnasium [dahs gewm-**nahz**-yuhm]
junior high ~	die Hauptschule/Realschule [dii **haupt**-Soolə / rey-**ahl**-Soolə]
secondary ~	das Gymnasium [dahs gewm-**nahz**-yuhm]
schoolboy/-girl	Schüler/in [Sewlər / -ihn]
scientist	Wissenschaftler/in [**vihs**ən-Sahft-lər / -ihn]
secretary	Sekretär/in [zehk-reh-**tehr** / -ihn]
shoemaker	Schuhmacher/in [**Soo**-mahxər / -ihn]
salesclerk, salesperson	Verkäufer/in [fehr-**koyf**ər / -ihn]
skilled worker	Facharbeiter/in [**fahx**-ahr-baytər / -ihn]
Slavic studies	die Slawistik [dii slah-**vih**-stihk]
social worker	Sozialarbeiter/in [zoht-**syahl**-ahr-baytər / -ihn]
sociology	die Soziologie [dii zoht-syoh-loh-**gii**]
steward/stewardess	Steward/ess [styoo-ərt / -ehs]
student	Student/in [Stoo-**dehnt** / -ihn]

studies	das Studium [dahs **Stood**-yuhm]
subject	das Studienfach [dahs **Stood**-yehn-fahx]
tailor	Schneider/in [Snaydər / -ihn]
tax consultant	Steuerberater/in [**Stoy**ərbərahtər / -ihn]
taxi driver	Taxifahrer/in [**tahk**-sii-fahrər / -ihn]
teacher	Lehrer/in [lehrər / -ihn]
technical college	Technische Hochschule [**tehç**-nihSə **hohx**-Soolə]
technician	Techniker/in [**tehç**-nihkər / -ihn]
theater studies	die Theaterwissenschaft [dii tey-**aht**ər-vihsən-Sahft]
theology	die Theologie [dii tey-oh-loh-**gii**]
therapist	Therapeut/in [tehrə**poyt** / -ihn]
toolmaker	Werkzeugmacher/in [**vehrk**-tsoyg-mahxər / -ihn]
tour guide	Reiseleiter/in [**rayz**əlaytər / -ihn]
trainee	Auszubildende/r [**aus**-tsoo-bihld-ehndə / ər
translator	Übersetzer/in [ew-behr-**zehts**ər / -ihn]
university	die Universität; die Hochschule [dii oo-nii-vehr-zih-**teyt**, dii **hohx**-Soolə]
vet(erinarian)	Tierarzt/-ärztin [**tiir**-artst / ehrts-tihn]
vicar	Pfarrer/in [pfahrər / -ihn]
vocational school	die Berufsschule [dii bə**roofs**-Soolə]
waiter/waitress	Kellner/in [kehlnər / -ihn]
watchmaker	Uhrmacher/in [**oor**-mahxər / -ihn]
white-collar worker	Angestellte/r [**ahn**-gə-Stehltə / -ər
writer	Schriftsteller/in [**Srihft**-Stehlər / -ihn]

3 **On the Go**
Unterwegs

Giving Directions

Ortsangaben

left	links [lihŋks]
right	rechts [rehçts]
straight ahead	geradeaus [gərahdə-**aus**]
in front of	vor [fohr]
in back of, behind	hinter [hihntər]
after	nach [nahx]
next to	neben [neybən]
across from, opposite	gegenüber [gey-gənewbər]
here	hier [hiir]
there	dort [dort]
near	nah [nah]
far	weit [vayt]
street, road	die Straße [dii Strahsə]
narrow street, alley	die Gasse [dii gahsə]
intersection, crossroads, junction	die Kreuzung [dii **kroyt**-suhŋ}
fork	die Gabelung [dii **gahb**əluhŋ]
curve	die Kurve [dii kuhrvə]

Car/Motorcycle/Bicycle

Auto/Motorrad/Fahrrad

Information	Auskunft
Excuse me, how do I get to …, please?	Entschuldigung, wie komme ich nach …? [ehnt-**Suhl**-dih-guhŋ, vii komə ihç nahx]
Can you show me …	Können Sie mir … [kœnən zii miir]
the town …	den Ort … [deyn ort]
the way …	die Strecke … [dii Strehkə]
that …	das … [dahs]
on the map, please?	auf der Karte zeigen? [auf dehr kahrtə tsaygən]
How far is it?	Wie weit ist das? [vii vayt ihst dahs]

Excuse me, is this the road to …?	Bitte, ist das die Straße nach …? [bihtə, ihst dahs dii Strahsə nahx]
How do I get to the expressway to …?	Wie komme ich zur Autobahn nach …? [vii komə ihç tsuhr **au**-toh-bahn nahx]
Straight ahead until you get to …	Immer geradeaus bis … [ihmər gərahdə-**aus** bihs]
Then turn left/right.	Dann links/rechts abbiegen. [dahn liŋks / rehçts **ahp**-biigən]
Follow the signs.	Folgen Sie den Schildern. [folgən zii deyn **Sihld**-ehrn]
Is there a quiet road to …?	Gibt es auch eine wenig befahrene Straße nach …? [gihpt ehs aux aynə veyniç bə-**fah**-rehnə Strahsə nahx]
Is there a scenic road to …?	Gibt es auch eine landschaftlich schöne Straße nach …? [gihpt ehs aux aynə **lahnt**-Sahft-lihç Sœnə Strahsə nahx]
You're on the wrong road. Drive back to …	Sie sind hier falsch. Sie müssen zurückfahren bis … [zii zihnt hiir fahlS. zii mewsən tsuh-**rewk**-fahrən bihs]

In German-speaking countries people drive on the right side of the road and pass on the left. There are three main categories of roads: "Landstraßen" [**lahnt**-Strahsən] (ordinary roads), "Bundesstraßen" [**buhnd**əs-Strahsən] (highways), and "Autobahnen" [**au**-toh-bahnən] (superhighways/freeways/expressways).
On Swiss and Austrian expressways motorists have to pay a toll. Speed limits vary:

	Germany	Austria	Switzerland
In towns:	50 km/h	50 km/h	50 km/h
Open road:	90 km/h	100 km/h	80 km/h
Expressways:	—	130 km/h	120 km/h

Safety belts ("Sicherheitsgurte" [**zihç**ərhayts-guhrtə]) are compulsory, and small children must use special car seats.

At the Gas Station | An der Tankstelle

Where's the nearest gas station, please?	Wo ist bitte die nächste Tankstelle? [voh ihst bihtə dii nehkstə **tahŋk**-Stehlə]

… liters of …	Ich möchte … Liter … [ihç mœçtə … lii-tər]
regular,	Normalbenzin. [nor-**mahl**-behnt-siin]
super,	Super. [**zoo**-pehr]
diesel,	Diesel. [diizəl]
unleaded/leaded,	
please.	bleifrei/verbleit. [**blay**-fray / fehr-**blayt**]
Fill it up, please.	Volltanken, bitte. [**fol**-tahŋkən bihtə]
Please check …	Prüfen Sie bitte … [prewfən zii bihtə]
the oil.	den Ölstand. [deyn **œl**-Stahnt]
the tire pressure.	den Reifendruck. [deyn **rayf**əndruhk]
Please check the water, too.	Sehen Sie auch das Kühlwasser nach. [zeyən zii aux dahs **kewl**-vahsər nahx]
Could you change the oil, please?	Könnten Sie mir einen Ölwechsel machen? [kœntən zii miir aynən **œl**-vehksəl mahxən]
I'd like to have the car washed, please.	Ich möchte den Wagen waschen lassen. [ihç mœçtə deyn vahgən vahSən lahsən]
I'd like a road map of this area, please.	Ich möchte eine Straßenkarte dieser Gegend, bitte. [ihç mœçtə aynə **Strahs**ənkahrtə diizər geygənt bihtə]
Where are the rest rooms, please?	Wo sind bitte die Toiletten? [voh zihnt bihtə dii toy-**leht**ən]

Parking Parken

Parking can be a problem in inner cities, where it's usually restricted by parking meters (Parkuhren [**pahrk**-oorən]) or blue zones, for which you need a parking disc (Parkscheibe [**pahrk**-Saybə]). Discs are available at service stations, hotels, or local tourist offices. You set the dial to show the time you arrived, so both you and the traffic police know when you have to leave again!

Is there a parking lot near here?	Gibt es hier in der Nähe eine Parkmöglichkeit? [gihpt ehs hiir ihn dehr neyə aynə **pahrk**-mœg-lihç-kayt]

| Can I park my car here? | Kann ich den Wagen hier abstellen? [kahn ihç deyn vahgən hiir **ahp**-Stehlən] |
| Could you give me change for … marks/shillings/francs for the parking meter? | Könnten Sie mir … Mark/Schilling/Franken für die Parkuhr wechseln? [kœntən zii miir … mahrk / **Sih**-lihŋ / frahŋkən fewr dii **pahrk**-oor **vehk**-sehln] |

View of Zürich

Is there an attendant?	Ist der Parkplatz bewacht? [ihst dehr **pahrk**-plahts bəvahxt]
I'm afraid we're full up.	Wir sind leider voll besetzt. [viir zihnt laydər fol bəzehtst]
How long can I park here?	Wie lange kann ich hier parken? [vii lahŋə kahn ihç hiir pahrkən]
How much is it …	Wie hoch ist die Parkgebühr pro … [vii hohx ihst dii **pahrk**-gəbewr proh]
by the hour?	Stunde? [Stuhndə]
per day?	Tag? [tahk]
per night?	Nacht? [nahxt]
Is the parking garage open all night?	Ist das Parkhaus die ganze Nacht geöffnet? [ihst dahs **pahrk**-haus dii gantsə nahxt gəœfnət]

A Breakdown	**Eine Panne**
My car's broken down.	Ich habe eine Panne. [ihç hahbə aynə pahnə]
I have a flat tire.	Ich habe einen Platten. [ihç hahbə aynən plahtən]

Three main automobile associations, the ADAC in Germany, the ÖAMTC in Austria, and the TCS in Switzerland, will assist you if your vehicle breaks down on an expressway. They can be called from emergency telephones on expressways and many main roads.

My registration number is …	Meine Auto-/Motorradnummer ist … [maynə **au**-toh / **moh**-toh-raht-nuhmər ihst]
Would you send a mechanic/a tow truck, please?	Würden Sie mir bitte einen Mechaniker/einen Abschleppwagen schicken? [vewrdən zii miir bihtə aynən meh-**çah**-nihkər / aynən **ahp**-Slehp-vahgən Sihkən]
Could you lend me some gas, please?	Könnten Sie mir mit Benzin aushelfen? [kœntən zii miir miht behnt-**siin** aus-hehlfən]
Could you help me change the tire, please?	Könnten Sie mir beim Reifenwechsel helfen? [kœntən zii miir baym **rayf**ənvehksəl hehlfən]
Could you give me a lift to the nearest repair shop/gas station?	Würden Sie mich bis zur nächsten Werkstatt/Tankstelle mitnehmen? [vewrdən **zii** mihç bihs tsuhr nehkstən vehrk-Shtaht / **tahŋk**-Stehlə miht-neymən]

At the Repair Shop	**In der Werkstatt**
Is there a repair shop near here?	Wo ist hier in der Nähe eine Werkstatt? [voh ihst hiir ihn dehr neyə aynə **vehrk**-Shtaht]
Can you … come with me? give me a tow?	Können Sie … [kœnən zii] mit mir kommen? [miht miir komən] mich abschleppen? [mihç **ahp**-Slehpən]

My car won't start.	Mein Wagen springt nicht an. [mayn vahgən Sprihŋt nihçt ahn]
Do you know what the problem is?	Wissen Sie, woran es liegt? [vihsən zii, vor-**ahn** ehs liikt]
There's something wrong with the engine.	Mit dem Motor stimmt was nicht. [miht deym **moh**-tor Stihmt vahs nihçt]
The brakes don't work.	Die Bremsen funktionieren nicht. [dii brehmzən fuhŋk-tsyohn-**iir**ən nihçt]
The battery is empty.	Die Batterie ist leer. [dii Bahtərii ihst leyr]
… is/are faulty.	… ist/sind defekt. [ihst / zihnt deh-**fehkt**]
The car's losing oil.	Der Wagen verliert Öl. [dehr vahgən fehr-**liirt** œl]
Could you have a look?	Können Sie mal nachsehen? [kœnən zii mahl nahx-zeyən]
Change the spark plugs, please.	Wechseln Sie bitte die Zündkerzen aus. [vehksəln zii bihtə dii **tsewnt**-kehrtsən aus]
Do you have spare parts for this model?	Haben Sie Ersatzteile für diesen Wagen? [hahbən zii ehr-**zahts**-taylə fewr diizən vahgən]
Just make the essential repairs, please.	Machen Sie bitte nur die nötigsten Reparaturen. [mahxən zii bihtə noor dii **nœ**-tihkstən reh-pah-rətoorən]
When will the car/the motorcycle be ready?	Wann ist der Wagen/das Motorrad fertig? [vahn ihst dehr vahgən / dahs **moh**-toh-raht **fehrt**-ihç]
How much will it be?	Was wird es kosten? [vahs vihrt ehs kostən]

A Traffic Accident	**Verkehrsunfall**
There's been an accident.	Es ist ein Unfall passiert. [ehs ihst ayn uhn-fahl pah-**siirt**]
Please call …	Rufen Sie bitte … [roofən zii bihtə]
an ambulance.	einen Krankenwagen. [aynən krahŋkən-vahgən]
the police.	die Polizei. [dii poh-lih-**tsay**]
the fire department.	die Feuerwehr. [dii foyərvehr]

Can you take care of the injured?	Können Sie sich um die Verletzten kümmern? [kœnən zii zihç uhm dii fehr-**leht**stən kewm-ehrn]
Do you have a first-aid kit?	Haben Sie Verbandszeug? [hahbən zii fehr-**bahnts**-tsoyk]

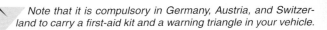

Note that it is compulsory in Germany, Austria, and Switzerland to carry a first-aid kit and a warning triangle in your vehicle.

It was my/your fault.	Es war meine/Ihre Schuld. [ehs vahr maynə / iirə Suhlt]
You ... didn't yield the right of way. cut the curve. changed lanes without signaling.	Sie haben ... [zii hahbən] die Vorfahrt nicht beachtet. [dii for-fahrt nihçt bə-**ahxtət**] die Kurve geschnitten. [dii kuhrvə gə**Snih**tən] die Fahrspur gewechselt, ohne zu blinken. [dii **fahr**-Spuhr gəvehk-sehlt, ohnə tsuh blihŋkən]
You ... were driving too fast. were tailgating. went through a red light.	Sie sind ... [zii zihnt] zu schnell gefahren. [tsuh Snehl gəfahrən] zu dicht aufgefahren. [tsuh dihçt **auf**-gəfahrən] bei Rot über die Kreuzung gefahren. [bay roht ewbər dii **kroyt**-suhŋ gəfahrən]
I was doing ... kilometers an hour.	Ich bin ... km/h gefahren. [ihç bihn ... kii-loh-**mey**-tər proh Stuhndə gəfahrən]
Shall we call the police, or can we settle things ourselves?	Sollen wir die Polizei holen, oder können wir uns so einigen? [zolən viir dii poh-liht-**say** hohlən, ohdər kœnən viir uhns zoh **ayn**-ih-gən]
I'd like my insurance company to ascertain the damage.	Ich möchte den Schaden durch meine Versicherung regeln lassen. [ihç mœçtə deyn Sahdən duhrç maynə fehr-**zih**çəruhŋ **rey**-gehln lahsən]
I'll give you my address and insurance number.	Ich gebe Ihnen meine Anschrift und Versicherungsnummer. [ihç geybə iinən maynə **ahn**-Srihft uhnt fehr-**sih**çəruhŋz-nuhmər]

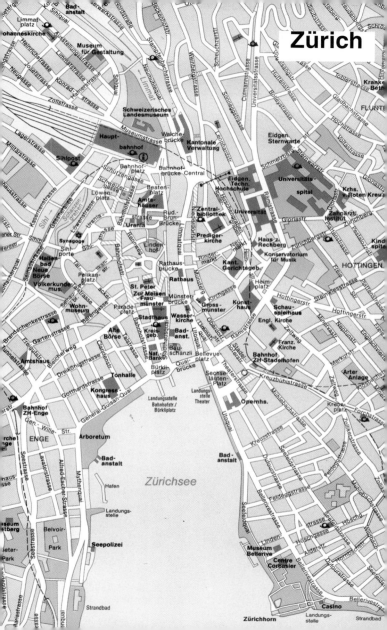

Please give me ...

Geben Sie mir bitte ... [geybən zii miir bihtə]

    your name and address.

    Ihren Namen und Ihre Anschrift [iirən nahmən uhnt iirə **ahn**-Srihft]

    the name and address of your insurance company.

    Namen und Anschrift Ihrer Versicherung. [nahmən uhnt **ahn**-Srihft iirər fehr-**sihç**əruhŋ]

Will you act as a witness for me?

Können Sie für mich Zeuge sein? [kœnən zii fewr mihç tsoygə zayn]

Thank you very much for your help.

Vielen Dank für Ihre Hilfe. [fiilən dahŋk fewr iirə hihlfə]

Car/Motorcycle/Bicycle Rental

Auto-/Motorrad-/Fahrradvermietung

I'd like to rent ...

Ich möchte ... mieten. [ihç mœçtə ... miitən]

    a car

    einen Wagen [aynən vahgən]

    a cross-country vehicle

    einen Geländewagen [aynən gə**lehnd**əvahgən]

    a moped

    ein Moped [ayn **moh**-peht]

    a motorcycle

    ein Motorrad [ayn **moh**-toh-raht]

    a motor scooter

    einen Roller [aynən rolər]

    a bike

    ein Fahrrad [ayn **fah**-raht]

for ... days.

für ... Tage. [fewr ... tahgə]

for a week.

für eine Woche [fewr aynə vohxə]

How much does it cost per day/week?

Wie hoch ist die Tagespauschale/Wochenpauschale? [vii hohx ihst dii **tahg**əs-pau-Sahlə / **vohx**ən-pau-Sahlə]

What do you charge per kilometer?

Wie viel verlangen Sie pro gefahrenen km? [vii fiil fehr-**lahŋ**ən zii proh gə**fahr**ənən kah-ehm]

A rough guide:
1 mile = 1.6093 km
10 miles = 16 km

How much is the deposit?

Wie hoch ist die Kaution? [vii hohx ihst dii kaut-**syohn**]

I'll take the …	Ich nehme den … [ihç neymə deyn] *(make of car)*/die … [dii] *(make of motorcycle)*.
Does the vehicle have full-coverage insurance?	Ist das Fahrzeug vollkaskoversichert? [ihst dahs **fahr**-tsoyk **fol**-kahs-koh-fehr-zihçərt]
Would you like supplementary insurance?	Möchten Sie eine Zusatzversicherung? [mœçtən zii aynə **tsuh**-zahts-fehr-zihçəruhŋ]
May I see your driver's license?	Darf ich Ihren Führerschein sehen? [dahrf ihç iirən **fewr**ər-Sayn zeyən]
Can I have the car right away?	Kann ich den Wagen gleich mitnehmen? [kahn ihç deyn vahgən glayç **miht**-neymən]
Is it possible to leave the car in …?	Ist es möglich, das Fahrzeug in … abzugeben? [ihst ehs **mœg**-lihç, dahs **fahr**-tsoyk ihn … **ahp**-tsuh-geybən]

Word List: Car/Motorcycle/Bicycle

to accelerate	Gas geben [gahs geybən]
accelerator	das Gaspedal [dahs **gahs**-peh-dahl]
air filter	der Luftfilter [dehr **luhft**-fihltər]
alarm system	die Alarmanlage [dii ah-**lahrm**-ahn-lagə]
alcohol level	Promille [proh-**mihl**ə]
alternator	die Lichtmaschine [dii **lihçt**-ma-Siinə]
antifreeze	das Frostschutzmittel [dahs **frost**-Suhts-mihtəl]
auto repair shop	die Werkstatt [dii **vehrk**-Staht]
automatic (transmission)	das Automatik(getriebe) [dahs au-toh-**mah**-tihk(-gətriibə)]
axle	die Achse [dii ahksə]
backfire	die Fehlzündung [dii **feyl**-tsewn-duhŋ]
backpedal brake	Rücktritt [**rewk**-triht]
ball bearing	das Kugellager [dahs **kuhg**əl-lahgər]
bell	die Klingel [dii klihŋəl]

bicycle, bike	das Fahrrad [dahs **fah**-raht]
racing bike	das Rennrad [dahs **rehn**-raht]
three-speed/ten-speed bike	Drei-/Zehngangrad [**dray** / **tseyn**-gahŋ-raht]
bicycle stand	der Ständer [dehr Stehndər]
bike path	der Fahrradweg [dehr **fah**-raht-veyk]
to blind	blenden [blehndən]
blinker	der Blinker [dehr blihŋkər]
box wrench	der Steckschlüssel [dehr **Stehk**-Slewsəl]
brake	die Bremse [dii brehmzə]
to brake	bremsen [brehmzən]
brake fluid	die Bremsflüssigkeit [**brehmz**-flewsik-kayt]
brake lever	der Bremshebel [dehr **brehmz**-heybəl]
brake lights	die Bremslichter [dii **brehmz**-lihçtər]
brake lining/brake pad	der Bremsbelag [dehr **brehmz**-bəlahk]
breakdown	die Panne [dii pahnə]
bright lights	das Fernlicht [dahs **fehrn**-lihçt]
broken	gebrochen [gəbroxən]
bumper	die Stoßstange [dii **Stos**-Stahŋə]
cable	das Kabel [dahs kahbəl]
car body	die Karosserie [dii kar-o-sə-**rii**]
car wash	die Wagenwäsche [dii **vahgən**-vehSə]
carburetor	der Vergaser [dehr fehr-**gahz**ər]
carrier	der Gepäckträger [dehr gə**pehk**-treygər]
chain	die Kette [dii kehtə]
clutch	Kupplung, Kupplungshebel [**kuhp**-luhŋ, **kuhp**-luhŋs-heybəl]
coolant, cooling water	das Kühlwasser [dahs **kewl**-vahsər]
crash helmet	der Sturzhelm [dehr **Stuhrts**-hehlm]
cylinder	der Zylinder [dehr tsew-**lihn**dər]
cylinder head	der Zylinderkopf [dehr tsew-**lihn**dər-kopf]
to dazzle	blenden [blehndən]
	auskuppeln [**aus**-kuhp-ehln]

defect, flaw	der Defekt [dehr dey-**fehkt**]
detour	die Umleitung [dii **uhm**-lay-tuhŋ]
to dim one's headlights	abblenden [**ahp**-blehndən]
dipstick	der Ölmess-Stab [dehr œl-mehs-Stahp]
to disengage the clutch	auskuppeln [**aus**-kuhp-ehln]
distributor	der Verteiler [dehr fehr-**taylə**r]
driver's license	der Führerschein [dehr **fewrə**r-Sayn]
emergency flashers	der Warnblinker [dehr **vahrn**-blihŋkər]
emergency road service	der Pannendienst [dehr **pahnə**ndiinst]
emergency telephone	die Notrufsäule [dii **noht**-ruhf-zoylə]
engine	der Motor [dehr **moh**-tor]
exhaust	der Auspuff [dehr **aus**-puhf]
expressway	die Autobahn [dii **au**-toh-bahn]
fan belt	der Keilriemen [dehr **kayl**-riimən]
fault	der Defekt [dehr dey-**fehkt**]
fender	der Kotflügel [dehr **kot**-flewgəl]
filling station	die Tankstelle [dii **tahŋk**-Stehlə]
fine	das Bußgeld [dahs **buhs**-gehlt]
flat (tire)	die (Reifen-)Panne [dii (**rayf**ən-)pahnə], der Plattfuß [dehr **plaht**-fuhs]
footbrake	die Fußbremse [dii **fuhs**-brehmzə]
four-lane	vierspurig [**fiir**-Spuh-riç]
four-wheel drive	der Allradantrieb [dehr **ahl**-raht-ahn-triip]
freeway	die Autobahn [dii **au**-toh-bahn]
front axle	die Vorderachse [dii **for**-dər-aksə]
front light	das Vorderlicht [dahs **for**-dər-lihçt]
front wheel	das Vorderrad [dahs **for**-də-raht]
front-wheel drive	der Vorderradantrieb [dehr **for**-dəraht-ahn-triip]
fuel injector	die Einspritzpumpe [dii **ayn**-Sprihts-puhmpə]
full-coverage insurance	Vollkaskoversicherung [**fol**-kahs-koh-fehr-zihçəruhŋ]
fuse	die Sicherung [dii **zihç**əruhŋ]
gas	das Benzin [dahs behn-**tsiin**]

gas canister	der Benzinkanister [dehr behn-**tsiin**-kah-nih-stər]
gas pump	die Benzinpumpe [dii behn-**tsiin**-puhmpə]
gas station	die Tankstelle [dii **tahŋk**-Stehlə]
gas tank	der Benzintank [dehr behnt-**siin**-tahŋk]
gear	der Gang [dehr gahŋ]
first gear	erster Gang [ehrstər gahŋ]
neutral	der Leerlauf [dehr **leyr**-lauf]
reverse gear	der Rückwärtsgang [dehr **rewk**-vehrts-gahŋ]
gear lever	der Schalthebel [dehr **Sahlt**-heybəl]
gearbox	das Getriebe [dahs gətriibə]
gearshift	die Gangschaltung [dii **gahŋ**-Sahlt-tuhŋ]
gearshift lever	der Schalthebel [dehr **Sahlt**-heybəl]
generator	die Lichtmaschine [dii **lihçt**-mah-Siinə]
to grease	schmieren [Smiirən]
green insurance card	die grüne Versicherungskarte [grewnə fehr-**zihçə**ruhŋs-kahrtə]
handbrake	die Handbremse [**hahnt**-brehmzə]
handlebars	(Fahrrad-)Lenker [(**fah**-raht-)lehŋkər]
hazard warning light	der Warnblinker [**vahrn**-blihŋkər]
headlight	der Scheinwerfer [**Sayn**-vehrfər]
headlight flash(er)	die Lichthupe [**lihçt**-huhpə]
heating	die Heizung [**hayt**-suhŋ]
high beam	das Fernlicht [**fehrn**-lihçt]
highway	die Landstraße [**lahnt**-Strahsə]
to hitchhike	trampen [trahmpən]
hitchhiker	der Tramper [trahmpər]
hood	die Motorhaube [**moh**-tor-haubə]
horn	die Hupe [huhpə]
hp (horsepower)	PS [pey-**ehs**]
hub	die Nabe [nahbə]
ignition	die Zündung [tsewnd-uhŋ]
ignition key	der Zündschlüssel [tsewnd-Slewsəl]

ignition switch/lock	das Zündschloss [tsewnd-Slos]
indicator	der Blinker [blihŋkər]
inner tube	der Schlauch [Slaux]
interstate	die Autobahn [au-toh-bahn]
jack	der Wagenheber [vahgən-heybər]
jet	die Düse [dewzə]
jumper cable	das Starthilfekabel [Stahrt-hihlfə-kahbəl]
kickstand	der Ständer [stehndər]
to knock	klopfen [klopfən]
lane	die Fahrspur [fahr-spuhr]
lever	der Hebel [heybəl]
license plate	das Nummernschild [nuhmərn-Sihlt]
low beam	das Abblendlicht [ahp-blehnt-lihçt]
luggage rack	der Gepäckträger [gəpehk-treygər]
moped	das Moped [moh-peht]
motor, engine	der Motor [moh-tor]
motorcycle	das Motorrad [moh-tor-raht]
mountain bike	Mountainbike [moun-tən-bayk]
mudguard	das Schutzblech [Suhts-blehç]
muffler	der Auspuff [aus-puhf]
no-fault and liability insurance	voll versichert [fol fehr-zihçərt]
nut	die Schraubenmutter [Sraubən-muhtər]
octane number	die Oktanzahl [ok-tahn-tsahl]
oil	das Öl [œl]
oil change	der Ölwechsel [œl-vehksəl]
outer tire	der Mantel [mahntəl]
pannier	die Packtasche [pahk-tahSə]
papers	die Papiere [pah-piirə]
parking brake	die Handbremse [hahnt-brehmzə]
parking disc	die Parkscheibe [pahrk-Saybə]
parking garage	das Parkhaus [pahrk-haus]
parking lights	das Standlicht [Stahnt-lihçt]

parking lot	der Parkplatz [**pahrk**-plahts]
parking meter	die Parkuhr [**pahrk**-oor]
parking place	der Parkplatz [**pahrk**-plahts]
pedal	das Pedal [peh-**dahl**]
picnic area	die Raststätte [**rahst**-Stehtə]
piston	der Kolben [kolbən]
pump	die Luftpumpe [**luhft**-puhmpə]
puncture	die (Reifen-)Panne [(**rayf**ən-)pahnə]
puncture repair kit	das Flickzeug [**flihk**-tsoyk]
radar speed check	die Radarkontrolle [rah-**dahr**-kon-trohlə]
radiator	der Kühler [kewlər]
radiator water	das Kühlwasser [**kewl**-vahsər]
rainwear	Regenkombi [**reyg**ən-kom-bii]
rear axle	die Hinterachse [**hihnt**ər-ahksə]
rear light	das Rücklicht [**rewk**-lihçt]
rear wheel	das Hinterrad [**hihnt**ər-raht]
rearview mirror	der Rückspiegel [**rewk**-Spiigəl]
rear-wheel drive	der Hinterradantrieb [**hihnt**ər-raht-ahn-triip]
reflector	der Reflektor [rey-**flehk**-tor]
repair shop	die Werkstatt [**vehrk**-Staht]
rest area	die Raststätte [**rahst**-Stehtə]
rim	die Felge [fehlgə]
road construction site	die Baustelle [**bau**-Stehlə]
road map	die Straßenkarte [**Strahs**ən-kahrtə]
road patrol	der Pannendienst [**pahn**ən-diinst]
saddle	der Sattel [zahtəl]
saddlebag	die Packtasche [**pahk**-tahSə]
sandpaper	das Schmirgelpapier [**Smiirg**əl-pah-piir]
scooter	der Motorroller [**moh**-tor-rolər]
screw	die Schraube [Sraubə]
screwdriver	der Schraubenzieher [**Sraub**ən-tsiiər]
sealing	die Dichtung [**dihç**-tuhŋ]
seatbelt	der Sicherheitsgurt [**zihç**ərhayts-guhrt]

shock absorber	der Stoßdämpfer [**Stos**-dehmpfər]
short circuit	der Kurzschluss [**kuhrts**-Sluhs]
sign	der Wegweiser [**veyk**-vaysər]
snow tire	der Winterreifen [**vihnt**ər-rayfən]
socket wrench	der Steckschlüssel [**Stehk**-Slewsəl]
spare tire, spare wheel	das Ersatzrad [ehr-**zahts**-raht]
spare parts	die Ersatzteile (pl) [ehr-**zahts**-taylə]
sparkplug	die Zündkerze [**tsewnt**-kehrtsə]
speedometer	der Tachometer [tahx-oh-**mey**-tər]
spoke	die Speiche [Spayçə]
starter	der Anlasser [**ahn**-lahsər]
state highway	die Bundesstraße [**buhnd**əs-Strahsə]
station	die Tankstelle [**tahŋk**-Stehlə]
steering wheel	das Lenkrad [**lehŋk**-raht]
stickshift	die Gangschaltung [**gahŋ**-Sahl-tuhŋ]
sunroof	das Schiebedach [**Sii**-bədahx]
supercharger	das Gebläse [gə**blehz**ə]
tail light	das Rücklicht [**rewk**-lihçt]
toll	die Maut [maut]
tool	das Werkzeug [**vehrk**-tsoyk]
to tow (away)	abschleppen [**ahp**-Slehpən]
tow rope	das Abschleppseil [**ahp**-Slehp-zayl]
tow truck	der Abschleppwagen [**ahp**-Slehp-vahgən]
towing service	der Abschleppdienst [**ahp**-Slehp-diinst]
traffic jam	der Stau [Stau]
traffic light	die Ampel [ahmpəl]
trailer	der Anhänger [**ahn**-hehŋər]
transmission	das Getriebe [gə**trii**bə]
truck	der Lastwagen [**lahst**-vahgən]
trunk	der Kofferraum [**kof**ər-raum]
turbo, fan	das Gebläse [gə**blehz**ə]
to turn (left/right)	abbiegen [**ahp**-biigən]
tire	der (Auto)reifen [(**au**-toh-)rayfən]

tire iron	das Radkreuz [**raht**-kroyts]
tire repair kit	das Flickzeug [**flihk**-tsoyk]
valve	das Ventil [fehn-**tiil**]
warning triangle	das Warndreieck [**vahrn**-dray-ehk]
wheel	das Rad [raht]
wheel brace	das Radkreuz [**raht**-kroyts]
windshield	die Windschutzscheibe [**vihnt**-Suhts-Saybə]
windshield wiper	der Scheibenwischer [**Sayb**ən-vihSər]
winter tire	der Winterreifen [**vihnt**ər-rayfən]
wrench	der Schraubenschlüssel [**Sraub**ən-Slewsəl]

Signs and Notices

Achtung	caution
Anlieger frei	residents only
Anfänger	student driver
Ausfahrt	exit
Ausfahrt freihalten	keep clear
… ausgenommen	except for …
Autofähre	car ferry
Begrenztes Parkverbot	restricted parking
Behelfsausfahrt	temporary exit
Bis zur Haltelinie vorfahren	drive up to the stop line
Bitte einordnen	get into the correct lane
Bushaltestelle	bus stop
Einbahnstraße	one-way street
Einfahrt	entrance
Einmündung	junction
Einspuriger Verkehr	single-lane traffic
Fahrbahn wechseln	change lane
Fahrbahnverengung	road narrows
Feuerwehrzufahrt	fire department access
Frauenparkplätze	parking spaces for women only

Fußgängerzone	pedestrian zone
Gefahr	danger
Gefährliche Kurve	dangerous curve
Gegenverkehr	two-way traffic
Geisterfahrer	wrong-way drivers
Geschwindigkeits-begrenzung	speed limit
Gesperrt (für Fahrzeuge aller Art)	closed (to all vehicles)
Gewichtsgrenze	weight limit
Glatteis	black ice
Haarnadelkurve	hairpin curve
Halten verboten	no stopping
Hochwasser	flooding
Industriegebiet	industrial area
Innenstadt	city center, downtown
Keine Einfahrt	no entry
Krankenhaus	hospital
Kreisverkehr	rotary traffic
Kreuzung	crossroads
Kurzparkzone	limited parking zone
Ladezone	loading zone
Langsam fahren	reduce speed, slow down
Licht	headlights
Nachtfahrverbot	no driving at night
Nebel	fog
Niedrige Brücke	low bridge
Notruf	emergency phone
Ölspur	oil slick
Parken verboten	no parking
Parkhaus	parking garage
Parkplatz	parking
Parkscheinautomat	ticket machine
Rechts (Links) fahren	keep right (left)

Rechtsabbiegen verboten	no right turn
Rutschgefahr	slippery road
Sackgasse	dead end
Schritt fahren	drive at walking pace
Schule	school
Schulkinder überqueren	children crossing
Seitenwind	sidewind
Signalanlage	traffic signals ahead
Spielstraße	children playing
Starkes Gefälle	steep hill
Stau	traffic jam
Steinschlag	falling rocks
die Straßenarbeiten	construction
die Straßeneinmündung	road junction
der Tunnel	tunnel
Überholverbot	no passing
die Umleitung	detour
Unbeschrankter Bahnübergang	crossing – no gates
Unfall	accident
die Verkehrsampel	traffic lights
Verschmutzte Fahrbahn	muddy road surface
Vorfahrt beachten	yield right of way
Vorsicht	caution
Wenden verboten	no U-turn
Wildwechsel	deer crossing
Zebrastreifen	zebra crossing (meaning a striped piece of pavement for use by crossing pedestrians)
Zweispuriger Verkehr	two-way traffic

Airplane

Flugzeug

Lufthansa

At the Travel Agency/ At the Airport	**Im Reisebüro/Am Flughafen**
Where's the … counter?	Wo ist der Schalter der … Fluggesellschaft? [voh ihst dehr Sahltər dehr … **fluhk**-gəzehl-Sahft]
When's the next flight to …?	Wann fliegt die nächste Maschine nach …? [vahn fliikt dii nehkstə mah-**Siin**ə nahx …]
I'd like to book a …	Ich möchte einen … [ihç mœçtə aynən]
one-way flight/ round-trip flight	einfachen Flug [**ayn**-fahxən fluhk] Hin- und Rückflug [**hihn**- uhnt **rewk**-fluhk]
to …	nach … buchen. [nahx … buhxən]
Are there still seats available?	Sind noch Plätze frei? [zihnt nox plehtsə fray]
Are there charter flights, too?	Gibt es auch Charterflüge? [gihpt ehs aux **tSahrt**ər-flewgə]
How much is an economy (coach) class/ a first class flight?	Was kostet der Flug Touristenklasse/ 1. Klasse? [vahs kostət dehr fluhk tuh-**rihst**ən-klahsə / ehrstə klahsə]
How much baggage can I take with me?	Wie viel Gepäck ist frei? [vii fiil gəpehk ihst fray]
How much does excess baggage cost per kilo?	Was kostet das Kilo Übergepäck? [vahs kostət dahs **kii**-loh **ewb**ərgəpehk]
I'd like to cancel this flight/change the reservation.	Ich möchte diesen Flug stornieren/umbuchen. [ihç mœçtə diizən fluhk Storn-**iir**ən / **uhm**-buhxən]

When do I have to be at the airport?	Wann muss ich am Flughafen sein? [vahn muhs ihç ahm **fluhk**-hahfən zayn]
Where's the information desk?	Wo ist der Informationsschalter? [voh ihst dehr ihn-for-maht-**syohns**-Sahltər]
Can I take this as carry-on baggage?	Kann ich das als Handgepäck mitnehmen? [kahn ihç dahs ahls **hahnt**-gəpehk **miht**-neymən]
Is the plane to … late?	Hat die Maschine nach … Verspätung? [haht dii mah-**Siin**ə nahx … fehr-**Spey**-tuhŋ]
How late is it going to be?	Wie viel Verspätung hat sie? [vii fiil fehr-**Spey**-tuhŋ haht zii]
Has the plane from … already landed?	Ist die Maschine aus … schon gelandet? [ihst dii mah-**Siin**ə aus … Sohn gəlahndət]
Last call. Passengers for … on flight number …, please proceed to exit …	Letzter Aufruf. Die Passagiere nach …, Flug-Nr. …, werden gebeten, sich zum Ausgang … zu begeben. [lehts-tər **auf**-roof. dii pah-sə-**Ziir**ə nahx …, fluhk nuhmər …, vehrdən gəbehtən, zihç tsuhm **aus**-gahŋ … tsuh bə**geyb**ən]

On Board / An Bord

No smoking, please. Fasten your seat belts, please.	Bitte das Rauchen einstellen! [bihtə dahs rauxən **ayn**-Stehlən] Anschnallen, bitte! [**ahn**-Snahlən bihtə]
What river/lake/mountain is that?	Was ist das für ein Fluss/See/Gebirge? [vahs ihst dahs fewr ayn fluhs / zey / gə**birg**ə]
Where are we now?	Wo sind wir jetzt? [voh zihnt viir yehtst]
When do we land in …?	Wann landen wir in …? [vahn lahndən viir ihn]
We'll be landing in about … minutes.	Wir landen in etwa … Minuten. [viir lahndən ihn eht-vah … mih-**noot**ən]
What's the weather like in …?	Wie ist das Wetter in …? [vii ihst dahs vehtər ihn…]

Arrival   Ankunft

► also Chapter 9 – Lost and Found Office

I can't find my baggage/suitcase.	Ich finde mein Gepäck/meinen Koffer nicht. [ihç fihndə mayn gə**pehk** / maynən kofər nihçt]
My baggage is missing.	Mein Gepäck ist verloren gegangen. [mayn gə**pehk** ihst fehr-**lor**ən gəgahŋən]
My suitcase has been damaged.	Mein Koffer ist beschädigt worden. [mayn kofər ihst bə**Seh**-dihkt vordən]
Where can I report it?	An wen kann ich mich wenden? [ahn veyn kahn ihç mihç vehndən]
Where does the air terminal bus leave from?	Wo fährt der Bus zum Air Terminal ab? [voh fehrt dehr buhs tsuhm ehr **tehr**-mihnəl ahp]

Word List: Airplane   ► also Word List: Train

airline	die Fluggesellschaft [**fluhk**-gəzehl-Sahft]
airport bus/shuttle	der Flughafenbus [**fluhk**-hahfən-buhs]
airport tax	die Flughafengebühr [**fluhk**-hahfən-gəbewr]
aisle	Gang [gahŋ]
approach	der Anflug [**ahn**-fluhk]
arrival	die Ankunft [**ahn**-kuhnft]
baggage	das Gepäck [gə**pehk**]
baggage cart	der Kofferkuli [**kof**ər-koo-lii]
baggage check-in	die Gepäckabfertigung [gə**pehk**-ahp-fehr-tih-guhŋ]
baggage claim	die Gepäckausgabe [gə**pehk**-aus-gahbə]
boarding card	die Bordkarte [**bort**-kahrtə]
booking	die Buchung [**buhx**-uhŋ]
business class	Business class [**bihz**-nihs klahs]
to cancel	stornieren [Storn-**iir**ən]
captain	der Kapitän [kah-pih-**tehn**]

carry-on baggage	das Handgepäck [**hahnt**-gəpehk]
to change the booking/ reservation	umbuchen [**uhm**-buh-xuhŋ]
charter flight	der Charterflug [**tSart**ər-fluhk]
to check in	einchecken [**ayn**-tSehkən]
connection	der Anschluss [**ahn**-Sluhs]
counter	der Schalter [Sahltər]
crew	die Besatzung [bəzaht-suhŋ]
delay	die Verspätung [fehr-**Spey**-tuhŋ]
destination	das Reiseziel [**rayz**ə-tsiil]
direct flight	der Direktflug [dih-**rehkt**-fluhk]
domestic flight	der Inlandsflug [**ihn**-lahnts-fluhk]
duty-free shop	zollfreier Laden [**tsol**-frayər lahdən]
emergency chute	die Notrutsche [**noht**-ruhtSə]
emergency exit	der Notausgang [**noht**-aus-gahŋ]
emergency landing	die Notlandung [**noht**-lahn-duhŋ]
to fasten one's seatbelt	anschnallen, sich [**ahn**-Snahlən zihç]
flight	der Flug [fluhk]
flight attendant	Steward/ess [styooərt/styooər-dehs]
flight schedule	der Flugplan [**fluhk**-plahn]
gate	der Flugsteig [**fluhk**-Stayk]
hand baggage	das Handgepäck [**hahnt**-gəpehk]
helicopter	der Hubschrauber [**huhp**-Sraubər]
identification tag	der Anhänger [**ahn**-hehŋər]
international flight	der Auslandsflug [**aus**-lahnts-fluhk]
to land	landen [lahndən]
landing	die Landung [**lahn**-duhŋ]
last-minute flight	der Last-Minute-Flug [lahst-**mih**-niht-fluhk]
layover	die Zwischenlandung [**tsvih**Sən-lahn-duhŋ]
life-jacket	die Schwimmweste [**Svihm**-vehstə]
nonsmoker	Nichtraucher [**nihçt**-rauxər]
on board	an Bord [ahn bort]
passenger	der Fluggast [**fluhk**-gahst] der Passagier [pah-sə-**Ziir**]

pilot	Pilot/in [pih-**loht** / -ihn]
plane	das Flugzeug [**fluhk**-tsoyk]
plane ticket	der Flugschein [**fluhk**-Sayn]
rear, tail	das Heck [hehk]
regular flight	der Linienflug [**lihn**-yihn-fluhk]
reservation	die Buchung [**buh**-xuhŋ]
route	die Flugstrecke [**fluhk**-Strehkə]
runway	das Rollfeld [**rol**-fehlt]
scheduled time of departure	planmäßiger Abflug [**plahn**-meh-sihgər **ahp**-fluhk]
seatbelt	der Anschnallgurt [**ahn**-Snahl-guhrt]
security check	die Sicherheitskontrolle [**zihç**ərhayts-kon-trohlə]
smoker	Raucher [rauxər]
steward/stewardess	Steward/ess [styooərt/styooər-dehs]
stopover	die Zwischenlandung [**tsvih**-Sən-lahn-duhŋ]
tail, rear	das Heck [hehk]
take-off	der Abflug [**ahp**-fluhk]
time of arrival	die Ankunftszeit [**ahn**-kuhnfts-tsayt]
window seat	der Fenstersitz [**fehnst**ər-zihts]

View of Heidelberg

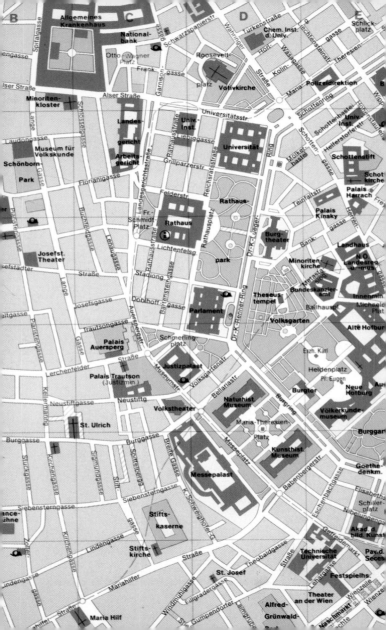

Wien

Train

Eisenbahn

At the Travel Agency/ At the Station	Im Reisebüro/Auf dem Bahnhof
A second-class/ first-class one-way ticket to …, please.	Eine einfache Fahrt 2. Klasse/ 1. Klasse nach …, bitte. [aynə **ayn**-fahxə fahrt tsvaytər klahsə / erstər klahsə nahx … bihtə]
Two round-trip tickets to …, please.	Zweimal … hin und zurück, bitte. [**tsvay**-mahl … hihn uhnt tsuh-**rewk** bihtə]
Are there cheap weekend round-trip tickets?	Gibt es verbilligte Wochenendkarten? [gihpt ehs fehr-**bih**-lihçtə **vohx**ən- ehnt-kahrtən]
Is there a reduction for children/students?	Gibt es eine Ermäßigung für Kinder/Studenten? [gihpt ehs aynə ehr-**meh**-sih-guhŋ fewr kihndər / Stoo- **dehnt**ən]
I'd like to reserve a seat on the … o'clock train to …	Bitte eine Platzkarte für den Zug um … Uhr nach … [bihtə aynə **plahts**- kahrtə fewr deyn tsuhk uhm … oor nahx …]
A window seat?	Einen Fensterplatz? [aynən **fehnst**ər- plahts]
I'd like to reserve a couchette/a sleeper on the eight o'clock train to …	Ich möchte einen Liegewagenplatz/ Schlafwagenplatz für den Zug um 20 Uhr nach … [ihç mœçtə aynən **liig**əvahgən-plahts / **Slahf**-vahgən- plahts fewr deyn tsuhk uhm **tsvahn**- zihç oor nahx …]
Is there a car train to …?	Gibt es einen Autoreisezug nach …? [gihpt ehs aynən **au**-toh-rayzə-tsuhk nahx …]
How much is it for a car and four people?	Was kostet das für ein Auto mit vier Personen? [vahs kostət dahs fewr ayn **au**-toh miht fiir pehr-**zohn**ən]
I'd like to check this suitcase.	Ich möchte diesen Koffer als Reisegepäck aufgeben. [ihç mœçtə diizən kofər ahls **rayz**əgəpehk **auf**- geybən]

Where can I check my bike?	Wo kann ich mein Fahrrad aufgeben? [voh kahn ihç mayn **fah**-raht **auf**-geybən]
Do you want to insure your baggage?	Wollen Sie Ihr Gepäck versichern? [volən zii iir gə**pehk** fehr-**zih**çərn]
Will the baggage be on the … o'clock train?	Geht das Gepäck mit dem …-Uhr Zug ab? [geyt dahs gəpehk miht deym …-oor tsuhk ahp]
When will it arrive in …?	Wann kommt es in … an? [vahn komt ehs ihn … ahn]
Is the train from … running late?	Hat der Zug aus … Verspätung? [haht dehr tsuhk aus … fehr-**Spey**-tuhŋ]
Is there a connection to … at …?	Habe ich in … Anschluss nach …? [hahbə ihç ihn … **ahn**-Sluhs nahx …]
Is there a ferry to …?	Gibt es eine Fähre nach …? [gihpt ehs aynə fehrə nahx …]
(Where) Do I have to change?	(Wo) Muss ich umsteigen? [(voh) muhs ihç **uhm**-Staygən]
Which track does the … train leave from?	Von welchem Gleis fährt der Zug nach … ab? [fon vehlçəm glays fehrt dehr tsuhk nahx … ahp]
The train from … going on to … is now arriving on track 1.	Der Zug aus … nach … fährt auf Gleis 1 ein. [dehr tsuhk aus … nahx … fehrt auf glays ayns ayn]
The train from … is running 10 minutes late.	Der Zug aus … hat 10 Minuten Verspätung. [dehr tsuhk aus … haht tseyn mih-**noot**ən fehr-**Spey**-tuhŋ]
All aboard, please!	Bitte einsteigen! [bihtə **ayn**-Staygən]

On the Train | Im Zug

Excuse me, is this seat free?	Verzeihung, ist dieser Platz noch frei? [fehr-**tsay**-uhŋ, ihst diizər plahts nox fray]
Can you help me, please?	Können Sie mir bitte helfen? [kœntən zii miir bihtə helfən]
May I open/shut the window?	Darf ich das Fenster öffnen/schließen? [dahrf ihç dahs fehnstər œfnən / Sliisən]

Excuse me, this is a nonsmoker.	Entschuldigen Sie, bitte. Dies ist ein Nichtraucherabteil. [ehnt-**Suhl**-dih-gən zii, bihtə. Diis ihst ayn **nihçt**-rauxər-ahp-tayl]
Excuse me, that's my seat. I have a reservation.	Entschuldigen Sie, das ist mein Platz. Ich habe eine Platzkarte. [ehnt-**Suhl**-dih-gən zii, dahs ihst mayn plahts. ihç hahbə aynə **plahts**-kahrtə]
Tickets, please.	Die Fahrkarten, bitte. [dii **fahr**-kahrtən bitə]
Any more tickets, please?	Ist noch jemand zugestiegen? [ihst nox **yey**-mahnt **tsuh**-gəStiigən]
Does this train stop in …?	Hält dieser Zug in …? [hehlt diizər tsuhk ihn …]
Where are we now?	Wo sind wir jetzt? [voh zihnt viir yehtst]

Ponte Dei Salti near Lavertezzo, Ticino/Switzerland

How long are we stopping here?	Wie lange haben wir hier Aufenthalt? [vii lahŋə hahbən viir hiir **auf**-ehnt-hahlt]
Will we arrive on time?	Kommen wir pünktlich an? [komən viir **pewŋkt**-lihç ahn]

Word List: Train	▶ also Word List: Airplane
additional charge	der Zuschlag [**tsuh**-Slahk]
to arrive	ankommen [**ahn**-komən]
baggage	das Gepäck [gəpehk]
baggage car	der Gepäckwagen [gəpehk-vahgən]
baggage cart	der Gepäckkarren [gəpehk-kahrən]
baggage check	der Gepäckschein [gəpehk-Sayn]
baggage locker	das Gepäckschließfach [gəpehk-Sliis-fahx]
baggage rack	die Gepäckablage [gəpehk-ahp-lahgə]
baggage room	die Gepäckaufbewahrung [gəpehk-auf-bəvah-ruhŋ]
car train	der Autoreisezug [**au**-toh-rayzə-tsuhk]
child's ticket	die Kinderfahrkarte [**kihnd**ər-fahr-kahrtə]
compartment	das Abteil [ahp-tayl]
corridor	der Gang [gahŋ]
couchette reservation	die Liegewagenkarte [**liigə**-vahgən-kahrtə]
departure	die Abfahrt [ahp-fahrt]
dining car	der Speisewagen [**Spayz**ə-vahgən]
emergency brake	die Notbremse [**noht**-brehmsə]
engine	die Lokomotive [loh-koh-moh-**tiiv**ə]
fare	der Fahrpreis [**fahr**-prays]
fast train	der D-Zug [**dey**-tsuhk]
free	frei [fray]
to get on	einsteigen [**ayn**-Staygən]
to get off/out	aussteigen [**aus**-Staygən]
group ticket	der Sammelfahrschein [**zahm**əl-fahr-Sayn]
high-speed train	der Hochgeschwindigkeitszug [**hohx**-gəSvihn-dihç-kayts-tsuhk]
InterCity	der IC [ee-**tsey**] (InterCity) [ihntər-si-htii]
large-capacity car	der Großraumwagen [**gros**-raum-vahgən]
local train	der Eilzug [**ayl**-tsuhk]

"InterCity" trains (IC) connect most large cities on a regular basis. "EuroCity" (EC) trains are the international equivalent. The fastest trains are the "InterCity Express" (ICE), but they cover fewer destinations. All three trains require a special supplement. In addition there are "InterRegio" (IR) trains and the normal "D-Zug" or "Schnellzug" connections. For a small fee it is possible to reserve seats in advance.

locker	das Gepäckschließfach [gə**pehk**-Sliis-fahx]
luggage	das Gepäck [gə**pehk**]
main station	der Hauptbahnhof [**haupt**-bahn-hohf]
motorail service	der Autoreisezug [**au**-toh-rayzə-tsuhk]
nonsmoking compartment	das Nichtraucherabteil [**nihçt**-rauxər-ahp-tayl]
occupied	besetzt [bə**zeht**st]
to pay on the train	nachlösen [**nahx**-lœzən]
platform ticket	die Bahnsteigkarte [**bahn**-Stayk-kahrtə]
porter	der Gepäckträger [gə**pehk**-treygər]
powder room	der Waschraum [**vahS**-raum]
railroad	die Eisenbahn [**ayz**ən-bahn]
railroad car number	die Wagennummer [**vahg**ən-nuhmər]
redcap	der Gepäckträger [gə-**pehk**-treygər]
reduction	die Ermäßigung [ehr-**meh**-sih-guhŋ]
reservation	die Reservierung [rey-zehr-**vii**-ruhŋ]
reservation for a reclining chairseat	die Liegewagenkarte [**liig**ə-vahgən-kahrtə]
restaurant car	der Speisewagen [**Spayz**ə-vahgən]
rest room	der Waschraum [**vahS**-raum]
round-trip ticket	die Rückfahrkarte [**rewk**-fahr-kahrtə]
seat reservation	die Platzkarte [**plahts**-kahrtə]
sleeping car/sleeper reservation	die Schlafwagenkarte [**Slahf**-vahgən-kahrtə]
smoking compartment	das Raucherabteil [**raux**ər-ahp-tayl]
station	der Bahnhof [**bahn**-hohf]
station restaurant	Bahnhofsrestaurant [**bahn**-hohf-reh-stoh-rahnt]

stop	der Aufenthalt [**auf**-ehnt-hahlt]
subject to a supplement	zuschlagpflichtig [**tsuh**-Slahk-pflihç-tihç]
supplement	der Zuschlag [**tsuh**-Slahk]
taken	besetzt [bə**zeht**st]
through coach	der Kurswagen [**kuhrs**-vahgən]
ticket	die Fahrkarte [**fahr**-kahrtə]
ticket office	der Fahrkartenschalter [**fahr**-kahrtən-Sahltər]
time of departure	die Abfahrtszeit [**ahp**-fahrts-tsayt]
timetable	der Fahrplan [**fahr**-plahn]
toilet	die Toilette [toy-**leht**ə]
track	das Gleis [glays]
train	die Eisenbahn [**ayz**ən-bahn]
train crew	das Zugbegleitpersonal [**tsuhk**-bəglayt-pehr-zoh-nahl]
train station	der Bahnhof [**bahn**-hohf]
train ferry	die Eisenbahnfähre [**ayz**ən-bahn-fehrə]
vacant	frei [fray]
waiting room	der Wartesaal [**vahrt**ə-zahl]
washroom	der Waschraum [**vahS**-raum]
window seat	der Fensterplatz [**fehnst**ər-plahts]

Ship

Schiff

Information   ### Auskunft

Which is the best way to get to … by ship?	Welche ist die beste Schiffsverbindung nach …? [vehlçə ihst dii behstə **Sihfs**-fehr-bihn-duhŋ nahx …]
When does the next ship/the next ferry leave for …?	Wann fährt das nächste Schiff/die nächste Fähre nach … ab? [vahn fehrt dahs nehkstə Sihf / dii nehkstə fehrə nahx … ahp]
How long does the crossing take?	Wie lange dauert die Überfahrt? [vii lahŋə dauərt dii **ewb**ərfahrt]

What ports do we call at?	Welche Häfen werden angelaufen? [vehlçə hehfən vehrdən **ahn**-gə-laufən]
When do we land at …?	Wann legen wir in … an? [vahn leygən viir ihn … ahn]
How long are we stopping at …?	Wie lange haben wir Aufenthalt in …? [vii lahŋə hahbən viir **auf**-ehnt-hahlt ihn …]
I'd like a ticket to …	Ich möchte eine Schiffskarte nach … [ihç mœçtə aynə **Sihfs**-kahrtə nahx …]
first class	1. Klasse [ehrstə klahsə]
tourist class	Touristenklasse [too-**rihs**-tən-klahsə]
a single cabin	eine Einzelkabine [**aynts**əl-kah-biinə]
a double cabin	eine Zweibettkabine [aynə **tsvay**-beht-kah-biinə]
I'd like a ticket for the round trip at … o'clock.	Ich möchte eine Karte für die Rundfahrt um … Uhr. [ihç mœçtə aynə kahrtə fewr dii **ruhnt**-fahrt uhm … oor]

On Board — An Bord

Excuse me, I'm looking for cabin number …	Bitte, ich suche Kabine Nr. … [bihtə, ihç zuhxə kah-**biin**ə nuhmər …]
Can I have a different cabin?	Kann ich eine andere Kabine haben? [kahn ihç aynə kah-**biin**ə hahbən]
Where's my suitcase/baggage?	Wo ist mein Koffer/Gepäck? [voh ihst mayn kofər / gəpehk]
Where's the restaurant/lounge?	Wo ist der Speisesaal/der Aufenthaltsraum? [voh ihst dehr **Spayz**əzahl / dehr **auf**-ehnt-hahlts-raum]
When are the meals served?	Wann wird gegessen? [vahn vihrt gəgehsən]
Steward, would you bring me …, please.	Steward, bringen Sie mir bitte … [styooərt, brihŋən zii miir bihtə]
I don't feel well.	Ich fühle mich nicht wohl. [ihç fewlə mihç nihçt vohl]
Call the ship's doctor, please.	Rufen Sie bitte den Schiffsarzt! [roofən zii bihtə deyn **Sihfs**-artst]

Could you give me something for seasickness, please?	Geben Sie mir bitte ein Mittel gegen Seekrankheit. [geybən zii miir bihtə ayn mihtəl geybən **zey**-krahŋk-hayt]

Word List: Ship ► also Word List: Airplane, Train

anchor	der Anker [ahŋkər]
to board	einschiffen [**ayn**-Sihfən]
booking	die Buchung [**buh**-xuhŋ]
bow	der Bug [buhk]
cabin	die Kabine [kah-**biin**ə], die Kajüte [kah-**yewt**ə]
to call at	anlaufen [**ahn**-laufən]
captain	der Kapitän [kah-pih-**tehn**]
circular trip	die Rundfahrt [**ruhnt**-fahrt]
coast	die Küste [kewstə]
connection	die Bootsverbindung [**bohts**-fehr-bihn-duhŋ]
course	der Kurs [kuhrs]
crew	die Mannschaft [**mahn**-Sahft]
cruise	die Kreuzfahrt [**kroyts**-fahrt]
deck	das Deck [dehk]
to disembark	ausschiffen [**aus**-Sihfən]
dock	der Anlegeplatz [**ahn**-leygə-plahts]
to dock at	anlegen in [**ahn**-leygən ihn]
dry land	das Festland [**fehst**-lahnt]
to embark	einschiffen [**ayn**-Sihfən]
excursion	der Landausflug [**lahnt**-aus-fluhk]
ferry	die Fähre [fehrə]
car ferry	die Autofähre [**au**-toh-fehrə]
train ferry	die Eisenbahnfähre [**ayz**ən-bahn-fehrə]
to go ashore	ausschiffen [**aus**-Sihfən]
harbor	der Hafen [hahfən]
harbor fees	die Hafengebühr [**hahf**əngəbewr]
hovercraft	das Luftkissenboot [**luhft**-kihsən-boht]

hydrofoil, jetfoil	das Tragflächenboot [**trak**-flehçən-boht]
knot	der Knoten [knohtən]
to land at, to dock at	anlegen in [**ahn**-leygən ihn]
life buoy	der Rettungsring [**reh**-tuhŋs-rihŋ]
life preserver/jacket/vest	die Schwimmweste [**Svihm**-vehstə]
life preserver (ring-shaped)	der Rettungsring [**reh**-tuhŋs-rihŋ]
lifeboat	das Rettungsboot [**reh**-tuhŋs-boht]
lighthouse	der Leuchtturm [**loyçt**-tuhrm]
mainland	das Festland [**fehst**-lahnt]
motorboat	das Motorboot [**moh**-tor-boht]
on board	an Bord [ahn bort]
passenger	der Passagier [pah-sə-**Ziir**]
pier	der Landesteg [**lahnd**ə-Steyk]
port	der Hafen [hahfən]
promenade deck	das Promenadendeck [proh-mə**nahd**ən-dehk]
quay	der Kai [kay]
rough seas	der Seegang [**zey**-gahŋ]
round trip	die Rundfahrt [**ruhnt**-fahrt]
rowboat	das Ruderboot [**rood**ərboht]
rudder	das Ruder [**rood**ər]
to (set) sail	auslaufen [**aus**-laufən]
sailboat	das Segelboot [**zeyg**əlboht]
sailor	der Matrose [mah-**trohz**ə]
seasick	seekrank [**zey**-krahŋk]
starboard	Steuerbord [**Stoy**ər-bort]
steamer, steamship	der Dampfer [dahmpfər]
stern	das Heck [hehk]
steward	der Steward [styooərt]
to stop at	anlaufen [**ahn**-laufən]
sun deck	das Sonnendeck [**zon**əndehk]
ticket	die Fahrkarte [**fahr**-kahrtə]
'tween deck	das Zwischendeck [**tsvihS**ən-dehk]

wave	die Welle [vehlə]
wharf	der Landesteg [**lahnd**əSteyk]
yacht	die Jacht [yahxt]

At the Border

An der Grenze

Passport Control

Passkontrolle

Your passport, please.	Ihren Pass, bitte! [iirən pahs bihtə]
Your passport has expired.	Ihr Pass ist abgelaufen. [iir pahs ihst **ahp**-gəlaufən]
I'm with the tour group from …	Ich gehöre zu der Reisegesellschaft aus … [ihç gəhœrə tsuh dehr **rayz**əgəzehl-Sahft aus …]
Do you have a visa?	Haben Sie ein Visum? [hahbən zii ayn **vii**-zuhm]
Can I get the visa here?	Kann ich das Visum hier bekommen? [kahn ihç dahs **vii**-zuhm hiir bəkomən]

Customs

Zollkontrolle

Do you have anything to declare?	Haben Sie etwas zu verzollen? [hahbən zii **eht**-vahs tsuh fehr-**tsol**ən]
No, I only have a few presents.	Nein, ich habe nur ein paar Geschenke. [nayn, ihç hahbə nuhr ayn pahr gə**Sehŋ**kə]
Pull over to the right/the left, please.	Fahren Sie bitte rechts/links heran. [fahrən zii bihtə rehks / lihŋks hehr-**ahn**]
Open the trunk/this suitcase, please.	Öffnen Sie bitte den Kofferraum/diesen Koffer. [œfnən zii bihtə deyn **kof**ər-raum / diizən kofər]
Do I have to pay duty on this?	Muss ich das verzollen? [muhs ihç dahs fehr-**tsol**ən]
How much duty do I have to pay?	Wie viel Zoll muss ich bezahlen? [vii feel tsol muhs ihç bə**tsahl**ən]

Word List: Border

border crossing	der Grenzübergang [**grehnts**-ewbər-gahŋ]
Christian name	der Vorname [**for**-nahmə]
customs	Zoll(amt) [**tsol**(ahmt)]
customs check	die Zollkontrolle [**tsol**-kon-trohlə]
customs office	das Zollamt [**tsol**-ahmt]
customs official	Zollbeamter/Zollbeamtin [**tsol**-bəahmtər / **tsol**-bəahmt-ihn]
date of birth	das Geburtsdatum [gə**buhrts**-dah-tuhm]
driver's license	der Führerschein [**fewr**ər-Sayn]
duty	Zoll(gebühr) [**tsol**(gəbewr)]
duty-free	zollfrei [**tsol**-fray]
endorsement	der Sichtvermerk [**zihçt**-fehr-mehrk]
to enter the country	einreisen [**ayn**-rayzən]
export	die Ausfuhr [**aus**-fuhr]
first name	der Vorname [**for**-nahmə]
green insurance card	die grüne Versicherungskarte [grewnə fehr-**zihç**əruhŋs-kahrtə]
identity card	der Personalausweis [pehr-zoh-**nahl**-aus-vays]
import	die Einfuhr [**ayn**-fuhr]
international vaccination certificate	internationaler Impfpass [ihntər-naht-syoh-**nahl**ər **ihmpf**-pahs]
to leave the country	ausreisen [**aus**-rayzən]
liable to duty	zollpflichtig [**tsol**-pflihç-tiç]
maiden name	der Geburtsname [gə**buhrts**-nahmə]
marital status	der Familienstand [fah-**mihl**-yehn-Stahnt]
single	ledig [**ley**-dihç]
married	verheiratet [fehr-**hay**-rah-tət]
widowed	verwitwet [fehr-**viht**-veht]
nationality	die Staatsangehörigkeit [**Stats**-ahn-gəhœriç-kayt]
nationality plate	das Nationalitätskennzeichen [nat-syoh-nah-lih-**teyts**-kehn-tsayçən]

passport	der Reisepass [**rayz**əpahs]
passport control	die Passkontrolle [**pahs**-kon-trohlə]
place of birth	der Geburtsort [gə**buhrts**-ort]
place of residence	der Wohnort [**vohn**-ort]
rabies	die Tollwut [**tol**-vuht]
regulations	die Bestimmungen *(pl)* [bə**Stih**-muhŋən]
subject to duty	zollpflichtig [**tsol**-pflihç-tihç]
surname	der Familienname [fah-**mihl**-yehn-nahmə]
valid	gültig [**gewl**-tihç]
visa	das Visum [**vii**-zuhm]

Local Transportation

Nahverkehrsmittel

There are various forms of public transportation in most towns and cities, and they are usually coordinated so that tickets are valid on all of them. With streetcars and trains you usually have to buy a ticket from a machine before you get on. If the machine doesn't print a date and time, you have to stamp it yourself at a separate machine labeled "entwerten." Multiple tickets, family tickets ("Familienkarte"), and day passes for all lines ("Netzkarte") are often available.

Note that there's no ticket collector on most German buses or streetcars. You pay your fare to the bus driver/streetcar driver. It's often worthwhile to buy a booklet of tickets or a pass for one or more days from automatic ticket dispensers found at each station. Most major cities operate an underground transportation system (U-Bahn).

Which bus/streetcar/ subway line goes to …?	Welcher Bus/Welche Straßenbahn/ Welche U-Bahnlinie fährt nach …? [vehlçər buhs / vehlçə **Strahs**ənbahn / vehlçə **oo**-bahn-lihnyə fehrt nahx …]

Excuse me, where's the nearest … ?	Bitte, wo ist die nächste … ? [bihtə, voh ihst dii nehkstə …]
bus stop?	Bushaltestelle? [**buhs**-hahltə-Stehlə]
streetcar stop?	Straßenbahnhaltestelle? [**Strahsən**-bahn-hahltə-Stehlə]
subway station?	U-Bahnstation? [**oo**-bahn-Stat-syohn]
Which line goes to … ?	Welche Linie fährt nach …? [vehlçə lihnyə fehrt nahx …]

Dusk falling on Salzburg

Does this bus go to …?	Ist dies der richtige Bus nach …? [ihst diis dehr **rihç**-tihgə buhs nahx …]
What time does the bus leave?	Wann fährt der Bus ab? [vahn fehrt dehr buhs ahp]
Where does the bus leave from?	Wo fährt der Bus ab? [voh fehrt dehr buhs ahp]
When's the first/last subway to …?	Wann fährt die erste/letzte U-Bahn nach …? [vahn fehrt dii ehrstə / lehtstə **oo**-bahn nahx …]
Which direction do I take?	In welche Richtung muss ich fahren? [ihn vehlçə **rihç**-tuhŋ muhs ihç fahrən]

How many stops is it?	Wie viele Haltestellen sind es? [vii fiilə **hahltə**-Stehlən zihnt ehs]
Where do I have to get out/change?	Wo muss ich aussteigen/ umsteigen? [voh muhs ihç **aus**-Staygən / **uhm**-Staygən]
Will you tell me when we're there, please?	Sagen Sie mir bitte, wenn ich aussteigen muss. [zahgən zii miir bihtə, vehn ihç **aus**-Staygən muhs]
Where can I buy a ticket?	Wo kann ich den Fahrschein kaufen? [voh kahn ihç deyn **fahr**-Sayn kaufən]
To …, please.	Bitte, einen Fahrschein nach … [bihtə, aynən **fahr**-Sayn nahx]
Are there one-day/ weekly tickets?	Gibt es auch Tages-/Wochenkarten? [gihpt ehs aux **tahg**əs- / **vohx**ən-kahrtən]

Taxi

Taxi

Where's the nearest taxi stand?	Wo ist der nächste Taxistand? [voh ihst dehr nehkstə **tahk**-sii-Stahnt]
To the station.	Zum Bahnhof. [tsuhm **bahn**-hohf]
To the … Hotel.	Zum … Hotel. [tsuhm … hoh-**tehl**]
To … Street.	In die …-Straße. [ihn dii …-Strahsə]
To …, please.	Nach …, bitte. [nahx … bihtə]
How much will it cost to …?	Wie viel kostet es nach …? [vii fiil kostət ehs nahx …]
Could you stop here, please?	Halten Sie bitte hier. [hahltən zii bihtə hiir]
Could you wait, please? I'll be back in five minutes.	Warten Sie bitte. Ich bin in 5 Minuten zurück. [vahrtən zii bihtə. ihç bihn ihn fewnf mih-**noot**ən tsuh-**rewk**]
That's for you.	Das ist für Sie. [dahs ihst fewr zii]

On Foot

Zu Fuß

Excuse me, where's …, please?	Bitte, wo ist …? [bihtə voh ihst]
Could you tell me how to get to …, please?	Können Sie mir sagen, wie ich nach … komme? [kœnən zii miir zahgən, vii ihç nahx ... komə]
I'm sorry, I don't know.	Tut mir Leid, das weiß ich nicht. [tuht miir layt, dahs vays ihç nihçt]
What's the shortest way to … ?	Welches ist der kürzeste Weg nach/zu …? [vehlçəs ihst dehr kewrtsəstə veyk nahx / tsuh ...]
How far is it to … ?	Wie weit ist es zum/zur …? [vii vayt ihst ehs tsuhm / tsuhr]
It's a long way. (It's not far.)	Es ist (nicht) weit. [ehs ihst (nihçt) vayt]
Go straight ahead.	Gehen Sie geradeaus. [geyən zii gərah-də-**aus**]
Turn left/right.	Gehen Sie nach links/rechts. [geyən zii nahx lihŋks / rehçts]
The first/second street on the left/right.	Erste/Zweite Straße links/rechts. [ehrstə / tsvaytə Strahsə lihŋks / rehçts]
Cross …	Überqueren Sie … [ewbər**kvehr**ən zii ...]
the bridge.	die Brücke. [dii brewkə]
the square.	den Platz. [deyn plahts]
the street.	die Straße. [dii Strahsə]
Then ask again.	Dann fragen Sie noch einmal. [dahn frahgən zii nox **ayn**-mahl]
You can't miss it.	Sie können es nicht verfehlen. [zii kœnən ehs nihçt fehr-**feyl**ən]
You can take …	Sie können … nehmen. [zii kœnən ... neymən]
the bus.	den Bus [deyn buhs]
the streetcar.	die Straßenbahn [dii **Strahs**ən-bahn]
the subway.	die U-Bahn [dii **oo**-bahn]

Word List: In the City

alley	die Gasse [gahsə]
building	das Gebäude [gəboydə]
bus	der Bus [buhs]
bus station/depot	der Busbahnhof [**buhs**-bahn-hohf]
to buy a ticket	(einen Fahrschein) lösen [(aynən **fahr**-Sayn) lœzən]
church	die Kirche [kihrçə]
conductor	der Schaffner [Sahfnər]
departure	die Abfahrt [**ahp**-fahrt]
direction	die Richtung [**rihç**-tuhŋ]
district	der Stadtteil [**Stat**-tayl]
downtown	die Innenstadt [**ihn**ən-Staht] das Stadtzentrum [**Staht**-tsehn-truhm]
driver	der Fahrer [fahrər]
end of the line	die Endstation [**ehnt**-Stat-syohn]
fare	der Fahrpreis [**fahr**-prays]
flat rate	der Pauschalpreis [pau-**Sahl**-prays]
to get in/on	einsteigen [**ayn**-Staygən]
to get off/out	aussteigen [**aus**-Staygən]
house	das Haus [haus]
house number	die Hausnummer [**haus**-nuhmər]
inspector	der Kontrolleur [kon-tro-**lœr**]
interurban bus	der Überlandbus [**ewb**ər-lahnt-buhs]
lane	die Gasse [gahsə]
last stop	die Endstation [**ehnt**-Staht-syohn]
local train	der Nahverkehrszug [**nah**-fehr-kehrs-tsuhk]
main street	die Hauptstraße [**haupt**-Strahsə]
one-day travel pass	die Tageskarte [**tahg**əs-kahrtə]
park	der Park [pahrk]
pedestrian zone	die Fußgängerzone [**fuhs**-gehŋər-tsohnə]
to press the button	Knopf drücken [knopf drewkən]
receipt	die Quittung [**kvih**-tuhŋ]

Berlin

road	die Straße [Strahsə]
side street	die Nebenstraße [**neyb**ən-Strahsə]
sidewalk	der Gehsteig [**gey**-Stayk]
sightseeing tour	die Stadtrundfahrt [**Staht**-ruhnt-fahrt]
to stop	halten [hahltən]
stop	die Haltestelle [**hahlt**ə-Stehlə]
street	die Straße [Strahsə]
streetcar	die Straßenbahn [**Strahs**ən-bahn]
suburb	der Vorort [**for**-ort]
subway	die U-Bahn [**oo**-bahn]
taxi stand	der Taxistand [**tahk**-sii-Stahnt]
taxi driver	der Taxifahrer [**tahk**-sii-fahrər]
terminus	die Endstation [**ehnt**-Staht-syohn]
ticket	der Fahrschein [**fahr**-Sayn]
ticket agent	der Fahrkartenverkäufer [**fahr**-kahrtən-fehr-koyfər]
ticket collector	der Schaffner [Sahfnər]
ticket machine, ticket vendor	der Fahrkartenautomat [**fahr**-kahrtən-au-toh-maht]
timetable	der Fahrplan [**fahr**-plahn]
tip	das Trinkgeld [**trihŋk**-gehlt]
travel pass	die Netzkarte [**nehts**-kahrtə]
weekly ticket	die Wochenkarte [**vohx**ən-kahrtə]

4 **Accommodations**
Unterkunft

Information

Auskunft

Can you recommend ..., please?	Können Sie mir bitte ... empfehlen? [kœnən zii miir bihtə ... ehmp-**feylən**]
a good hotel	ein gutes Hotel [ayn gootəs hoh-**tehl**]
a cheap hotel	ein einfaches Hotel [ayn **ayn**-fahxəs hoh-**tehl**]
a pension, boarding house	eine Pension [aynə pehn-**zyohn**]
a bed-and-breakfast place	ein Privatzimmer [ayn prii-**vaht**-tsihmər]
Is it centrally located/quiet/near the beach?	Ist es zentral/ruhig/in Strandnähe gelegen? [ihst ehs tsehn-**trahl** / **roo**-ihç / ihn **Strahnt**-neyə]
How much will it cost a night?	Was wird eine Übernachtung kosten? [vahs vihrt aynə ewbər**nahx**-tuhŋ kostən]
Is there a youth hostel/a campground here?	Gibt es hier eine Jugendherberge/einen Campingplatz? [gihpt ehs hiir aynə **yoo**-gənt-hehr-behrgə / aynən **kehm**-pihŋ-plahts]

Hotel/Pension/Bed and Breakfast

Hotel/Pension/Privatzimmer

At the Reception Desk	**An der Rezeption**
I've reserved a room. My name's ...	Ich habe bei Ihnen ein Zimmer reserviert. Mein Name ist ... [ihç hahbə bay iinən ayn tsihmər rey-zehr-**viirt**. mayn nahmə ihst ...]
Do you have any vacancies?	Haben Sie noch Zimmer frei? [hahbən zii nox tsihmər fray]
... for one night.	... für eine Nacht. [fewr aynə nahxt]
... for two days.	... für zwei Tage. [fewr tsvay tahgə]
... for a week.	... für eine Woche. [fewr aynə vohxə]

No, I'm afraid we're full up.	Nein, wir sind leider vollständig belegt. [nayn, viir zihnt laydər **fol**-Stehn-dihç bə-**leykt**]
Yes, what kind of room would you like?	Ja, was für ein Zimmer wünschen Sie? [yah, vahs fewr ayn tsihmər vewnSən zii]
a single room	ein Einzelzimmer [ayn **ayn**tsəl-tsihmər]
a double room	ein Doppelzimmer [ayn **dop**əl-tsihmər]
a twin room	ein Zweibettzimmer [ayn **tsvay**-beht-tsihmər]
a quiet room	ein ruhiges Zimmer [ayn **roo**-ihgəs tsihmər]
with a sink	mit Waschbecken [miht **vahS**-behkən]
with a shower	mit Dusche [miht duhSə]
with a bath	mit Bad [miht baht]
with a balcony	mit Balkon [miht bahl-**kohn**]
with a terrace	mit Terrasse [miht teh-**rahs**ə]
with a view of the sea	mit Blick aufs Meer [miht blihk aufs meyr]
at the front	zur Straße (hin) gelegen [tsuhr Strahsə (hihn) gəleygən]
at the back	zum Hof (hin) gelegen [tsuhm hohf (hihn) gəleygən]
Do you have a nonsmoking room?	Haben Sie ein Nichtraucherzimmer? [hahbən zii ayn **nihçt**-rauxər-tsihmər]
Can I see the room?	Kann ich das Zimmer ansehen? [kahn ihç dahs tsihmər **ahn**-zeyən]
I don't like this room. Show me another one, please.	Dieses Zimmer gefällt mir nicht. [diizəs tsihmər gə**fehlt** miir nihçt] Zeigen Sie mir bitte ein anderes. [tsaygən zii miir bihtə ayn ahndərəs]
This room's very nice. I'll take it.	Dieses Zimmer ist sehr hübsch. [diizəs tsihmər ihst zeyr hewpS] Ich nehme es. [ihç neymə ehs]
Can you put a third bed/a crib in the room?	Können Sie noch ein drittes Bett/Kinderbett dazustellen? [kœnən zii nox ayn drihtəs beht / **kihnd**ər-beht daht-**suh**-Stehlən]

How much is the room with …	Was kostet das Zimmer mit … [vahs kostət dahs tsihmər miht]
breakfast?	Frühstück? [**frew**-Stewk]
breakfast and evening meal?	Halbpension? [**hahlp**-pehn-zyohn]
full board?	Vollpension? [**fol**-pehn-zyohn]
Would you fill in the registration form, please?	Würden Sie bitte den Anmeldeschein ausfüllen? [vewrdən zii bihtə deyn **ahn**-mehldə-Sayn **aus**-fewlən]
May I see your passport/ identity card?	Darf ich Ihren Reisepass/ Personalausweis sehen? [dahrf ihç iirən **rayzə**-pahs / pehr-zoh-**nahl**-aus-vays zeyən]
Please have the baggage taken up to my room.	Bitte lassen Sie das Gepäck auf mein Zimmer bringen. [bihtə lahsən zii dahs gə**pehk** auf mayn tsihmər brihŋən]
Where can I park the car?	Wo kann ich den Wagen abstellen? [voh kahn ihç deyn vahgən **ahp**-Stehlən]
In our garage/parking lot.	In unserer Garage./Auf unserem Parkplatz. [ihn uhnzərər gah-**rah**-Zə / auf uhn-zərəm **pahrk**-plahts]
Does the hotel have a swimming pool/a private beach?	Hat das Hotel ein Schwimmbad/einen eigenen Strand? [haht dahs hoh-**tehl** ayn **Svihm**-baht / aynən aygənən Strahnt]

As well as "Hotels," you will encounter "Seehotels," "Alpenhotels," and other types of hotels. The terms "Gasthaus" and "Gasthof" are also common. "Hotel Garni" is a hotel that only serves breakfast. "Fremdenzimmer" means bed and breakfast in a private home. Look for the sign "Zimmer frei" (vacancies).

Talking to the Hotel Staff	**Gespräche mit dem Hotelpersonal**
What time is breakfast?	Wann gibt es Frühstück? [vahn gihpt ehs **frew**-Stewk]
Where's the breakfast room?	Wo kann man frühstücken? [voh kahn mahn **frew**-Stewkən]
Where's the restaurant?	Wo ist der Speisesaal? [voh ihst dehr **Spayzə**-zahl]

Downstairs.	Die Treppe runter. [dii trehpə ruhntər]
Would you like breakfast in your room?	Sollen wir Ihnen das Frühstück aufs Zimmer schicken? [zolən viir iinən dahs **frew**-Stewk aufs tsihmər Sihkən]
I'd like breakfast in my room at … o'clock, please.	Schicken Sie mir bitte das Frühstück um … Uhr aufs Zimmer. [Sihkən zii miir bihtə dahs **frew**-Stewk uhm … oor aufs tsihmər]
For breakfast I'd like …	Zum Frühstück nehme ich … [tsuhm **frew**-Stewk neymə ihç]
black coffee.	schwarzen Kaffee. [Svahrtsən **kah**-fey]
coffee with milk.	Kaffee mit Milch. [**kah**-fey miht mihlç]
decaffeinated coffee.	koffeinfreien Kaffee. [ko-fey-**iin**-frayən **kah**-fey]
tea with milk/lemon.	Tee mit Milch/Zitrone. [tey miht mihlç / tsih-**trohn**ə]
hot chocolate.	Schokolade. [Soh-koh-**lahd**ə]
fruit juice.	einen Fruchtsaft. [aynən **fruhxt**-zahft]
a soft-boiled egg.	ein weiches Ei. [ayn vayçəs ay]
scrambled eggs.	Rühreier. [**rewr**-ayər]
bread/rolls.	Brot/Brötchen. [broht / **brœt**-çehn]
toast.	Toast. [tohst]
butter.	Butter. [buhtər]
honey.	Honig. [**hohn**-ihç]
jam/orange marmelade.	Marmelade/Orangenmarmelade. [(oh-**rahn**-Zən-)mahr-məlahdə]
muesli.	Müsli. [**mews**-lii]
yogurt.	Joghurt. [**yoh**-guhrt]
some fruit.	etwas Obst. [**eht**-vahs ohpst]

Most hotels have a breakfast buffet. Poached and fried eggs are rare, as is bacon, except in large international hotels. Slices of cheese and sausage are standard. Tea is usually served in a glass with a slice of lemon, and you will have to ask for milk separately. Coffee is served with cream unless you order milk.

Could I have a packed lunch tomorrow?	Könnte ich für morgen ein Lunchpaket bekommen? [kœntə ihç fewr morgən ayn **ləntS**-pahkət bəkomən]

Please wake me at … o'clock in the morning.	Wecken Sie mich bitte morgen früh um … Uhr. [vehkən zii mihç bihtə morgən frew uhm ... oor]
My key, please.	Bitte meinen Schlüssel. [bihtə maynən Slewsəl]
Could you bring me …, please?	Würden Sie mir bitte … bringen? [vewrdən zii miir bihtə ... brihŋən]
another towel	noch ein Handtuch [nox ayn **hant**-tuhx]
some soap	ein Stück Seife [ayn Stewk zayfə]
some coathangers	einige Kleiderbügel [**ayn**-ihgə **klayd**ərbewgəl]
How does … work?	Wie funktioniert …? [vii fuhŋk-tsyoh-**niirt**]
Did anyone ask for me?	Hat jemand nach mir gefragt? [haht **yey**-mahnt nahx miir gəfrahkt]
Are there any letters for me?	Ist Post für mich da? [ihst pohst fewr mihç dah]
Do you have any postcards/stamps?	Haben Sie Ansichtskarten/Briefmarken? [hahbən zii **ahn**-zihçts-kahrtən / **briif**-mahrkən]
Where can I mail this letter?	Wo kann ich diesen Brief einwerfen? [voh kahn ihç diizən briif **ayn**-vehrfən]
Where can I rent/borrow …	Wo kann ich … mieten/ausleihen? [voh kahn ihç ... miitən / **aus**-layən]
Where can I make a phone call?	Wo kann ich telefonieren? [voh kahn ihç teh-leh-foh-**niir**ən]
Can I leave my valuables in your safe?	Kann ich meine Wertsachen bei Ihnen in den Safe geben? [kahn ihç maynə **vehrt**-zahxən bay iinən ihn deyn zeyf (or: seyf) geybən]
Can I leave my things here until I get back?	Kann ich meine Sachen hier lassen, bis ich wiederkomme? [kahn ihç maynə zahxən hiir lahsən, bihs ihç **viid**ərkomə]

Beds usually have duvets instead of sheets and blankets. In the wardrobe you will find a blanket for extra warmth. Tea- and coffee-making facilities in rooms are rare.

Complaints	**Beanstandungen**

The room hasn't been cleaned.

Das Zimmer ist nicht gereinigt worden. [dahs tsihmər ihst nihçt gə**ray**-nihçt]

The shower …

Die Dusche … [dii duhSə]

The toilet flush …

Die Spülung … [dii **Spew**-luhŋ]

The heating …

Die Heizung … [dii **hayt**-suhŋ]

The light …

Das Licht … [dahs lihçt]

The radio …

Das Radio … [dahs **rahd**-yoh]

The television …

Der Fernseher … [dehr **fehrn**-zeyər]

… doesn't work.

… funktioniert nicht. [fuhŋk-tsyoh-**niirt** nihçt]

The faucet drips.

Der Wasserhahn tropft. [dehr **vahs**ərhahn tropft]

There's no (warm) water.

Es kommt kein (warmes) Wasser. [ehs komt kayn (vahrməs) vahsər]

The toilet/sink is stopped up.

Die Toilette/Das Waschbecken ist verstopft. [dii toy-**leht**ə / dahs **vahS**-behkən ihst fehr-**Stopft**]

The towels haven't been changed.

Die Handtücher wurden nicht gewechselt. [dii **hahnt**-tewxər vuhrdən nihçt gə**vehks**əlt]

The window doesn't shut.

Das Fenster schließt nicht. [dahs fehnstər Sliist nihçt]

The window won't open.

Das Fenster geht nicht auf. [dahs fehnstər geyt nihçt auf]

The key doesn't fit.

Der Schlüssel passt nicht. [dehr Slewsəl pahst nihçt]

Departure	**Abreise**

I'm leaving this evening/tomorrow at … o'clock.

Ich reise heute Abend/Morgen um … Uhr ab. [ihç rayzə hoytə ah-bənt / morgən uhm … oor ahp]

By what time must I be out of the room?

Bis wann muss ich das Zimmer räumen? [bihs vahn muhs ihç dahs tsihmər roymən]

I'd like my bill, please.	Machen Sie bitte die Rechnung fertig. [mahxən zii bihtə dii **rehx**-nuhŋ **fehr**-tihç]
Do you accept eurocheques?	Nehmen Sie Euroschecks? [neymən zii **oy**-roh-Sehks]
Can I pay by credit card?	Kann ich mit Kreditkarte bezahlen? [kahn ihç miht krey-**diit**-kahrtə bə**tsahl**ən]
Please forward any letters to me at this address.	Bitte senden Sie noch ankommende Post an diese Adresse nach. [bihtə zehndən zii nox **ahn**-koməndə pohst ahn diizə ah-**drehs**ə nahx]
Please have my baggage brought down.	Lassen Sie bitte mein Gepäck herunterbringen. [lahsən zii bihtə mayn gə**pehk** heh-**ruhnt**ər-brihŋən]
Would you call a taxi for me, please?	Rufen Sie mir bitte ein Taxi. [roofən zii miir bihtə ayn **tahk**-sii]
Thank you very much for everything. Goodbye!	Vielen Dank für alles. [fiilən dahŋk fewr alləs] Auf Wiedersehen. [auf **viid**ərzeyən]

Word List: Hotel/Pension/Bed and Breakfast

adapter	der Zwischenstecker [**tsvih**Sən-Stehkər]
air-conditioning	die Klimaanlage [**kliim**ə-ahn-lahgə]
armchair	der Sessel [**zehs**əl]
ashtray	der Aschenbecher [**ah**Sən-behçər]
babysitting service	die Kinderbetreuung [**kihnd**ər-bətroy-uhŋ]
balcony	der Balkon [bahl-**kohn**]
bathroom	das Badezimmer [**bahd**ə-tsihmər]
bathtub	die Badewanne [**bahd**ə-vahnə]
bed	das Bett [beht]
bed and breakfast	das Fremdenzimmer [**frehmd**ən-tsihmər]
bedclothes	die Bettwäsche [**beht**-vehSə]
bedside table	der Nachttisch [**nahxt**-tihS]
blanket	die Wolldecke [**vol**-dehkə]
bolster	die Nackenrolle [**nahk**ən-rolə]

breakfast	das Frühstück [**frew**-Stewk]
breakfast room	der Frühstücksraum [**frew**-Stewks-raum]
chambermaid	das Zimmermädchen [**tsihm**ər-meht-çən]
children's playground	der Kinderspielplatz [**kihn**dər-Spiil-plahts]
to clean	reinigen [**rayn**-ihgən]
closet	der Schrank [Srahŋk]
clothes closet	der Kleiderschrank [**klayd**ər-Srahŋk]
coathanger	der Kleiderbügel [**klayd**ər-bewgəl]
crib	das Kinderbett [**kihnd**ər-beht]
cupboard	der Schrank [Srahŋk]
dining room	der Speisesaal [**Spayz**ə-zahl]
dinner	das Abendessen [**ah**-bənt-ehsən]
duvet	die Bettdecke [**beht**-dehkə]
elevator	der Aufzug [**auf**-tsuhk]
extension cord	die Verlängerungsschnur [fehr-**lehŋ**ər-uhŋz-Snuhr]
fan	der Ventilator [veh-tih-**lah**-tor]
faucet	der Wasserhahn [**vahs**ər-hahn]
floor	die Etage [ey-**tahZ**ə]
full board	die Vollpension [**fol**-pehn-zyohn]
glass	das Wasserglas [**vahs**ər-glahs]
half board	die Halbpension [**hahlp**-pehn-zyohn]
heating	die Heizung [**hayt**-suhŋ]
high season	die Hauptsaison [**haupt**-zeh-zoh]
housekeeper	das Zimmermädchen [**tsihm**ər-meht-çən]
indoor swimming pool	das Hallenbad [**hahl**ən-baht]
key	der Schlüssel [Slysəl]
lamp	die Lampe [lahmpə]
light switch	der Lichtschalter [**lihçt**-Sahltər]
lounge	der Aufenthaltsraum [**auf**-ehnt-hahlts-raum]
low season, off season	die Vorsaison/Nachsaison [**for**-zeh-zoh / **nahx**-zeh-zoh]
lunch	das Mittagessen [**mih**-tahk-ehsən]

mattress	die Matratze [mah-**trahts**ə]
mirror	der Spiegel [Spiigəl]
motel	das Motel [moh-**tehl**]
outlet	die Steckdose [**Stehk**-dohzə]
patio	die Terrasse [teh-**rahs**ə]
pension, small hotel	die Pension [pehn-**zyohn**]
pillow	das Kopfkissen [**kopf**-kihsən]
playground	der Kinderspielplatz [**kihnd**ər-Spiil-plahts]
plug	der Stecker [Stehkər]
porter	der Portier [port-**yey**]
radio	das Radio [**rahd**-yoh]
reading lamp	die Nachttischlampe [**nahx**-tihS-lahmpə]
reception (desk)	die Empfangshalle [ehmp-**fahŋz**-hahlə] die Rezeption [rey-tsehp-**tsyohn**]
registration	die Anmeldung [**ahn**-mehl-duhŋ]
reservation	die Reservierung [rey-zehr-**viir**-uhŋ]
room	das Zimmer [dahs tsihmər]
room and board	Kost und Logis [kost uhnt loh-**Zii**]
safe	der Safe [zeyf (or) seyf]
sheet	das Bettlaken [**beht**-lahkən]
shower	die Dusche [duhSə]
sink	das Waschbecken [**vahS**-behkən]
story	die Etage [ey-**tahZ**ə]
swimming pool	das Schwimmbad [**Svihm**-baht]
tap	der Wasserhahn [**vahs**ər-hahn]
television	der Fernseher [**fehrn**-zeyər]
television lounge	der Fernsehraum [**fehrn**-zey-raum]
terrace	die Terrasse [teh-**rahs**ə]
toilet	die Toilette [toy-**leht**ə]
toilet paper	das Toilettenpapier [toy-**leht**ən-pah-piir]
towel	das Handtuch [**hahnt**-tuhx]
tumbler	das Wasserglas [**vahs**ər-glahs]
TV	der Fernseher [**fehrn**-zeyər]

Summer morning in Austria

ventilator	der Ventilator [vehn-tih-**lah**-tor]
wall socket	die Steckdose [**Stehk**-dohzə]
wardrobe	der Kleiderschrank [**klaydə**-Srahŋk]
wastepaper basket	der Papierkorb [pah-**piir**-korp]
water	das Wasser [vahsər]
cold water	kaltes Wasser [kahltəs vahsər]
warm water	warmes Wasser [vahrməs vahsər]
window	das Fenster [dahs fehnstər]

Vacation Rentals: Houses/Apartments

Ferienhäuser/Ferienwohnungen

Is electricity/water included in the price?	Ist der Stromverbrauch/ Wasserverbrauch im Mietpreis enthalten? [ihst dehr **Strom**-fehr-braux / **vahs**ər-fehr-braux ihm **miit**-prays ehnt-**hahlt**ən]

Are pets allowed?	Sind Haustiere erlaubt? [zihnt **haus**-tiirə ehr-**laupt**]
Where can we pick up the keys to the house/the apartment?	Wo bekommen wir die Schlüssel für das Haus/die Wohnung? [voh bəkomən viir dii Slewsəl fewr dahs haus / dii **voh**-nuhŋ]
Do we have to return them to the same place?	Müssen wir sie dort auch wieder abgeben? [mewsən viir zii dort aux viidər **ahp**-geybən]
Where are the garbage cans?	Wo befinden sich die Mülltonnen? [voh bə**fihnd**ən zihç dii **mewl**-tohnən]
Do we have to clean the place before we leave?	Müssen wir die Endreinigung selbst übernehmen? [mewsən viir dii **ehnt**-ray-nih-guhŋ zehlpst ewbər**neym**ən]

Word List: Vacation Rentals: Houses/Apartments

▶ **also Word List: Hotel/Pension/Bed and Breakfast**

additional costs	die Nebenkosten [**neyb**ən-kostən]
apartment	das Apartment [ə-**pahrt**-mənt]
bedroom	das Schlafzimmer [**Slahf**-tsihmər]
brochure	der Prospekt [proh-**spehkt**]
bungalow	der Bungalow [**buhŋ**-gəloh]
bunk bed	das Etagenbett [ey-**tahZ**ən-beht]
cabin, cottage	das Ferienhaus [**fehr**-yən-haus]
central heating	die Zentralheizung [tsehn-**trahl**-hayt-suhŋ]
coffee machine/maker	die Kaffeemaschine [**kah**-fey-mah-Siinə]
day of arrival	der Anreisetag [**ahn**-rayzə-tahk]
dishwasher	die Geschirrspülmaschine [gə**Siir**-spewl-mah-Siinə]
dish towel	das Geschirrhandtuch [gə**Siir**-hahnt-tuhx]
electricity	der Strom [Strom]
extras	die Nebenkosten [**neyb**ən-kostən]
fridge	der Kühlschrank [**kewl**-Srahŋk]
garbage	der Müll [mewl]

iron	das Bügeleisen [**bewg**əl-ayzən]
kitchenette	die Kochnische [**kox**-nihSə]
landlord/landlady	der Hausbesitzer/die Hausbesitzerin [**haus**-bəziht-sər / -ihn]
living room	das Wohnzimmer [**vohn**-tsihmər]
owner	der Hausbesitzer/die Hausbesitzerin [**haus**-bəziht-sər / -ihn]
pets	die Haustiere n pl [**haus**-tiirə]
refrigerator	der Kühlschrank [**kewl**-Srahŋk]
rent	die Miete [miitə]
to rent	vermieten [fehr-**miit**ən]
resort	die Ferienanlage [**fehr**-yən-ahn-lahgə]
sofa bed	die Schlafcouch [**Slahf**-kautS]
stove	der Herd [hehrt]
electric stove	der Elektroherd [eh-**lehk**-troh-hehrt]
gas stove	der Gasherd [**gahs**-hehrt]
studio couch	die Schlafcouch [**Slahf**-kautS]
toaster	der Toaster [toh-stər]
vacation apartment	die Ferienwohnung [**fehr**-yən-voh-nuhŋ]
vacation house	das Ferienhaus [**fehr**-yən-haus]
voltage	die Stromspannung [**Strom**-Spah-nuhŋ]
washing machine	die Waschmaschine [**vahS**-mah-Siinə]

Camping

Camping

Is there a campground nearby?	Gibt es in der Nähe einen Campingplatz? [gihpt ehs ihn dehr neyə aynən **kehm**-pihŋ-plahts]
Do you have room for another camping trailer/tent?	Haben Sie noch Platz für einen Wohnwagen/ein Zelt? [hahbən zii nox plahts fewr aynən **vohn**-vahgən / ayn tsehlt]
How much does it cost per day and person?	Wie hoch ist die Gebühr pro Tag und Person? [vii hohx ihst dii gəbewr proh tahk uhnt pehr-**zohn**]

What's the charge for …	Wie hoch ist die Gebühr für … [vii hohx ihst dii gəbewr fewr]
the car?	das Auto? [dahs au-toh]
the camping trailer?	den Wohnwagen? [deyn **vohn**-vahgən]
the camper?	das Wohnmobil? [dahs **vohn**-moh-biil]
the tent?	das Zelt? [dahs tsehlt]
Do you rent cabins/camping trailers?	Vermieten Sie Ferienhäuser/Wohnwagen? [fehr-**miit**ən zii fehr-yən-hoyzər / **vohn**-vahgən]
Where can I park my camping trailer?	Wo kann ich meinen Wohnwagen aufstellen? [voh kahn ihç maynən **vohn**-vahgən **auf**-Stehlən]
Where can I put up my tent?	Wo kann ich mein Zelt aufschlagen? [voh kahn ihç mayn tsehlt **auf**-Slahgən]
We'll be staying for … days/weeks.	Wir bleiben … Tage/Wochen. [viir blaybən … tahgə / vohxən]
Is there a food store here?	Gibt es hier ein Lebensmittelgeschäft? [gihpt ehs hiir ayn **leyb**ənz-mihtəl-gəSehft]
Where are the …	Wo sind die … [voh zihnt dii]
toilets?	Toiletten? [toy-**leht**ən]
washrooms?	Waschräume? [**vahS**-roymə]
showers?	Duschen? [duhSən]
Are there electrical hook-ups here?	Gibt es hier Stromanschluss? [gihpt ehs hiir **Strom**-ahn-Sluhs]
Where can I exchange/rent gas bottles?	Wo kann ich Gasflaschen umtauschen/ausleihen? [voh kahn ihç **gahs**-flahSən **uhm**-tauSən / **aus**-layən]
Is the campground guarded at night?	Ist der Campingplatz bei Nacht bewacht? [ihst dehr **kehm**-pihŋ-plahts bay nahxt bə**vahxt**]
Is there a children's playground here?	Gibt es hier einen Kinderspielplatz? [gihpt ehs hiir aynən **kihnd**ər-Spiil-plahts]
Is there a swimming pool?	Gibt es ein Schwimmbad? [gihpt ehs ayn **Svihm**-baht]
Could you lend me …, please?	Können Sie mir bitte … leihen? [kœnən zii miir bihtə … layən]

Youth Hostel

Jugendherberge

Can I rent bedclothes/a sleeping bag?	Kann ich bei Ihnen Bettwäsche/ einen Schlafsack leihen? [kahn ihç bay iinən **beht**-vehSə / aynən **Slahf**-zahk layən]
The front door is locked at midnight.	Die Eingangstür wird um 24 Uhr abgeschlossen. [dii **ayn**-gahns-tewr vihrt uhm **fiir**-uhnt-tsvahn-tsihç oor **ahp**-gəSlosən]

> *Hikers and mountaineers find a large range of mountain huts, usually run by the national alpine clubs. Many serve meals, but some are also self-catering huts.*

Word List: Camping/Youth Hostel

to camp	zelten [tsehltən]
camper	das Wohnmobil [**vohn**-moh-biil]
campground	der Campingplatz [**kehm**-pihŋ-plahts]
camping	das Camping [**kehm**-pihŋ]
camping guide	der Campingführer [**kehm**-pihŋ-fewrər]
camping site	der Campingplatz [**kehm**-pihŋ-plahts]
camping trailer	der Wohnwagen [**vohn**-vahgən]
campstove	der Kocher [koxər]
(rental) charge	die Benutzungsgebühr [bənuht-suhŋs-gəbewr]
children's playground	der Kinderspielplatz [**kihnd**ər-Spiil-plahts]
day room	der Tagesraum [**tahg**əs-raum]
dormitory	der Schlafsaal [**Slahf**-zahl]
dryer	der Wäschetrockner [**vehS**ə-troknər]
drinking water	das Trinkwasser [**triŋk**-vahsər]
electrical hook-up	der Stromanschluss [**Strom**-ahn-Sluhs]
electricity	der Strom [Strom]

farm	der Bauernhof [**bau**ərn-hohf]
gas bottle/cylinder	die Gasflasche [**gahs**-flahSə]
gas stove	der Gaskocher [**gahs**-koxər]
hall of residence	das Studentenwohnheim [Stoo-**dehnt**ən-vohn-haym]
hook-up	der Stromanschluss [**Strom**-ahn-Sluhs]
hostel warden	Herbergsmutter/-vater [**hehr**-behrks-muhtər / -fahtər]
kerosene lamp	die Petroleumlampe [peh-**troh**-leh-uhm-lahmpə]
membership card	die Mitgliedskarte [**miht**-gliits-kahrtə]
playground	der Kinderspielplatz [**kihnd**ər-Spiil-plahts]
plug	der Stecker [Stehkər]
propane gas	das Propangas [proh-**pahn**-gahs]
rent	leihen [layən]
rental charge/fee	die Leihgebühr [**lay**-gəbewr]
reservation	die Voranmeldung [**for**-ahn-mehl-duhŋ]
sink	das Geschirrspülbecken [gə-**Siir**-Spewl-behkən]
sleeping bag	der Schlafsack [**Slahf**-zahk]
stove	der Kocher [koxər]
tent	das Zelt [tsehlt]
tent peg	der Zeltpflock [**tsehlt**-pflok]
tent pole	die Zeltstange [**tsehlt**-Stahŋə]
wall socket	die Steckdose [**Stehk**-dohzə]
washroom	der Waschraum [**vahS**-raum]
water	das Wasser [vahsər]
youth hostel	die Jugendherberge [**yoo**-gənt-hehr-behrgə]
Youth Hostel Association	der Jugendherbergsverband [**yoo**-gənt-hehr-behrks-fehr-bahnt]
youth hostel card	der Jugendherbergsausweis [**yoo**-gənt-hehr-behrks-aus-vays]

Weingut

Willi Schackert
Weinverkauf

5 Eating and Drinking
Gastronomie

Eating Out

Essen gehen

Is there … here?	Wo gibt es hier … [voh gihpt ehs hiir]
a good restaurant	ein gutes Restaurant? [ayn gootəs reh-stoh-**rahnt**]
a restaurant with local specialties	ein typisches Restaurant? [ayn **tew**-pihSəs reh-stoh-**rahnt**]
an Italian/a Greek/a Chinese restaurant	ein italienisches/ griechisches/ chinesisches Restaurant? [ayn ih-tahl-**yey**-nihSəs / grii-çihSəs / çih-**ney**-zihSəs reh-stoh-**rahnt**]
an inexpensive restaurant	ein nicht zu teures Restaurant? [ayn nihçt tsuh toyərəs reh-stoh-**rahnt**]
a fast-food restaurant	einen Schnellimbiss? [aynən **Snehl**-ihm-bihs]

Mediterranean food (in particular Italian and Greek) is common. Popular take-out items include pizzas, sausages and French fries, Turkish shish kebabs, and American-style food.

At the Restaurant

Im Restaurant

When looking for a place to eat or drink, you may come across any of the following names: "Gasthaus"/ "Gasthof" (an inn or small hotel offering both regional and international cuisine); "Gartenwirtschaft" or "Biergarten" (beer garden with tables outside); "Ratskeller" (a restaurant inside or next to the town hall, or "Rathaus"). A "Bistro" is a small bar with snacks and a limited range of food; "Kneipe" is colloquial for "bar" or "tavern"; an "Imbissstube" is a fast-food outlet; a "Konditorei" is a pastry and cake shop, often inside a café. In Austria you may also encounter restaurants called "Beisel" (deriving from "beißen" = "essen"/to eat).

Would you reserve us a table for four for this evening, please?	Reservieren Sie uns bitte für heute Abend einen Tisch für vier Personen. [rey-zehr-**viir**ən zii uhns bihtə fewr hoytə ah-bənt aynən tihS fewr fiir pehr-**zohn**ən]

Is this table/seat free?	Ist dieser Tisch/Platz noch frei? [ihst diizər tihS / plahts nox fray]
A table for two/three, please.	Einen Tisch für zwei/drei Personen, bitte. [aynən tihS fewr tsvay / dray pehr-**zohn**ən bihtə]
Where are the rest rooms/toilets, please?	Wo sind bitte die Toiletten? [voh zihnt bihtə dii toy-**leht**ən]
This way, please.	Bitte hier entlang. [bihtə hiir ehnt-**lahŋ**]

In all but the most expensive restaurants it is usual for guests to choose their own table and not to wait to be seated.

Ordering

Breakfast ▶ also Chapter 4

Bestellung

Waiter, may I have … the menu, the wine list, please?	Herr Ober, … [hehr ohbər] die Speisekarte, [dii **Spayzə**-kahrtə] die Weinkarte, bitte. [dii **vayn**-kahrtə bihtə]
What can you recommend?	Was können Sie mir empfehlen? [vahs kœnən zii miir ehmp-**feyl**ən]
Do you serve vegetarian dishes?	Haben Sie vegetarische Gerichte? [hahbən zii veh-geh-**tah**-rihSə gərihçtə]
Do you serve children's portions?	Gibt es auch Kinderportionen? [gihpt ehs aux **kihnd**ər-port-syohnən]
Are you ready to order?	Haben Sie schon gewählt? [hahbən zii Sohn gə**vehlt**]
What would you like as an appetizer/for your main course/for dessert?	Was nehmen Sie als Vorspeise/ Hauptgericht/ Nachtisch? [vahs neymən zii ahlz **for**-Spayzə / **haupt**-gərihçt / **nahx**-tihS]
I'll have …	Ich nehme … [ihç neymə]
I don't want an appetizer, thank you.	Ich möchte keine Vorspeise, danke. [ihç mœçtə kaynə **for**-Spayzə, dahŋkə]
I'm afraid we've run out of …	Wir haben leider kein/e … mehr. [viir hahbən laydər kayn/ -ə mehr]

Could I have Y instead of X?	Könnte ich statt … … haben? [kœntə ihç Shtaht X, Y hahbən]
I'm allergic to …	Ich vertrage kein/e… [ihç fehr-**trahgə** kayn/ -ə]
How would you like your steak?	Wie möchten Sie Ihr Steak haben? [vii mœçtən zii iir Steyk hahbən]
well done	durchgebraten [**duhrç**-gəbrahtən]
medium rare	medium [**meyd**-yuhm]
rare	englisch [**ehŋ**-lihS]
What would you like to drink?	Was wollen Sie trinken? [vahs volən zii trihŋkən]
A glass of…, please.	Bitte ein Glas… [bihtə ayn glahs]
A bottle of/Half a bottle of…, please.	Bitte eine Flasche/eine halbe Flasche … [bihtə aynə flahSə / aynə hahlbə flahSə]
With ice, please.	Mit Eis, bitte. [miht ays, bihtə]
Would you like anything else?	Haben Sie noch einen Wunsch? [hahbən zii nox aynən vewnS]
Bring us…, please.	Bitte bringen Sie uns… [bihtə brihŋən zii uhns]
Could we have some more bread/water/wine, please?	Könnten wir noch etwas Brot/ Wasser/ Wein bekommen? [kœntən viir nox **eht**-vahs broht/ vahsər/ vayn bəkomən]

> You usually address a waiter as "Herr Ober," [hehr ohbər] a waitress as "Fräulein." [**froy**-layn]

Complaints

Beanstandungen

We need another…	Hier fehlt ein/e… [hiir feylt ayn/ə]
Have you forgotten my…?	Haben Sie mein/e… vergessen? [hahbən zii mayn/ə… fehr-**gehs**ən]
I didn't order that.	Das habe ich nicht bestellt. [dahs hahbə ihç nihçt bə**Shtehl**t]
The food's cold/too salty.	Das Essen ist kalt/versalzen. [dahs ehsən ihst kahlt / fehr-**zahl**-tsən]

The meat's tough/too fat(ty).	Das Fleisch ist zäh/zu fett. [dahs flayS ihst tseh / tsuh feht]
The fish isn't fresh.	Der Fisch ist nicht frisch. [dehr fihS ihst nihçt frihS]
Take it back, please.	Nehmen Sie es bitte zurück. [neymən zii ehs bihtə tsuh-**rewk**]
Ask the manager to come here, please.	Holen Sie bitte den Chef. [hohlən zii bihtə deyn Sehf]

> *Don't confuse the German word "Chef" (= manager) with the English "chef" (= Koch).*

The Check

Die Rechnung

May I have the check, please?	Bezahlen, bitte. [bətsahlən bihtə]
We're in a hurry.	Wir haben es eilig. [viir hahbən ehs **ay**-lihç]
All together, please./ Could we have that on one check, please.	Bitte alles zusammen. [bihtə ahləs tsuh-**zahm**ən]
Separate checks, please.	Getrennte Rechnungen, bitte. [gətrehntə **rehç**-nuhŋən bihtə]
Is service included?	Ist die Bedienung inklusive? [ihst dii bədii-nuhŋ ihn-kluh-**ziiv**ə]
There seems to be a mistake in the check.	Die Rechnung scheint mir nicht zu stimmen. [dii **rehç**-nuhŋ Saynt miir nihçt tsuh Stihmən]
I didn't have that. I had...	Das habe ich nicht gehabt. Ich hatte ... [dahs hahbə ihç nihçt gə**hahpt**. ihç hahtə]
Did you enjoy your meal?	Hat es Ihnen geschmeckt? [haht ehs iinən gə**Smehkt**]
The food was excellent.	Das Essen war ausgezeichnet. [dahs ehsən vahr **aus**-gətsayçnət]
That's for you.	Das ist für Sie. [dahs ihst fewr zii]

Give me change for 80 marks, please.	Geben Sie mir bitte auf achtzig Mark raus. [geybən zii miir bihtə auf **axt**-sihç mahrk raus]
Keep the change.	(Es) stimmt so. [(ehs) Stihmt zoh]

All your drinks will be included in the check with your food. Tipping is not absolutely necessary, but it is customary to round up the total by about 5 to 10 percent.

As a Dinner Guest

Einladung zum Essen/Essen in Gesellschaft

Thank you very much for the invitation.	Vielen Dank für die Einladung! [fiilən dahŋk fewr dii **ayn**-lah-duhŋ]
Help yourself!	Greifen Sie zu! [grayfən zii tsuh]
To your health!, Cheers!	Zum Wohl! [tsuhm vohl!] Prost! [Prohst!]
Could you pass me the ..., please?	Können Sie mir bitte ... reichen? [kœnən zii miir bihtə ... rayçən]
Would you like some more ... ?	Noch etwas ...? [nox **eht**-vahs]
No, thank you. It was plenty.	Danke, es war reichlich. [dahŋkə ehs vahr **rayç**-lihç]
I'm full, thank you.	Ich bin satt, danke. [ihç bihn zaht dahŋkə]
Do you mind if I smoke?	Darf ich rauchen? [dahrf ihç rauxən]

Word List: Eating and Drinking

▶ **also Chapter 8, Word List: Groceries**

appetizer	die Vorspeise [**for**-Spayzə]
ashtray	der Aschenbecher [**ah**Sən-behçər]
baked	gebacken [gəbahkən]
bar	die Bar [bahr]
bay leaves	die Lorbeerblätter *n pl* [**lor**-beyr-blehtər]

beer	das Bier [biir]
to boil	kochen [koxən]
boiled	gekocht [gə**koxt**]
bone	der Knochen [knoxən]
bowl	die Schüssel [Slewsəl]
braised	geschmort [gə**Smort**]
bread	das Brot [broht]
breakfast	das Frühstück [**frew**-Stewk]
carafe	die Karaffe [kah-**rahfə**]
caraway seed(s)	der Kümmel [kewməl]
children's portion	der Kinderteller [**kihnd**ər-tehlər]
cloves	die Nelken *f pl* [nehlkən]
coffee pot	die Kaffeekanne [**kah**-fey-kahnə]
cold	kalt [kahlt]
to cook	kochen [koxən]
cook	der Koch [kox]
corkscrew	der Korkenzieher [**kork**ən-tsiiər]
course	der Gang [ganŋ]
cup	die Tasse [tahsə]
cutlery: knife, fork, and spoon	das Besteck [bə**Stehk**]
dessert	der Nachtisch [**nahx**-tihS]
diabetic	der Diabetiker [diiə-**beh**-tih-kər]
diet	die Schonkost [**Sohn**-kost]
dinner	das Abendessen [**ah**-bənt-ehsən]
dish	das Gericht [gərihçt]
dish *(food)*	die Speise [Spayzə]
dish *(for serving)*	die Schüssel [Sewsəl]
dish of the day	das Tagesgericht [**tahg**əs-gərihçt]
done *(cooked)*	gar [gahr]
draft, on tap	vom Fass [fom fahs]
draft beer	Bier vom Fass [biir fom fahs]
to dress *(salad)*	anmachen [**ahn**-mahxən]
dressing	das Dressing [**dreh**-sihŋ]
drink	das Getränk [gətrehŋk]

dry *(wine)*	trocken [trokən]
egg cup	der Eierbecher [**ay**ər-beçər]
fat	das Fett [feht]
fish bone	die Gräte [grehtə]
fork	die Gabel [gahbəl]
French fries	Pommes frites [pom friit]
fresh	frisch [frihS]
fried	(in der Pfanne) gebraten [(ihn dehr pfahnə) gə**braht**ən]
garlic	der Knoblauch [**knohp**-laux]
glass	das Glas [glahs]
gravy	(Braten-)Soße [(**braht**ən-)zohsə]
grill	der Rost [rohst]
grilled	vom Grill [fom grihl]
hard-boiled	hart(gekocht) [**hahrt**(gəkoxt]]
to help oneself	sich bedienen [zihç bə**diin**ən]
herbs	die Kräuter *pl* [kroytər]
homemade	hausgemacht [**haus**-gəmahxt]
hors d'oeuvre	die Vorspeise [**for**-Spayzə]
hot *(spicy)*	scharf [Sahrf]
hot *(temperature)*	heiß [hays]
to be hungry	hungrig sein [**huhŋ**-rihç zayn]
ice cream parlor	die Eisdiele [**ays**-diilə]
juicy	saftig [**zahf**-tihç]
ketchup	das Ketschup [**keh**-tSuhp]
knife	das Messer [mehsər]
lean	mager [mahgər]
lemon	die Zitrone [tsih-**trohn**ə]
lentils	die Linsen *f pl* [lihn-zən]
lunch	das Mittagessen [**mih**-tahk-ehsən]
main course	die Hauptspeise [**haupt**-Spayzə]
mayonnaise	die Majonäse [mah-yoh-**neyz**ə]
menu	die Speisekarte [**Spayz**ə-kahrtə]
menu of the day	das Tagesmenü [**tag**əs-meh-new]
mustard	der Senf [zehnf]

napkin	die Serviette [zehrv-**yeht**ə]
nonalcoholic	alkoholfrei [**ahl**-koh-hohl-fray]
noodles, pasta	die Nudeln *f pl* [**noo**-dehln]
nutmeg	die Muskatnuss [**muhs**-kaht-nuhs]
oil	das Öl [œl]
olive oil	das Olivenöl [oh-**lii**-vən-œl]
olives	die Oliven *f pl* [oh-**lii**-vehn]
onion	die Zwiebel [tsviibəl]
to order	bestellen [bə**Stehl**ən]
order	die Bestellung [bə**Steh**-luhŋ]
paprika	die Paprika [**pah**-priikə]
parsley	die Petersilie [pey-tər-**zih**-liə]
pepper *(seasoning)*	der Pfeffer [pfeh-fər]
pepper *(vegetable)*	die Paprika [**pah**-prii-kə]
pepper shaker	der Pfefferstreuer [**pfehf**ər-Stroyər]
plate	der Teller [tehlər]
portion	die Portion [port-**syohn**]
potatoes	die Kartoffeln *f pl* [kahr-**to**-fehln]
raw	roh [roh]
rice	der Reis [rays]
roasted	gebraten [gə**braht**ən]
salad	der Salat [zah-**laht**]
salad bar	das Salatbüfett [zah-**laht**-bew-fey]
salt	das Salz [zahlts]
salt shaker	der Salzstreuer [**zahlts**-Stroyər]
sauce	die Soße [zohsə]
saucer	die Untertasse [**uhnt**ər-tahsə]
to season	würzen [vewrt-sən]
seasoning	das Gewürz [gəvewrts]
set meal/menu	das Menü [meh-**new**]
side dish	die Beilage [**bay**-lahgə]
slice	die Scheibe [Saybə]
smoked	geräuchert [gə**royç**ərt]
soft-boiled	weich(gekocht) [**vayç**(gəkoxt)]
soup	die Suppe [zuhpə]

sour	sauer [zauər]
specialty	die Spezialität [Speht-syah-lih-**teyt**]
spice	das Gewürz [gə**vewrts**]
spit-roasted	am Spieß [ahm Spiis]
spoon	der Löffel [lœfəl]
stain	der Fleck [flehk]
steamed	gedämpft [gə**dehmpft**] gedünstet [gə**dewn**-stət]
straw	der Strohhalm [**Stroh**-hahlm]
stuffed	gefüllt [gə**fewlt**]
stuffing	die Füllung [**few**-luhŋ]
sugar	der Zucker [tsuhkər]
sweet	süß [zews]
sweetener	der Süßstoff [**zews**-Stof]
tablecloth	das Tischtuch [**tihS**-tux]
tap, on ~	vom Fass [fom fahs]
taste	der Geschmack [gə**Smahk**]
teapot	die Teekanne [**tey**-kahnə]
teaspoon	der Teelöffel [**tey**-lœfəl]
tender	zart [tsahrt]
tip	das Trinkgeld [**trihŋk**-gehlt]
toasted *(bread)*	geröstet [gə**rœstət**]
today's dinner	das Tagesmenü [**tahgəs**-meh-new]
today's special	das Tagesgericht [**tahgəs**-gə-rihçt]
toothpick	der Zahnstocher [**tsahn**-Stoxər]
tough	zäh [tseh]
to try	probieren [proh-**biir**ən]
to uncork	entkorken [ehnt-**kork**ən]
vegetarian	vegetarisch [vey-geh-**tah**-rihS]
vinegar	der Essig [**eh**-sihç]
waiter/waitress	der Kellner/die Kellnerin [**kehl**nər / **kehl**-nə-rihn]
water	das Wasser [vahsər]
well done	durchgebraten [**duhrç**-gə-brahtən]
wine	der Wein [vayn]
wine glass	das Weinglas [**vayn**-glahs]

Menu

Speisekarte

Vorspeisen	Appetizers
Austern *f pl* [**aus**-tehrn]	oysters
Avocado [ah-və-**kah**-doh]	avocado
Garnelencocktail [gahr-**ney**-lən-kok-teyl]	prawn cocktail
Hummer [humər]	lobster
Krabbencocktail [**krahb**ən-kok-teyl]	shrimp cocktail
Melone mit Schinken [meh-**lohn**ə miht **Sih**ŋkən]	melon with ham
Muscheln *f pl* [**muhS**əln]	mussels
Räucherlachs [**roy**çər-lahks]	smoked salmon
Schinken [**Sih**ŋkən]	ham
Weinbergschnecken [**vayn**-behrk-Snehkən]	snails in garlic butter

Salate	Salads
Bohnensalat [**bohn**ən-zah-laht]	bean salad
Gemischter Salat [gə**mihSt**ər zah-laht]	mixed salad
Gurkensalat [**guhrk**ən-zah-laht]	cucumber salad
Karottensalat [ka-**roht**ən-zah-laht]	carrot salad
Kartoffelsalat [kar-**to**-fehl-zah-laht]	potato salad
Krautsalat [**kraut**-zah-laht]	cabbage salad

Suppen	Soups
Champignoncremesuppe [**Sahm**-pihn-yon-krehm-zuhpə]	cream of mushroom soup
Erbsensuppe [**ehrp**-sən-zuhpə]	pea soup
Fleischbrühe [**flayS**-brewə] Bouillon [bool-**yohn**]	clear soup/consommé

Französische Zwiebelsuppe [frahnt-**sœ**-zihSə **tsviibəl**-zuhpə]	French onion soup
Gemüsesuppe [gə**mewz**ə-zuhpə]	vegetable soup
Gulaschsuppe [**goo**-lahS-zuhpə]	goulash soup
Hühnersuppe [**hewn**ər-zuhpə]	chicken soup
Ochsenschwanzsuppe [**oks**ən-Svahnts-zuhpə]	oxtail soup
Spargelcremesuppe [**Sparg**əl-krehm-zuhpə]	cream of asparagus soup
Tomatencremesuppe [toh-**mah**-tən-krehm-zuhpə]	cream of tomato soup

Eierspeisen — **Egg Dishes**

harte/weiche Eier [hahrtə / vayçə ayər]	hard-boiled/soft-boiled eggs
(Käse-/Champignon-/Tomaten-)? Omelett [(kayzə- / **Sahm**-pihn-yohn- / toh-**mah**-tən-)om(ə)**leht**]	(cheese/mushroom/tomato) omelette
Rühreier [**rewr**-ayər]	scrambled eggs
Spiegeleier [**Spiig**əl-ayər]	fried eggs
Spiegeleier mit Schinken [... miht Sihŋkən]	fried eggs and ham
Spiegeleier mit Speck [... miht Spehk]	fried eggs and bacon
verlorene Eier [fehr-**lor**ənə ayər]	poached eggs

Fisch — **Fish**

gekocht [gə**koxt**]	boiled
gebraten [gə**braht**ən]	fried
gebacken [gə**bahk**ən]	
geräuchert [gə**royç**ərt]	smoked
Aal [ahl]	eel
Forelle [fo-**rehl**ə]	trout
Kabeljau [**kahb**əl-yau]	cod
Karpfen [kahrp-fən]	carp

Lachs [lahks]	salmon
Makrele [mah-**krehl**ə]	mackerel
Matjesfilet [**maht**-yəs-fih-ley]	herring filet
Räucherhering [**roy**çər-heh-rihŋ] Bückling [**bewk**-lihŋ]	kipper, bloater
Scholle [Sohlə]	plaice
Seezunge [**zey**-tsuhŋə]	sole
Tunfisch [**tuhn**-fihS]	tuna
Tintenfisch [**tihnt**ən-fihS]	squid

Geflügel

Poultry

Ente [ehntə]	duck
Fasan [fah-**zahn**]	pheasant
Gans [gahns]	goose
Huhn [huhn] Hähnchen [**hehn**-çən]	chicken
Rebhuhn [**rehp**-huhn]	partridge
Truthahn [**truht**-hahn] Pute [pootə]	turkey
Wachtel [vaxtəl]	quail

Fleisch

Meat

Filet(steak) [fih-**ley**(-Steyk])	filet (steak)
Fleischsoße [**flayS**-zohsə]	gravy
Frikadellen [frih-kə-**dehl**ən]	meat croquettes
Hackfleisch (vom Rind) [**hahk**-flayS (vom rihnt)]	ground beef
Hamburger [**hahm**-buhrgər]	hamburger
Hirsch [hihrS]	venison (stag)
Kalbfleisch [**kahlp**-flayS]	veal
Kaninchen [kah-**nihn**-çen]	rabbit
Kotelett [kot(ə)**leht**]	chop/cutlet
Kutteln [**kuh**-tehln]	tripe

Lamm [lahm]	lamb
Leber [leybər]	liver
Nieren [niirən]	kidneys
Reh [rey]	venison (deer)
Rindfleisch [**rihnt**-flayS]	beef
Rumpsteak [**ruhmp**-Steyk]	rump steak
Schinken [Sihŋkən]	ham
Schweinefleisch [**Svaynə**-flayS]	pork
Spanferkel [**Spahn**-fehrkəl]	suckling pig
Wildschwein [**vihlt**-Svayn]	wild boar
Würstchen [**vewrst**-çən]	sausages
Zunge [tsuhŋə]	tongue

Gemüse

Vegetables

Blumenkohl [**bloom**ən-kohl]	cauliflower
Bratkartoffeln [**braht**-kahr-to-fehln]	fried potatoes
Brokkoli [**bro**-koh-lii]	broccoli
Champignons [**Sahm**-pihn-yohns]	mushrooms
Chicorée [Sih-koh-**rey**]	chicory
Erbsen [ehrpsən]	peas
Fenchel [fehnçəl]	fennel
Folienkartoffel [**fohl**-yən-kar-to-fəl]	baked potato
Frühlingszwiebeln [**frew**-lihŋs-tsvii-behln]	green onions
grüne Bohnen [grewnə bohnən]	green beans
Gurke [guhrkə]	cucumber
Karotten [kah-**roht**ən]	carrots
Kartoffelbrei [kahr-**to**-fəl-bray]	mashed potatoes
Kartoffeln [kahr-**to**-fehln]	potatoes
Kopfsalat [**kopf**-zah-laht]	lettuce

German	Pronunciation	English
Kresse [krehsə]		cress
Kürbis [**kewr**-bihs]		pumpkin
Lauch [laux]		leek
Maiskolben [**mays**-kolbən]		corn on the cob
Möhren [mœrən]		carrots
Ofenkartoffel [**oh**-fən-kahr-to-fəl]		oven-roasted potato
Paprikaschoten [**pah**-priikə-Sohtən]		peppers
Pommes frites [pom **friht**]		French fries
Rosenkohl [**rohz**ən-kohl]		Brussels sprouts
Rösti [**rœs**-tii]		hash brown potatoes
rote Beete [rohtə beytə]		beets
rote Rüben [rohtə rewbən]		
Rotkohl [**roht**-kohl]		red cabbage
Salat [zah-**laht**]		salad
Salzkartoffeln [**zahlts**-kahr-to-fehln]		boiled potatoes
Schwenkkartoffeln [**Svehŋk**-kahr-to-fehln]		potatoes tossed in butter
Spargel [Spargəl]		asparagus
Spinat [Spih-**naht**]		spinach
Stangenbohnen [**Stahŋ**ən-bohnən]		pole beans
Stangensellerie [**Stahŋ**ən-zehlərii]		celery
Tomaten [toh-**mah**-tən]		tomatoes
Weißkohl [**vays**-kohl]		cabbage
Zucchini [tsoo-**kii**-nii]		zucchini
Zwiebeln [**tsvii**-behln]		onions

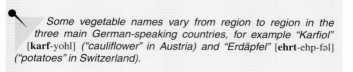

*Some vegetable names vary from region to region in the three main German-speaking countries, for example "Karfiol" [**karf**-yohl] ("cauliflower" in Austria) and "Erdäpfel" [**ehrt**-ehp-fəl] ("potatoes" in Switzerland).*

Käse	Cheese
Blauschimmelkäse [**blau**-Sihmǝl-keyzǝ]	blue cheese
Frischkäse [**frihS**-]	cream cheese
Hüttenkäse [**hewt**ǝn-]	cottage cheese
Schafskäse [**Sahfs**-]	sheep's milk cheese
Ziegenkäse [**tsiig**ǝn-]	goat's milk cheese

*Typical hard cheeses are Emmentaler [**ehm**ǝn-tahlǝr] (Swiss), Appenzeller [**ahp**ǝn-tsehlǝr], and Greyerzer [**grey**-ehrt-sǝr] (Gruyere). Appenzeller and Greyerzer are sharper in flavor than the mild Emmentaler. Particularly pungent are Harzer [**hahrts**ǝr] (a type of hand cheese), Limburger [**lihm**-buhrgǝr] (a semisoft, strongly flavored cheese), and Handkäse [**hahnt**-keyzǝ] (hand cheese, a small, sour-milk cheese originally molded by hand). "Handkäse mit Musik" (miht moo-**zihk**] is served with caraway seeds, onions, and vinegar. Most soft cheeses come from France (Camembert, Brie).*

Nachtisch/Obst	Dessert/Fruit
Ananas [**ah**-nahnǝs]	pineapple
Birnen [biirnǝn]	pears
Eis [ays]	ice cream
Eisbecher [**ays**-beçǝr]	ice cream sundae
Erdbeeren [**ehrt**-beyrǝn]	strawberries
Gebäck [gǝbehk]	pastry
Kirschen [kihrSǝn]	cherries
Kompott [kom-**pot**]	stewed fruit
Obstsalat [**ohpst**-zah-laht]	fruit salad
Pfannkuchen [**pfahn**-kuhxǝn]	pancakes
Pfirsiche [**pfihr**-zihçǝ]	peaches
Pflaumen [pflaumǝn]	plums

Reisbrei [**rays**-bray]	rice pudding
Rhabarber [rah-**bahr**-bər]	rhubarb
Sahne [zahnə]	cream
Schlagsahne [**Slahk**-zahnə]	whipped cream
Schlagobers [**Slahg**-ohbərs]	whipped cream (in Austria)
Stachelbeeren [**Stahx**əl-beyrən]	gooseberries
Vanillesoße [vah-**nih**-lə-zoh-sə]	vanilla sauce

The choice of desserts is often limited to ice cream or fruit salad, but there are some typical desserts such as "Rote Grütze" [rohtə grewtsə] *(stewed red summer fruits served cold with cream or vanilla sauce) and "Kaiserschmarren"* [kayzər-Smahrən] *(Austrian cut-up, sugared pancakes with raisins). The range of cakes, on the other hand, is very large. As well as different types of fruit cakes such as "Apfelkuchen"* [**ahp**-fəl-kuhxən] *and cheesecake ("Käsekuchen")* [**keyz**ə-kuhxən]*, there are many "Torten"* [tortən] *(with layers of cream): "Schwarzwälder Kirschtorte"* [**Svahrts**-vehldər **kihrS**-tortə] *(Black Forest Cake), for example.*

List of Beverages

Getränke

Alkoholische Getränke	Alcoholic Beverages
Apfelwein [**ahp**-fəl-vayn]	hard cider
Bier [biir]	beer

*There are many different types of beer, varying from region to region. The most common are "Export" [**ehks**-port] or "Helles" [hehləs] (pale or light), "Pils" [pihls] (similar to Pilsner), "Alt" [ahlt] or "Bockbier" [**bok**-biir] (bock beer), and "Weizenbier" [**vayts**ən-biir] (a light wheat beer often drunk in summer with a slice of lemon). A shandy (beer with lemon soda) is generally known as "ein Radler" [ayn rahdlər].*

Weinbrand [**vayn**-brahnt]	brandy
Champagner [Sahm-**pahn**-yər]	champagne
Gin [dZihn] *(as in English)*	gin
Kognak [**kon**-yahk]	cognac
Likör [lih-**kœr**]	liqueur
Most [mohst]	cider
Rum [ruhm, room]	rum
Sekt [zehkt]	sparkling wine
Tafelwein [**tahf**əl-vayn]	table wine
Wein [vayn]	wine
leicht [layçt]	light
lieblich [**liip**-lihç]	sweet
rosé [roh-**zey**]	rosé
rot [roht]	red
trocken [trokən]	dry
weiß [vays]	white
Weinschorle sauer [**vayn**-Sorlə zauər]	wine with mineral water
Weinschorle süß [**vayn**-Sorlə zews]	wine with a soft drink

Whisky [**vih**-skii]	whiskey
Wodka [vot-kə]	vodka

After a meal you may be offered an "Obstler," [ohpstlər] a kind of fruit brandy or "Schnaps" [Snahps] distilled from pears, cherries, or plums.

*Most German wines are white or rosé. The red wines tend to be light. There are two basic categories: "Tafelwein" (table wine) and "Qualitätswein" [kvah-lih-**teyts**-vayn] (quality wine). "QbA" (Qualitätswein besonderer Anbaugebiete [...bəzondərər **ahn**-bau-gəbiitə]) means that the wine comes from one of eleven defined regions. Further quality levels are "Kabinett," [kah-bih-**neht**] "Spätlese" [**Speyt**-leyzə] (from a late harvest, with a richer flavor), and "Auslese" [**aus**-leyzə] (from selected very ripe grapes). A rare specialty is "Eiswein" [**ays**-vayn] (ice wine), made from grapes harvested after the frosts.*

Alcoholfreie Getränke

Nonalcoholic Beverages

alkoholfreies Bier [**ahl**-ko-hol-frayəs biir]	alcohol-free beer
Apfelsaft [**ahp**-fəl-zahft]	apple juice
Cola [kohlə]	coke
Eistee [**ays**-tey]	iced tea
Fruchtsaft [**fruhxt**-zahft]	fruit juice
Grapefruitsaft [**greyp**-froot-zahft]	grapefruit juice
Limonade [lih-moh-**nahdə**]	soft drink, carbonated drink
Mineralwasser [mih-ney-**rahl**-vahsər]	mineral water
mit Kohlensäure [miht **kohl**ən-zoyrə]	carbonated
ohne Kohlensäure [ohnə **kohl**ən-zoyrə]	still, with no carbonation
Orangensaft [oh-**rahŋ**-Zən-zahft]	orange juice
Tomatensaft [toh-**maht**ən-zahft]	tomato juice
Tonic [**to**-nihk]	tonic water

*Apple juice is often drunk diluted with mineral water ("Apfelsaftschorle" [**ahp**-fəl-zahft-Sorlə] or "gespritzter Apfelsaft" [gəS**priht**stər **ahp**-fəl-zahft]). Another popular drink is "Spezi" [**Speht**-sii] (a mixture of cola and orange soda).*

Kaffee & Tee

Eiskaffee [**ays**-kah-fey]
Früchtetee [**frewxt**ə-tey]
(eine Tasse) Kaffee
[(aynə tahsə) **kah**-fey]
koffeinfreier Kaffee
[kof-eh-**iin**-frayər **kah**-fey]
Kräutertee [**kroyt**ər-tey]
Milch [mihlç]
Pfefferminztee [**pfehf**ər-mihnts-tey]
Sahne [zahnə]
(eine Tasse/ein Glas) Tee
[(aynə tahsə / ayn glahs) tey]

Coffee & Tea

iced coffee
fruit tea
(a cup of) coffee

decaffeinated coffee

herbal tea
milk
peppermint tea
cream
(a cup/glass of) tea

> *Coffee is usually served with evaporated milk or cream. Often you can only order a "Kännchen" [kehn-çən] (small pot for two cups). "Schümli" [**Sewm**-lii] is Swiss-style frothy coffee. Italian coffees such as "Cappuccino" and "Espresso" are very popular. In Austrian coffeehouses you will encounter a wide range of specialties such as "Melange" [meh-**lahnZ**] (coffee with hot milk, café au lait), "Schwarzer" [S**vahrts**ər] (black coffee), and "kleiner Brauner" [klaynər braunər] (small cup of coffee with milk).*

Einige österreichische Spezialitaten

G'spritzter [gə**Sprihtst**ər]

Heuriger [**hoy**-rihgər]

Backhendl [**bahk**-hehndəl]
Brettljause [**breht**əl-yauzə]

Cevapcici [tSey-**vahp**-tSii-tSii]

Some Austrian Specialties

1/8 liter of wine diluted with the same amount of mineral water

young wine less than a year old

whole roasted chicken

a selection of cheeses and sliced cold meat

grilled sausages made with ground beef

Dampfnudeln [**dahmpf**-noo-dehln]	sweet dumplings filled with jam
Erdäpfel [**ehrt**-ehp-fəl]	potatoes
Faschiertes [fahS-**iirt**əs]	ground meat
Frittatensuppe [frih-**taht**ən-zuhpə]	clear soup with strips of pancake
Germknödel [**gehrm**-knœdəl]	a dumpling made from a yeast dough filled with plum jam and sprinkled with poppy seeds
Geselchtes [gə**zehlçt**əs]	smoked meat
Haxe [haksə]	leg of pork
Jause [yauzə]	afternoon snack
Kaiserschmarren [**kayz**ər-Smahrən]	cut-up sugared pancakes with almonds and raisins
Kren [krehn]	horseradish
Marillen [mah-**rihl**ən]	apricots
Mehlspeise [**mehl**-Spayzə]	general term for dessert
Nockerl [nokərl]	dumpling
Schlagobers [**Slahg**-ohbərs]	whipped cream
Palatschinken [**pah**-laht-Sihŋkən]	thin pancake filled with jam
Paradeiser [pah-rah-**dayz**ər]	tomatoes
Sachertorte [**zax**ər-tortə]	rich chocolate cake with thin layers of apricot jam
Schwammerl [Svamərl]	mushroom
Semmel [zehməl]	bread roll
Tafelspitz [**tahf**əl-Spihts]	boiled beef served with horseradish
Topfen [topfən]	farmer cheese
Topfenstrudel [**topf**ən-Stroodəl]	similar to apple strudel, but filled with farmer cheese

Einige Schweizer Spezialitaten	**Some Swiss Specialties**
Bündner Fleisch [**bewnt**-nər flayS]	paper-thin slices of air-dried beef
Berner Platte [behrnər plahtə]	platter with different kinds of meat, boiled tongue, sausages, and beans
Raclette [rah-**kleht**]	slices of melted raclette cheese served with potatoes and pickles
Käsefondue [**keyz**ə-fon-doo]	cheese fondue: hot melted cheese into which pieces of bread are dipped
Fondue bourguignonne [fon-**doo** buhr-gihn-**yohn**]	small pieces of beef dipped in a hot broth, served with various sauces
Züricher Rahmgeschnetzeltes [**tsew**-rihçər **rahm**-gəSnehtsəltəs]	strips of veal in a creamy wine and mushroom sauce
Rösti [**rœs**-tii]	hash brown potatoes
Rübli [**rewb**-lii]	carrots
Kabis [**kah**-bihs]	cabbage
Fladen [flahdən]	cake
Glacé [glah-**sey**]	ice cream
Schale [Sahlə]	coffee with milk
Café crème [kah-**fey** krehm]	coffee with cream
Rahm [rahm]	whipped cream
Bürli [**bewr**-lii]	bread rolls

Tourist Information

Auf dem Verkehrsbüro

For information about interesting sights, festivals, and events follow the i-sign to the Fremdenverkehrsamt [**frehmd**ən-fehr-kehrz-ahmt] (tourist office). There is one in nearly every town.

I'd like a map of the town (city), please.	Ich möchte einen Stadtplan haben. [ihç mœçtə aynən **Staht**-plahn hahbən]
Do you have brochures on …?	Haben Sie Prospekte von …? [hahbən zii proh-**spekt**ə fon]
Do you have a schedule of events for this week?	Haben Sie einen Veranstaltungskalender für diese Woche? [hahbən zii aynən fehr-**ahn**-Stahl-tuhŋz-kah-lehn-dər fewr diizə vohxə]
Are there sightseeing tours of the town (city)?	Gibt es Stadtrundfahrten? [gihpt ehs **Staht**-ruhnt-fahrtən]
How much does the tour cost?	Was kostet die Rundfahrt? [vahs kostət dii **ruhnt**-fahrt]

Places of Interest/Museums

Sehenswürdigkeiten/Museen

What places of interest are there here?	Welche Sehenswürdigkeiten gibt es hier? [vehlçə **zey**ənz-vewr-dihç-kaytən gihpt ehs hiir]
We'd like to visit …	Wir möchten … besichtigen. [viir mœçtən … bə**zihç**-tihgən]
When's the museum open?	Wann ist das Museum geöffnet? [vahn ihst dahs muh-**zey**-uhm gəœfnət]
When does the tour start?	Wann beginnt die Führung? [vahn bə**gihnt** dii **few**-ruhŋ]
Is there a tour in English, too?	Gibt es auch eine Führung auf Englisch? [gihpt ehs aux aynə **few**-ruhŋ auf **ehŋ**-lihS]
Are we allowed to take photographs here?	Darf man hier fotografieren? [dahrf mahn hiir foh-toh-grah-**fiir**ən]

What square/church is that?	Was für ein Platz/eine Kirche ist das? [vahs fewr ayn plahts / aynə kihrçə ihst dahs]
Is this (that) …?	Ist das …? [ihst dahs]
When was … built?	Wann wurde … erbaut? [vahn vuhrdə … ehr-**baut**]
Who's the artist/the sculptor?	Wie heißt der Künstler/ Bildhauer? [vii hayst dehr kewnst-lər / **bihlt**-hauər]
Is there an exhibition catalogue?	Gibt es einen Katalog zur Ausstellung? [gihpt ehs aynən kah-tah-**lohk** tsuhr **aus**-Steh-luhŋ]
Do you have a poster/ postcard/slide of …?	Haben Sie das Bild … als Poster/Postkarte/Dia? [hahbən zii dahs bihlt … ahls pos-tər / **post**-kahrtə / **dii**-ah]

Most museums and art galleries are closed on Mondays.

Word List: Places of Interest/Museums

abbey	die Abtei [ahp-**tay**]
aisle	das Seitenschiff [**zaytə**n-Sihf]
altar	der Altar [ahl-**tahr**]
ancient	antik [ahn-**tiik**]
arcade	der Bogengang [**bohgə**n-gahŋ]
arch	der Bogen [bohgən]
pointed arch	der Spitzbogen [**Spihts**-bohgən]
round arch	der Rundbogen [**ruhnt**-bohgən]
archaeology	die Archäologie [ahr-çeh-oh-loh-**gii**]
architect	Architekt/Architektin [ahr-çih-**tehkt** / -ihn]
architecture	die Architektur [ahr-çih-tehk-**toor**]
art collection	die Kunstsammlung [**kuhnst**-zahm-luhŋ]
Art Nouveau	der Jugendstil [**yoogə**nt-Stiil]
arts and crafts	das Kunstgewerbe [**kuhnst**-gəvehrbə]
balustrade	die Balustrade [bah-luh-**strahdə**]
Baroque	die Barockzeit [bah-**rok**-tsayt] / barock [bah-**rok**]

bay	der Erker [ehrkər]
bell	die Glocke [glokə]
birthplace	die Geburtsstätte [gəbuhrts-Stehtə]
bridge	die Brücke [brewkə]
bronze	die Bronze [brohn-sə]
Bronze Age	die Bronzezeit [**brohns**ə-tsayt]
building	das Bauwerk [**bau**-vehrk]
	das Gebäude [gəboydə]

State Gallery, Stuttgart

bust	die Büste [bewstə]
(flying) buttress	der Strebepfeiler [**Streyb**ə-pfaylər]
candlestick	der (Kerzen-)Leuchter [(**kehrts**ən-)loyçtər]
capital	das Kapitell [kah-pih-**tehl**]
carpet	der Teppich [**teh**-pihç]
castle	die Burg [buhrk]
	das Schloss [Slos]
catacombs	die Katakomben *f pl* [kah-tah-**komb**ən]
cathedral	der Dom [dohm]
	die Kathedrale [kah-tey-**drahl**ə]

Catholic *(noun)*	Katholik/Katholikin [kah-toh-**liik** / -ihn]
(adj)	katholisch [kah-**toh**-lihS]
ceiling	die Decke [dehkə]
ceiling fresco	die Deckenmalerei [**dehk**ən-mahləray]
Celtic	keltisch [**kehl**-tihS]
cemetery	der Friedhof [**friit**-hohf]
center of trade	die Handelsstadt [**hahnd**əls-Staht]
century	das Jahrhundert [yahr-**huhn**dərt]
ceramics	die Keramik [keh-**rah**-mihk]
chandelier	der (Kron-)Leuchter [(**kron**-)loyçtər]
chapel	die Kapelle [kah-**pehl**ə]
china	das Porzellan [port-seh-**lahn**]
choir	der Chor [kohr]
choir stalls	das Chorgestühl [**kohr**-gəStewl]
Christian *(noun)*	Christ/Christin [krihst / **krihs**-tihn]
(adj)	christlich [**krihst**-lihç]
Christianity	das Christentum [**krihst**ən-tuhm]
church	die Kirche [kihrçə]
citadel	die Zitadelle [tsih-tah-**dehl**ə]
city hall	das Rathaus [**raht**-haus]
classicism	der Klassizismus [klah-sih-**tsis**-muhs]
clergyman	der Geistliche [**gayst**-lihçə]
cloister	der Kreuzgang [**kroyts**-gahŋ]
colonnade	der Bogengang [**bohg**ən-gahŋ]
column	die Säule [zoylə]
convent	(Nonnen-)Kloster [(**non**ən-)klohstər]
copperplate	der Kupferstich [**kupf**ər-Stihç]
copy	die Kopie [koh-**pii**]
Corinthian	korinthisch [ko-**rihn**-tihS]
county/state fair	das Volksfest [**folks**-fehst]
court	der Hof [hohf]
covered market	die Markthalle [**mahrkt**-hahlə]
cross	das Kreuz [kroyts]
crucifix	das Kruzifix [kruht-sih-**fihks**]

crypt	die Krypta [**krewp**-tah]
customs	das Brauchtum [**braux**-tuhm]
denomination	die Konfession [kon-fehs-**yohn**]
design	das Design [dih-**zayn**]
dig	die Ausgrabungen *f pl* [**aus**-grah-buhŋən]
diocesan town	der Bischofssitz [**bih**-Sofs-zihts]
dome	die Kuppel [kuhpəl]
Doric	dorisch [**doh**-rihS]
downtown	die Innenstadt [**ihn**ən-Staht]
drawing	die Zeichnung [**tsayç**-nuhŋ]
dynasty	die Dynastie [dew-nahs-**tii**]
emblem	das Wahrzeichen [**vahr**-tsayçən]
emperor	der Kaiser [kayzər]
empress	die Kaiserin [**kayz**ərihn]
epoch	die Epoche [eh-**pox**ə]
etching	die Radierung [rah-**diir**-uhŋ]
excavations	die Ausgrabungen *f pl* [**aus**-grah-buhŋən]
exhibit	das Exponat [ehks-poh-**naht**]
exhibition	die Ausstellung [**aus**-Steh-luhŋ]
façade	die Fassade [fah-**sahd**ə]
find	der Fund [fuhnt]
font	das Taufbecken [**tauf**-behkən]
fortress	die Festung [**fehs**-tuhŋ]
foundations	das Fundament [fuhn-dah-**mehnt**]
founder	der Gründer [grewndər]
fountain	der Brunnen [bruhnən]
fresco	das Fresko [**frehs**-koh]
frieze	der Fries [friis]
gable	der Giebel [giibəl]
gallery	die Empore [ehm-**pohr**ə] die Galerie [gah-leh-**rii**]
gate	das Tor [tohr]
Germanic	germanisch [gehr-**mah**-nihS]

The Brandenburg Gate, Berlin

glass painting	die Glasmalerei [**glahs**-mah-lə-ray]
Gobelin	der Gobelin [goh-bə-**leh (as in French)**]
gold work	die Goldschmiedekunst [**golt**-Smiidə-kuhnst]
Gothic	die Gotik [**goh**-tihk] gotisch [**goh**-tihS]
Gothic revival	die Neugotik [**noy**-goh-tihk]
government building	das Regierungsgebäude [reh-**giir**-uhŋs-gəboydə]
graphic arts	die Grafik [**grah**-fihk]
grave	das Grab [grahp]
gravestone	der Grabstein [**grahp**-Stayn]
graveyard	der Friedhof [**friit**-hohf]
Greek *(noun)*; the Greeks; Greek *(adj)*	Grieche/Griechin[griiçə / **grii**-çihn] die Griechen *pl* [griiçən] griechisch [**grii**-çihS]
ground plan	der Grundriss [**gruhnt**-rihs]
guide	Fremdenführer/Fremdenführerin [**frehmd**ən-fewrər / -fewrərihn]
guided tour	die Führung [**fewr**-uhŋ]

heathen	heidnisch [**hayt**-nihS]
heyday	die Blütezeit [**blewt**ətsayt]
historic district	die Altstadt [**ahlt**-Staht]

*Half-timbered house,
South Germany*

history	die Geschichte [gə**Sihç**tə]
illustration	die Illustration [ih-luhs-traht-**syohn**]
impressionism	der Impressionismus [ihm-prehs-yoh-**nihs**-muhs]
influence	der Einfluss [**ayn**-fluhs]
inner courtyard	der Innenhof [**ihn**ən-hohf]
inscription	die Inschrift [**ihn**-Srihft]
Ionic	ionisch [ii-**oh**-nihS]
Jew	Jude/Jüdin [yoodə / **yew**-dihn]
Jewish	jüdisch [**yew**-dihS]
king	der König [**kœ**-nihç]
landscape painting	die Landschaftsmalerei [**lahnt**-Sahfts-mahləray]

library	die Bibliothek [bihb-lii-oh-**teyk**]
lithograph(y)	die Lithografie [lih-toh-grah-**fii**]
looting	die Plünderung [**plewn**-dəruhŋ]
marble	der Marmor [**mahr**-mor]
market	der Markt [markt]
marquetry	die Intarsien *f pl* [ihn-**tahrz**-yehn]
material	das Material [mah-tehr-**yahl**]
mausoleum	das Mausoleum [mau-zoh-**ley**-uhm]
mayor/mayoress	Bürgermeister/Bürgermeisterin [**bewrg**ər-maystər / -maystə-rihn]
medieval	mittelalterlich [**miht**əl-ahltər-lihç]
megalithic grave	das Hünengrab [**hewn**ən-grahp]
memorial	die Gedenkstätte [gə**dehŋk**-Stehtə]
Middle Ages	das Mittelalter [**miht**əl-ahltər]
model	das Modell [moh-**dehl**]
modern	modern [moh-**dehrn**]
monastery	(Mönchs-)Kloster [(**mœnks**-)kloh-stər]
monk	der Mönch [mœnç]
monument	das Denkmal [**dehŋk**-mahl] das Grabmal [**grahp**-mahl]
mosaic	das Mosaik [moh-zah-**iik**]
Moslem *(noun);* *(adj)*	Moslem/Moslemin [**mos**-lehm / -ihn] moslemisch [mos-**leh**-mihS]
mural (painting)	die Wandmalerei [**vahnt**-mahləray]
museum	das Museum [moo-**zey**-uhm]
museum of ethnology	das Völkerkundemuseum [**fœlk**ər-kuhndə-moo-zey-uhm]
natural history museum	das Naturkundemuseum [nah-**toor**-kuhndə-moo-zey-uhm]
nave	das Mittelschiff [**miht**əl-Sihf]
neo-Gothic style	die Neugotik [**noy**-goh-tihk]
Norman	normannisch [nor-**mah**-nihS]
nude	der Akt [ahkt]
nun	die Nonne [nonə]
obelisk	der Obelisk [oh-beh-**lihsk**]

oil painting	die Ölmalerei [œl-mahləray]
opera	die Oper [oh-pehr]

State Opera House, Wien (Vienna)

order (holy)	der (religiöse) Orden [(reh-lihg-**yœzə**) ordən]
organ	die Orgel [orgəl]
oriel	der Erker [ehrkər]
original	das Original [oh-rih-gih-**nahl**]
ornament	das Ornament [or-nah-**mehnt**]
outline	Grundriss [**gruhnt**-rihs] Abriss [**ahp**-rihs]
pagan	heidnisch [**hayd**-nihS]
painter	Maler/Malerin [mahlər / **mahl**ərihn]
painting	die Malerei [mahlə**ray**] die Gemälde [gə**mehld**ə]
palace	der Palast [pah-**lahst**]
panel	das Tafelbild [**taf**əl-bihlt]
parchment	das Pergament [pehr-gah-**mehnt**]
pastel	das Pastell [pahs-**tehl**]
pavilion	der Pavillon [pah-vihl-**yohn**]

Phoenician	phönizisch [fœ-**niht**-sihS]
photography	die Fotografie [foh-toh-grah-**fii**]
photomontage	die Fotomontage [**foh**-toh-mon-tahZə]
picture	das Bild [bihlt]
pilgrim	Pilger/Pilgerin [pihlgər / **pihlg**ərihn]
pilgrimage	die Pilgerfahrt [**pihlg**ər-fahrt]
pillage	die Plünderung [**plewn**-dəruhŋ]
pillar	die Säule [zoylə]
	der Pfeiler [pfaylər]
place of worship	die Kultstätte [**kuhlt**-Stehtə]
porcelain	das Porzellan [port-seh-**lahn**]
portal	das Portal [por-**tahl**]
portrait	das Porträt [por-**treht**]
poster	das Plakat [plah-**kaht**]
pottery	die Töpferei [tœp-fəray]
prehistoric	vorgeschichtlich [**forg**əSihçt-lihç]
prime	die Blütezeit [**blewt**ə-tsayt]
Protestant *(noun)*	der Protestant [proh-tehs-**tahnt**]
(adj)	protestantisch [proh-tehs-**tahn**-tihS]
pulpit	die Kanzel [kahnt-səl]
queen	die Königin [**kœ**-nih-gihn]
relief	das Relief [rey-**lyehf**]
religion	die Religion [rey-lihg-**yohn**]
remains	die Überreste *m pl* [**ewb**ər-rehstə]
Renaissance	die Renaissance [rəneh-**sahns**]
restoration	die Restaurierung [reh-stau-**rii**-ruhŋ]
Romanesque	romanisch [roh-**mah**-nihS]
Romanesque period	die Romanik [roh-**mahn**-tihk]
Romanticism	die Romantik [roh-**mahn**-tihk]
roof	das Dach [dahx]
rosette	die Rosette [roh-**zeht**ə]
ruin	die Ruine [roo-**iin**ə]
rune stone	der Runenstein [**roon**ən-Stayn]
runes	die Runen *f pl* [roonən]
sandstone	der Sandstein [**zahnt**-Stayn]

sarcophagus	der Sarkophag [zahr-koh-**fahk**]
school	die Schule [Soolə]
sculptor	Bildhauer/Bildhauerin [**bihlt**-hauər / -hauərihn]
sculpture	die Plastik [**plahs**-tihk]
	die Skulptur [skuhlp-**toor**]
(church) service	der Gottesdienst [**gotəs**-diinst]
sights	die Sehenswürdigkeiten [**zey**əns-vewr-dihç-kaytən]
sightseeing tour of the town/city	die Stadtrundfahrt [**Staht**-ruhnt-fahrt]
silk-screen print(ing)	der Siebdruck [**ziip**-druhk]
square	der Platz [plahts]
statue	die Statue [Staht-wə]

Marx-Engels monument, Berlin

"Next time we'll get it right."

steeple	der Kirchturm [**kihrç**-tuhrm]
still life	das Stillleben [**Stihl**-leybən]

Stone Age	die Steinzeit [**Stayn**-tsayt]
stucco	der Stuck [Stuhk]
style	der Stil [Stiil]
symbol	das Wahrzeichen [**vahr**-tsayçən]
symbolism	der Symbolismus [zewm-bo-**lihs**-muhs]
synagogue	die Synagoge [zew-nah-**gohg**ə]
tapestry	der Teppich [**teh**-pihç]
	der Gobelin [goh-bəleh]
temple	der Tempel [tehmpəl]
terracotta	die Terrakotta [teh-rah-**kot**ə]
theater	das Theater [tey-**aht**ər]
to rebuild	wieder aufbauen [viidər **auf**-bauən]
to reconstruct	rekonstruieren [rey-kon-Stroo-**iir**ən]
to restore	restaurieren [reh-stau-**riir**ən]
tomb	das Grab [grahp]
tombstone	der Grabstein [**grahp**-Stayn]
torso	der Torso [**tor**-zoh]
tour	die Besichtigung [bə-**zihç**-tih-guhŋ]
	die Rundfahrt [**ruhnt**-fahrt]
tower	der Turm [tuhrm]
(the old) town	die Altstadt [**ahlt**-Staht]
town hall	das Rathaus [**raht**-haus]
town wall	die Stadtmauer [**Staht**-mauər]
trading center	die Handelsstadt [**hahnd**əls-Staht]
traditions	das Brauchtum [**braux**-tuhm]
transept	das Querschiff [**kvehr**-Sihf]
treasure chamber	die Schatzkammer [**Sahts**-kamər]
university	die Universität [oo-nih-vehr-sih-**teyt**]
vase	die Vase [vahzə]
vault(s)	das Gewölbe [gə**vœlb**ə]
vestry	die Sakristei [zah-krihs-**tay**]
Vikings	die Wikinger *m pl* [**vii**-kihŋər]
wall	die Mauer [mauər]
watercolor	das Aquarell [ahk-vah-**rehl**]

weaving	die Weberei [vey-bəray]
window	das Fenster [fehnstər]
wing	der Flügel [flewgəl]
wood carving	die Schnitzerei [Snihtsəray]
woodcut	der Holzschnitt [holts-Sniht]
work	das Werk [vehrk]
early work	das Frühwerk [frew-vehrk]
late work	das Spätwerk [Speyt-vehrk]

Excursions   ▶ also Chapter 3, Ship

Ausflüge

Can you see … from here?	Kann man von hier aus … sehen? [kahn mahn fon hiir aus … zeyən]
What direction is …?	In welcher Richtung liegt …? [ihn vehlçər **rihç**-tuhŋ liikt …]
Will we pass …?	Kommen wir am/an … vorbei? [komən viir ahm/ahn … for-**bay**]

Neuschwanstein Castle, Bavaria

Are we going to see …, too?	Besichtigen wir auch …? [bəzihç-tihgən viir aux …]
How much free time do we have in …?	Wie viel freie Zeit haben wir in …? [vii fiil frayə tsayt hahbən viir ihn …]
When are we going back?	Wann fahren wir zurück? [vahn fahrən viir tsuh-**rewk**]
When will we be back?	Wann werden wir zurück sein? [vahn vehrdən viir tsuh-**rewk** zayn]

Word List: Excursions

amusement park	der Vergnügungspark [fehrg-**new**-guhŋs-pahrk]
bird sanctuary	das Vogelschutzgebiet [**fohg**əl-Suhts-gəbiit]
botanical gardens	der Botanische Garten [boh-**tah**-nihSə gahrtən]
brewery	die Brauerei [brau-ə**ray**]
cave	die Höhle [hœlə]
cliff	die Klippe [klihpə]
countryside	die Landschaft [**lahnt**-Sahft]
day trip	der Tagesausflug [**tahg**əs-aus-fluhk]

The "blue spring" of Blaubeuren, South Germany

environs	die Umgebung [uhm-**gey**-buhŋ]
excursion	der Ausflug [**aus**-fluhk]
fishing port	der Fischerhafen [**fihS**ər-hahfən]
flea market	der Flohmarkt [**floh**-mahrkt]
forest	der Wald [vahlt]
forest fire	der Waldbrand [**vahlt**-brahnt]
gorge	die Schlucht [Sluhxt]
grotto	die Grotte [grotə]
heath	die Heide [haydə]
lake	der See [zey]
manor house	das Herrenhaus [**hehrn**-haus]
market	der Markt [mahrkt]
mine	das Bergwerk [**behrk**-vehrk]
moor	die Heide [haydə]
mountains	das Gebirge [gə**bihrg**ə]
mud flats	das Watt [vaht]
national park	der Nationalpark [naht-syoh-**nahl**-pahrk]
nature reserve	das Naturschutzgebiet [nah-**toor**-Suhts-gəbiit]
observatory	die Sternwarte [**Stehrn**-vahrtə]
open-air museum	das Freilichtmuseum [**fray**-lihçt-moo-zey-uhm]
panorama	der Rundblick [**ruhnt**-blihk]
petting zoo	der Streichelzoo [**Stray**çəl-tsoh]
planetarium	das Planetarium [plah-neh-**tahr**-yuhm]
ravine	die Klamm [klahm]
recreation center	das Freizeitzentrum [**fray**-tsayt-tsehn-truhm]
reef	das Riff [rihf]
safari park	der Safaripark [zah-**fah**-rii-pahrk]
scenery	die Landschaft [**lahnt**-Sahft]
square	der Platz [plahts]
suburb	der Vorort [**for**-ort]
surroundings	die Umgebung [uhm-**gey**-buhŋ]

Linderhof Castle, Bavaria

tour	die Rundfahrt [**ruhnt**-fahrt]
trip	der Ausflug [**aus**-fluhk]
valley	das Tal [tahl]
vantage point	der Aussichtspunkt [**aus**-ziçts-puhŋkt]
vineyard	der Weinberg [**vayn**-behrk]
waterfall	der Wasserfall [**vahs**ər-fahl]
woods	der Wald [vahlt]
zoo	der Zoo [tsoo]
	das Tiergarten [**tiir**-gahrtən]

Events/Entertainment

Veranstaltungen/Unterhaltung

Theater/Concert/Movies	**Theater/Konzert/Kino**
What's on (at the theater) tonight?	Welches Stück wird heute Abend (im Theater) gespielt? [vehlçəs Stewk vihrt hoytə ah-bənt (ihm tey-**aht**ər) gə**Spiilt**]

What's on at the movies tomorrow night?	Was läuft morgen Abend im Kino? [vahs loyft morgən ah-bənt ihm **kii**-noh]
Are there concerts in the cathedral?	Werden im Dom Konzerte veranstaltet? [vehrdən ihm dohm kon-**tsehrt**ə fehr-**ahn**-Stahltət]
Can you recommend a good play/film (movie)?	Können Sie mir ein gutes Theaterstück/einen guten Film empfehlen? [kœnən zii miir ayn gootəs tey-**aht**ər-Stewk / aynən gootən fihlm ehmp-**feyl**ən]
When does the performance start?	Wann beginnt die Vorstellung? [vahn bəgihnt dii **for**-Steh-luhŋ]
Where can I get tickets?	Wo bekommt man Karten? [voh bəkomt mahn kahrtən]
Two tickets for this evening/tomorrow evening, please.	Bitte zwei Karten für heute/ morgen Abend. [bihtə tsvay kahrtən fewr hoytə / morgən ah-bənt]
Two seats at …, please.	Bitte zwei Plätze zu … [bihtə tsvay plehtsə tsuh …]
Two adults and one child.	Zwei Erwachsene, ein Kind. [tsvay ehr-**vaks**ənə, ayn kihnt]
Can I have a program, please?	Kann ich bitte ein Programm haben? [kahn ihç bihtə ayn proh-**grahm** hahbən]
What time does the performance end?	Wann ist die Vorstellung zu Ende? [vahn ihst dii **for**-Steh-luhŋ tsuh ehndə]
Where's the checkroom?	Wo ist die Garderobe? [voh ihst dii gahrdə-**rohb**ə]

Word List: Theater/Concert/Movies

accompaniment	die Begleitung [bəglay-tuhŋ]
act	der Akt [ahkt]
actor/actress	Schauspieler/Schauspielerin [**Sau**-Spiilər / -Spiilə-rihn]
advance sale	der Vorverkauf [**for**-fehr-kauf]
ballet	das Ballett [bah-**leht**]

box	die Loge [lohzə]
box office	die Kasse [kahsə]
cabaret	das Kabarett [kah-bah-**reht**,/**rey**]
calendar of events	der Veranstaltungskalender [fehr-**ahn**-Stahl-tuhŋs-kah-lehn-dər]
checkroom	die Garderobe [gahrdə-**rohb**ə]
choir	der Chor [kohr]
circus	der Zirkus [**tsihr**-kuhs]
comedy	die Komödie [ko-**mœ**-dyə]
composer	Komponist/Komponistin [kom-poh-**nihst**/-**nihs**-tihn]
concert	das Konzert [kon-**tsehrt**]
chamber music concert	das Kammerkonzert [**kahm**ər-]
jazz concert	das Jazzkonzert ("jazz" as in English)
pop concert	das Popkonzert [**pop**-]
symphony concert	das Sinfoniekonzert [zihn-foh-**nii**-]
conductor	Dirigent/Dirigentin [dih-rih-**gehnt**/-**gehn**-tihn]
curtain	der Vorhang [**for**-hahŋ]
dancer	Tänzer/Tänzerin [tehntsər/**tehnts**ərihn]
director	Regisseur/Regisseurin [reh-zih-**sœr**/-**sœ**-rihn]
drama	das Drama [drah-mə]
festival	das Festival [**fehs**-tih-vahl]
film	der Film [fihlm]
film actor/actress	Filmschauspieler [**fihlm**-Sau-Spiilər] Filmschauspielerin [-ihn]
intermission	die Pause [pauzə]
movie	der Film [fihlm]
movie theater	das Kino [**kii**-noh]
drive-in movie theater	das Freilichtkino [**fray**-lihçt-]
musical	das Musical (as in English)
open-air theater	das Freilichttheater [**fray**-lihçt-tey-ahtər]
opera	die Oper [ohpər]
opera glasses	das Opernglas [**oh**-pehrn-glahs]

operetta	die Operette [oh-peh-**reht**ə]
orchestra	das Orchester [or-**kehst**ər]
orchestra *(section of seats in a theater)*	das Parkett [pahr-**keht**]
part	die Rolle [rohlə]
performance	die Vorstellung [**for**-Steh-luhŋ]; die Aufführung [**auf**-few-ruhŋ]
play	das Schauspiel [**Sau**-Spiil]; das Theaterstück [tey-**aht**ər-Stewk]
premiere	die Premiere [prehm-**yeyr**ə]
production	die Inszenierung [ihns-tseh-**nii**-ruhŋ]
program	der Spielplan [**Spiil**-plahn]
program *(booklet)*	das Programmheft [proh-**grahm**-hehft]
role	die Rolle [rohlə]
leading role	die Hauptrolle [**haupt**-rohlə]
row	der Rang [rahŋ]
singer	Sänger/Sängerin [zehŋər / -ihn]
soloist	Solist/Solistin [zoh-**lihst** / -ihn]
stage	die Bühne [bewnə]
subtitle	der Untertitel [**uhnt**ər-tiitəl]
ticket	die Eintrittskarte [**ayn**-trihts-kahrtə]
tier	der Rang [rahŋ]
tragedy	die Tragödie [trah-**gœd**-yə]
variety (theater)	das Varietee [vahr-yə-**tey**]
vaudeville	das Varietee [vahr-yə-**tey**]

Bar/Discotheque/Nightclub

Bar/Disko/Nachtclub

What is there to do here in the evenings?	Was kann man hier abends unternehmen? [vahs kahn mahn hiir ah-bənts uhntər-**neym**ən]
Is there a nice bar here?	Gibt es hier eine gemütliche Kneipe? [gihpt ehs hiir aynə gə**mewt**-lihçə knaypə]
Where can we go dancing?	Wo kann man hier tanzen gehen? [voh kahn mahn hiir tahntsən geyən]

Is there a young crowd there, or is it more for older people?	Ist dort ein eher junges oder älteres Publikum? [ihst dort ayn eyər yuhŋəs ohdər ehltərəs **puhb**-lih-kuhm]
Is evening dress required?	Ist Abendgarderobe erwünscht? [ihst **ah**-bənt-gahrdə-rohbə ehr-**vewnSt**]
One drink is included in the price of admission.	Im Eintrittspreis ist ein Getränk enthalten. [ihm **ayn**-trihts-prays ihst ayn gətr**ehŋk** ehnt-**hahlt**ən]
A whiskey and soda, please.	Ein Whisky-Soda, bitte. [ayn **vihs**-kii-zohdə bihtə]
The same again.	Das gleiche noch mal. [dahs glayçə nox mahl]
This round's on me.	Diese Runde übernehme ich. [diizə ruhndə ewbər-**neym**ə ihç]
Shall we (have another) dance?	Wollen wir (noch mal) tanzen? [volən viir (nox mahl) tahntsən]
Shall we go for a walk?	Wollen wir noch einen Bummel machen? [volən viir nox aynən buhməl mahxən]

In bars you don't pay for each individual drink. The bartender will keep a record of your orders (sometimes on your beer coaster) and present you with the check when you leave. In larger cities, bars and taverns are open until well after midnight.

Word List: Bar/Discotheque/Nightclub

band	die Band [behnt]
bar	die Bar [bahr]
bouncer	der Türsteher [**tewr**-Steyər]
casino	das Spielcasino [**Spiil**-kah-zii-noh]
to dance	tanzen [tahntsən]
dance band	die Tanzkapelle [**tahnts**-kah-pehlə]
dance music	die Tanzmusik [**tahnts**-moo-ziik]
disc jockey	der Diskjockey (as in English)
disco(theque)	Disko(thek) [**dihs**-koh(-**tehk**)]
folk club	der Folkloreklub [folk-**lohr**ə-kluhp]

folk music	die Folkloremusik [folk-**lohr**ə-moo-ziik]
gambling arcade	die Spielhalle [**Spiil**-hahlə]
to go out	ausgehen [**aus**-geyən]
live music	die Livemusik [**layv**-moo-ziik]
nightclub	der Nachtclub [**nahxt**-kluhp]
show	die Show [Soh]
tavern	die Kneipe [knaypə]

At the Lake/Swimming Pool/On the Beach

Am See/Im Schwimmbad/Am Strand

Is there an outdoor/indoor pool here?	Gibt es hier ein Freibad/Hallenbad? [gihpt ehs hiir ayn **fray**-baht / **hahl**ən-baht]
Swimmers only!	Nur für Schwimmer! [noor fewr Svihmər]
No diving from the side of the pool!	Springen vom Beckenrand verboten! [Sprihŋən fom **behk**ən-rahnt fehr-**boht**ən]
No swimming!	Baden verboten! [bahdən fehr-**boht**ən]
Is the beach sandy/stony?	Ist der Strand sandig/steinig? [ihst dehr Strahnt **zahn**-dihç / **Stay**-nihç]
Are there any algae?	Gibt es Algen? [gihpt ehs ahlgən]
Is the water clean?	Ist das Wasser sauber? [ihst dahs vahsər zaubər]
How far out is it possible to swim?	Wie weit darf man hinausschwimmen? [vii vayt dahrf mahn hih-**naus**-Svihmən]
Is there a strong current?	Ist die Strömung stark? [ihst dii **Strœ**-muhŋ Stahrk]
Is it dangerous for children?	Ist es für Kinder gefährlich? [ihst ehs fewr kihndər gə**fehr**-lihç]
When's low tide/high tide?	Wann ist Ebbe/Flut? [vahn ihst ehbə / floot]
I'd like to rent …	Ich möchte … mieten. [ihç mœçtə … miitən]
a boat.	ein Boot [ayn boht]
a pair of waterskis.	ein Paar Wasserski [ayn pahr **vahs**ər-Sii]
a pedal boat.	ein Tretboot [ayn **treht**-boht]
a rowboat.	ein Ruderboot [ayn **rood**ər-boot]
a surfboard.	ein Surfbrett [ayn **sərf**-breht] ("surf" as in English)
How much is it per hour/day?	Was kostet es pro Stunde/pro Tag? [vahs kostət ehs proh Stuhndə / proh tahk]

*On many lakes and rivers you can find a boat rental ("Bootsverleih" [**bohts**-fehr-lay]). Bicycles can also be rented in most tourist areas. Try the local railroad station.*

Sports

Sport

What sports events are there here?	Welche Sportveranstaltungen gibt es hier? [vehlçə **Sport**-fehr-ahn-Stah-tuhŋən gihpt ehs hiir]
What sports facilities are there here?	Welche Sportmöglichkeiten gibt es hier? [vehlçə **Sport**-mœg-lihç-kaytən gihpt ehs hiir]
Is there a golf course/tennis court here?	Gibt es hier einen Golfplatz/einen Tennisplatz? [gihpt ehs hiir aynən **golf**-plahts / aynən **teh**-nihs-plahts]
Where can I go fishing?	Wo kann man hier angeln? [voh kahn mahn hiir ahŋəln]
I'd like to see the soccer match.	Ich möchte mir das Fußballspiel ansehen. [ih mœçtə miir dahs **fuhs**-bahl-Spiil **ahn**-zeyən]
When/Where is it?	Wann/Wo findet es statt? [vahn / voh fihndət ehs Staht]
How much does it cost to get in?	Was kostet der Eintritt? [vahs kostət dehr **ayn**-triht]
I'd like to go for a hike in the mountains.	Ich möchte eine Bergtour machen. [ihç mœçtə aynə **behrk**-toor mahxən]
Can you show me an interesting route on the map?	Können Sie mir eine interessante Route auf der Karte zeigen? [kœnən zii miir aynə ihn-teh-rəsahntə rootə auf dehr kahrtə tsaygən]
Where can I rent …?	Wo kann ich … ausleihen? [voh kahn ihç … **aus**-layən]
I'd like to take a … course.	Ich möchte einen …kurs machen. [ihç mœçtə aynən … kuhrs mahxən]
What sport do you go in for?	Welchen Sport treiben Sie? [vehlçən Sport traybən zii]

I play …	Ich spiele … [ihç Spiilə]
I'm a soccer fan.	Ich bin ein Fußballfan. [ihç bihn ayn **fuhs**-bahl-fehn] (or "fan" as in English)
I like to go to …	Ich gehe gern … [ihç geyə gehrn]
Can I play too?	Kann ich mitspielen? [kahn ihç **miht**-Spiilən]

> *The most popular sports are soccer, tennis, and bicycling in summer and skiing in winter. Golf is becoming quite popular now, although golf courses usually admit members only.*

Word List: Sports

activity vacation	der Aktivurlaub [ahk-**tiif**-oor-laup]
aerobics	das Aerobic [ah-eh-**roh**-bihk]
air mattress	die Luftmatratze [**luhft**-mah-trahtsə]
athlete	Sportler/Sportlerin [**Sport**-lər / **Sport**-lə-rihn]
athletic field	der Sportplatz [**Sport**-plahts]
attendant *(swimming)*	Bademeister/Bademeisterin [**bahdə**-maystər / -maystə-rihn]
badminton	das Badminton (as in English), der Federball [**feydə**r-bahl]
badminton racket	der Badmintonschläger [-Sleygər]
ball	der Ball [bahl]
basketball	der Basketball [**bahsk**ət-bahl]
beach umbrella	der Sonnenschirm [**zon**ən-Sihrm]
beginner	Anfänger/Anfängerin [**ahn**-fehŋər / -ihn]
to bicycle	Rad fahren [raht fahrən]
bicycle racing	das Radrennen [**raht**-rehnən]
bicycle tour	die Radtour [**raht**-toor]
bicycling	der Radsport [**raht**-Sport]

boat rental	der Bootsverleih [**bohts**-fehr-lay]
cable car	die Seilbahn [**zayl**-bahn]
canoe	das Kanu [kah-**noo**], das Paddelboot [**pahd**əl-boht]
chairlift	der Sessellift [**zehs**əl-lihft]
championship	die Meisterschaft [**mayst**ər-Sahft]
contest	der Wettkampf [**veht**-kahmpf]
course	der Kurs [kuhrs]
crew	die Mannschaft [**mahn**-Sahft]
cross-country skiing	der Langlauf [**lahŋ**-lauf]
deck chair	der Liegestuhl [**liig**ə-Stool]
deep-sea fishing	das Hochseefischen [**hohx**-zey-fihSən]
defeat	die Niederlage [**niid**ər-lahgə]
to dive	tauchen [**tauxən**]
diving board	das Sprungbrett [**Spruŋ**-breht]
diving equipment	die Taucherausrüstung [**taux**ər-aus-rews-tuhŋ]
diving goggles	die Taucherbrille [**taux**ər-brihlə]
doubles *(tennis)*	das Doppel [dohpəl]
fishing license	der Angelschein [**ahŋ**əl-Sayn]
fishing rod	die Angel [ahŋəl]
fitness center	das Fitnesscenter [**fiht**-nihs-tsehntər]
fitness training	das Konditionstraining [kon-diht-**syohns**-treh-nihŋ]
game	das Spiel [Spiil]
gliding	das Segelfliegen [**zeyg**əl-fliigən]
goal	das Tor [tohr]
goaltender, goalie	der Torwart [**tohr**-vahrt]
golf	das Golf [golf]
golf club	der Golfschläger [**golf**-Sleygər]
golf course	der Golfplatz [**golf**-plahts]

gymnastics	die Gymnastik [gewm-**nahs**-tihk]; das Turnen [turnən]
halftime	die Halbzeit [**hahlp**-tsayt]
handball	Handball [**hahnt**-bahl]
hang-gliding	das Drachenfliegen [**drahx**ən-fliigən]
hiking	das Wandern [vahndərn]
hockey	das Hockey [**ho**-kii]
hockey stick	der Hockeyschläger [-Sleygər]
horse	das Pferd [pfehrt]
horse racing	das Pferderennen [**pfehrd**ə-rehnən]
ice hockey	das Eishockey [**ays**-ho-kii]
ice rink	die Eisbahn [**ays**-bahn]
ice skates	die Schlittschuhe *m pl* [**Sliht**-Sooə]
ice skating	der Eiskunstlauf [**ays**-kuhnst-lauf]
indoor pool	das Hallenbad [**hahl**ən-baht]
innertube	der Schwimmring [**Svihm**-rihŋ]
to jog	joggen (as in English)
jogging	das Jogging (as in English), das Laufen [laufən]
judo	das Judo [**yoo**-doh]
karate	das Karate [kah-**rah**-tə]
lifeguard	Rettungsschwimmer/ Rettungsschwimmerin [**reh**-tuhŋs-Svihmər / -ihn]
to lose	verlieren [fehr-**liir**ən]
match	das Spiel [Spiil]; der Wettkampf [**veht**-kahmpf]
minigolf	das Minigolf [**mih**-nii-golf]
motor sport	der Motorsport [**moh**-tor-Sport]
motorboat	das Motorboot [**moh**-tor-boht]
mountain bike	das Mountainbike (as in English)

mountain climbing	das Bergsteigen [**behrk**-Staygən]
net	das Netz [nehts]
ninepin bowling	das Kegeln [keygəln]
nonswimmer	der Nichtschwimmer [**nihçt**-Svihmər]
nude beach	FKK-Strand [ehf-kah-**kah**-Strahnt]
outdoor pool	das Freibad [**fray**-baht]
parachuting	das Fallschirmspringen [**fahl**-Sihrm-Sprihŋən]
path	der Wanderweg [**vahnd**ər-veyk]
pebbles	die Kiesel *m pl* [kiizəl]
pedal boat	das Tretboot [**treht**-boht]
private beach	der Privatstrand [prii-**vaht**-Strahnt]
race	das Rennen [rehnən]
referee	der Schiedsrichter [**Siits**-rihçtər]
regatta	die Regatta [reh-**gaht**ə]
result	das Ergebnis [ehr-**geyp**-nihs]
to ride	reiten [raytən]
riding	der Reitsport [**rayt**-Sport]
rock-climbing	das Bergsteigen [**behrk**-Staygən]
rowboat	das Ruderboot [**rood**ər-boht]
rowing	das Rudern [roodərn]
rubber boat	das Schlauchboot [**Slaux**-boht]
sailboat	das Segelboot [**zeyg**əl-boht]
sailing	das Segeln [zeygəln]
sand	der Sand [zahnt]
sand dune	die Düne [dewnə]
sauna	die Sauna [zaunə]
seaside resort	der Badeort [**bahd**ə-ort]
shower	die Dusche [duhSə]

shuttlecock	der Federball [**feyd**ər-bahl]
singles	das Einzel *(Tennis)* [**aynts**əl (teh-nihs)]

Skiing in the Alps

ski	der Ski [Sii]
ski poles/sticks	die Skistöcke *m pl* [**Sii**-Stœkə]
skiing	das Skilaufen [**Sii**-laufən]
sled	der Schlitten [Slihtən]
to go sledding	das Schlittenfahren [**Sliht**ən-fahrən]
snorkel	der Schnorchel [Snorçəl]
soccer	der Fußball [**fuhs**-bahl]
soccer field	der Fußballplatz [-plahts]
soccer match	das Fußballspiel [-Spiil]
soccer team	die Fußballmannschaft [-mahn-Sahft]
solarium	das Solarium [zoh-**lahr**-yuhm]
sports field	der Sportplatz [**Sport**-plahts]

sportsman/-woman	Sportler/Sportlerin [**Sportl**ər / -ihn]
squash	das Squash [skvahS]
start	der Start [Stahrt]
sunshade	der Sonnenschirm [**zon**ən-Sihrm]
surfboard	das Surfbrett ("surf" as in English, plus [breht])
surfing	das Surfen, das Wellenreiten [**vehl**ən-raytən]
swimmer	Schwimmer/ Schwimmerin [**Svihm**ər / -ihn]
swimming	das Schwimmen [Svihmən]
swimming pool	das Schwimmbad [**Svihm**-baht]
table tennis	das Tischtennis [**tihS**-teh-nihs]
table-tennis paddle	der Tischtennisschläger [-Sleygər]
T-bar lift	der Schlepplift [**Slehp**-lihft]
tennis	das Tennis [**teh**-nihs]
tennis racquet	der Tennisschläger [-Sleygər]
tenpin bowling	das Bowling [**boh**-lihŋ] (as in English)
ticket	die Eintrittskarte [**ayn**-trihts-kahrtə]
ticket office	die Kasse [kahsə]
tie	das Unentschieden [**uhn**-ehnt-Siidən]
to tie	unentschieden spielen [**uhn**-ehnt-Siidən Spiilən]
toboggan	der Schlitten [Slihtən]
(bath) towel	das Badetuch [**bahd**ə-tuhx]
track	der Wanderweg [**vahnd**ər-veyk]
track and field events	die Leichtathletik [**layçt**-aht-leh-tihk]
umpire	der Schiedsrichter [**Siitz**-rihçtər]
victory	der Sieg [ziik]
volleyball	das Volleyball (as in English)

water polo	der Wasserball [**vahs**ər-bahl]
water wings	die Schwimmflügel *m pl* [**Svihm**-flewgəl]
to win	gewinnen [gə**vihn**ən]
win	der Sieg [ziik]
windbreak	der Windschutz [**vihnt**-Suhts]
wrestling	der Ringkampf [**rihŋ**-kahmpf]

8 Shopping/Shops
Einkaufen/Geschäfte

Questions/Prices

Fragen/Preise

opening hours	die Öffnungszeiten *f pl* [dii œf-nuhŋs-tsaytən]
open/closed/closed for vacation	offen/ [ofən] geschlossen/ [gəSlosən] Betriebsferien [bətriips-fehr-yən]

It's usual to greet (and be greeted by) store employees when entering a store ("Guten Tag") and to say "Auf Wiedersehen" when leaving.

Where can I find …?	Wo finde ich … ? [voh fihndə ihç]
Can you recommend a … store?	Können Sie mir ein …geschäft empfehlen? [kœnən zii miir ayn … gəSehft ehmp-feylən]
Are you being helped?	Werden Sie schon bedient? [vehrdən zii Sohn bədiint]
Thank you, I'm just looking around.	Danke, ich sehe mich nur um. [dahŋkə, ihç zeyə mihç noor uhm]
I'd like …	Ich möchte … [ihç mœçtə]
Do you have …?	Haben Sie …? [hahbən zii]
Show me …, please.	Zeigen Sie mir bitte … [tsaygən zii miir bihtə]
Could you show me another …?	Können Sie mir bitte einen anderen (m)/eine andere (f) /ein anderes (n) … zeigen? [kœnən zii miir bihtə aynən ahndərən / aynə ahndərə / ayn ahndərəs … tsaygən]
Do you have anything cheaper?	Haben Sie auch etwas billigeres? [hahbən zii aux **eht**-vahs **bih**-lihgərəs]
Do you have anything of better quality?	Haben Sie auch etwas in besserer Qualität? [hahbən zii aux **eht**-vahs ihn behsərər kvah-lih-**teyt**]
I like that.	Das gefällt mir. [dahs gəfehlt miir]
I'll take it.	Ich nehme es. [ihç neymə ehs]
How much is it?	Wie viel kostet es? [vii fiil kostət ehs]
Do you take … eurocheques?	Nehmen Sie … [neymən zii] Euroschecks? [**oy**-roh-Sehks]

credit cards?	Kreditkarten? [kreh-**diht**-kahrtən]
traveler's checks?	Reiseschecks? [**rayz**ə-Sehks]
I'd like to exchange this, please.	Ich möchte dies umtauschen. [ihç mœçtə diis **uhm**-tauSən]

<hr />

Word List: Stores

antique store	das Antiquitätengeschäft [ahn-tih-kvih-**teyt**ən-gəSehft]
art dealer	der Kunsthändler [**kuhnst**-hehnd-lər]
arts and crafts	das Kunstgewerbe [**kuhnst**-gəvehrbə]
bakery	die Bäckerei [behkə-**ray**]
barber	der (Herren-)Friseur [(**hehrn**-) frih-**zœr**]
beauty parlor	der Kosmetiksalon [kos-**mey**-tihk-zah-lohn]
bookshop	die Buchhandlung [**buhx**-hahnt-luhŋ]
boutique	die Boutique [boo-**tiik**]
butcher store	die Metzgerei [mehtsgə-**ray**] die Fleischerei [flaySə-**ray**]
candy store	das Süßwarengeschäft [**zews**-vahrən-gəSehft]
confectioner's shop	die Konditorei [kon-dih-to-**ray**]
cosmetics store	die Parfümerie [pahr-fewmə-**rii**]
delicatessen	das Feinkostgeschäft [**fayn**-kost-gəSehft]
department store	das Kaufhaus [**kauf**-haus]
drugstore	die Drogerie [droh-gə-**rii**]
dry cleaners	die (chemische) Reinigung [(**çeh**-mihSə) **ray**-nih-guhŋ]
electrical goods	die Elektrohandlung [eh-**lehk**-troh-hahnt-luhŋ]
fish shop	das Fischgeschäft [**fihS**-gə-Sehft]
flea market	der Flohmarkt [**floh**-mahrkt]
florist's shop	das Blumengeschäft [**bloom**ən-gəSehft]
food store	das Lebensmittelgeschäft [**leyb**ənz-mihtəl-gəSehft]
fruit store	die Obsthandlung [**ohpst**-hahnt-luhŋ]

furniture store	das Möbelgeschäft [**mœb**əl-gəSehft]
fur store	das Pelzgeschäft [**pehlts**-gəSehft]
grocery store	das Lebensmittelgeschäft [**leyb**ənz-mihtəl-gəSehft]
hairdresser	der Friseur [frih-**zœr**]
hardware store	das Eisenwarengeschäft [**ayz**ən-vahrən-gəSehft]
health food store	das Reformhaus [rey-**form**-haus]
household goods	die Haushaltswaren *f pl* [**haus**-hahlts-vahrən]
jeweler	der Juwelier [yoo-veh-**liir**]
launderette, laundromat	der Waschsalon [**vahS**-zah-lohn]
laundry	die Wäscherei [vehSə**ray**]
leather goods store	das Lederwarengeschäft [**leyd**ər-vahrən-gəSehft]

market *(weekly)*	der (Wochen)-Markt [(**vohx**ən-)mahrkt]
music store	das Musikgeschäft [moo-**zihk**-gəSehft]

news dealer	der Zeitungshändler [**tsay**-tuhŋs-hehnd-lər]
optician	der Optiker [**op**-tihkər]
pharmacy	die Apotheke [ah-poh-**teyk**ə]
photographic materials	die Fotoartikel *m pl* [**foh**-toh-ahr-tihkəl]
second-hand bookstore	das Antiquariat [ahn-tihk-vahr-**yaht**]
second-hand store	der Secondhand-Laden [**zeh**-kont-hehnt-lahdən], der Trödler [trœdlər]
shoe store	das Schuhgeschäft [**Soo**-gəSehft]
shoemaker	der Schuhmacher [**Soo**-mahxər]
shopping center, mall	das Einkaufszentrum [**ayn**-kaufs-tsehn-truhm]
souvenir shop	das Souvenirgeschäft [zoo-vəniir-gəSehft]

"Gartenzwerge": A typical sight in German gardens

sporting goods store	das Sportgeschäft [**Sport**-gəSehft]
stationery store	das Schreibwarengeschäft [**Srayp**-vahrən-gəSehft]
supermarket	der Supermarkt [**zoo**-pər-mahrkt]
tailor	der Herrenschneider/in [**hehrn**-Snaydər / -ihn]
tobacco store	der Tabakladen [tah-**bahk**-lahdən]

toy store	das Spielwarengeschäft [**Spiil**-varən-gəSehft]
travel agency	das Reisebüro [**rayz**ə-bew-roh]
vegetable dealer	der Gemüsehändler [gə**mewz**ə-hehndlər]
watchmaker	der Uhrmacher [**oor**-mahxər]
wine store	die Weinhändlung [**vayn**-hehnd-luhŋ]

Groceries

Lebensmittel

What can I get you?	Was darf es sein? [vahs dahrf ehs zayn]
I'd like …	Geben Sie mir bitte … [geybən zii miir bihtə]
a pound of …	ein Pfund … [ayn pfuhnt]
ten slices of …	10 Scheiben … [tseyn Saybən]
a piece of …	ein Stück von … [ayn Stewk fon]
a package of …	eine Packung … [aynə **pah**-kuhŋ]
a jar of …	ein Glas … [ayn glahs]
a can of …	eine Dose … [aynə dohzə]
a bottle of …	eine Flasche … [aynə flahSə]
a bag, please.	eine Einkaufstüte. [aynə **ayn**-kaufs-tewtə]
Whole or sliced?	Am Stück oder geschnitten? [ahm Stewk ohdər gə**Snih**tən]
Can I get you anything else?	Darf es sonst noch etwas sein? [dahrf ehs zonst nox **eht**-vahs zayn] Sonst noch was? [zonst nox vahs]
Could I try some of this, please?	Dürfte ich vielleicht etwas hiervon probieren? [dewrftə ihç fih-**layçt eht**-vahs hiir-**fon** proh-**biir**ən]
No, thank you. That's all.	Danke, das ist alles. [dahŋkə dahs ihst ahləs]

Word List: Groceries

> Wine and liquor can be purchased in supermarkets and gas stations, as well as in specialized wine stores. In addition to the terms in the following list you will encounter a wide range of re-

gional words, especially for fruits, vegetables, sausages, types of bread rolls, and cakes.

almonds	die Mandeln *f pl* [**mahn**-dehln]
apples	die Äpfel *m pl* [ehp-fəl]
apricots	die Aprikosen *f pl* [ah-prih-**kohz**ən]
artichokes	die Artischocken *f pl* [ar-tih-**Sok**ən]
asparagus	der Spargel [Spargəl]
avocado	die Avocado [ah-voh-**kah**-doh]
baby food	die Kindernahrung [**kihnd**ər-nah-ruhŋ]
bananas	die Bananen *f pl* [bah-**nahn**ən]
bar of chocolate	der Schokoriegel [**So**-koh-riigəl] die Tafel Schokolade [tahfəl Soh-koh-**lahd**ə]

basil	das Basilikum [bah-**zih**-lih-kuhm]
beans	die Bohnen *f pl* [bohnən]
green beans	grüne Bohnen [grewnə bohnən]
beef	das Rindfleisch [**rihnt**-flayS]
beer	das Bier [biir]
alcohol-free beer	alkoholfreies Bier [**ahl**-koh-hol-frayəs biir]
blackberries	die Brombeeren *f pl* [**brom**-beyrən]
bread	das Brot [broht]
a loaf of bread	ein (Laib) Brot [(layp) broht]
roll	das Brötchen [brœt-çən]
white bread	das Weißbrot [**vays**-broht]
wholegrain bread	das Vollkornbrot [**fol**-korn-broht]
butter	die Butter [buhtər]
buttermilk	die Buttermilch [**buht**ər-mihlç]
cabbage	der Weißkohl [**vays**-kohl]
cake	der Kuchen [kuhxən]
candy	die Süßigkeiten *f pl* [**zew**-sihç-kaytən]
canned goods	die Konserven *f pl* [kon-**zehrv**ən]
carrots	die Karotten *f pl* [kah-**rot**ən]
cauliflower	der Blumenkohl [**bloom**ən-kohl]
celery	der Sellerie [zeh-lərii]
champagne	der Champagner [Sahm-**pahny**ər]
cheese	der Käse [keyzə]
cheese spread	der Streichkäse [**Stray**ç-keyzə]
goat's milk cheese	der Ziegenkäse [**tsiig**ən-keyzə]

cherries	die Kirschen *f pl* [kihrSən]
chicken	das Hähnchen [hehnçən]
chicory	der Chicorée [Sii-koh-**rey**]
chocolate	die Schokolade [Soh-koh-**lahd**ə]
chocolate bar	der Schokoriegel [**Soh**-koh-riigəl]
chop	das Kotelett [koht(ə-)**leht**]
coconut	die Kokosnuss [**koh**-kos-nuhs]
coffee	der Kaffee [**kah**-fey]
cold cuts	der Aufschnitt [**auf**-Sniht]
cookies	die Kekse *m pl* [kehksə]

A Christmas specialty:
Gingerbread house

corn	der Mais [mays]
cream	die Sahne [zahnə]
cucumber	die Gurke [guhrkə]
cutlet	das Kotelett [koht(ə-)**leht**]
Danish pastry	das süße Stück [zewsə Stewk]
dates	die Datteln *f pl* [**daht**-ehln]
eel	der Aal [ahl]

eggplant	die Aubergine *f* [oh-bər-**Ziin**ə]
eggs	die Eier *n pl* [ayər]
eggs from free-range hens	Eier von frei laufenden Hühnern [ayər fon fray laufəndən **hewn**-ehrn]
fennel	der Fenchel [fehnçəl]
figs	die Feigen *f pl* [faygən]
fish	der Fisch [fihS]
flour	das Mehl [meyl]
fresh	frisch [frihS]
fruit	das Obst [ohpst]
garlic	der Knoblauch [**knop**-laux]
grapefruit	die Pampelmuse [**pahmp**əl-**mooz**ə]
grapes	die Weintrauben *f pl* [**vayn**-traubən]
ground meat	das Hackfleisch [**hahk**-flayS]
ham	der Schinken [Sihŋkən]
cooked ham	gekochter Schinken [gəkoxtər ...]
smoked ham	geräucherter Schinken [gəroyxərtər ...]
health food	die Reformkost [rey-**form**-kost]
herring	der Hering [**heh**-rihŋ]
home-grown vegetables	Gemüse aus Eigenanbau [gəmewzə aus **aygə**n-ahn-bau]
honey	der Honig [**hoh**-nihç]
ice cream	Eis(krem) [**ays**(krehm)]
jam	die Marmelade [mahrmə-**lahd**ə]

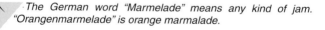
The German word "Marmelade" means any kind of jam. "Orangenmarmelade" is orange marmalade.

lamb	das Lammfleisch [**lahm**-flayS]
leek	der Lauch [laux]
lemon	die Zitrone [tsih-**trohn**ə]
lentils	die Linsen *f pl* [lihnzən]
lettuce	der Kopfsalat [**kopf**-zah-laht]
licorice	die Lakritze [lah-**krihts**ə]
liver pâté	die Leberpastete [**leyb**ər-pahstətə]
liver sausage, liverwurst	die Leberwurst [**leyb**ər-vuhrst]
mackerel	die Makrele [mah-**kreyl**ə]
margarine	die Margarine [mahr-gah-**riin**ə]

marmalade	die Orangenmarmelade [oh-**rahn**-Zən-mahrmə-lahdə]
mayonnaise	die Majonäse [mah-yoh-**neyz**ə]
meat	das Fleisch [flayS]
melon	die Melone [meh-**lohn**ə]
honeydew melon	die Honigmelone [**hoh**-nihç-meh-lohnə]
watermelon	die Wassermelone [**vahs**ər-meh-lohnə]
milk	die Milch [mihlç]
low-fat milk	fettarme Milch [**feht**-ahrmə ...]
mineral water	das Mineralwasser [mih-neh-**rahl**-vahsər], das Selterswasser **zehlt**ərs-vahsər], der Sprudel [Sproodəl]
muesli	das Müsli [**mews**-lii]
mussels	die Muscheln *f pl* [muh-Səln]
mustard	der Senf [zehnf]
nuts	die Nüsse *f pl* [newsə]
oil	das Öl [œl]
olive oil	das Olivenöl [oh-**lii**-vən-œl]
olives	die Oliven *f pl* [oh-**lii**-vən]
onion	die Zwiebel [tsviibəl]
orange juice	der Orangensaft [oh-**rahn**-Zən-zahft]
oranges	die Apfelsinen *f pl* [ahpfəl-**ziin**ən] die Orangen *f pl* [oh-**rahn**-Zən]
organic food	die Biokost [**bii**-oh-kost]
oysters	die Austern *f pl* [**aus**-tehrn]
paprika	die Paprika [**pah**-priikə]
parsley	die Petersilie [peytər-**ziil**-yə]
pasta	die Nudeln *f pl* [**noo**-dehln]
peaches	die Pfirsiche *m pl* [**pfihr**-zihçə]
pears	die Birnen *f pl* [biirnən]
peas	die Erbsen *f pl* [ehrpsən]
chickpeas	die Kichererbsen *f pl* [**kihç**ər-ehrpsən]
pepper	der Pfeffer [pfehfər]
peppers	die Paprikaschoten *f pl* [**pah**-priikə-Sohtən]

perch	der Barsch [bahrS]
pineapple	die Ananas [**ah**-nah-nəs]
plums	die Pflaumen *f pl* [pflaumən]
pork	das Schweinefleisch [**S**vaynə-flayS]
potatoes	die Kartoffeln *f pl* [kahr-**to**-fəln]
prawns	die Garnelen *f pl* [gahr-**neh**lən]
pumpkin	der Kürbis [**kewr**-bihs]
rabbit	das Kaninchen [kah-**nihn**-çən]
raisins	die Rosinen *f pl* [roh-**zii**-nən]
rice	der Reis *m* [rays]
rolled oats	die Haferflocken *f pl* [**hahf**ər-flokən]
rolls	die Brötchen *n pl* [brœt-çən]
saffron	der Safran [**zahf**-rahn]
salad	der Salat [zah-**laht**]
salami	die Salami [zah-**lah**-mii]
salt	das Salz [zahlts]
sandwiches	belegte Brote [bəleyktə brohtə]
sausages	die Würstchen *n pl* [vewrst-çən]
semolina	der Grieß [griis]
shrimp	die Krabben *f pl* [krahbən]
soft drink	die Limonade [lih-moh-**nahd**ə]
sole	die Seezunge [**zey**-tsuhŋə]
soup	die Suppe [zuhpə]
sour cream	der Sauerrahm [**zau**ər-rahm]
spaghetti	die Spaghetti *n pl* [Spah-**geh**-tii] (although note that the recent spelling reform has removed the "h," so "Spagetti")
spinach	der Spinat [Spih-**naht**]
squid	der Tintenfisch [**tihnt**ən-fihS]
strawberries	die Erdbeeren *f pl* [**ehrt**-beyrən]
sugar	der Zucker [tsuhkər]
sweet rolls	süße Stücke *n pl* [zewsə Stewkə]
tangerine	die Mandarine [mahn-dah-**riin**ə]

tea	der Tee [tey]
tea bag	der Teebeutel [**tey**-boytəl]
thyme	der Thymian [**tewm**-yahn]
toast	der Toast [tohst]
tomatoes	die Tomaten *f pl* [toh-**maht**ən]
tuna	der Tunfisch [**tuhn**-fihS]
untreated	ungespritzt [**uhn**-gəSpritst]
veal	das Kalbfleisch [**kahlp**-flayS]
vegetables	das Gemüse [gə**myz**ə]
vinegar	der Essig [**ehs**-ihç]
wine	der Wein [vayn]
alcohol-free wine	alkoholfreier Wein [**ahl**-koh-hol-frayər vayn]
red wine	der Rotwein [**roht**-vayn]
white wine	der Weißwein [**vays**-vayn]
yogurt	der Joghurt [**yoh**-guhrt]

Toiletries

Drogerieartikel

absorbent cotton	die Watte [vahtə]
after-shave lotion	das Rasierwasser [rah-**ziir**-vahsər]
Band-Aid®	das Pflaster [pflahstər]
blusher	das Rouge [rooZə]
body lotion	die Körpermilch [**kœr**pər-mihlç]
brush	die Bürste [bewrstə]
cleansing lotion	die Waschlotion [**vahS**-loht-syohn]
cleansing milk	die Reinigungsmilch [**ray**-nih-guhŋz-mihlç]
clothes brush	die Kleiderbürste [**klaydə**r-bewrstə]
comb	der Kamm [kahm]
condom	das Präservativ [preh-zehr-vah-**tiif**], das Kondom [**kon**-dohm]
cotton swab/Q-tip	das Wattestäbchen [**vahtə**-Stehp-çən]
cream	die Creme [krehm]
~ for dry/normal/oily skin	~ für [fewr] trockene [trokənə]/ normale [nor-**mahl**ə]/ fettige [**feh**-tihgə] Haut [haut]
hand ~	die Handcreme [**hahnt**-krehm]
moisturizing ~	die Feuchtigkeitscreme [**foyç**-tihç-kayts-krehm]
curlers	die Lockenwickler *m pl* [**lok**ən-vihklər]
deodorant	das Deo(dorant) [**dey**-oh(do-**rahnt**)]
detergent	das Waschmittel [**vahS**-mihtəl]
diapers	die Windeln *f pl* [vihndəln]
dishcloth	das Spültuch [**Spewl**-tuhx]
dishwashing liquid	das Spülmittel [**Spewl**-mihtəl]
eau de Cologne	das Kölnisch Wasser [**kœl**-nihS vahsər]
eyeshadow	der Lidschatten [**liht**-Sahtən]
eyebrow pencil	der Augenbrauenstift [**augə**n-brauən-Stihft]

feeding bottle	die Saugflasche [**zauk**-flahSə]
hair gel	das Haargel [**hahr**-gehl]
hair remover	der Haarentferner [**hahr**-ehnt-fehrnər]
hairband	das Haargummi [**hahr**-guh-mii]
hairbrush	die Haarbürste [**hahr**-bewrstə]
hairpins	die Haarklammern *f pl* [**hahr**-klahmərn]
hairspray	das Haarspray [**hahr**-Sprey]
lipstick	der Lippenstift [**lihp**ən-Stihft]
manicure set	das Nagelnecessaire [**nahg**əl-neh-seh-sehr]
mascara	die Wimperntusche [**vihm**-pehrn-tuhSə]
mirror	der Spiegel [Spiigəl]
mouthwash	das Mundwasser [**muhnt**-vahsər]
nail brush	die Nagelbürste [**nag**əl-bewrstə]
nail file	die Nagelfeile [-faylə]
nail scissors	die Nagelschere [-Seyrə]
nail polish	der Nagellack [-lahk]
nail-polish remover	der Nagellackentferner [-lahk-ehnt-fehrnər]
pacifier	der Schnuller [Snuhlər]
paper handkerchiefs/ Kleenex®	die Papiertaschentücher *n pl* [pah-**piir**-tahSən-tewxər]
perfume	das Parfüm [pahr-**fewm**]
powder face ~	der Puder [poodər] der Gesichtspuder [gə**zihçts**-poodər]
protection factor *(sunscreen)*	der Lichtschutzfaktor [**lihçt**-Suhts-fahk-tor]
razor electric ~	der Rasierer [rah-**ziir**ər] elektrischer Rasierapparat [eh-**lehk**-trihSər rah-**ziir**-ah-pah-raht]
razor blade	die Rasierklinge [rah-**ziir**-klihŋə]
safety pins	die Sicherheitsnadeln *f pl* [**zihç**ər-hayts-nah-dehln]
sanitary napkins	die Damenbinden *f pl* [**dahm**ən-bihndən]
setting lotion	der Haarfestiger [**hahr**-fehs-tihgər]

shampoo	das Haarwaschmittel [**hahr**-vahS-mihtəl]
~ for oily/normal/dry hair	~ für [fewr] fettiges [**feh**-tihgəs]/ normales [nor-**mahl**əs]/ trockenes [trokənəs] Haar [hahr]
~ to prevent/fight dandruff	~ gegen Schuppen [geygən Suhpən]
shaving brush	der Rasierpinsel [rah-**ziir**-pihnzəl]
shaving soap/stick	die Rasierseife [rah-**ziir**-zayfə]
shower gel	das Duschgel [**duhS**-gehl]
soap	die Seife [zayfə]
sponge	der Schwamm [Svahm]
stain remover	das Fleckenwasser [**flehk**ən-vahsər]
styling mousse	der Schaumfestiger [**Saum**-feh-stihgər]
suntan lotion	die Sonnencreme [**zon**ən-krehm]
suntan oil	das Sonnenöl [**zon**ən-œl]
tampons	die Tampons *m pl* [**tahm**-pon]
toilet paper	das Toilettenpapier [toy-**leht**ən-pah-piir]
toothbrush	die Zahnbürste [**tsahn**-bewrstə]
toothpaste	die Zahnpasta [**tsahn**-pahstə]
towelettes	die Erfrischungstücher *n pl* [ehr-**frih**-Suhŋs-tewxər]
tweezers	die Pinzette [pihnt-**seht**ə]
washcloth	der Waschlappen [**vahS**-lahpən]

At the Tobacconist

Tabakwaren

A pack/carton of filter-tipped/plain … cigarettes, please.	Ein Päckchen [ayn pehkçən]/Eine Stange [aynə Stahŋə]… Zigaretten [tsih-gah-**reht**ən] mit/ohne Filter, bitte. [miht / ohnə fihltər bihtə]
Do you have American/menthol cigarettes?	Haben Sie amerikanische/Menthol-Zigaretten? [hahbən zii ah-meh-rih-**kah**-nihSə / **mehn**-tohl-tsih-gah-rehtən]

Which brand (of mild/strong cigarettes) would you recommend?	Welche Marke (leichter/starker Zigaretten) können Sie mir empfehlen? [vehlçə mahrkə (layçtər / Stahrkər tsih-gah-**reht**ən) kœnən zii miir ehmp-**feyl**ən]
Ten cigars/cigarillos, please.	Zehn Zigarren/Zigarillos, bitte. [tseyn tsih-**gahr**ən / tsih-gah-**rih**-lohs, bihtə]
A package/can of cigarette/pipe tobacco, please.	Ein Päckchen/Eine Dose Zigaretten-/Pfeifentabak, bitte. [ayn pehkçən / aynə dohzə tsih-gah-**reht**ən- / **pfayf**ən-tah-bahk bihtə]
A box of matches/A lighter, please.	Eine Schachtel Streichhölzer/Ein Feuerzeug, bitte. [aynə Sahxtəl **Strayç**-hœltsər / ayn **foy**ər-tsoyk bihtə]

Clothing/Leather Goods/Dry Cleaning

Kleidung/Lederwaren/Reinigung

Can you show me ...?	Können Sie mir ... zeigen? [kœnən zii miir ... tsaygən]
Do you have a particular color in mind?	Denken Sie an eine bestimmte Farbe? [dehŋkən zii ahn aynə bə**Stihmt**ə fahrbə]
I'd like something in ...	Ich möchte etwas in ... [ihç mœçtə **eht**-vahs ihn ...]
I'd like something to match this.	Ich möchte etwas Passendes hierzu. [ihç mœçtə **eht**-vahs pahsəndəs hiir-**tsuh**]
Can I try it on?	Kann ich es anprobieren? [kahn ihç ehs **ahn**-proh-biirən]
What size do you take?	Welche (Konfektions-)Größe haben Sie? [vehlçə (kon-fehk-**tsyohnz**-) grœsə hahbən zii]
It's too ... tight/big. short/long. small/big.	Das ist mir zu ... [dahs ihst miir tsuh] eng/weit. [ehŋ / vayt] kurz/lang. [kurts / lahŋ] klein/groß. [klayn / grohs]
It's a good fit. I'll take it.	Das passt gut. Ich nehme es. [dahs pahst goot. ihç neymə ehs]

It's not quite what I want.	Das ist nicht ganz, was ich möchte. [dahs ihst nihçt gants, vahs ihç mœçtə]
I'd like a pair of … shoes.	Ich möchte ein Paar … schuhe. [ihç mœçtə ayn pahr … Sooə]
Size …	Schuhgröße … [**Soo**-grœsə]
They're too narrow/wide.	Sie sind zu eng/weit. [zii zihnt tsuh ehŋ / vayt]
And a tube of shoe cream/a pair of shoelaces, please.	Bitte noch eine Tube Schuhcreme [bihtə nox aynə toobə **Soo**-krehm] /ein Paar Schnürsenkel. [ayn pahr **Snewr**-zehŋkəl]

Conversion of German sizes

women's suits, dresses, coats, etc.

Continent	USA
34	6
36	8
38	10
40	12
42	14
44	16
46	18
48	20
50	22

men's suits, coats, sweaters, etc.

Continent	USA
44	34
46	36
48	38
50	40
52	42
54	44
56	46
58	48

men's shirts (collar size)

Continent	USA
38	15 (S)
39–40	15½ (M)
41	16 (L)
42	16½ (L)
43	17 (XL)
44	17½ (XL)
45–46	18 (XXL)

shoes

Continent	Women's	Men's
37	6–6½	–
38	7–7½	5–5½
39	8–8½	6–6½
40	9–9½	7–7½
41	10–10½	8–8½
42	11–11½	9–9½
43	12–12½	10–10½
44	13–13½	11–11½
45	–	12–12½
46	–	13–13½

I'd like to have new soles put on these shoes.
Ich möchte diese Schuhe neu besohlen lassen. [ihç mœçtə diizə Sooə noy bəzohlən lahsən]

Could you put new heels on, please?
Können Sie bitte die Absätze neu machen? [kœnən zii bihtə dii **ahp**-zehtsə noy mahxən]

I'd like to have these things cleaned/washed.
Ich möchte diese Sachen reinigen/waschen lassen. [ihç mœçtə diizə zahxən **ray**-nihgən / vahSən lahsən]

When will they be ready?
Wann sind sie fertig? [vahn zihnt zii **fehr**-tihç]

Word List: Clothing/Leather Goods/Dry Cleaning

bathing cap	die Bademütze [**bahd**ə-mewtsə]
bathrobe	der Bademantel [**bahd**ə-mahntəl]
belt	der Gürtel [gewrtəl]
bikini	der Bikini [bih-**kii**-nii]
blazer	der Blazer [bleyzər]
blouse	die Bluse [bloozə]
boots	die Stiefel *m pl* [Stiifəl]
bow tie	die Fliege [fliigə]
bra(ssiere)	der Büstenhalter [**bewst**ən-hahltər]
briefs	der Herrenslip [**hehrn**-slihp]
button	der Knopf [knopf]
cap	die Mütze [mewtsə]
cardigan	die Strickjacke [**Strihk**-yahkə]
checked	kariert [kah-**riirt**]
children's shoes	die Kinderschuhe *m pl* [**kihnd**ər-Sooə]
coat	der Mantel [mahntəl]
collar	der Kragen [krahgən]
color	die Farbe [fahrbə]
cotton	die Baumwolle [**baum**-volə]
dress	das Kleid [klayt]
dressing gown	der Morgenrock [**morg**ən-rok]
to dry clean	chemisch reinigen [**çeh**-mihS ray-nihgən]
evening dress	das Abendkleid [**ah**-bənt-klayt]
fur coat	der Pelzmantel [**pehlts**-mahntəl]
fur jacket	die Pelzjacke [**pehlts**-yahkə]
gloves	die Handschuhe *m pl* [**hahnt**-Sooə]
handbag	die Handtasche [**hahnt**-tahSə]
handkerchief	das Taschentuch [**tahS**ən-tuhx]
hat	der Hut [hoot]
to iron	bügeln [bewgəln]
jacket	die Jacke [yahkə]
sports jacket	der Sakko [**zah**-koh]
jeans	die Jeans (as in English)
leather coat	der Ledermantel [**leyd**ər-mahntəl]
leather jacket	die Lederjacke [**leyd**ər-yahkə]

leather trousers	die Lederhose [**leyd**ər-hohzə]
linen	das Leinen [**layn**ən]
lining	das Futter [**fuht**ər]
machine washable	waschmaschinenfest [**vahS**-mah-Siinən-fehst]
men's shorts *(underwear)*	die Herrenunterhose [**hehrn**-uhntər-hohzə]
miniskirt	der Minirock [**mih**-nii-rok, **mii**-nii-]
nightdress	das Nachthemd [**nahxt**-hehmt]
non-iron	bügelfrei [**bewg**əl-fray]
pajamas	das Pyjama (as in English)
panties	der Damenslip [**dahm**ən-slihp]
pants	die Hose [hohzə]
panty hose	die Strumpfhose [**Struhmpf**-hohzə]
parka	der Anorak [**ah**-noh-rahk]
petticoat/slip	der Unterrock [**uhnt**ər-rok]
pullover	der Pullover [puh-**loh**-vər]
raincoat	der Regenmantel [**reyg**ən-mahntəl]
robe	der Morgenrock [**morg**ən-rok]
rubber boots	die Gummistiefel *m pl* [**guh**-mii-Stiifəl]
sandals	die Sandalen *f pl* [zahn-**dahl**ən]
scarf	das Halstuch [**hahls**-tuhx], der Schal [Sahl]
shirt	das Hemd [hehmt]
shoecream	die Schuhcreme [**Soo**-krehm]
shoes	die Schuhe *m pl* [Sooə]
shorts	die kurze Hose [kuhrtsə hohzə]
silk	die Seide [zaydə]
skirt	der Rock [rok]
sleeve	der Ärmel [ehrməl]
slippers	die Hausschuhe *m pl* [**haus**-Sooə]
sneakers	die Turnschuhe *m pl* [**tuhrn**-Sooə]
socks	die Socken *f pl* [zokən]
sole	die Sohle [zohlə]
stockings	die Strümpfe *m pl* [Strewmpfə]
striped	gestreift [gə**Strayft**]

suede coat	der Wildledermantel [**vihlt**-leydər-mahntəl]
suede jacket	die Wildlederjacke [**vihlt**-leydər-yahkə]
suit *(for men)*	der Anzug [**ahn**-tsuhk]
suit *(for women)*	das Kostüm [kos-**tewm**]
summer dress	das Sommerkleid [**zom**ər-klayt]
sunhat	der Sonnenhut [**zon**ən-hoot]
sweater	der Pullover [puh-**loh**-vər]
swim trunks	die Badehose [**bahd**ə-hohzə]
swimsuit	der Badeanzug [**bahd**ə-ahn-tsuhk]
synthetic fiber	die Kunstfaser [**kuhnst**-fahzər]
tee shirt	T-Shirt (as in English)
terry cloth	das Frottee [fro-**tey**]
tie	die Krawatte [krah-**vaht**ə]
track suit	der Jogginganzug, der Trainingsanzug (as in English, plus [ahn-tsuhk])
trousers	die Hose [**hohz**ə]
umbrella	der Schirm [**Sihrm**]
undershirt	das Unterhemd [**uhnt**ər-hehmt]
underwear	die Unterwäsche [**uhnt**ər-vehSə]
vest	die Weste [**vehst**ə]
waistcoat	die Weste [**vehst**ə]
wool	die Wolle [**vol**ə]
zipper	der Reißverschluss [**rays**-fehr-Sluhs]

Books and Stationery

Bücher und Schreibwaren

Do you sell English/ American newspapers/ magazines?	Haben Sie englische/ amerikanische Zeitungen/ Zeitschriften? [hahbən zii **ehŋ**-lihSə / ah-meh-rih-**kah**-nihSə **tsay**-tuhŋən / **tsayt**-Srihftən]
I'd like a guide to …	Ich hätte gern einen Reiseführer über … [ihç hehtə gehrn aynən **rayz**ə-fewrər ewbər …]

Word List: Books and Stationery

air-mail paper	das Luftpostpapier [**luhft**-pohst-pah-piir]
ballpoint pen	der Kugelschreiber [**koog**əl-Sraybər] der Kuli [**koo**-lii]
city map	der Stadtplan [**Staht**-plahn]
colored pencil	der Farbstift [**fahrp**-Stihft]
coloring book	das Malbuch [**mahl**-buhx]
envelope	der Briefumschlag [**briif**-uhm-Slahk]
eraser	der Radiergummi [rah-**diir**-guh-mii]
felt-tip pen	der Filzstift [**fihlts**-Stihft]
fountain pen	der Füllfederhalter [**fewl**-feydər-hahltər]
gift wrap	das Geschenkpapier [gə**Sehŋk**-pah-piir]
glue	der Klebstoff [**klep**-Stof]
magazine	die Illustrierte [ih-luhs-**triirt**ə] die Zeitschrift [**tsayt**-Srihft]
map	die Landkarte [**lahnt**-kahrtə]
newspaper	die Zeitung [**tsay**-tuhŋ]
notebook	das Notizbuch [noh-**tiits**-buhx]
notepad	der Notizblock [noh-**tiits**-blok]
novel	der Roman [roh-**mahn**]
detective story	der Kriminalroman [krih-mih-**nahl**-roh-mahn]
paper	das Papier [pah-**piir**]
paperback	das Taschenbuch [**tahS**ən-buhx]
pencil	der Bleistift [**blay**-Stihft]
pencil sharpener	der Bleistiftspitzer [**blay**-Stihft-Spihtsər]
picture postcard	die Ansichtskarte [**ahn**-zihçts-kahrtə]
playing cards	die Spielkarten *f pl* [**Spiil**-kahrtən]
road map	die Straßenkarte [**Strahs**ən-kahrtə]
Scotchtape®	der Tesafilm® [**tey**-zah-fihlm]
sketchbook	der Zeichenblock [**tsayç**ən-blok]
stamp	die Briefmarke [**briif**-mahrkə]
stationery, writing paper	das Briefpapier [**briif**-pah-piir]

Housewares

Haushaltswaren

Word List: Housewares

aluminum foil	die Alufolie [**ah**-loo-foh-lyə]
bottle opener	der Flaschenöffner [**flahS**ən-œfnər]
broom	der Besen [beyzən]
brush	der Handfeger [**hahnt**-feygər]
bucket	der Eimer [aymər]
can opener	der Dosenöffner [**dohz**ən-œfnər]
candles	die Kerzen f pl [kehrtsən]
charcoal	die Grillkohle [**grihl**-kohlə]
clothespins	die Wäscheklammern f pl [**vehS**ə-klahmərn]
clothes line	die Wäscheleine [**vehS**ə-laynə]
cold bag	die Kühltasche [**kewl**-tahSə]
corkscrew	der Korkenzieher [**kork**ən-tseeər]
cutlery	das Essbesteck [**ehs**-bəStehk]
dustpan	das Kehrblech [**kehr**-blehç]
garbage bag	der Abfallbeutel [**ahp**-fahl-boytəl]
glass	das Glas [glahs]
grill	der Grill [grihl]
grill lighter	der Grillanzünder [**grihl**-ahn-tsewndər]
ice pack	das Kühlelement [**kewl**-eh-leh-mehnt]
kerosene	das Petroleum [peh-**troh**-ley-uhm]
methyl alcohol	der Brennspiritus [**brehn**-Spih-rih-tuhs]
paper napkins	die Papierservietten f pl [pah-**piir**-zehrv-yehtən]
plastic bag	der Plastikbeutel [**plah**-stihk-boytəl]
plastic wrap	die Frischhaltefolie [**frihS**-hahltə-foh-lyə]
pocket knife	das Taschenmesser [**tahS**ən-mehsər]
saucepan	der Kochtopf [**kox**-topf]
sunshade	der Sonnenschirm [**zon**ən-Sihrm]
thermos	die Thermosflasche [**tehr**-mohs]

tin foil	die Alufolie [**ah**-luh-foh-lyə]
trash bag	der Abfallbeutel [**ahp**-fahl-boytəl]

Electrical Goods and Photographic Materials

Elektro- und Fotoartikel

I'd like …
  (a) film for this camera.

Ich möchte … [ihç mœçtə]
  einen Film für diesen Fotoapparat.
  [aynən fihlm fewr diizən **foh**-toh-ah-pah-raht]

(a) color film for prints/slides.

einen Farbfilm für Papierbilder/Dias.
[aynən **fahrp**-fihlm fewr pah-**piir**-bihldər / **dii**-ahs]

(a) film with 36/24/12 exposures.

einen Film mit sechsunddreißig/ vierundzwanzig/ zwölf Aufnahmen.
[aynən fihlm miht zehks-uhnt-**dray**-sihç / fiir-uhnt-**tsvahn**-tsihç / tsvœlf **auf**-nahmən]

Could you put the film in the camera for me, please?

Könnten Sie mir bitte den Film einlegen? [kœntən zii miir bihtə deyn fihlm **ayn**-leygən]

Would you develop this film for me, please?

Würden Sie mir bitte diesen Film entwickeln? [vewrdən zii miir bihtə diizən fihlm ehnt-**vihk**əln]

I'd like one print of each of these negatives, please.

Ich möchte bitte je einen Abzug von diesen Negativen. [ihç mœçtə bihtə yey aynən **ahp**-tsuhk fon diizən ney-gah-**tiiv**ən]

What size?

Welches Format bitte? [vehlçəs for-**maht**, bihtə]

Ten by thirteen/nine by nine centimeters.

Zehn mal dreizehn./Neun mal neun Zentimeter. [tseyn mahl **dray**-tseyn / noyn mahl noyn tsehn-tih-**meyt**ər]

Glossy or matte?

Hochglanz oder Matt? [**hohx**-glahnts ohdər maht]

When can I pick up the photos?

Wann kann ich die Bilder abholen?
[vahn kahn ihç dii bihldər **ahp**-hohlən]

The viewfinder/shutter doesn't work.

Der Sucher/Der Auslöser funktioniert nicht. [dehr zuhxər / dehr **aus**-lœzər fuhŋk-tsyoh-**niirt** nihçt]

Can you fix it?	Können Sie es reparieren? [kœnən zii ehs reh-pah-**riir**ən]

Word List: Electrical Goods and Photographic Materials

adapter	der Adapter [ah-**dahp**-tər]
aperture (setting)	die Blende [blehndə]
automatic release	der Selbstauslöser [**zehlpst**-aus-lœzər]
battery	die Batterie [bah-tə-**rii**]
black-and-white film	der Schwarzweißfilm [**Svahrts-vays**-fihlm]
bulb	die Glühbirne [**glew**-bihrnə]
cassette	die Kassette [kah-**sehtə**]
cassette recorder	der Kassettenrekorder [kah-**sehtən**-rey-kordər]
CD	die CD, Compact disc [sey-**dey**], or as in English
CD-ROM	die CD-ROM (as in English)
extension cord	die Verlängerungsschnur [fehr-**lehŋə**ruhŋs-Snuhr]
film camera	die Filmkamera [**fihlm**-kah-mey-rah]
film speed	die Filmempfindlichkeit [**fihlm**-ehmp-fihnt-lihç-kayt]
flash	das Blitzgerät [**blihts**-gəreht]
flashcube	der Blitzwürfel [**blihts**-vewrfəl]
flashlight	die Taschenlampe [**tahS**ən-lahmpə]
hairdryer	der Föhn® [fœn]
headphones	der Kopfhörer [**kopf**-hœrər]
lens	das Objektiv [op-yehk-**tiif**], die Linse [lihnzə]
light meter	der Belichtungsmesser [bə**lihç**-tuhŋz-mehsər]
passport photo	das Passbild [**pahs**-bihlt]
personal stereo, walkman	der Walkman® (as in English)
plug	der Stecker [Stehkər]
pocket calculator	der Taschenrechner [**tahS**ən-rehçnər]
record	die Schallplatte [**Sahl**-plahtə]

shutter	der Verschluss [fehr-**Sluhs**]
speaker	der Lautsprecher [**laut**-Sprehçər]
telephoto lens	das Teleobjektiv [**teh**-leh-op-yehk-tiif]
tripod	das Stativ [Stah-**tiif**]
video camera	die Videokamera [**vii**-dey-oh-kah-mey-rah]
videotape	der Videofilm [-fihlm]
video recorder	der Videorekorder [-rey-kordər]
videocassette	die Videokassette [-kah-sehtə]
viewfinder	der Sucher [zuhxər]

At the Optician

Beim Optiker

Could you repair these glasses for me, please?	Würden Sie mir bitte diese Brille reparieren? [vewrdən zii miir bihtə diizə brihlə reh-pah-**riirən**]
One of the lenses of my glasses is broken.	Mir ist ein Glas meiner Brille zerbrochen. [miir ihst ayn glahs maynər brihlə tsehr-**broxən**]
I'm near-sighted/far-sighted.	Ich bin kurzsichtig/weitsichtig. [ihç bihn **kuhrts**-zihç-tihç / **vayt**-zihç-tihç]
What's your eye prescription?	Wie ist Ihre Sehstärke? [vii ihst iirə **zey**-Stehrkə]
Plus/minus … in the right eye, … in the left eye …	Rechts plus/minus …, links … [rehçts pluhs / **mii**-nuhs …/ lihŋks …]
When can I pick up the glasses?	Wann kann ich die Brille abholen? [vahn kahn ihç dii brihlə **ahp**-hohlən]
I need … some cleansing solution for hard/ soft contact lenses.	Ich brauche … [ihç brauxə] Reinigungslösung [**ray**-nih-guhŋz-lœ-zuhŋ] für harte/weiche Kontaktlinsen. [fewr hahrtə / vayçə kon-**tahkt**-lihnzən]
I'm looking for … some sunglasses.	Ich suche … [ihç zooxə] eine Sonnenbrille. [aynə **zon**ən-brihlə]
some binoculars.	ein Fernglas. [ayn **fehrn**-glahs]

At the Watchmaker/Jeweler

Beim Uhrmacher/Juwelier

My watch doesn't work. Could you take a look at it?	Meine Uhr geht nicht mehr. Können Sie mal nachsehen? [maynə oor geyt nihçt mehr. kœnən zii mahl **nahx**-zeyən]
I'd like a nice souvenir/present.	Ich möchte ein hübsches Andenken/Geschenk. [ihç mœçtə ayn hewpSəs **ahn**-dehŋkən / gə**Sehŋk**]
How much do you want to spend?	Wie viel wollen Sie ausgeben? [vii fiil volən zii **aus**-geybən]
I'd like something not too expensive.	Ich möchte etwas nicht zu Teures. [ihç mœçtə **eht**-vahs nihçt tsuh toyrəs]

Word List: Watchmaker/Jeweler

bracelet	das Armband [**ahrm**-bahnt]
brooch	die Brosche [brohSə]
crystal	der Kristall [krihs-**tahl**]

earrings	die Ohrringe *m pl* [**ohr**-rihŋə]
gold	das Gold [golt]
jewelry	der Schmuck [Smuhk]
necklace	die Kette [kehtə]
pearl	die Perle [pehrlə]
pendant	der Anhänger [**ahn**-hehŋər]
ring	der Ring [rihŋ]
silver	das Silber [zihlbər]
wristwatch	die Armbanduhr [**ahrm**-bahnt-oor]

At the Hairdresser/Barber

Beim Friseur

Can I make an appointment for tomorrow?	Kann ich mich für morgen anmelden? [kahn ihç mihç fewr mor-gən **ahn**-mehldən]
How would you like your hair done?	Wie hätten Sie gern Ihr Haar? [vii hehtən zii gehrn iir hahr]
Shampoo and blow dry/set, please.	Waschen und föhnen/legen, bitte. [vahSən uhnt fœnən / leygən bihtə]
Wash and cut/Dry cut, please.	Schneiden mit/ohne Waschen, bitte. [Snaydən miht / ohnə vahSən bihtə]
I'd like …	Ich möchte … [ihç mœçtə]
a perm(anent).	eine Dauerwelle. [aynə **dau**ər-vehlə]
to have my hair dyed/tinted.	mir die Haare färben/tönen lassen. [miir dii hahrə fehrbən / tœnən lahsən]
to have my hair highlighted/toned down.	mir (helle/dunkle) Strähnchen färben lassen. [miir (hehlə / duhŋklə) Strehnçən fehrbən lahsən]
Leave it long, please.	Lassen Sie es bitte lang. [lahsən zii ehs bihtə lahŋ]
Just trim the ends.	Nur die Spitzen. [noor dii Spihtsən]
Not too short/Very short/A bit shorter, please.	Nicht zu kurz/Ganz kurz/Etwas kürzer, bitte. [nihçt tsuh kuhrts / gahnts kuhrts / **eht**-vahs kewrtsər bihtə]
A bit (more) off the back/front/top/sides, please.	Bitte hinten/vorn/oben/an den Seiten (noch) etwas wegnehmen. [bihtə hihntən / forn / ohbən / ahn deyn zaytən (nox) eht-vahs **vehk**-neymən]

Cut above/below the ears, please.	Die Ohren sollen bitte frei sein/ bedeckt bleiben. [dii ohrən zolən bihtə fray zayn / bədehkt blaybən]
The part on the left/ right, please.	Den Scheitel links/rechts, bitte. [deyn Saytəl lihŋks / rehçts bihtə]
A razor cut, please.	Einen Messerschnitt, bitte. [aynən **mehs**ər-Sniht, bihtə]
Would you backcomb it a bit, please.	Bitte etwas toupieren. [bihtə eht-vahs too-**piir**ən]
No/Not too much hairspray, please.	Bitte kein/nur wenig Haarspray. [bihtə kayn / noor **vey**-nihç **hahr**-Sprey]
I'd like a shave, please.	Rasieren, bitte. [rah-**ziir**ən bihtə]
Would you trim my beard, please?	Stutzen Sie mir bitte den Bart. [Stuhtsən zii miir bihtə deyn bahrt]
Can you give me a manicure?	Können Sie mir Maniküre machen? [kœnən zii miir mah-nih-**kewr**ə mahxən]
Thank you. That's fine.	Vielen Dank. So ist es gut. [fiilən dahŋk. zoh ihst ehs goot]

Word List: Hairdresser/Barber

bangs	der Pony [**poh**-nii]
beard	der Bart [bahrt]
blond	blond [blont]
to blow dry	föhnen [fœnən]
to comb	kämmen [kehmən]
conditioner	die Haarkur [**hahr**-koor]
curlers	die Lockenwickler *m pl* [**lok**ən-vihklər]
curls	die Locken *f pl* [lokən]
dandruff	die Schuppen *f pl* [Suhpən]
to do someone's hair	frisieren [frih-**ziir**ən]
to dye	färben [fehrbən]
eyebrows	die Augenbrauen *f pl* [**aug**ən-brauən]
hair	das Haar [hahr]
dry hair	trockenes Haar [trokənəs ...]
oily hair	fettiges Haar [feh-tigəs ...]
haircut	der Haarschnitt [**hahr**-Sniht]

hairspray	der Haarspray [**hahr**-Sprey]
hairstyle	die Frisur [frih-**zoor**]
layered cut	der Stufenschnitt [**Stoof**ən-Sniht]
moustache	der Schnurrbart [**Snuhr**-bahrt]
part	der Scheitel [Saytəl]
perm(anent wave)	die Dauerwelle [**dauə**r-vehlə]
to pluck one's eyebrows	die Augenbrauen zupfen [**aug**ən-brauən tsuhpfən]
to set	legen [laygən]
set	die Wasserwelle [**vahs**ər-vehlə]
shampoo	das Shampoo (as in English)
to have a shave	sich rasieren lassen [zihç rah-**ziir**ən lahsən]
sideburns	die Koteletten *f pl* [kot(ə)**leht**ən]
to tint	tönen [tœnən]
toupee	das Toupet [too-**pey**]
to trim	stutzen [Stuhtsən]
wig	die Perücke [peh-**rewk**ə]

Money

Geldangelegenheiten

Where's the nearest bank/exchange office/ automatic teller machine?	Wo ist hier bitte eine Bank/eine Wechselstube/ein Geldautomat? [voh ihst hiir bihtə aynə bahŋk / aynə **vehksəl**-Stoobə / ayn **gehlt**-au-toh-maht]
What time does the bank open/close?	Wann öffnet/schließt die Bank? [vahn œfnət / Sliist dii bahŋk]
I'd like to change … \$ into marks (Austrian shillings, Swiss francs).	Ich möchte … Dollar in DM (Schilling, Schweizer Franken) wechseln. [ihç mœçtə … **doh**-lahr ihn dey-**ehm** / **doytS**-mahrk (**Sih**-lihŋ , Svaytsər frahŋkən) vehksəln]
What's the current exchange rate?	Wie ist heute der Wechselkurs? [vii ihst hoytə dehr **vehksəl**-kuhrs]
How many marks/ shillings/francs do I get for \$100?	Wie viel Mark/Wie viele Schillinge/Wie viele Franken bekomme ich für hundert Dollar? [vii fiil mahrk / vii fiilə **Sih**-lihŋə / vii fiilə frahŋkən bəkomə ihç fewr **huhn**-dehrt **doh**-lahr]

I'd like to cash this traveler's check/ eurocheque/money order.	Ich möchte diesen Reisescheck/ diesen Euroscheck/ diese Postanweisung einlösen. [ihç mœçtə diizən **rayzə**-Sehk / diizən **oy**-roh-Sehk / diizə **post**-ahn-vay-zuhŋ **ayn**-lœzən]
What's the maximum I can write it for?	Auf welchen Betrag kann ich ihn maximal ausstellen? [auf vehlçən bətrahk kahn ihç iin mahk-sih-**mahl aus**-Stehlən]
Can I see your check card, please?	Ihre Scheckkarte, bitte. [iirə **Sehk**-kahrtə, bihtə]
May I see your passport/ identity card, please?	Darf ich bitte Ihren Pass/Ausweis sehen? [dahrf ihç bihtə iirən pahs / **aus**-vays zeyən]
Sign here, please.	Würden Sie bitte hier unterschreiben? [vewrdən zii bihtə hiir uhntər-**Sraybən**]

Has any money been transferred for me?	Ist Geld für mich überwiesen worden? [ihst gehlt fewr mihç ewbər-**vayz**ən vordən]
Go to the cashier, please.	Gehen Sie bitte zur Kasse. [geyən zii bihtə tsuhr kahsə]
How would you like the money?	Wie wollen Sie das Geld haben? [vii volən zii dahs Gehlt hahbən]
Bills/Notes, please.	Bitte nur Scheine. [bihtə noor Saynə]
Some small change, too, please.	Auch etwas Kleingeld. [aux **eht**-vahs **klayn**-gehlt]
I'd like three fifty mark bills/notes and the rest in small change, please.	Geben Sie mir bitte drei Fünfzigmarkscheine und den Rest in Kleingeld. [geybən zii miir bihtə dray **fewnf**-tsihç-mahrk-Saynə uhnt deyn rehst ihn **klayn**-gehlt]
I've lost my traveler's checks. What do I have to do?	Ich habe meine Reiseschecks verloren. Was muss ich tun? [ihç hahbə maynə **rayz**ə-Sehks fehr-**lohr**ən. vahs muhs ihç toon.

Word List: Money

amount	der Betrag [bətrahk]
Austrian shillings	die Schillinge *m pl* [**Sih**-lihŋ]
automatic teller machine, ATM	der Geldautomat [**gehlt**-au-toh-maht]
bank	die Bank [**bahŋk**]
bank account	das Bankkonto [-kon-toh]
bank charges	die Bankgebühren [-gəbewrən]
bank code number	die Bankleitzahl [-layt-tsahl]
banknote	der Geldschein [**gehlt**-Sayn]
bureau de change	die Wechselstube [**vehks**əl-Stoobə]
cash	bar [bahr]; das Bargeld [**bahr**-gehlt]
change	das Kleingeld [**klayn**-gehlt]
to change	umtauschen [**uhm**-tauSən]
check	der Scheck [Sehk]
to cash a check	einen Scheck einlösen [**ayn**-lœzən]
to write a check	einen Scheck ausstellen [**aus**-Stehlən]

check card	die Scheckkarte [**Sehk**-kahrtə]
checkbook	das Scheckbuch [**Sehk**-buhx]
coin	die Münze [mewntsə]
counter	der Schalter [Sahltər]
credit card	die Kreditkarte [kreh-**diht**-kahrtə]
currency	die Währung [**veh**-ruhŋ]
to deposit	einzahlen [**ayn**-tsahlən]
eurocheque	der Euroscheck [**oy**-roh-Sehk]
exchange	der Geldwechsel [**gehlt**-vehksəl]
exchange office	die Wechselstube [**vehksəl**-Stoobə]
exchange rate	der Wechselkurs [**vehksəl**-kuhrs]
foreign currency	die Devisen *f pl* [deh-**viiz**ən]
form	das Formular [for-moo-**lahr**]
German marks	D-Mark *f pl* [**dey**-mahrk]
giro transfer form	die Zahlkarte [**tsahl**-kahrtə]
giro transfer order	die Zahlungsanweisung [**tsah**-luhŋz-ahn-vay-zuhŋ]
money	das Geld [gehlt]
postal money order	die Postanweisung [**post**-ahn-vay-zuhŋ]
to pay	zahlen [tsahlən]
to pay in	einzahlen [**ayn**-tsahlən]
to pay out	auszahlen [**aus**-tsahlən]
payment	die Zahlung [**tsah**-luhŋ]
PIN number	die Geheimzahl [gə**haym**-tsahl]
post office savings bank	die Postsparkasse [**post**-Spahr-kahsə]
post office savings book	das Postsparbuch [**post**-Spahr-buhx]
rate of exchange	der Kurs [kurs]
receipt	die Quittung [**kvih**-tuhŋ]
remittance	die Überweisung [ewbər-**vay**-zuhŋ]
savings account	das Sparkonto [**Spahr**-kon-toh]
savings bank	die Sparkasse [**Spahr**-kahsə]
savings book	das Sparbuch [**Spahr**-buhx]
signature	die Unterschrift [**uhnt**ər-Srihft]
Swiss francs	Schweizer Franken *m pl* [Svaytsər frahŋkən]

teller	der Schalter [Sahltər]
transfer	die Geldanweisung [**gehlt**-ahn-vay-zuhn], die Überweisung [ewbər-**vay**-zuhn]
traveler's check	der Reisescheck [**rayzə**-Sehk]
window (in a bank)	der Schalter [Sahltər]
to withdraw	abheben [**ahp**-heybən]

At the Post Office

Auf der Post

Where's the nearest post office/mailbox?	Wo ist das nächste Postamt/der nächste Briefkasten? [voh ihst dahs nekstə **post**-ahmt / dehr nehkstə **briif**-kahstən]
How much does a letter/postcard …	Was kostet ein Brief/eine Postkarte … [vahs kostət ayn briif / aynə **post**-kahrtə]
… to Great Britain	… nach Großbritannien? [nahx **grohs**-brih-**tahn**-yən]
… to the USA	… in die Vereinigten Staaten? [ihn dii fehr-**ayn**-ihçtən Stahtən] (or, … in die USA [ihn dii oo-ehs-**ah**])
… to Ireland	… nach Irland? [nahx **iir**-lahnt]
cost?	
Three … DM stamps, please.	Drei Briefmarken zu … DM, bitte. [dray **briif**-mahrkən tsuh … dey-**ehm** bihtə]
I'd like to send this letter …	Diesen Brief bitte per … [diizən briif bihtə pehr …]
registered.	Einschreiben. [**ayn**-Sraybən]
by airmail.	Luftpost. [**luhft**-post]
express.	Express. [ehk-**sprehs**]
How long does a letter to the USA take?	Wie lange braucht ein Brief nach USA? [vii lahnə brauxt ayn briif nax oo-ehs-**ah**]

Some other English-speaking countries:

Australia	Australien [aus-**trahl**-yən]
Canada	Kanada [**kah**-nah-dah]

England	England [**ehŋ**-lahnt]
Great Britain	Großbritannien [**grohs**-brih-**tahn**-yən]
Ireland	Irland [**iir**-lahnt]
New Zealand	Neuseeland [noy-**zey**-lahnt]
Scotland	Schottland [**Sot**-lahnt]
South Africa	Südafrika [**zewt-ah**-frih-kah]
Do you have special issues, too?	Haben Sie auch Sondermarken? [hahbən zii aux **zond**ər-mahrkən]
This set/One each of those, please.	Diesen Satz/Je eine Marke, bitte. [diizən zahts / yey aynə mahrkə bihtə]

General Delivery

Postlagernd

Are there any letters for me? My name's ...	Ist Post für mich da? Mein Name ist ... [ihst post fewr mihç dah? mayn nahmə ihst]
No, there's nothing for you.	Nein, es ist nichts da. [nayn ehs ihst nihçts dah]
Yes, there is something for you. May I see your passport, please?	Ja, es ist etwas da. Ihren Ausweis, bitte. [yah, ehs ihst **eht**-vas dah. iirən **aus**-vays bihtə]

Word List: Post Office

▶ also Word List: Money

address	die Adresse [ah-**drehs**ə]
addressee	der Empfänger [ehmp-**fehŋ**ər]
by airmail	mit Luftpost [**luhft**-post]
cash on delivery (COD)	per Nachnahme [**nahx**-nahmə]
charge	die Gebühr [gə**bewr**]
collection	die Leerung [**ley**-ruhŋ]
counter	der Schalter [**Sahl**tər]
customs declaration	die Zollerklärung [**tsol**ər-kleh-ruhŋ]
declaration of value	die Wertangabe [**vehrt**-ahn-gahbə]
destination	der Bestimmungsort [bə**Stih**-muhŋz-ort]
envelope	der Briefumschlag [**briif**-uhm-Slahk]

express letter	der Eilbrief [**ayl**-briif]
fax	das (Tele)fax [(**teh**-leh-)fahks]
fee	die Gebühr [gə**bewr**]
to fill in	ausfüllen [**aus**-fewlən]
form	das Formular [for-moo-**lahr**], der Vordruck [**for**-druhk]
to forward	nachsenden [**nahx**-zehndən]
letter	der Brief [briif]
to mail	absenden [**ahp**-zehndən], aufgeben [**auf**-geybən]
mail carrier	der Briefträger/die Briefträgerin [**briif**-treygər / -ihn]
mailbox	der Briefkasten [**briif**-kahstən]
main post office	das Hauptpostamt [**haupt**-post-ahmt]
opening hours	die Schalterstunden *f pl* [**Sahlt**ər-Stuhndən]
package, parcel	das Paket [pah-**keyt**]
parcel bill	die Paketkarte [pah-**keyt**-kahrtə]
post office	das Postamt [**post**-ahmt]
postage	das Porto [**por**-toh]
postcard	die Postkarte [**post**-kahrtə]
poste restante	postlagernd [**post**-lahgərnt]
printed matter	die Drucksache [**druhk**-zahxə]
receipt	die Empfangsbestätigung [ehmp-**fahŋz**-bəSteh-tih-guhŋ]
registered letter	der Einschreibebrief [**ayn**-Sraybə-briif]
to send	absenden [**ahp**-zehndən]
sender	der Absender/die Absenderin [**ahp**-zehndər / -ihn]
small parcel	das Päckchen [**pehk**çən]
special issue stamp	die Sondermarke [**zond**ər-mahrkə]
stamp	die Briefmarke [**briif**-mahrkə]
to stamp	frankieren [frahŋ-**kiir**ən]
stamp machine	der Briefmarkenautomat [**briif**-mahrkən-au-toh-maht]

telex	das Telex [**teh**-lehks]
weight	das Gewicht [gə**vihçt**]
window	der Schalter [**Sahl**tər]
zip code	die Postleitzahl [**post**-layt-tsahl]

Telephoning

Telefonieren

Could I use your telephone?	Dürfte ich wohl Ihr Telefon benutzen? [dewrftə ihç vohl iir teh-leh-**fohn** bə**nuht**sən]
Where's the nearest phone booth?	Wo ist die nächste Telefonzelle? [voh ihst dii nehkstə teh-leh-**fohn**-tsehlə]
Can I have a phonecard, please?	Können Sie mir bitte eine Telefonkarte geben? [kœnən zii miir bihtə aynə teh-leh-**fohn**-kahrtə geybən]
Can you change this for me? I need to make a phone call.	Können Sie mir bitte wechseln? Ich muss telefonieren. [kœnən zii miir bihtə vehksəln? ihç muhs teh-leh-foh-**nii**rən]
Do you have a … telephone directory?	Haben Sie ein Telefonbuch von …? [hahbən zii ayn teh-leh-**fohn**-buhx fon …]
What's the prefix for …?	Wie ist die Vorwahl von …? [vii ihst dii **for**-vahl fon …]
I'd like to make a long-distance call to …	Bitte ein Ferngespräch nach … [bihtə ayn **fehrn**-gəSprehç nahx]
I'd like to make a collect call.	Ich möchte ein R-Gespräch anmelden. [ihç mœçtə ayn **ehr**-gəSprehç **ahn**-mehldən]

For direct international calls from Germany, Austria, and Switzerland:
1. *Dial the country code;*
2. *Then dial the area code without the 0 or 9 at the beginning of the code;*
3. *Now dial the telephone number.*

Country codes:	Great Britain 0044
	Ireland 00353
	USA 001
	Canada 001
	Australia 0061
	New Zealand 0064

Can you connect me with …, please?	Können Sie mich bitte mit … verbinden? [kœnən zii mihç bihtə miht … fehr-**bihnd**ən?]
Booth number …	Gehen Sie in Kabine Nr. … [geyən zii ihn kah-**bii**nə nuhmər]
The line's busy.	Die Leitung ist besetzt. [dii lay-tuhŋ ihst bə**zetst**]
There's no answer.	Es meldet sich niemand. [ehs mehldət zihç **nii**-mahnt]
Hold the line, please.	Bleiben Sie bitte am Apparat. [blaybən zii bihtə ahm ah-pah-**raht**]
This is … speaking.	Hier spricht … [hiir Sprihçt]
Hello, who's speaking?	Hallo, mit wem spreche ich? [hah-**loh**, miht veym Sprehçə ihç]
Can I speak to Mr./Mrs., Ms./Miss …, please?	Kann ich bitte Herrn/ Frau/ Fräulein … sprechen? [kahn ihç bihtə hehrn/ frau/ **froy**-layn … Sprehçən]
Speaking.	am Apparat. [ahm ah-pah-**raht**]
I'll connect you.	Ich verbinde. [ihç fehr-**bihnd**ə]
I'm sorry, he's/she's not here/at home.	Tut mir Leid, er/sie ist nicht da/zu Hause. [toot miir layt, ehr/ zii ihst nihçt dah / tsuh hauzə]
When will he/she be back?	Wann wird er/sie zurück sein? [vahn vihrt ehr / zii tsuh-**rewk** zayn]
Can he/she call you back?	Kann er/sie Sie zurückrufen? [kahn ehr/zii zii tsuh-**rewk**-roofən]
Yes, my number's …	Ja, meine Nummer ist … [yah, maynə nuhmər ihst]
Would you like to leave a message?	Möchten Sie eine Nachricht hinterlassen? [mœçtən zii aynə **nahx**-rihçt hihntər-**lahs**ən]
Would you tell him/her that I called?	Würden Sie ihm/ihr bitte sagen, ich hätte angerufen? [vewrdən zii iim / iir bihtə zahgən, ihç hehtə **ahn**-gəroofən]

Could you give him/her a message?	Könnten Sie ihm/ihr etwas ausrichten? [kœntən zii iim/iir **eht**-vahs **aus**-rihçtən]
I'll call back later.	Ich rufe später noch mal an. [ihç roofə **Spey**tər nox mahl ahn]
Sorry, wrong number.	Falsch verbunden. [fahlS fehr-**buhnd**ən]
Can I send a fax to …?	Kann ich bei Ihnen ein Telefax nach … schicken? [kahn ihç bay iinən ayn **teh**-leh-fahks nahx … Sihkən]

Word List: Telephoning

to answer the phone	abnehmen [**ahp**-neymən]
answering machine	der Anrufbeantworter [**ahn**-roof-bəahnt-vortər]
area code	die Vorwahlnummer [**for**-vahl-nuhmər]
busy	besetzt [bə**zehtst**]
busy signal	das Besetztzeichen [bə**zehtst**-tsayçən]
to call	anrufen [**ahn**-roofən]
(phone) call	der Anruf [**ahn**-roof], das Gespräch [gə**Sprehç**]
charge	die Gebühr [gə**bewr**]
collect call	das R-Gespräch [**ehr**-gəSprehç]
country code	die Vorwahlnummer [**for**-vahl-nuhmər]
to dial	wählen [**vehl**ən]
to dial direct	durchwählen [**duhrç**-vehlən]
dial tone	das Freizeichen [**fray**-tsayçən]
directory information	die Auskunft [**aus**-kuhnft]
exchange	die Vermittlung [fehr-**miht**-luhŋ], das Amt [ahmt]
international call	das Auslandsgespräch [**aus**-lahnts-gəSprehç]
line	die Verbindung [fehr-**bihn**-duhŋ]
local call	das Ortsgespräch [**orts**-gəSprehç]

long-distance call	das Ferngespräch [**fehrn**-gəSprehç]
operator	die Vermittlung [fehr-**miht**-luhŋ]
pay phone	der Münzfernsprecher [**mewnts**-fehrn-Sprehçər]
to phone	anrufen [**ahn**-roofən]
phone booth	die Telefonzelle [teh-leh-**fohn**-tsehlə]
phone call	das Telefongespräch [-gəSprehç]
phone number	die Telefonnummer [-nuhmər]
phonecard	die Telefonkarte [-kahrtə]
receiver	der Hörer [hœrər]
telephone	das Telefon [teh-leh-**fohn**]
telephone directory	das Telefonbuch [-buhx]
telephone office, central	das Fernsprechamt [**fehrn**-Sprehç-ahmt]
unit	die Gebühreneinheit [gəbewrən-ayn-hayt]
yellow pages	das Branchenverzeichnis [**brahn**-Sən-fehr-tsayç-nihs]

At the Police Station

Auf dem Polizeirevier

Where's the nearest police station, please?	Wo ist bitte das nächste Polizeirevier? [voh ihst bihtə dahs nehkstə poh-liht-**say**-reh-viir]
I'd like to report an accident.	Ich möchte einen Unfall anzeigen. [ihç mœçtə aynən **uhn**-fahl **ahn**-tsaygən]
My ...	Mir ist ... [miir ihst]
... handbag/purse	... die Handtasche [dii **hahnt**-tahSə]
... wallet	... die Brieftasche [dii **briif**-tahSə]
... camera	... mein Fotoapparat [mayn **foh**-toh-ah-pah-raht]
... car/bike	... mein Auto/ Fahrrad [mayn **au**-toh / **fah**-raht]
has been stolen.	gestohlen worden. [gə**Stohl**ən vordən]
My car has been broken into.	Mein Auto ist aufgebrochen worden. [mayn **au**-toh ihst **auf**-gəbroxən vordən]

… has been stolen from my car.	Aus meinem Auto ist … gestohlen worden. [aus maynəm **au**-toh ihst … gə**Stohl**ən vordən]
I've lost …	Ich habe … verloren. [ihç hahbə … fehr-**lohr**ən]
My son/daughter has been missing since …	Mein Sohn/Meine Tochter ist seit … verschwunden. [mayn zohn / maynə toxtər ihst zayt … fehr-**Svuhnd**ən]
Can you help me, please?	Können Sie mir bitte helfen? [kœntən zii miir bihtə hehlfən]
When exactly did it happen?	Wann genau ist das passiert? [vahn gənau ihst dahs pah-**siirt**]
We'll look into the matter.	Wir werden der Sache nachgehen. [viir vehrdən dehr zahxə **nahx**-geyən]
I don't have anything to do with it.	Ich habe damit nichts zu tun. [ihç hahbə dah-**miht** nihçts tsuh toon]
Your name and address, please.	Ihren Namen und Ihre Anschrift, bitte. [iirən nahmən uhnt iirə **ahn**-Srihft bihtə]
Get in touch with the American/Australian/ British/Canadian/Irish consulate.	Wenden Sie sich an das amerikanische/ australische/ britische/ kanadische/ irische Konsulat. [vehndən zii zihç ahn dahs ah-meh-rih-**kah**-nihSə / au-**strah**-lihSə / **brih**-tihSə / kah-**nah**-dihSə / ii-rihSə kon-zuh-**laht**]

Word List: Police	► Chapter 3 – A Traffic Accident
to arrest	verhaften [fehr-**hahft**ən]
attack	der Überfall [**ewb**ər-fahl]
to beat up	zusammenschlagen [tsuh-**zahm**ən-Slahgən]
billfold	die Geldbörse [**gehlt**-bœrsə]
to break into/open	aufbrechen [**auf**-brehçən]
car documents	die Autopapiere *n pl* [**au**-toh-pah-piirə]
car key	der Autoschlüssel [**au**-toh-Slewsəl]
car radio	das Autoradio [**au**-toh-rahd-yoh]
check	der Scheck [Sehk]

check card	die Scheckkarte [**Sehk**-kahrtə]
to confiscate	beschlagnahmen [bə**Slahk**-nahmən]
court	das Gericht [gə**rihçt**]
crime	das Verbrechen [fehr-**brehç**ən]
documents	die Papiere *n pl* [pah-**piir**ə]
drugs	das Rauschgift [**rauS**-gihft]
to harass	belästigen [bə**lehs**-tihgən]
identity card	der Personalausweis [pehr-zoh-**nahl**-aus-vays]
judge	Richter/in [**rihçt**ər / -ihn]
key	der Schlüssel [**Slews**əl]
lawyer	der Rechtsanwalt/die Rechtsanwältin [**rehçts**-ahn-vahlt / vehl-tihn]
to lose	verlieren [fehr-**liir**ən]
money	das Geld [gehlt]
mugging	der Überfall [**ewb**ər-fahl]
papers	die Papiere *n pl* [pah-**piir**ə]
passport	der Reisepass [**rayz**ə-pahs]
pickpocket	der Taschendieb/die Taschendiebin [**tahS**ən-diip / -dii-bihn]
police	die Polizei [poh-liht-**say**]
police car	der Polizeiwagen [-**vahg**ən]
policeman/policewoman	der Polizist/die Polizistin [poh-liht-**sihst** / ihn]
police station	das Polizeirevier [poh-liht-**say**-reh-viir]
prison	das Gefängnis [gə**fehŋ**-nihs]
rape	die Vergewaltigung [fehr-gə**vahl**-tih-guhŋ]
to rape	vergewaltigen [fehrgə**vahl**-tihgən]
to report	anzeigen [**ahn**-tsaygən]
shoplifter	der Ladendieb/die Ladendiebin [**lahd**ən-diip / -dii-bihn]
theft	der Diebstahl [**diip**-Stahl]
thief	der Dieb/die Diebin [**diip** / **dii**-bihn]
wallet	die Brieftasche [**briif**-tahSə]

Lost and Found Office

Fundbüro

Where's the lost and found office, please?	Wo ist das Fundbüro, bitte? [voh ihst dahs **fuhnt**-bew-roh bihtə]
I've lost …	Ich habe … verloren. [ihç hahbə … fehr-**lohr**ən]
I left my purse on the train/on the streetcar/on the bus.	Ich habe meine Handtasche im Zug/in der Straßenbahn/im Bus vergessen. [ihç hahbə maynə **hahnt**-tahSə ihm tsuhk / ihn dehr **Strahs**ən-bahn / ihm buhs fehr-**gehs**ən]
Please let me know if it's turned in.	Benachrichtigen Sie mich bitte, wenn sie abgegeben werden sollte. [bə**nahx**-rihç-tihgən zii mihç bihtə, vehn zii **ahp**-gəgeybən vehrdən zoltə]
Here's the address of my hotel/my home address.	Hier ist meine Hotelanschrift/ Heimatadresse. [hiir ihst maynə hoh-**tehl**-ahn-Srihft / **hay**-maht-ah-drehsə]

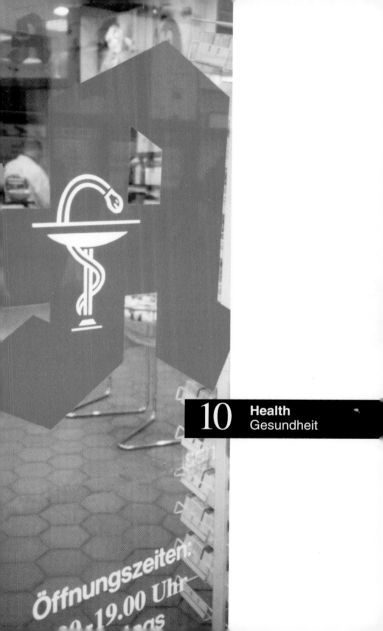

10 **Health**
Gesundheit

Öffnungszeiten:
19.00 Uhr

At the Pharmacy

In der Apotheke

Where's the nearest pharmacy (with all-night service)?	Wo ist die nächste Apotheke (mit Nachtdienst)? [voh ihst dii nehkstə ah-poh-**teyk**ə (miht **nahxt**-diinst)]
Can you give me something for …?	Geben Sie mir bitte etwas gegen … [geybən zii miir bihtə **eht**-vahs geygən]
You need a prescription for this.	Sie brauchen ein Rezept dafür. [zii brauxən ayn reyt-**sehpt** dah-**fewr**]
Can I wait?	Kann ich darauf warten? [kahn ihç da-**rauf** vahrtən]
When can I pick it up?	Wann kann ich es abholen? [vahn kahn ihç ehs **ahp**-hohlən]

Word List: Pharmacy   ▶ also Word List: Doctor/Dentist/Hospital

Useful expressions when taking medicine:

after/before meals	nach/vor dem Essen [nahx / for deym ehsən]
for external use	äußerlich [**oys**ər-lihç]
gargle	gurgeln [**guhrg**əln]
for internal use	innerlich [**ihn**ər-lihç]
inhale	inhalieren [ihn-hah-**liir**ən]
let dissolve in your mouth	im Mund zergehen lassen [ihm muhnt tsehr-**gey**ən lahsən]
swallow whole	unzerkaut schlucken [**uhn**-tsehr-kaut Sluhkən]
on an empty stomach	auf nüchternen Magen [auf **newç**tərnən mahgən]

absorbent cotton	die Watte [vahtə]
adhesive bandage, Band-Aid®	das Pflaster [pflahstər]

antibiotics	das Antibiotikum [ahn-tii-bii-**oh**-tih-kuhm]
antidote	das Gegengift [**geyg**ən-gihft]
aspirin	das Aspirin [ahs-pih-**rihn**]
birth control pills	die Antibabypillen *f pl* [ahn-tii-**bey**-bii-pihlən]
camomile tea	der Kamillentee [kah-**mihl**ən-tey]
cardiac stimulant	das Kreislaufmittel [**krays**-lauf-mihtəl]
charcoal tablets	die Kohletabletten *f pl* [**kohl**ə-tah-blehtən]
condom	das Präservativ, das Kondom [preh-zehr-vah-**tiif**, **kon**-dohm]
cough syrup	der Hustensaft [**hoo**-stən-zahft]
disinfectant	das Desinfektionsmittel [dehs-ihn-fehk-**tsyohnz**-mihtəl]
drops	die Tropfen *m pl* [tropfən]
ear drops	die Ohrentropfen *m pl* [**ohr**ən-tropfən]
elastic bandage	die Elastikbinde [ey-**lah**-stihk-bihndə]
eye drops	die Augentropfen *m pl* [**aug**ən-tropfən]
gauze bandage	die Mullbinde [**muhl**-bihndə]
glucose	der Traubenzucker [**traub**ən-tsuhkər]
headache tablets/pills	die Kopfschmerztabletten *f pl* [**kopf**-Smehrts-tah-blehtən]
insect repellent	das Insektenmittel [ihn-**zehkt**ən-mihtəl]
insulin	das Insulin [ihn-zoo-**liin**]
iodine	das Jod [yoht]
laxative	das Abführmittel [**ahp**-fewr-mihtəl]
medicine	das Medikament [meh-dih-kah-**mehnt**]
ointment	die Salbe [zahlbə]
ointment for burns	die Brandsalbe [**brahnt**-zahlbə]
pain-killing tablets/pills	die Schmerztabletten *f pl* [**Smehrts**-tah-blehtən]

pill	die Tablette [tah-**bleht**ə]
powder	der Puder [**pood**ər]
prescription	das Rezept [reyt-**sehpt**]
remedy	das Mittel [**miht**əl]
sedative	das Beruhigungsmittel [bəroo-ih-**guhŋz**-mihtəl]
side effects	die Nebenwirkungen *f pl* [**neyb**ən-vihr-kuhŋən]
sleeping pills	die Schlaftabletten *f pl* [**Slahf**-tah-blehtən]
sunburn	der Sonnenbrand [**zon**ən-brahnt]
suppository	das Zäpfchen [**tsehpf**çən]
tablet	die Tablette [tah-**bleht**ə]
to take	einnehmen [**ayn**-neymən]
thermometer	das Fieberthermometer [**fiib**ər-tehr-moh-meytər]
throat lozenges	die Halstabletten *f pl* [**hahls**-tah-blehtən]
tranquilizer	das Beruhigungsmittel [bəroo-ih-**guhŋz**-mihtəl]

Visitors from the United States and other non-EU countries should take out medical insurance before traveling.

At the Doctor

Arztbesuch

Can you recommend a good ...?	Können Sie mir einen guten ... empfehlen? [kœnən zii miir aynən gootən ... ehmp-**feyl**ən]
doctor	Arzt/Ärztin [ahrtst / **ehrt**-stihn]
dentist	Zahnarzt [**tsahn**-]
dermatologist	Hautarzt [**haut**-]
ear, nose, and throat specialist	Hals-Nasen-Ohren-Arzt [**hahls**-nahzən-ohrən-]

eye specialist	Augenarzt [**augən**-]
GP (general practitioner)	praktischen Arzt [**prahk**-tihSən]
gynecologist	Frauenarzt [**frauən**-]
internist	Internisten [ihn-tehr-**nihst**]
neurologist	Nervenarzt [**nehrv**ən-]
pediatrician	Kinderarzt [**kihnd**ər-]
urologist	Urologen [oo-roh-**loh**-gən]

Where's his/her practice?
Wo ist seine/ihre Praxis? [voh ihst zaynə / iirə **prahk**-sihs]

What are his/her office hours?
Wann hat er/sie Sprechstunde? [vahn haht ehr / zii **Sprehç**-Stuhndə]

What's the trouble?
Was für Beschwerden haben Sie? [vahs fewr bə**Svehrd**ən hahbən zii]

I don't feel well.
Ich fühle mich nicht wohl. [ihç fewlə mihç nihçt vohl]

I have a temperature.
Ich habe Fieber. [ihç hahbə fiibər]

I can't sleep.
Ich kann nicht schlafen.[ihç kahn nihçt Slahfən]

I often feel nauseous.
Mir ist oft schlecht. [miir ihst oft Slehçt]

I often feel faint.
Mir ist oft schwindelig. [miir ihst oft **Svihn**-də-lihç]

I fainted.
Ich bin ohnmächtig geworden. [ihç bihn **ohn**-mehç-tihç gə**vord**ən]

I have a bad cold.
Ich bin stark erkältet. [ihç bihn Stahrk ehr-**kehlt**ət]

I have …
Ich habe … [ihç hahbə]
  a headache.
  Kopfschmerzen. [**kopf**-Smehrtsən]
  a sore throat.
  Halsschmerzen. [**hahls**-Smehrtsən]
  a cough.
  Husten. [hoostən]

I've been stung/bitten.
Ich bin gestochen/gebissen worden. [ihç bihn gə**Stox**ən / gə**bihs**ən]

I have an upset stomach.
Ich habe mir den Magen verdorben. [ihç hahbə miir deyn mahgən fehr-**dorb**ən]

I have diarrhea./I'm constipated.	Ich habe Durchfall/Verstopfung. [ihç hahbə **duhrç**-fahl / fehr-**Stop**-fuhŋ]
The food doesn't agree with me./I can't stand the heat.	Ich vertrage das Essen/die Hitze nicht. [ihç fehr-**trahgə** dahs ehsən / dii hihtsə nihçt]
I've hurt myself.	Ich habe mich verletzt. [ihç hahbə mihç fehr-**lehtst**]
I fell down.	Ich bin gestürzt. [ihç bihn gə**Stewrtst**]
I think I've broken/sprained ...	Ich glaube, ich habe mir ... gebrochen/verstaucht. [ihç glaubə, ihç hahbə miir ... gə**brox**ən / fehr-**Stauxt**]
Where does it hurt?	Wo tut es weh? [voh toot ehs vey]
I have pain here.	Ich habe hier Schmerzen. [ihç hahbə hiir Smehrtsən]
Does that hurt?	Tut es hier weh? [toot ehs hiir vey]
I have high/low blood pressure.	Ich habe einen hohen/niedrigen Blutdruck. [ihç hahbə aynən hoh-ən / **nii**-drihgən / **bloot**-druhk]
I'm a diabetic.	Ich bin Diabetiker/Diabetikerin. [ihç bihn dii-ah-**beh**-tihkər / -ihn]
I'm pregnant.	Ich bin schwanger. [ihç bihn Svahŋər]
I had ... recently.	Ich hatte vor kurzem ... [ihç hahtə for kuhrtsəm]
Get undressed, please.	Bitte, machen Sie sich frei. [bihtə mahxən zii zihç fray]
Take ... off, please.	Ziehen Sie bitte ... aus. [tsiiən zii bihtə ... aus]
Take a deep breath. Hold your breath, please.	Bitte tief einatmen. Atem anhalten. [bihtə tiif **ayn**-ahtmən. Ahtəm **ahn**-hahltən]
Open your mouth.	Öffnen Sie den Mund. [œfnən zii deyn muhnt]
Show me your tongue.	Zeigen Sie die Zunge. [tsaygən zii dii tsuhŋə]
Cough, please.	Husten, bitte. [hoostən, bihtə]

How long have you been feeling like this?	Wie lange fühlen Sie sich schon so? [vii lahŋə fewlən zii sihç Sohn zoh]
I've lost my appetite.	Ich habe keinen Appetit. [ihç hahbə kaynən Ahpə-**tiit**]
Do you have a vaccination card?	Haben Sie einen Impfpass? [hahbən zii aynən **ihmpf**-pahs]
I've been vaccinated against …	Ich bin gegen … geimpft. [ihç bihn geygən … gə-**ihmpft**]
You'll have to be X-rayed.	Sie müssen geröntgt werden. [zii mewsən gə**rœntkt** vehrdən]
I need a blood/urine sample.	Ich brauche eine Blut-/Urinprobe. [ihç brauxə aynə **bloot**- / oo-**riin**-prohbə]
I'll have to send you to a specialist.	Ich muss Sie an einen Facharzt überweisen. [ihç muhs zii ahn aynən **fahx**-ahrtst ewbər-**vayzən**]
You'll have to have an operation.	Sie müssen operiert werden. [zii mewsən oh-pə-**riirt** vehrdən]
You need a few days in bed.	Sie brauchen ein paar Tage Bettruhe. [zii brauxən ayn pahr tahgə **beht**-rooə]
It's nothing serious.	Es ist nichts Ernstes. [ehs ihst nihçts ehrnstəs]
Can you give me/ prescribe something for …?	Können Sie mir bitte etwas gegen … geben/verschreiben? [kœnən zii miir bihtə **eht**-vahs geygən … geybən / fehr-**Sraybən**]
I usually take …	Normalerweise nehme ich … [nor-**mahlər**-vayzə neymə ihç]
Take one tablet/pill before you go to bed.	Nehmen Sie eine Tablette vor dem Schlafengehen. [neymən zii aynə tah-**blehtə** for deym **Slahf**ən-geyən]
Here's my international medical insurance card.	Hier ist mein internationaler Krankenschein. [hiir ihst mayn ihntər-naht-syoh-**nahlər krahŋk**ən-Sayn]
Can you give me a doctor's certificate, please?	Können Sie mir bitte ein ärztliches Attest ausstellen? [kœnən zii miir bihtə ayn **ehrtst**-lihçəs ah-**tehst aus**-Stehlən]

At the Dentist

Beim Zahnarzt

I have a (terrible) toothache.	Ich habe (starke) Zahnschmerzen. [ihç hahbə (Stahrkə) **tsahn**-Smehrtsən]
This tooth (at the top/bottom/front/back) hurts.	Dieser Zahn (oben/ unten/ vorn/ hinten) tut weh. [diizər tsahn (ohbən/ uhntən/ forn/ hihntən) toot vey]
I've lost a filling.	Ich habe eine Füllung verloren. [ihç hahbə aynə **few**-luhŋ fehr-**lohr**ən]
I've broken a tooth.	Mir ist ein Zahn abgebrochen. [miir ihst ayn tsahn **ahp**-gəbroxən]
I'll have to fill it.	Ich muss ihn plombieren. [ihç muhs iin plom-**biir**ən]
I'll only do a temporary job.	Ich behandle ihn nur provisorisch. [ihç bəhahndlə iin noor proh-vii-**zoh**-rihS]
It'll have to come out.	Ich muss ihn ziehen. [ihç muhs iin tsiiən]
This tooth needs a crown.	Dieser Zahn muss eine Krone bekommen. [diizər tsahn mews aynə krohnə bəkomən]
I'd like an injection, please./I don't want an injection.	Geben Sie mir bitte eine/keine Spritze. [geybən zii miir bihtə aynə/ kaynə Sprihtsə]
Rinse well, please.	Bitte gut spülen. [bihtə goot Spewlən]
Can you repair these dentures, please?	Können Sie diese Prothese reparieren? [kœnən zii diizə proh-**teyz**ə reh-pah-**riir**ən]
Come back in two days for a follow-up.	Kommen Sie in zwei Tagen bitte noch mal zum Nachsehen. [komən zii ihn tsvay tahgən bihtə nox mahl tsuhm **nahx**-zeyən]
See your dentist as soon as you get home.	Suchen Sie dann zu Hause gleich Ihren Zahnarzt auf. [zooxən zii dahn tsuh hauzə glayç iirən **tsahn**-ahrtst auf]

In the Hospital

Im Krankenhaus

How long will I have to stay here?	Wie lange muss ich hier bleiben? [vii lahŋə muhs ihç hiir blaybən]
I can't sleep. Could you give me a pain-killing tablet/a sleeping pill, please.	Ich kann nicht einschlafen. Geben Sie mir bitte eine Schmerztablette/ Schlaftablette. [ihç kahn nihçt **ayn**-Slahfən. geybən zii miir bihtə aynə **Smehrts**-tah-blehtə / **Slahf**-tah-blehtə]
When can I get up?	Wann darf ich aufstehen? [vahn dahrf ihç **auf**-Steyən]
Could you give me a certificate stating how long I was in the hospital, together with the diagnosis, please?	Geben Sie mir bitte eine Bescheinigung über die Dauer des Krankenhausaufenthalts mit Diagnose. [geybən zii miir bihtə aynə bə**Say**-nih-guhŋ ewbər dii dauər dehs **krahŋk**ən-haus-auf-ehnt-hahlts miht dii-ahg-**nohz**ə]

Word List: Doctor/Dentist/Hospital

abdomen	der Unterleib [**uhnt**ər-liip]
abscess	der Abszess [ahps-**tsehs**]
AIDS	Aids [eydz]
to be allergic to	allergisch sein gegen [ah-**lehr**-gihS zayn geygən]
allergy	die Allergie [ah-lehr-**gii**]
anesthetic	die Narkose [nahr-**kohz**ə]
angina	die Angina [ahn-**giin**ə]
ankle	der Knöchel [knœçəl]
appendicitis	die Blinddarmentzündung [**blihnt**-dahrm-ehn-tsewn-duhŋ]
appendix	der Blinddarm [**blihnt**-dahrm]
arm	der Arm [ahrm]

artifical limb	die Prothese [proh-**teyz**ə]
asthma	das Asthma [**ahst**-mah]
attack	der Anfall [**ahn**-fahl]
back	der Rücken [rewkən]
backache	die Rückenschmerzen *m pl* [**rewk**ən-Smehrtsən]
bandage	der Verband [fehr-**bahnt**]
bladder	die Blase [blahzə]
to bleed	bluten [blootən]
bleeding	die Blutung [**bloo**-tuhŋ]
blood	das Blut [**bloot**]
blood group	die Blutgruppe [**bloot**-groopə]
blood pressure	der Blutdruck [**bloot**-druhk]
blood test/sample	die Blutprobe [**bloot**-prohbə]
blood transfusion	die Bluttransfusion [**bloot**-trahns-fooz-yohn]
blood poisoning	die Blutvergiftung [**bloot**-fehr-gihf-tuhŋ]
bone	der Knochen [knoxən]
bowel movement	der Stuhlgang [**Stool**-gahŋ]
brain	das Gehirn [gə**hihrn**]
breast	die Brust [bruhst]
to breathe difficulty in breathing	atmen [**aht**-mehn] die Atembeschwerden *f pl* [**ah**-tehm-bəSvehrdən]
broken	gebrochen [gə**brox**ən]
bronchial tubes	die Bronchien *f pl* [**bron**-çiiən]
bronchitis	die Bronchitis [bron-**çii**-tihs]
burn	die Verbrennung [fehr-**breh**-nuhŋ]
bypass (operation)	der Bypass (as in English)
cancer	der Krebs [krehps]
cardiac infarction	der Herzinfarkt [**hehrts**-ihn-fahrkt]
cavity	das Loch [lox]

certificate	das Attest [ah-**tehst**], die Bescheinigung [bəSay-nih-guhŋ]
chest	die Brust [bruhst]
chickenpox	die Windpocken *f pl* [**vihnt**-pokən]
cholera	die Cholera [**koh**-leh-rah]
circulatory disorder	die Kreislaufstörung [**krays**-lauf-Stœ-ruhŋ]
cold	die Erkältung [ehr-**kehl**-tuhŋ], der Schnupfen [Snuhpfən]
to catch a cold	sich erkälten [zihç ehr-**kehlt**ən]
to have a cold	erkältet sein [ehr-**kehlt**ət zayn]
colic	die Kolik [**koh**-lihk]
collarbone	das Schlüsselbein [**Slews**əl-bayn]
concussion	die Gehirnerschütterung [gəhihrn-ehr-Sewtə-ruhŋ]
constipation	die Verstopfung [fehr-**Stop**-fuhŋ]
contagious	ansteckend [**ahn**-Stehkənt]
contusion	die Prellung [**preh**-luhŋ], die Quetschung [**kveht**-Suhŋ]
cough	der Husten [hoostən]
cramp	der Krampf [krahmpf]
crown *(tooth)*	die Krone [krohnə]
cut	die Schnittwunde [**Sniht**-vuhndə]
denture	die Zahnprothese [**tsahn**-proh-teyzə]
diabetes	Diabetes [dii-ah-**bey**-tehs]
diagnosis	die Diagnose [dii-ahg-**noz**ə]
diarrhea	der Durchfall [**duhrç**-fahl]
diet	die Diät [dii-**eht**]
digestion	die Verdauung [fehr-**dau**-uhŋ]
diphtheria	die Diphtherie [dif-teh-**rii**]
to disinfect	desinfizieren [dehs-ihn-fiht-**siir**ən]
dizziness	das Schwindelgefühl [**Svihnd**əl-gəfewl]
to dress	verbinden [fehr-**bihnd**ən]

dressing	der Verband [fehr-**bahnt**]
ear	das Ohr [ohr]
eardrum	das Trommelfell [**trom**əl-fehl]
elbow	der Ellbogen [**ehl**-bohgən]
examination	die Untersuchung [uhntər-**zoo**-xuhŋ]
to extract *(tooth)*	ziehen *(Zahn)* [tsiiən (tsahn)]
eye	das Auge [augə]
face	das Gesicht [gə**zihçt**]
to faint	in Ohnmacht fallen [ihn **ohn**-mahxt fahlən]
to fester	eitern [**ay**-tehrn]
fever	das Fieber [fiibər]
filling *(tooth)*	die Plombe [plombə]
finger	der Finger [fihŋər]
fit	der Anfall [**ahn**-fahl]
fit of shivering	der Schüttelfrost [**Sewt**əl-frost]
flu	die Grippe [grihpə]
food poisoning	die Lebensmittelvergiftung [**leyb**ənz-mihtəl-fehr-gihf-tuhŋ]
foot	der Fuß [fuhs]
fracture	der Knochenbruch [**knox**ən-bruhx]
gall bladder	die Gallenblase [**gahl**ən-blahzə]
gas	die Blähungen *f pl* [**bley**-uhŋən]
German measles	die Röteln *f pl* [**rœ**-tehln]
gland	die Drüse [drewzə]
growth	die Geschwulst [gə**Svuhlst**]
gullet	die Speiseröhre [**Spayz**ə-rœrə]
gums	das Zahnfleisch [**tsahn**-flayS]
hematoma	der Bluterguss [**bloot**-ehr-guhs]
hemorrhoids	die Hämorrhoiden *f pl* [heh-mo-roh-**iid**ən]
hand	die Hand [hahnt]

hay fever	der Heuschnupfen [**hoy**-Snuhpfən]
head	der Kopf [kopf]
headache	die Kopfschmerzen *m pl* [**kopf**-Smehrtsən]

> *In German-speaking countries many people spend a few weeks from time to time on a "Kur," or health cure, often in a town with the word "Bad" in its name (Bad Gastein, for example). There are various forms of diet and treatment, often involving mineral water.*

health resort	der Kurort [**koor**-ort]
hearing	das Gehör [gə**hœr**]
heart	das Herz [hehrts]
heart attack	der Herzanfall [-**ahn**-fahl], der Herzinfarkt [-**ihn**-fahrkt]
heart defect	der Herzfehler [-**feylər**]
heart specialist	der Herzspezialist [-Speht-syah-lihst]
heart trouble	die Herzbeschwerden *f pl* [-bə**Svehrdən**]
heartburn	das Sodbrennen [**zot**-brehnən]
hernia	der Leistenbruch [**laystən**-bruhx]
hip	die Hüfte [hewftə]
to be hoarse	heiser sein [hayzər zayn]
hospital	das Krankenhaus [**krahŋkən**-haus]
to hurt	weh tun [vey toon]
to hurt oneself	sich verletzen [zihç fehr-**lehtsən**]
ill	krank [krahŋk]
illness	die Krankheit [**krahŋk**-hayt]
indigestion	die Verdauungsstörung [fehr-**dau**-uhŋs-Stœ-ruhŋ]
infection	die Infektion [ihn-fehkt-**syohn**]
inflammation	die Entzündung [ehnt-**tsewn**-duhŋ]

inflammation of the middle ear	die Mittelohrentzündung [**miht**əl-ohr-ehnt-tsewn-duhŋ]
infusion	die Infusion [ihn-fooz-**yohn**]
injection	die Spritze [Sprihtsə]
to injure	verletzen [fehr-**lehts**ən]
injury	die Verletzung [fehr-**leht**-suhŋ]
insomnia	die Schlaflosigkeit [**Slahf**-loh-zihç-kayt]
intestine	der Darm [dahrm]
jaundice	die Gelbsucht [**gehlp**-zuhxt]
jaw	der Kiefer [kiifər]
joint	das Gelenk [gəlehŋk]
kidney	die Niere [niirə]
kidney stone	der Nierenstein [**niir**ən-Stayn]
knee	das Knie [knii]
lack of appetite	die Appetitlosigkeit [ah-peh-**tiit**-loh-zihç-kayt]
leg	das Bein [bayn]
limbs	die Glieder *n pl* [gliidər]
lip	die Lippe [lihpə]
liver	die Leber [leybər]
lumbago	der Hexenschuss [**hehks**ən-Suhs]
lungs	die Lunge [luhŋə]
massage	die Massage [mah-**sahZ**ə]
to massage	massieren [mah-**siir**ən]
masseur/masseuse	der Masseur/die Masseurin [mah-**sœr** / -ihn]
measles	die Masern *f pl* [**mah**-zehrn]
medical insurance	die Krankenkasse [**krahŋk**ən-kahsə]
medical insurance form	der Krankenschein [**krahŋk**ən-Sayn]
menstruation	die Menstruation [mehns-troo-aht-**syohn**]
migraine	die Migräne [mii-**grehn**ə]

miscarriage	die Fehlgeburt [**feyl**-gəbuhrt]
mouth	der Mund [muhnt]
mumps	der Mumps [muhmps]
muscle	der Muskel [muskəl]
nausea	der Brechreiz [**brehx**-rayts], die Übelkeit [**ewb**əl-kayt]
neck	der Hals [hahls]
nephritis	die Nierenentzündung [**niir**ən-ehnt-tsewn-duhŋ]
nerve	der Nerv [nehrf]
nervous	nervös [nehr-**vœs**]
nose	die Nase [nahzə]
nose bleed	das Nasenbluten [**nahz**ən-blootən]
nurse	die Krankenschwester [**krahŋk**ən-Svehstər]
office hours	die Sprechstunde [**Sprehç**-Stuhndə]
operation	die Operation [oh-peh-raht-**syohn**]
pacemaker	der Herzschrittmacher [**hehrts**-Sriht-mahxər]
pain	die Schmerzen *m pl* [Smehrtsən]
to be painful	weh tun [vey toon]
paralysis	die Lähmung [**ley**-muhŋ]
perspiration	der Schweiß [Svays]
to perspire	schwitzen [Svihtsən]
physiotherapy	die Krankengymnastik [**krahŋk**ən-gewm-nahs-tihk]
piles	die Hämorrhoiden *f pl* [heh-moh-roh-**iid**ən]
pneumonia	die Lungenentzündung [**luhŋ**ən-ehnt-tsewn-duhŋ]
poisoning	die Vergiftung [fehr-**gihf**-tuhŋ]
polio	die Kinderlähmung [**kihnd**ər-ley-muhŋ]
practice	die Praxis [**prahk**-sihs]
pregnancy	die Schwangerschaft [**Svahŋ**ər-Sahft]

to prescribe	verschreiben [fehr-**Srayb**ən]
pulled ligament/muscle	die Zerrung [**tseh**-ruhŋ]
pulse	der Puls [puhls]
pus	der Eiter [aytər]
radiotherapy, radiation	die Bestrahlung [bə**Strah**-luhŋ]
rash	der Ausschlag [**aus**-Slahk]
rheumatism	das Rheuma [**roy**-mah]
rib	die Rippe [rihpə]
rupture	der Leistenbruch [**layst**ən-bruhx]
salmonella	die Salmonellen *f pl* [zahl-moh-**nehl**ən]
scan	die Ultraschalluntersuchung [**uhl**-trah-Sahl-uhntər-zoo-xuhŋ]
scar	die Narbe [nahrbə]
scarlet fever	das Scharlach [**Sahr**-lahx]
sciatica	der Ischias [ihS-yəs]
sexual organs	die Geschlechtsorgane *n pl* [gə**Slehçts**-or-gahnə]
shin	das Schienbein [**Siin**-bayn]
shoulder	die Schulter [**Suhl**tər]
sick	krank [krahŋk]
sinusitis	die Stirnhöhlenentzündung [**Stihrn**-hœlən-ehnt-tsewn-duhŋ]
skin	die Haut [haut]
skin disease	die Hautkrankheit [**haut**-krahŋk-hayt]
skull	der Schädel [**Sehd**əl]
sleeplessness	die Schlaflosigkeit [**Slahf**-loh-Sihç-kayt]
smallpox	die Pocken *f pl* [pokən]
sore throat	die Halsschmerzen *m pl* [**hahls**-Smehrtsən]
spa	das Mineralbad [mih-neh-**rahl**-baht]

specialist	der Facharzt/die Fachärztin [**fahx**-artst / -ehrts-tihn]
spine	das Rückgrat [**rewk**-graht], die Wirbelsäule [**vihrb**əl-zoylə]
splint	die Schiene [Siinə]
sprained	verstaucht [fehr-**Stauxt**]
sting	der Stich [Stihç]
stitch	das Seitenstechen [**zayt**ən-Stehçən]
to stitch up	nähen [neyən]
stomach	der Bauch [baux], der Magen [mahgən]
stomachache	die Magenschmerzen *m pl* [**mahg**ən-Smehrtsən]
stroke	der Schlaganfall [**Slahk**-ahn-fahl]
sunstroke	der Sonnenstich [**zon**ən-Stihç]
surgeon	der Chirurg/die Chirurgin [çih-**ruhrk** / **ruhr**-gihn]
sweat	der Schweiß [Svays]
to sweat	schwitzen [Svihtsən]
swelling	die Schwellung [**Sveh**-luhŋ]
swollen	geschwollen [gə**Svol**ən]
to take out *(tooth)*	ziehen [tsiiən]
temperature	das Fieber [fiibər]
tetanus	der Tetanus [**tey**-tah-nuhs]
therapy	die Behandlung [bə**hahnt**-luhŋ]
thorax	der Brustkorb [**bruhst**-korp]
throat	der Hals [hahls], die Kehle [keylə]
toe	die Zehe [tseyə]
tongue	die Zunge [tsuhŋə]
tonsillitis	die Mandelentzündung [**mahnd**əl-ehnt-tsewn-duhŋ]
tonsils	die Mandeln *f pl* [**mahn**-dehln]

tooth	der Zahn [tsahn]
incisor	der Schneidezahn [**Snayd**ə-tsahn]
molar	der Backenzahn [**bahk**ən-tsahn]
toothache	die Zahnschmerzen *m pl* [**tsahn**-Smehrtsən]
torn ligament	der Bänderriss [**behnd**ə-rihs]
tumor	die Geschwulst [gə**S**vuhlst]
typhoid (fever)	der Typhus [**tew**-fuhs]
ulcer	das Geschwür [gə**S**vewr]
ultrasound	der Ultraschall [**uhl**-trah-Sahl]
ultraviolet light	die Höhensonne [**hoh**-ən-zonə]
unconscious	bewusstlos [bə**vuhst**-lohs]
urine	der Urin [oo-**riin**]
to vaccinate	impfen [ihmpfən]
vaccination	die Impfung [**ihmp**-fuhŋ]
vaccination card	der Impfpass [**ihmpf**-pahs]
vein	die Ader [ah-dər]
venereal disease	die Geschlechtskrankheit [gə**Sleçts**-krahŋk-hayt]
virus	das Virus [**vii**-ruhs]
visiting hours	die Besuchszeit [bə**zuhks**-tsayt]
to vomit	sich erbrechen [zihç ehr-**brehç**ən]
waiting room	das Wartezimmer [**vahrt**ə-tsihmər]
ward	die Station [Staht-**syohn**]
whooping cough	der Keuchhusten [**koyç**-hoostən]
wind	die Blähungen *f pl* [**bley**-uhŋən]
wound	die Wunde [vuhndə]
to X-ray	röntgen [**rœnt**gən]
X ray	die Röntgenaufnahme [**rœnt**gən-auf-nahmə]
yoga	das Yoga [**yoh**-gah]

On the Way to a Business Meeting

Der Weg zum Geschäftstreffen

Can you tell me how to get to … please?
Wie komme ich bitte zu …? [vii komə ihç bihtə tsuh…]

Where's the main entrance?
Wo ist der Haupteingang? [voh ihst dehr **haupt**-ayn-gahŋ]

My name's … I'm from …
Mein Name ist … Ich komme von der Firma … [mayn nahmə ihst … ihç komə fon dehr fihrmə]

Can I speak to …, please?
Kann ich bitte … sprechen? [kahn ihç bihtə … Sprehçən]

Could you tell … I'm here, please?
Melden Sie mich bitte bei … an. [mehldən zii mihç bihtə bay … ahn]

I have an appointment with …
Ich habe einen Termin bei … [ihç hahbə aynən tehr-**miin** bay …]

… is expecting you.
… erwartet Sie bereits. [… ehr-**vahrt**ət zii bərayts]

He's/She's still in a meeting.
Er/Sie ist noch in einer Sitzung. [ehr/zii ihst nox ihn aynər **ziht**-suhŋ]

I'll take you to …
Ich führe Sie zu … [ihç fewrə zii tsuh …]

I'm sorry I'm late.
Entschuldigen Sie bitte, dass ich zu spät komme. [ehnt-**Suhl**-dih-gən zii bihtə, dahs ihç tsuh Speyt komə]

Please sit down.
Bitte setzen Sie sich. [bihtə zehtsən zii zihç]

Would you like something to drink?
Darf ich Ihnen etwas zu trinken anbieten? [dahrf ihç iinən **eht**-vahs tsuh trihŋkən **ahn**-biitən]

Did you have a good trip?
Hatten Sie eine angenehme Reise? [hahtən zii aynə **ahn**-gəneymə rayzə]

How much time do we have?
Wie viel Zeit haben wir? [vii fiil tsayt hahbən viir]

When does your flight leave?
Wann geht Ihre Maschine? [vahn geyt iirə mah-**Siin**ə]

I need an interpreter.
Ich brauche einen Dolmetscher. [ihç brauxə aynən **dol**-mehtSər]

Word List: On the Way to a Business Meeting

appointment	der Termin [tehr-**miin**]
building	das Gebäude [gə**boy**də]
company	die Firma [**fihr**mə]
conference center	das Konferenzzentrum [kon-feh-**rehnts**-tsehn-truhm]
conference room	der Konferenzraum [kon-feh-**rehnts**-raum]
department	die Abteilung [**ahp**-tay-luhŋ]
doorman	der Pförtner [**pfœrt**nər]
entrance	der Eingang [**ayn**-gahŋ]
firm	die Firma [**fihr**mə]
floor	das Stockwerk [**Stok**-vehrk]
interpreter	der Dolmetscher/die Dolmetscherin [**dol**-mehtSər / -ihn]
meeting	die Sitzung [**ziht**-suhŋ]
office	das Büro [bew-**roh**]
reception	der Empfang [ehmp-**fahŋ**]
secretary	der Sekretär/die Sekretärin [zehk-reh-**tehr** / -ihn]
secretary's office	das Sekretariat [zehk-reh-tahr-**yaht**]

Negotiations/Conferences/Trade Fairs

Verhandlung/Konferenz/Messe

I'm looking for the … stand.	Ich suche den Messestand der Firma … [ihç zooxə deyn **mehs**ə-Stahnt dehr **fihr**mə …]
They're in hall …, stand number …	Sie sind in Halle …, Stand Nr. … [zii zihnt ihn **hah**lə …, Stahnt **nuh**mər …]
We manufacture …	Wir sind Hersteller von … [viir zihnt **hehr**-Stehlər fon …]
We deal in …	Wir handeln mit … [viir **hahn**dəln miht …]

Do you have information on …?	Haben Sie Informationsmaterial über …? [hahbən zii ihn-for-maht-**syohnz**-mah-tehr-yahl ewbər]
We can send you detailed information on …	Wir können Ihnen ausführliches Material über … zusenden. [viir kœnən iinən **aus**-fewr-lihçəs mah-tehr-**yahl** ewbər … **tsuh**-zehndən]
Whom should I contact about …?	Wer ist Ansprechpartner für …? [vehr ihst **ahn**-Sprehç-pahrtnər fewr …]
Could you let us have a quote?	Könnten Sie uns ein Angebot zukommen lassen? [kœntən zii uhns ayn **ahn**-gəboht **tsuh**-komən lahsən]
We should arrange a meeting.	Wir sollten ein Treffen vereinbaren. [viir zoltən ayn trehfən fehr-**ayn**-bahrən]
Here's my business card.	Hier ist meine Visitenkarte. [hiir ihst maynə vih-**ziit**ən-kahrtə]

Word List: Negotiations/Conferences/Trade Fairs

advertising	die Werbung [**vehr**-buhŋ]
advertising campaign	die Werbekampagne [**vehr**bə-kahm-pahnyə]
advertising material	das Werbematerial [**vehr**bə-mah-tehr-yahl]
agenda	die Tagesordnung [**tahg**əs-ord-nuhŋ]
agreement	der Vertrag [fehr-**trahk**]
authorized dealer	der Vertragshändler [fehr-**trahks**-hehndlər]
bill	die Rechnung [**rehç**-nuhŋ]
bill of sale	der Kaufvertrag [**kauf**-fehr-trahk]
booth	die Kabine [kah-**biin**ə]
brochure	der Prospekt [proh-**spehkt**]
business card	die Visitenkarte [vih-**ziit**ən-kahrtə]
business connections	die Geschäftsbeziehungen [gə**Sehfts**-bətsii-uhŋən]

business partner/associate	der Geschäftspartner [gə**Sehfts**-pahrt-nər]
cash discount	der Skonto [**skon**-toh]
catalogue	der Katalog [kah-tah-**lohk**]
commercial traveler	der Handelsvertreter/die Handelsvertreterin [**hahnd**əlz-fehr-trehtər / -ihn]
concern	der Konzern [kon-**tsehrn**]
condition	die Kondition [kon-diht-**syohn**]
conference	die Konferenz [kon-feh-**rehnts**]
confirmation of order	die Auftragsbestätigung [**auf**-trahks-bəSteh-tih-guhŋ]
contact person	der Ansprechpartner/die Ansprechpartnerin [**ahn**-Sprehç-pahrt-nər / -ihn]
contract	der Vertrag [fehr-**trahk**]
cooperation	die Kooperation [koh-opəraht-**syohn**]
cost(s)	Kosten [kostən]
customer	der Kunde/die Kundin [kuhndə / **kuhn**-dihn]
delivery	die Lieferung [**liif**əruhŋ]
delivery time	die Lieferzeit [**liif**ər-tsayt]
discount	der Preisnachlass [**prays**-nahx-lahs]
distribution	der Vertrieb [fehr-**triip**]
distribution network	das Vertriebsnetz [fehr-**triips**-nehts]
estimate	der Kostenvoranschlag [**kost**ən-for-ahn-Slahk]
exhibition center	das Messezentrum [**mehs**ə-tsehn-truhm]
exhibition stand	der Messestand [**mehs**ə-Stahnt]
exhibitor	der Aussteller [**aus**-Stehlər]
exhibitor's pass	der Messeausweis (für Aussteller) [**mehs**ə-aus-vays (fewr **aus**-Stehlər)]
export	der Export [ehks-**port**]

to export	exportieren [ehks-port-**tiir**ən]
exporter	der Exporteur [ehks-por-**tœr**]
(trade) fair	die Messe [mehsə]
financing	die Finanzierung [fih-nahnt-**sii**-ruhŋ]
freight	die Fracht [frahxt]
group (company)	der Konzern [kon-**tsehrn**]
guarantee	die Garantie [gah-rahn-**tii**]
hall	die Halle [hahlə]
head office	die Zentrale [tsehn-**trahl**ə]
import	der Import [ihm-**port**]
to import	importieren [ihm-por-**tiir**ən]
importer	der Importeur [im-por-**tœr**]
industrial fair	die Industriemesse [ihn-duhs-**trii**-mehsə]
information stand	der Informationsstand [ihn-for-maht-**syohns**-Stahnt]
insurance	die Versicherung [fehr-**zihç**əruhŋ]
to be interested in	interessiert sein an [ihntəreh-**siirt** zayn ahn]
invoice	die Rechnung [**rehç**-nuhŋ]
joint venture	das Jointventure (as in English)
leasing	das Leasing [**lii**-sihŋ, -zihŋ]
license	die Lizenz [liht-**sehnts**]
licensing agreement	das Lizenzabkommem [liht-**sehnts**-ahp-komən]
list of exhibitors	das Ausstellerverzeichnis [**aus**-Stehlər-fehr-tsayç-nihs]
manager	die Führungskraft [**few**-ruhŋs-krahft]
managing director	der Geschäftsführer/die Geschäftsführerin [gə**Sehfts**-fewrər / -ihn]
manufacturer	der Hersteller [**hehr**-Stehlər]
marketing	das Marketing (as in English)

meeting	das Treffen [trehfən]
minutes (of a meeting)	das Protokoll [proh-toh-**kol**]
negotiations	die Verhandlungen *f pl* [fehr-**hahnt**-luhŋən]
offer	das Angebot [**ahn**-gəboht]
order	der Auftrag [**auf**-trahk]
packing, packaging	die Verpackung [fehr-**pah**-kuhŋ]
price	der Preis [prays]
price list	die Preisliste [**prays**-lihstə]
pro forma invoice	die Proforma-Rechnung [proh-**formə**-rehç-nuhŋ]
product	die Ware [vahrə]
production	die Produktion [pro-duhkt-**syohn**]
public relations (PR)	die Öffentlichkeitsarbeit [**œf**ənt-lihç-kayts-ahr-bayt]
quote	das Angebot [**ahn**-gəboht]
report	der Bericht [bərihçt]
retailer	der Einzelhändler/die Einzelhändlerin [**ayn**-tsəl-hehnd-lər / -ihn]
royalties	*(from books …)* Tantiemen *(pl)* [tahnt-**yeh**-mən]; *(from patent)* Lizenzgebühren *(pl)* [liht-**sehnts**-gəbewrən]
sales department	die Vertriebsabteilung [fehr-**triips**-ahp-tay-luhŋ]
sales promotion	die Verkaufsförderung [fehr-**kaufs**-fœrdə-ruhŋ]
sales representative	der Vertreter/die Vertreterin [fehr-**treht**ər / -ihn]
sales tax	die Umsatzsteuer [**uhm**-zahts-Stoyər]
salesperson *(in a shop)*	der Verkäufer/die Verkäuferin [fehr **koyf**ər / -ihn]
sample	das Muster [mustər]
seller	der Verkäufer/die Verkäuferin [fehr-**koyf**ər / -ihn]

shipment	Fracht [frahxt], Transport [trahns-**port**]
sole agency/agents	die Generalvertretung [geh-neh-**rahl**-fehr-treh-tuhŋ]
stand	der (Messe-)Stand [(**mehsə**)-Stahnt]
stocklist	das Warenverzeichnis [**vahrə**n-fehr-tsayç-nihs]
subsidiary	die Tochtergesellschaft [**toxt**ər-gəzehl-Sahft]
supplier	der Lieferant [liifə-**rahnt**]
supply	die Lieferung [**liif**ə-ruhŋ]
talk	der Vortrag [**for**-trahk]
terms of a contract	die Vertragsbedingungen *f pl* [fehr-**trahks**-bə-dihŋ-uhŋən]
terms of payment	die Zahlungsbedingungen *f pl* [**tsah**-luhŋs-bədihŋ-uhŋən]
terms of supply	die Lieferbedingungen *f pl* [**liif**ər-bədihŋ-uhŋən]
trade fair	die Fachmesse [**fahx**-mehsə]
training	die Schulung [**Soo**-luhŋ]
transportation	der Transport [trahns-**port**]
transportation costs	die Transportkosten *pl* [-kostən]
traveling sales representative	der Handelsvertreter/die Handelsvertreterin [**hahnd**əls-fehr-trehtər / -ihn]
value added tax (VAT)	die Mehrwertsteuer [**mehr**-vehr-stoyər]
wholesaler	der Großhändler [**grohs**-hehndlər]

Equipment

Ausstattung

Could you make me some copies of this, please?	Könnten Sie mir hiervon einige Kopien machen? [kœntən zii miir **hiir**-fon ay-nihgə koh-**pii**-ən mahxən]
I need an overhead projector for my talk.	Für meinen Vortrag benötige ich einen Tageslichtprojektor. [fewr maynən **for**-trahk bənœ-tihgə ihç aynən **tahgəs**-lihçt-proh-yehk-tor]
Could you get me ..., please?	Würden Sie mir bitte ... besorgen? [vewrdən zii miir bihtə ... bə**zorg**ən]

Word List: Equipment

catalogue	der Katalog [kah-tah-**lohk**]
color copier	der Farbkopierer [**farp**-koh-piirər]
copy	die Kopie [koh-**pii**]
disk	die Diskette [dihs-**keht**ə]
display material	das Ausstellungsmaterial [**aus**-Steh-luhŋz-mah-tehr-yahl]
extension cord	die Verlängerungsschnur [fehr-**lehŋ**ə-ruhŋs-Snuhr]
fax	das (Tele)fax [(**teh**-leh-)fahks]
felt-tip pen	der Filzstift [**fihlts**-Stihft]
flip chart	der Flipchart (as in English)
lectern	das Rednerpult [**reydn**ər-puhlt]
microphone	das Mikrofon [mii-kroh-**fohn**]
modem	das Modem [**moh**-dehm]
overhead pen	der Folienstift [**fohl**-yən-Stihft]
overhead projector	der Tageslichtprojektor [**tahgəs**-lihçt-proh-yehk-tor]

(writing) pad	der Schreibblock [**Srayp**-blok]
pen	der Stift [Stihft]
pencil	der Bleistift [**blay**-Stihft]
personal computer	der PC [pey-**tsey**]
phone	das Telefon [teh-leh-**fohn**]
photocopier	der Fotokopierer [**foh**-toh-ko-piirər]
printer	der Drucker [druhkər]
telephone	das Telefon [teh-leh-**fohn**]
video recorder	der Videorekorder [**vii**-dey-oh-rey-kordər]
word processor	das Textverarbeitungssystem [**tehkts**-vehr-ahr-bay-tuhŋs-zews-teym]

A Short Guide to German Grammar

Articles

The article indicates the gender of a noun. There are three genders in German: masculine, feminine, and neuter, as well as four cases: nominative, accusative, genitive, and dative.

	definite article				indefinite article			
	m	f	n	pl	m	f	n	pl
nom.	der	die	das	die	ein	eine	ein	*no article*
acc.	den	die	das	die	einen	eine	ein	*used with*
gen.	des	der	des	der	eines	einer	eines	*plural nouns*
dat.	dem	der	dem	den	einem	einer	einem	

Nouns

All German nouns are written with a capital letter.

There are three declensions: strong, weak, and mixed. (These terms classify nouns according to their endings in the genitive case.)

Nouns that end in s, sch, ß/ss, and z always have an -es in the genitive case.

Some nouns are declined like adjectives.

1. Strong masculine and neuter nouns

	nom. plural: + e	nom. plural: umlaut + e	nom. plural: + er	nom. plural: umlaut + er
singular				
nom.	der Tag	der Traum	das Kind	das Dach
	(the day)	(the dream)	(the child)	(the roof)
acc.	den Tag	den Traum	das Kind	das Dach
gen.	des Tag(e)s	des Traum(e)s	des Kind(e)s	des Dach(e)s
dat.	dem Tag(e)	dem Traum(e)	dem Kind(e)	dem Dach(e)
plural				
nom.	die Tage	die Träume	die Kinder	die Dächer
acc.	die Tage	die Träume	die Kinder	die Dächer
gen.	der Tage	der Träume	der Kinder	der Dächer
dat.	den Tagen	den Träumen	den Kindern	den Dächern

	nom. plural: + s	nom. plural: umlaut only	nom. plural: no change	nom. plural: no change
singular				
nom.	das Auto (the car)	der Vogel (the bird)	der Tischler (the carpenter)	der Lappen (the cloth)
acc.	das Auto	den Vogel	den Tischler	den Lappen
gen.	des Autos	des Vogels	des Tischlers	des Lappens
dat.	dem Auto	dem Vogel	dem Tischler	dem Lappen
plural				
nom.	die Autos	die Vögel	die Tischler	die Lappen
acc.	die Autos	die Vögel	die Tischler	die Lappen
gen.	der Autos	der Vögel	der Tischler	der Lappen
dat.	den Autos	den Vögeln	den Tischlern	den Lappen

2. Strong feminine nouns

	nom. plural: umlaut + e	nom. plural: umlaut only	nom. plural: + s
singular			
nom.	die Wand (the wall)	die Mutter (the mother)	die Bar (the bar)
acc.	die Wand	die Mutter	die Bar
gen.	der Wand	der Mutter	der Bar
dat.	der Wand	der Mutter	der Bar
plural			
nom.	die Wände	die Mütter	die Bars
acc.	die Wände	die Mütter	die Bars
gen.	der Wände	der Mütter	der Bars
dat.	den Wänden	den Müttern	den Bars

3. Weak masculine nouns

singular			
nom.	der Bauer (the farmer)	der Bär (the bear)	der Hase (the hare)
acc.	den Bauern	den Bären	den Hasen
gen.	des Bauern	des Bären	des Hasen
dat.	dem Bauern	dem Bären	dem Hasen
plural			
nom.	die Bauern	die Bären	die Hasen
acc.	die Bauern	die Bären	die Hasen
gen.	der Bauern	der Bären	der Hasen
dat.	den Bauern	den Bären	den Hasen

4. Weak feminine nouns

singular				
nom.	die Uhr	die Feder	die Gabe	die Ärztin
	(the clock)	(the feather)	(the gift)	(the doctor)
acc.	die Uhr	die Feder	die Gabe	die Ärztin
gen.	der Uhr	der Feder	der Gabe	der Ärztin
dat.	der Uhr	der Feder	der Gabe	der Ärztin
plural				
nom.	die Uhren	die Federn	die Gaben	die Ärztinnen
acc.	die Uhren	die Federn	die Gaben	die Ärztinnen
gen.	der Uhren	der Federn	der Gaben	der Ärztinnen
dat.	den Uhren	den Federn	den Gaben	den Ärztinnen

5. Mixed masculine and neuter nouns

These are declined as strong nouns in the singular and weak nouns in the plural.

singular				
nom.	das Auge	das Ohr	der Name	das Herz
	(the eye)	(the ear)	(the name)	(the heart)
acc.	das Auge	das Ohr	den Namen	das Herz
gen.	des Auges	des Ohr(e)s	der Namens	des Herzens
dat.	dem Auge	dem Ohr(e)	dem Namen	dem Herzen
plural				
nom.	die Augen	die Ohren	die Namen	die Herzen
acc.	die Augen	die Ohren	die Namen	die Herzen
gen.	der Augen	der Ohren	der Namen	der Herzen
dat.	den Augen	den Ohren	den Namen	den Herzen

6. Nouns declined as adjectives

masculine singular		
nom.	der Reisende	ein Reisender
	(the traveler)	
acc.	den Reisenden	einen Reisenden
gen.	des Reisenden	eines Reisenden
dat.	dem Reisenden	einem Reisenden
plural		
nom.	die Reisenden	Reisende
acc.	die Reisenden	Reisende
gen.	der Reisenden	Reisender
dat.	den Reisenden	Reisenden

feminine singular		
nom.	die Reisende	eine Reisende
acc.	die Reisende	eine Reisende
gen.	der Reisenden	einer Reisenden
dat.	der Reisenden	einer Reisenden

plural		
nom.	die Reisenden	Reisende
acc.	die Reisenden	Reisende
gen.	der Reisenden	Reisender
dat.	den Reisenden	Reisenden

neuter singular		
nom.	das Neugeborene (the newborn [baby])	ein Neugeborenes
acc.	das Neugeborene	ein Neugeborenes
gen.	des Neugeborenen	eines Neugeborenen
dat.	dem Neugeborenen	einem Neugeborenen

plural		
nom.	die Neugeborenen	Neugeborene
acc.	die Neugeborenen	Neugeborene
gen.	der Neugeborenen	Neugeborener
dat.	den Neugeborenen	Neugeborenen

Declension of proper names

The genitive of names of people, cities, and countries observes the following rules:

proper name with article	remains unchanged	des Aristoteles des (schönen) Berlin
proper name without article	adds an s	Marias Auto die Straßen Berlins
proper name ends in s, ß, x, z	adds an apostrophe	Aristoteles' (Schriften) die Straßen Calais'
several proper names in a row	adds an s to the last name	Johann Sebastian Bachs (Musik)
proper name in apposition	is declined like a noun	nom.: Karl der Große acc.: Karl den Großen gen.: Karls des Großen dat.: Karl dem Großen

- Family names take an s in the plural: die Schneiders.
- When family names end in s, ß, x, or z, -ens is added to the name: die Kurzens.
- Names of roads, buildings, companies, ships, newspapers, and organizations are always declined.

Adjectives

There are three types of adjective declension: strong, weak, and mixed.

The strong declension

is used when there is no article, pronoun, or other word preceding the adjective indicating the case (manch(e), mehrere, etc.). It is also used with cardinal numbers and expressions like ein paar and ein bißchen.

	m	f	n
singular			
nom.	guter Wein (good wine)	schöne Frau (beautiful woman)	liebes Kind (well-behaved child)
acc.	guten Wein	schöne Frau	liebes Kind
gen.	guten Wein(e)s	schöner Frau	lieben Kindes
dat.	gutem Wein(e)	schöner Frau	liebem Kind(e)
plural			
nom.	gute Weine	schöne Frauen	liebe Kinder
acc.	gute Weine	schöne Frauen	liebe Kinder
gen.	guter Weine	schöner Frauen	lieber Kinder
dat.	guten Weinen	schönen Frauen	lieben Kindern

The weak declension

is used with adjectives preceded by the definite article or with any other word already clearly showing the case of the noun (diese(r,s), folgende(r,s), etc.).

	m	f	n
singular			
nom.	der gute Wein	die schöne Frau	das liebe Kind
acc.	den guten Weine	die schöne Frau	das liebe Kind
gen.	des guten Wein(e)s	der schönen Frau	des lieben Kindes
dat.	dem guten Wein	der schönen Frau	dem lieben Kind
plural			
nom.	die guten Weine	die schönen Frauen	die lieben Kinder
acc.	die guten Weine	die schönen Frauen	die lieben Kinder
gen.	der guten Weine	der schönen Frauen	der lieben Kinder
dat.	den guten Weinen	den schönen Frauen	den lieben Kindern

The mixed declension

is used with singular masculine and neuter nouns and the indefinite articles ein and kein and with the possessive pronouns mein, dein, sein, unser, euer, ihr.

	m	**n**
singular		
nom.	ein guter Wein (a good wine)	ein liebes Kind (a well-behaved child)
acc.	einen guten Wein	ein liebes Kind
gen.	eines guten Wein(e)s	eines lieben Kindes
dat.	einem guten Wein(e)	einem lieben Kind

4. Adjectives ending in -abel, -ibel, -el

drop the -e- when declined.

	m **miserabel**	**f** **penibel**	**n** **heikel**
singular			
nom.	ein miserabler Film (a poor film)	eine penible Frau (an exacting woman)	ein heikles Problem (a thorny problem)
acc.	einen miserablen Film	eine penible Frau	ein heikles Problem
gen.	eines miserablen Film	einer peniblen Frau	eines heiklen Problems
dat.	einem miserablen Film	einer peniblen Frau	einem heiklen Problem
plural			
nom.	miserable Filme	penible Frauen	heikle Probleme
acc.	miserable Filme	penible Frauen	heikle Probleme
gen.	miserabler Filme	penibler Frauen	heikler Probleme
dat.	miserablen Filmen	peniblen Frauen	heiklen Problemen

5. Adjectives ending in -er and -en

usually keep the -e- when declined, except when the adjective is of foreign origin:

e.g. makaber eine makabre Geschichte (a macabre story)
integer ein integrer Mensch (a reliable person)

6. Adjectives ending in -auer and -euer

usually drop the -e- when declined.

e.g. teuer ein teures Geschenk (an expensive present)
sauer saure Gurken (pickled gherkins)

7. Comparison

Adjectives and adverbs add -er for the comparative and -ste(r,e) for the superlative.

	m	**f**	**n**
	schön (beautiful)	schöne	schönes
comparative	schöner	schönere	schöneres
superlative	der schönste	die schönste	das schönste

- Most adjectives containing an -a-, -o-, -u- change to -ä-, -ö-,-ü- in the comparative and superlative forms.

arm	ärmer	der/die/das ärmste	(poor/poorer/the poorest)
groß	größer	der/die/das größte	(big/bigger/the biggest)
klug	klüger	der/die/das klügste	(smart/smarter/the smartest)

- The German word for "than" is als:
  Sie ist älter als Jim.   (She's older than Jim.)

- Some comparative and superlative forms of adjectives are completely irregular:

gut	besser	beste(r,s)
viel	mehr	meiste(r,s)
hoch	höher	höchste(r,s)

Adverbs

- For the adverbial use of adjectives, the unchanged basic form of the adjective is employed.

  Das Bild ist schön.   (The picture is beautiful.)
  Die Sängerin singt schön.   (The singer sings beautifully.)

- The comparative of adverbs follows the same rules as adjectives:

  Sie schreibt schöner.   (She writes nicer.)
  Er läuft schneller.   (He runs faster.)

- The superlative is formed using am ...sten:

  Er läuft am schnellsten.   (He runs fastest.)

Verbs

Present Tense

The basic ending of German verbs is -en (machen, sagen, essen, etc.). To form the present tense remove the -en and add the corresponding personal endings to the stem of the verb. There is no continuous form in German; that is „Ich gehe um acht Uhr ins Büro" can be translated as "I go to the office at eight o'clock" (routine) or "I'm going to the office at eight o'clock" (single event).

		machen (to do)	**legen** (to put)	**sagen** (to say)
I	ich	mache	lege	sage
you	du	machst	legst	sagst
he she } it	er sie es	macht	legt	sagt
we	wir	machen	legen	sagen
you	ihr	macht	legt	sagt
they	sie	machen	legen	sagen

- The vowel -a- in some verbs changes to the umlaut -ä-.
  tragen   ich trage, du trägst, er/sie/es trägt,
  wir tragen, ihr tragt, sie tragen

Auxiliary verbs *haben*, *sein*, and *werden*

Present tense

	sein (to be)	**haben** (to have)	**werden** (to become)
ich	bin	habe	werde
du	bist	hast	wirst
er sie } es	ist	hat	wird
wir	sind	haben	werden
ihr	seid	habt	werdet
sie	sind	haben	werden

Imperfect tense and past participle

	sein (to be)	haben (to have)	werden (to become)
ich	war	hatte	wurde
du	warst	hattest	wurdest
er sie es	war	hatte	wurde
wir	waren	hatten	wurden
ihr	wart	hattet	wurdet
sie	waren	hatten	wurden
past participle	bin gewesen	habe gehabt	bin geworden

Modal auxiliaries

Here is a list of the most important ones. Note that most are irregular.

Present tense

	können (be able to)	dürfen (be allowed to)	mögen (like)	müssen (have to)	sollen (should)	wollen (want to)
ich	kann	darf	mag	muß	soll	will
du	kannst	darfst	magst	mußt	sollst	willst
er sie es	kann	darf	mag	muß	soll	will
wir	können	dürfen	mögen	müssen	sollen	wollen
ihr	könnt	dürft	mögt	müßt	sollt	wollt
sie	können	dürfen	mögen	müssen	sollen	wollen

Imperfect tense

	können	dürfen	mögen	müssen	sollen	wollen
ich	konnte	durfte	mochte	mußte	sollte	wollte
du	kon- ntest	durftest	moch- test	mußtest	solltest	wolltest
er sie } es	konnte	durfte	mochte	mußte	sollte	wollte
wir	konnten	durften	moch- ten	mußten	sollten	wollten
ihr	konntet	durftet	mochtet	mußtet	solltet	wolltet
sie	konnten	durften	moch- ten	mußten	sollten	wollten

Past Tense

There are two basic past tenses in German, the imperfect and the present perfect. Both describe events that took place in the past. There is no past continuous form.

| Gestern war ich krank. | Yesterday I was ill. |
| Letztes Jahr sind wir in Berlin gewesen. | Last year we were in Berlin. |

To form the **imperfect**, the following verb endings are added to the stem of the verb:

	machen (to do)	**begegnen** (to meet)	**wetten** (to bet)
ich	mach**te**	begegne**te**	wett**ete**
du	mach**test**	begegne**test**	wett**etest**
er sie } es	mach**te**	begegne**te**	wett**ete**
wir	mach**ten**	begegne**ten**	wett**eten**
ihr	mach**tet**	begegne**tet**	wett**etet**
sie	mach**ten**	begegne**ten**	wett**eten**

The **present perfect** is the most common way of referring to the past and is formed with the present tense of either haben (to have) or sein (to be), followed by the past participle of the verb. The past participle of regular verbs is formed by adding the prefix ge- and the ending -t to the stem.

machen	**ge**-mach-**t**	fragen	**ge**-frag-**t**
(to do)	(done)	(to ask)	(asked)

(For some of the more common irregular verbs, see page 241.)

Most verbs use haben to form the present perfect:

Er hat es gemacht.	He's done it. / He did it.
Ich habe es gesagt.	I've said it. / I said it.

sein is used with verbs of motion and verbs that indicate a transition from one state to another. Many irregular verbs form the present perfect with the prefix ge-, a vowel change, and the ending -en.

Wir sind gefahren.	We drove.

	kommen (to come)		**fahren** (to drive)		**sterben** (to die)	
ich	bin	gekommen	bin	gefahren	bin	gestorben
du	bist	gekommen	bist	gefahren	bist	gestorben
er sie es	ist	gekommen	ist	gefahren	ist	gestorben
wir	sind	gekommen	sind	gefahren	sind	gestorben
ihr	seid	gekommen	seid	gefahren	seid	gestorben
sie	sind	gekommen	sind	gefahren	sind	gestorben

!

Future

The future tense is formed with the auxiliary verb werden and the infinitive.

	fahren (to drive)	**sein** (to be)	**haben** (to have)	**können** (to be able to)
ich	werde fahren	werde sein	werde haben	werde können
du	wirst fahren	wirst sein	wirst haben	wirst können
er sie es	wird fahren	wird sein	wird haben	wird können
wir	werden fahren	werden sein	werden haben	werden können
ihr	werdet fahren	werdet sein	werdet haben	werdet können
sie	werden fahren	werden sein	werden haben	werden können

- Often the present tense is also used to express the future:

Ich komme morgen.	I'll come tomorrow.

Conditional

Present and perfect subjunctive of the auxiliary verbs sein, haben, and werden:

	sein (to be)	**haben** (to have)	**werden** (to become)
ich	sei/wäre	habe/hätte	werde/würde
du	seist/wärst	habest/hättest	werdest/würdest
er sie es	sei/wäre	habe /hätte	werde/würde
wir	seien/wären	haben/hätten	werden/würden
ihr	seiet/wärt	habet/hättet	werdet/würdet
sie	seien/wären	haben/hätten	werden/würden

- The conditional form is used in indirect speech and to make statements or express ideas that may not necessarily be true.

Er sagt, er sei krank.	He says he is ill.
Er sagte, er wäre krank.	He said he was ill.
Ich würde gehen, wenn ich Zeit hätte.	I would go if I had the time.

Imperative

The imperative is used to express a command or warning (come here!, watch out!). The imperative is formed by inverting the verb and the personal pronoun:

Sie schreiben einen Brief.	They are writing a letter.
Schreiben Sie einen Brief!	Write a letter!

infinitive	singular (familiar)	plural (familiar)	imperative (Sie) (polite)
schreiben	schreibe	schreibt	schreiben Sie
trinken	trinke	trinkt	trinken Sie
atmen	atme	atmet	atmen Sie
sein	sei	seid	seien Sie
haben	habe	habt	haben Sie
werden	werde	werdet	werden Sie

Questions

Simple questions are formed by changing the order of subject and verb.

Es regnet.	It's raining.
Regnet es?	Is it raining?
Der Laden macht um 9 Uhr auf.	The store opens at 9 o'clock.
Macht der Laden um 9 Uhr auf?	Does the store open at 9 o'clock?

Negation

To negate a sentence, add **nicht** after the main verb.

Sie wohnt in Berlin.	She lives in Berlin.
Er wohnt **nicht** in Berlin	He doesn't live in Berlin.

Nicht + ein, eine, einen, etc. becomes **kein, keine, keinen,** etc.

Ich habe eine Fahrkarte	I have a ticket.
Ich habe keine Fahrkarte	I don't have a ticket.

Pronouns

Pronouns agree with the gender and case/number of the noun they refer to.

1. Personal pronouns

nominative	accusative	genitive	dative
ich (I)	mich (me)	meiner	mir
du (you)	dich (you)	deiner	dir
er (he)	ihn (him)	seiner	ihm
sie (she)	sie (her)	ihrer	ihr
es (it)	es (it)	seiner	ihm
wir (we)	uns (us)	unser	uns
ihr (you)	euch (you)	euer	euch
sie (they)	sie (them)	ihrer	ihnen
Sie (you)	Sie (you)	Iher	Ihnen

- **du** is the familiar form of address when speaking to family, friends, and children.
- **Sie** is the polite form of address (for both singular and plural).
- **ihr** is the familiar form of address used when speaking to more than one person.

2. Reflexive pronouns

These are used with reflexive verbs such as sich freuen, sich waschen, sich bedanken.

myself	mich	ich freue mich
yourself	dich (familiar)	du freust dich
	sich (polite)	Sie freuen sich
himself/herself/itself	sich	er/sie/es freut sich
ourselves	uns	wir freuen uns
yourselves	euch (familiar)	ihr freut euch
	sich (polite)	Sie freuen sich
themselves	sich	sie freuen sich

3. Possessive pronouns

singular	m	f	n	pl
nom.	mein	meine	mein	meine
acc.	meinen	meine	mein	meine
gen.	meines	meiner	meines	meiner
dat.	meinem	meiner	meinem	meinen

- dein (your), sein (his), ihr (her), sein (its) are declined like mein (my).

1st person plural (our)			
nom.	unser	uns(e)re	unser	uns(e)re
acc.	uns(e)ren unsern	uns(e)re	unser	unsre
gen.	uns(e)res	uns(e)rer	uns(e)res	uns(e)rer
dat.	uns(e)rem unserm	uns(e)rer	uns(e)rem unserm	uns(e)ren

2nd person plural (your)			
nom.	euer	eure	euer	eure
acc.	euren	eure	euer	eure
gen.	eures	eurer	eures	eurer
dat.	eurem	eurer	eurem	euren

3rd person plural (their)			
nom.	ihr	ihre	ihr	ihre
acc.	ihren	ihre	ihr	ihre
gen.	ihres	ihrer	ihres	ihrer
dat.	ihrem	ihrer	ihrem	ihren

4. Interrogative pronouns

Interrogative pronouns referring to people (who, whose, whom) are declined in German, but not when they refer to things (what).

	people	things
nom.	*Wer* spielt mit?	*Was* ist das ?
acc.	*Wen* liebst du?	*Was* höre ich da?
gen.	*Wessen* Haus ist das?	
dat.	*Wem* gehört das Haus?	

Was für ein Mensch ist Peter?	What kind of person is Peter?
Welche Schuhe soll ich nehmen?	Which shoes/ones should I take?
Welches (Kleid) gefällt dir besser?	Which (dress) do you prefer?

welcher/welche/welches
which (one of more than two)

	m	f	n	plural
nom.	welcher	welche	welches	welche
acc.	welchen	welche	welches	welche
gen.	welches	welcher	welches	welcher
dat.	welchem	welcher	welchem	welchen

Prepositions

Most prepositions take either the accusative or the dative or both.

accusative only

bis	gegen	durch
ohne	für	um

dative only

ab	mit	aus
nach	außer	nächst
bei	seit	entgegen
von	gegenüber	zu

accusative and dative

an	neben	auf
unter	entlang	über
hinter	vor	in
zwischen		

The accusative is used to indicate **motion** and the dative **position**.

Er hängt die Uhr an die Wand. (acc.)	He hangs the clock on the wall.
Die Uhr hängt an der Wand. (dat.)	The clock is hanging on the wall.

Several prepositions combine with the definite article to produce short forms:

an/in	+	dem	→	am/im	(am Weg, im Haus)
bei	+	dem	→	beim	(beim Frisör)
von	+	dem	→	vom	(vom Theater)
zu	+	dem/der	→	zum/zur	(zum Bahnhof, zur Tankstelle)
an/in	+	das	→	ans/ins	(ans Meer, ins Kino)

a) Prepositions indicating position (Where?)
take the dative: „Das Auto steht vor dem Haus."

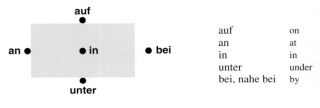

auf	on
an	at
in	in
unter	under
bei, nahe bei	by

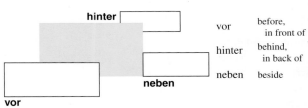

vor	before, in front of
hinter	behind, in back of
neben	beside

über	over
über, oberhalb von	above
unter	below
unterhalb von	underneath

zwischen (zweien)   zwischen (zweien)   between

zwischen (mehreren),   zwischen (mehreren), among
unter   unter

um ... herum   um ... herum   round, around

b) Prepositions indicating direction (where to?, where from?)
take the accusative: „Sie geht in den Keller."

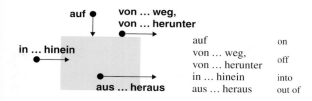

auf	on
von … weg,	
von … herunter	off
in … hinein	into
aus … heraus	out of

zu … (hin)	to, toward
von … (her)	from

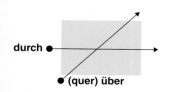

durch	through
(quer) über	across

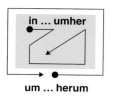

in … umher	about
um … herum	round, around

über	over
unter	under

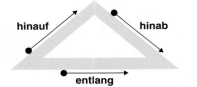

hinauf	up
herab	down
entlang	along

Dictionary English-German

See also the thematic word lists in each chapter.

Unless otherwise indicated, the stress falls on the first syllable.

A

abbreviation die Abkürzung [ahp-kurt-suhŋ]

able fähig [fey-ihç], im Stande [ihm Stahndə]; **be able to** (v) im Stande sein, [ihm Stahndə zayn] können [kœnən]

about ungefähr [uhn-gəfehr], etwa [eht-vah]; (time) gegen [geygən]

above all vor allem [for ahləm]

abroad im/ins Ausland [ihm / ihns auslahnt]

absent abwesend [ahp-veyzənd]

accelerate (v) beschleunigen [bəSloy-nihgən]

accept (v) annehmen [ahn-neymən]; (invitation) (v) zusagen [tsoo-zahgən]

acceptance die Annahme [ahn-nahmə]

accident der Unfall [uhn-fahl]; **have an accident** (v) verunglücken [fehr-uhn-glewkən]

accommodations die Unterkunft [uhntər-kuhnft]

accompany (v) begleiten [bəglaytən]

account die Rechnung [rehç-nuhŋ]; das Konto [kon-toh]; **on no account** keinesfalls [kaynəs-fahls]

accuracy die Genauigkeit [gənau-ihç-kayt]

acquaintance die Bekanntschaft [bəkahnt-Sahft]; (person) der/die Bekannte [bəkahntə]

across quer durch [kvehr duhrç]

act die Tat [taht]; (v) handeln [hahn-dəln]

action die Tat [taht], die Handlung [hahnd-luhŋ]

activity die Tätigkeit [tey-tihç-kayt]

actual(ly) eigentlich [aygənt-lihç]

add (v) hinzufügen [hihn-tsoo-fewgən]; **add up** (v) zusammenrechnen [tsuh-zahmən-rehçnən]; **in addition** zusätzlich [tsoo-zehts-lihç]; **additional** zusätzlich [tsoo-zehts-lihç]

address die Anschrift [ahn-Srihft], die Adresse [ah-drehsə]; (v) adressieren [ah-dreh-siirən]

administration die Verwaltung [fehr-**vahl**-tuhŋ]

admire (v) bewundern [bəvuhn-dehrn]

admission charge der Eintrittspreis [ayn-trihts-prays]

(admission) ticket die Eintrittskarte [ayn-trihts-kahrtə]

adult Erwachsene(r) [ehr-**vahks**ənə(r)]

advance (v) vorrücken [fohr-rewkən]; **in advance** im voraus [ihm for-aus]

advantage der Vorzug [for-tsuhk]; der Vorteil [for-tayl]

advantageous vorteilhaft [for-tayl-hahft]

advertisement die Anzeige [ahn-tsaygə]; die Reklame [reh-**klahm**ə]

advice der Rat [raht]

advise (v) raten [rahtən]

affair (matter) die Sache [zahxə]

afraid erschrocken [ehr-**Srok**ən]; **be afraid (of)** (v) s. fürchten (vor) [fewrçtən (for)]; befürchten [bə**fewrçt**ən]

after nach [nahx]

afternoon der Nachmittag [nahx-mih-tahk]; **in the afternoon** nachmittags [nahx-mih-tahks]

afterward nachher [nahx-hehr], danach [dah-**nahx**]

again wieder [viidər]

against gegen [geygən]; **be against it** (v) dagegen sein [dah-**geygən**]

age das Alter [ahltər]

agency die Agentur [ah-gehn-**toor**]

agent der Vermittler [fehr-**mihtl**ər]

agree (v) s. einigen [ay-nihgən], einig sein [ay-nihç zayn]; (on a date, time etc.) ausmachen [aus-mahxən]; **agree (to)** zustimmen [tsoo-Stihmən]; **agree on** vereinbaren [fehr-**ayn**-bahrən]

agreeable angenehm [ahn-gəneym]

agreement das Einverständnis [ayn-fehr-Steht-nihs]

aid die Hilfe [hihlfə]; **first aid** erste Hilfe [ehrstə hihlfə]

aim das Ziel [tsiil]

air die Luft [luhft]; (v) lüften [lewftən]

alarm clock der Wecker [vehkən]
alarmed erschrocken [ehr-**Sro**kən]
algae die Algen [ahl-gehn] *f pl*
alive lebend [leybənt]
all alle [ahlə]; ganz [gahnts]; jede(r, s) [yeydə(r,s)]
allow *(v)* erlauben [ehr-**lau**bən]
allowed zulässig [tsoo-leh-sihç]; **be allowed** *(v)* dürfen [dewrfən]
almost fast [fahst], beinahe [bay-nah-ə]
alone allein [ah-**layn**]
along entlang [ehnt-**lahŋ**]
already bereits [bə-**rayts**], schon [Sohn]
also auch [aux], gleichfalls [glayç-fahls]
alter *(v)* ändern [ehndərn]
although obwohl [op-**vohl**]
always immer [ihmər], stets [Stehts]
ambulance der Krankenwagen [krahŋkən-vahgən]
America Amerika [ah-**meh**-rih-kah]
American der/die Amerikaner/in [ah-meh-rih-**kahn**ər / -ihn]
among zwischen [tsvih**S**ən]; **among other things** unter anderem [uhntər ahndərəm]
amount der Betrag [bə**trahk**]
ample reichlich [rayç-lihç]
amusing unterhaltend [uhntər-**hahlt**ənd]
and und [uhnt]
and so on und so weiter [uhnt zoh vaytər]
angry zornig [tsor-nihç]; böse [bœzə]
animal das Tier [tiir]
announce *(v)* melden [mehldən], anmelden [ahn-mehldən]
announcement die Mitteilung [miht-tay-luhŋ]
annoying lästig [lehs-tihç]
annual(ly) jährlich [yehr-lihç]
another time ein andermal [ayn ahndər-mahl]
answer die Antwort [ahnt-vort]; *(v)* antworten [ahnt-vortən], beantworten [bə-**ahnt**-vortən]
anxious besorgt [bə**zorkt**]
any jeder Beliebige [yeydər bə**lii**-bihgə]
anybody *(in questions)* jemand [yey-mahnt]
anything *(in questions)* etwas [eht-vahs]
apartment die Wohnung [voh-nuhŋ]
apologize *(v)* s. entschuldigen [ehnt-**Suhl**-dihgən]

apparently anscheinend [ahn-Saynənt]
appear *(v)* erscheinen [ehr-**Sayn**ən]
appearance der Schein [Sayn]
appetite der Appetit [ah-pə-**tiit**]
applause der Beifall [bay-fahl]
appointment der Termin [tehr-**miin**]; *(meeting)* die Verabredung [fehr-**ahp**-rey-duhŋ]
approach *(v)* s. nähern [ney-ərn]
arcade die Ladenpassage [lahdən-pah-sah**Z**ə]
area die Gegend [geygənt]
argue *(v)* streiten [Straytən]
argument der Streit [Strayt]
around herum [heh-**ruhm**]
arrange *(v)* veranstalten [fehr-**ahn**-Stahltən]
arrive (at) *(v)* eintreffen [ayn-trehfən]
article der Artikel [ahr-**tih**kəl]
as *(reason)*; **as if** als ob [ahls op]; **just as you like** nach Belieben [nahx bə**liib**ən]
ask *(v)* fragen [frahgən], fordern [fordərn], auffordern [auf-fordərn]; **ask for** verlangen [fehr-**lahŋ**ən]; **ask s. o. for s. th.** jdn um etw. bitten [bihtən]
assault *(v)* überfallen [ewbər-**fahl**ən]
association der Verein [feh-**rayn**]
assume *(v)* vermuten [fehr-**moot**ən]
assumption die Vermutung [fehr-**moo**-tuhŋ], die Annahme [ahn-nahmə]
assure *(say)* *(v)* versichern [fehr-**zihç**ərn]
at *(time)* um [uhm]; **at table** bei Tisch [bay tihS]
athletic field der Sportplatz [Sport-plahts]
Atlantic der Atlantik [aht-**lahn**-tihk]
attack *(v)* überfallen [ewbər**fahl**ən]
attempt der Versuch [fehr-**zuhx**]
attend to *(v)* bedienen [bə**diin**ən]
attendant der/die Aufseher/in [auf-zeyər / -ihn]
attention die Achtung [ahx-tuhŋ]; **pay attention (to)** *(v)* aufpassen [auf-pahsən], beachten [bə**ahxt**ən]
attentive(ly) aufmerksam [auf-mehrk-zahm]
audience der Zuschauer [tsoo-Sauər], das Publikum [puh-blih-kuhm]
aunt die Tante [tahntə]
Austria Österreich [œstər-rayç]
Austrian der/die Österreicher/in [œstər-rayçər / -ihn]

authorities die Behörde [bəhœrdə]

automatic(ally) automatisch [au-toh-**mah**-tihS]

automobile der Wagen [vahgən]

available erhältlich [ehr-**hehlt**-lihç]

average durchschnittlich [duhrç-Sniht-lihç]; **on the average** durchschnittlich [duhrç-Sniht-lihç]

avoid *(v)* vermeiden [fehr-**mayd**ən]

awake wach [vahx]

aware bewusst [bəvuhst]; **be aware of** *(v)* merken [mehrkən]

away weg [vehk], fort [fort]; **go away** *(v)* weggehen [vehk-geyən]; **send away** *(v)* wegschicken [vehk-Sihkən]; **take away** *(v)* wegnehmen [vehk-neymən]

awful schrecklich [Srehk-lihç]

B

baby das Baby [bey-bii]

bachelor der Junggeselle [yuhŋ-gəzehlə]

back zurück [tsuh-**rewk**]; **at the back** hinten [hihntən]; **bring back** *(v)* zurückbringen [tsuh-**rewk**-brihŋən]; **come back** *(v)* zurückkehren [tsuh-**rewk**-kehrən], wiederkommen [viidər-komən]; **drive back** *(v)* zurückfahren [tsuh-**rewk**-fahrən]; **get back** *(v)* wiederbekommen [viidər-bəkomən]; **give back** *(v)* wiedergeben [viidərgeybən], zurückgeben [tsuh-**rewk**-geybən]; **pay back** *(v)* zurückzahlen [tsuh-**rewk**-tsahlən]

backpack der Rucksack [ruhk-zahk]

backwards rückwärts [rewk-vehrts]

bad schlimm [Slihm], schlecht [Slehçt], übel [ewbəl]; **go bad** *(v)* verderben [fehr-**dehrb**ən]

badly schlecht [Slehçt]

bag der Sack [zahk], die Tüte [tewtə], der Beutel [boytəl]; *(hand-)* die Handtasche [hahnt-tahSə]

ball der Ball [bahl]; *(festivity)* der Ball [bahl]

ban das Verbot [fehr-**boht**]

band die (Musik-)Gruppe [moo-**ziik**-gruhpə]

bandage der Verband [fehr-**bahnt**]; *(v)* verbinden [fehr-**bihnd**ən]

bank die Bank [bahŋk]; *(river)* das Ufer [oofər]

bar *(chocolate)* der Riegel [riigəl]

barely kaum [kaum]

barrier *(train)* die Sperre [Spehrə]

bars das Gitter [gihtər]

basket der Korb [korp]

bath das Bad [baht]; **take a bath** *(v)* baden [bahdən]

bathroom die Toilette [toy-**leht**ə]; das Badezimmer [bahdə-tsihmər]

baths die Badeanstalt [bahdə-ahn-Stahlt]

battery die Batterie [bah-teh-**rii**]

bay die Bucht [buhxt]

be *(v)* sein [zayn]; betragen [bətrahgən]; s. befinden [zihç bəfihndən]

beach der Strand [Strahnt]

beach resort der Badeort [bahdə-ort]

beam der Strahl [Strahl]

bear *(v)* ertragen [ehr-**trahg**ən]

beat *(v)* schlagen [Slahgən]

beautiful schön [Sœn]

beauty die Schönheit [Sœn-hayt]

because weil [vayl]; da [dah]; **because of** wegen [veygən]

become *(v)* werden [vehrdən]

bed das Bett [beht]; **go to bed** *(v)* ins Bett gehen [ihns beht geyən]

bedroom das Schlafzimmer [Slahf-tsihmər]

bee die Biene [biinə]

before vor [for]; *(conj)* bevor [bə**for**]; *(previously)* vorher [for-hehr]

begin *(v)* anfangen [ahn-fahŋən], beginnen [bəgihnən]

beginning der Anfang [ahn-fahŋ], der Beginn [bəgihn]

behavior das Benehmen [bəneymən]

behind hinter [hihntər]

Belgian der/die Belgier/in [behlgyər / -ihn]

Belgium Belgien [behlg-yən]

believe *(v)* glauben [glaubən]

bell die Klingel [klihŋəl]

belong to *(v)* gehören [gə**hœr**ən]

below unterhalb [uhntər-hahlp], unten [uhntən]

bench die (Sitz-)Bank [(zihts-)bahŋk]

bend die Kurve [kurvə]; *(v)* biegen [biigən]

beside neben [neybən]

besides außerdem [ausərdehm]

A/Z

best beste(r, s) [behstə(r,s)]; **at best** höchstens [hœkstəns]

bet die Wette [vehtə]; *(v)* wetten [vehtən]

better besser [behsər]

between zwischen [tsvihSən]

beyond jenseits [yehn-zayts], außerhalb [ausər-hahlp]

big groß [grohs]

bill die Rechnung [rehç-nuhŋ]

billfold die Brieftasche [briif-tahSə]

binoculars das Fernglas [fehrn-glahs]

bird der Vogel [fohgəl]

birth die Geburt [gəbuhrt]

birthday der Geburtstag [gəbuhrts-tahk]

birthplace der Geburtsort [gəbuhrts-ort]

bit bisschen [bihSən]; **a bit of ...** ein wenig von ... [ayn vey-nihç fon]

bite *(v)* beißen [baysən]

bitter bitter [bihtər]

blanket die Decke [dehkə]

blind blind [bliht]

bloom *(v)* blühen [blewən]

blossom *(v)* blühen [blewən]

blow der Schlag [Slahk]

board das Brett [breht]; das Bord [bort]; **go on board** *(v)* an Bord gehen [ahn bort geyən]

boat das Boot [boht], der Kahn [kahn]

body der Körper [kœrpər]

boil *(v)* kochen [koxən]

bolt *(lock)* der Riegel [riigəl]

book das Buch [buhx]

border die Grenze [grehntsə]

boring langweilig [lahŋ-vay-lihç]

born geboren [gəbohrən]

borrow *(v)* (aus-)leihen [(aus-)layən]

boss der/die Leiter/in [laytər / -ihn], der/die Chef/in [Sehf / -ihn]

both beide [baydə]

bother *(v)* belästigen [bəlehs-tihgən], stören [Stœrən]

bottle die Flasche [flahSə]

box die Kiste [kihstə], die Schachtel [Sahxtəl], die Packung [pah-kuhŋ]

boy der Junge [yuhŋə]

brains der Verstand [fehr-**Stahnt**]

branch *(office)* die Filiale [fihl-**yahlə**]

brand *(cigarettes)* die Sorte [zortə]; die (Handels-)Marke [(hahndəlz-)mahrkə]

break *(v)* zerbrechen [tsehr-**brehçən**], brechen [brehçən]; **break off** *(v)* abbrechen [ahp-brehçən]; **break open** *(v)* aufbrechen [auf-brehçən]

breakfast das Frühstück [frew-Stewk]; **have breakfast** *(v)* frühstücken [frew-Stewkən]

breath der Atem [ahtəm]

breathing das Atmen [ahtmən]

breathless atemlos [atəm-lohs]

briefcase die Mappe [mahpə]

bright hell [hehl], leuchtend [loyçtənt]; *(weather)* heiter [haytər]

brilliant glänzend [glehntsənt]

bring *(v)* mitbringen [miht-brihŋən]; (her-)bringen [hehr-brihŋən]

brink der Rand [rahnt]

broad breit [brayt]

broadcast *(v)* senden [zehndən]

brochure der Prospekt [proh-**spehkt**]

broken kaputt [kah-**puht**]

brother der Bruder [broodər]

brother-in-law der Schwager [Svahgər]

brown braun [braun]

brush die Bürste [bewrstə]; *(v)* bürsten [bewrstən]

build bauen [bauən]

building das Gebäude [gəboydə]

bulb *(electricity)* die (Glüh-)Birne [(glew-)bihrnə]

bunch *(carrots, etc.)* der Bund [buhnt]; **bunch of flowers** der Blumenstrauß [bloomən-Straus]

bureau de change *(sign)* der Geldwechsel [gehlt-vehksəl]

burn *(v)* brennen [brehnən]; verbrennen [fehr-**brehnən**]

burst *(v)* platzen [plahtsən]

bush der Busch [buhS]

business das Geschäft [gəSehft]

busy beschäftigt [bəSehf-tihkt]; *(telephone)* besetzt [bəzehtst]

but aber [ahbər]; sondern [zondərn]

button der Knopf [knopf]

buy *(v)* kaufen [kaufən], einkaufen [ayn-kaufən]

buyer der Käufer [koyfər]

by von [fon]; **by (means of)** durch [duhrç]; **by day/night** bei Tag/Nacht [bay tahk / nahxt]

bye-bye tschüs [tSews]

C

cab das Taxi [tahk-sii]

cabin die Kabine [kah-**biin**ə], die Hütte [hewtə]

café das Café [kah-**fey**]

calculate (v) rechnen [reçnən], berechnen [bəreçnən]

call (v) rufen [roofən]; aufrufen [aufroofən]; anrufen [ahn-roofən]; nennen [nehnən]; **call on s. o.** (v) jdn besuchen [yey-mahndən bəzo000xən]; **be called** (v) heißen [haysən]

calm die Ruhe [rooə]; (adj) ruhig [rooihç], still [Stihl]; **calm down** (v) s. beruhigen [bəroo-ihgən]

camera die Kamera [kah-meh-rah]

can die Büchse [bewksə], die Dose [dohzə]; **can opener** der Dosenöffner [dohzən-œfnər], der Büchsenöffner [bewksən-œfnər]

canal der Kanal [kah-**nahl**]

cancel (v) (tickets etc.) abbestellen [ahp-behStehlən]; (appointment) absagen [ahp-zahgən]

candle die Kerze [kehrtsə]

capable tüchtig [tewç-tihç]; **capable of** fähig [fey-ihç]

capital die Hauptstadt [haupt-Staht]

car das Auto [au-toh], der Wagen [vahgən], der PKW [pey-kah-**vey**]; (train) der Wagen [vahgən]

card die Karte [kahrtə]

care die Sorge [zorgə]; die Sorgfalt [zork-fahlt]; **take care (of s. o./s. th.)** (v) s. (um jdn./etw.) kümmern [uhm ... kewmərn], aufpassen (auf jdn./etw.) [auf-pahsən]

careful vorsichtig [for-zihç-tihç], sorgfältig [zork-fehl-tihç]

careless unvorsichtig [uhn-for-zihç-lihç], nachlässig [nahx-leh-sihç]

carry (v) tragen [trahgən]; **carry out** (v) (work) ausführen [aus-fewrən]

carton (of 200 cigarettes) die Stange (Zigaretten) [Stahŋə (tsih-gah-**reht**ən)]

case (incident) der Fall [fahl]; (box) der Behälter [bəhehltər]; **in any case** auf alle Fälle [auf allə fehlə]

cashier's desk die Kasse [kahsə]

castle das Schloss [Slos]

cat die Katze [kahtsə]

catch (v) fangen [fahŋən]; (train ...) kriegen [kriigən]

cause die Ursache [oor-zahxə], der Anlass [ahn-lahs], der Grund [gruhnt]; (v) verursachen [fehr-**oor**-zahxən]

caution die Vorsicht [for-zihçt]

cautious vorsichtig [for-zihç-tihç]

CD die CD [tsey-**dey**]

CD player der CD-Spieler [tsey-**dey**-Spiilər]

ceiling die (Zimmer-)Decke [(tsihmər-)dehkə]

celebration das Fest [fehst]

central zentral [tsehn-**trahl**]

center das Zentrum [tsehn-truhm]

certain (adj) gewiss [gə**vihs**], bestimmt [bə**Stihmt**], sicher [zihçər]; **certainly** (adv) gewiss [gə**vihs**], unbedingt [uhn-bədihŋt]

certificate das Zeugnis [tsoyk-nihs], die Urkunde [oor-kuhndə], die Bescheinigung [bə**Sayn**-ih-guhhŋ]

certify (v) bescheinigen [bə**Say**-nihgən]

chain die Kette [kehtə]

chair der Stuhl [Stool]

chance der Zufall [tsoo-fahl]; **by chance** zufällig [tsoo-feh-lihç]

change der Wechsel [vehksəl], die Veränderung [fehr-**ehnd**ə-ruhŋ]; das Wechselgeld [vehksəl-gehlt]; (v) verändern [fehr-**ehnd**ərn], (Geld) wechseln [(gehlt) vehksəln]; umsteigen [uhm-Staygən]; s. umziehen [uhm-tsiiən]; **give change for** (v) (Geld) herausgeben [her-**aus**-geybən]

changeable (weather) unbeständig [uhn-bəStehn-dihç]

channel der Kanal [kah-**nahl**]

chapel die Kapelle [kah-pehlə]

characteristic die Eigenschaft [aygən-Sahft]

charming entzückend [ehnt-**tsewk**ənt], bezaubernd [bə**tsaub**ərnt]

cheap billig [bih-lihç]

cheat (v) schwindeln [Svihndəln], betrügen [bə**trewg**ən]

check (v) kontrollieren [kon-troh-**liir**ən], nachprüfen [nahx-prewfən], nachsehen [nahx-zeyən]; **check through (baggage)** (v) (Gepäck) aufgeben [(gəpehk) auf-geybən]

cheeky unverschämt [uhn-fehr-Sehmt]

cheerful heiter [haytər]

chest *(box)* die Kiste [kihstə]

chewing gum der Kaugummi [kau-guh-mii]

child das Kind [kihnt]; **children** *(pl)* die Kinder [kihndər] n pl

choice die Auswahl [aus-vahl], die Wahl [vahl]

choir der Chor [kohr]

choose *(v)* wählen [vehlən]

cigar die Zigarre [tsih-**gahr**ə]

cigarette die Zigarette [tsih-gah-**reht**ə]

cigarillo das Zigarillo [tsih-gah-**rih**-loh]

circumstances die Umstände [uhm-Stehndə] m pl

city map der Stadtplan [Staht-plahn]

claim die Forderung [fordə-ruhŋ]

class die Klasse [klahsə]

clean sauber [zaubər]; *(washing)* frisch [frihS]; *(v)* putzen [puhtsən], reinigen [ray-nihgən]; **(dry) cleaners** die Reinigung [ray-nih-guhŋ]

clear klar [klahr], *(weather)* heiter [haytər]

clever klug [kluhk], schlau [Slau]

cliff der Fels [fehls], die Klippe [klihpə]

climate das Klima [kliimə]

climax der Höhepunkt [hœə-puhŋkt]

climb *(v)* steigen [Staygən]; der Aufstieg [auf-Stiik]

clock die (Wand-)Uhr [(vahnt-)oor]

close nahe [nah-ə]; *(v)* schließen [Sliisən], zumachen [tsoo-mahxən]; **close to** nahe bei [nah-ə bay]

closed geschlossen [gəSlosən]

cloth das Tuch [tuhx]

clothes hook der Kleiderhaken [klaydər-hahkən]

clothing die Kleidung [klay-duhŋ]

cloudy *(liquid)* trüb [trewp]; *(weather)* bewölkt [bə**vœl**kt]

club der Verein [feh-**rayn**]

coach *(train)* der Wagen [vahgən]

coal die Kohle [kohlə]

coast die Küste [kewstə]

cock der Hahn [hahn]

cockroach die Kakerlake [kahkər-lahkə]

coffee der Kaffee [kah-fey]

coin das Geldstück [gehlt-Stewk], die Münze [mewntsə]

coincidence der Zufall [tsoo-fahl]

cold kalt [kahlt]; **be cold** *(v)* frieren [friirən]

colleague der/die Kollege/Kollegin [koh-**ley**gə / koh-**ley**-gihn]

collect *(v)* sammeln [zahməln]

collection die Sammlung [zahm-luhŋ]

collision der Zusammenstoß [tsoo-zahmən-Stos]

color die Farbe [fahrbə]

colored farbig [fahr-bihç]

colorful bunt [buhnt]

come *(v)* kommen [komən]; **come from** *(v)* stammen aus [Stahmən aus]; **come to** *(v)* betragen [bətrahgən]; **come in!** herein! [heh-**rayn**!]; **come out** *(book)* *(v)* erscheinen [ehr-**Sayn**ən]

comfort die Bequemlichkeit [bə**kvehm**-lihç-kayt]

comfortable bequem [bə**kvehm**], gemütlich [gə**mewt**-lihç]

common *(adj)* gemeinsam [gə**mayn**-zahm]; gebräuchlich [gə**broyç**-lihç], gewöhnlich [gə**vœn**-lihç]

company die Firma [fiirmə]; *(people)* die Gesellschaft [gə**zehl**-Sahft]

compare *(v)* vergleichen [fehr-**glayç**ən]

comparison der Vergleich [fehr-**glayç**]

compass der Kompass [kom-pahs]

compel *(v)* zwingen [tsvihŋən]

compensation der Ersatz [ehr-**zahts**], der Schadenersatz [Sahd(ə)nər-zahts]

competition der Wettbewerb [veht-bəvehrp]

complain *(v)* reklamieren [reh-klah-miirən]; schimpfen [Sihmpfən]; **complain (of/about)** *(v)* s. beklagen (über) [bəklahgən (ewbər), s. beschweren [bəSvehrən]

complaint die Beanstandung [bə-**ahn**-Stah-duhŋ], die Beschwerde [bəSvehrdə]

complete ganz [gahnts]; *(v)* vollenden [folɛndən]

compulsion der Zwang [tsvahŋ]

conceal *(v)* verheimlichen [fehr-**haym**-lihçən]

concerned besorgt [bəzorkt]

concerning betreffend [bətrehfənt]

conclusion der Schluss [Sluhs]

condition die Bedingung [bədihŋ-uhŋ]; der Zustand [tsoo-Stahnt]

condolence(s) das Beileid [bay-layt]

condom das Kondom [kon-dohm]

confidence das Vertrauen [fehr-**trauən**]
confident vertrauensvoll [fehr-**trauəns**-fol]
confirm (v) bestätigen [bəSteh-tihgən]
congratulate (v) gratulieren [grah-tyə-**liirən**]
congratulations der Glückwunsch [glewk-vuhnS]
connect (v) (telephone) verbinden [fehr-**bihnd**ən]
connection die Verbindung [fehr-**bihn**-duhŋ]
conscientious gewissenhaft [gəvihsən-hahft]
conscious bewusst [bəvuhst]
consent das Einverständnis [ayn-fehr-Stehnt-nihs]; **consent to** (v) einwilligen [ayn-vih-lihgən]
consider (v) betrachten [bətrahxtən]
considerable beträchtlich [bətrehçt-lihç]
consideration die Rücksicht [rewk-zihçt]
consist of (v) bestehen aus [bəSteyən aus]
constitution die (Staats-)Verfassung [(Stahts-)fehr-**fah**-suhŋ]
consulate das Konsulat [kon-zuh-**laht**]
consult (v) konsultieren [kon-zul-**tiirən**]
consumption der Verbrauch [fehr-**braux**]
contact der Kontakt [kon-**tahkt**], die Berührung [bərew-ruhŋ]
contain (v) enthalten [ehnt-**hahlt**ən]
container der Behälter [bəhehltər], das Gefäß [gəfehs]
contents der Inhalt [ihn-hahlt]
continue (v) fortsetzen [fort-zehtsən]
contraceptive das Verhütungsmittel [fehr-**hew**-tuhŋz-mihtəl]
contract der Vertrag [fehr-**trahk**]
contrary das Gegenteil [geygən-tayl]
control (v) kontrollieren [kon-troh-**liirən**]
conversation das Gespräch [gəSprehç], die Unterhaltung [uhntər-**hahl**-tuhŋ]
conversion die Umrechnung [uhm-rehç-nuhŋ]
convince (v) überzeugen [ewbər-**tsoyg**ən]
cook (v) kochen [koxən]; zubereiten [tsoo-bəraytən]; **cooked** gar [gahr]
cool frisch [frihS], kühl [kewl]

copy die Kopie [koh-**pii**]
cord (electricity) die Schnur [Snuhr]
corner die Ecke [ehkə], der Winkel [vihŋkəl]
corporation das Unternehmen [uhntər-neymən]
correct korrekt [ko-**rehkt**]; (v) verbessern [fehr-**behs**ərn]
correspondence der Briefwechsel [briif-vehksəl]
corridor der Gang [gahŋ]
corrupt verdorben [fehr-**dorb**ən], bestechlich [bəStehç-lihç]; (v) bestechen [bəStehçən]
cost (v) kosten [kostən]
costs die Kosten [kostən] pl
cottage die Hütte [hewtə]
cotton die Baumwolle [baum-volə], das Baumwollgarn [baum-vol-gahrn]
cough (v) husten [hoostən]
count (v) zählen [tsehlən]
counter (bank) der Schalter [Sahltər]
country das Land [lahnt]; **native country** das Vaterland [fahtər-lahnt]; **fellow countryman** der Landsmann [lahnts-mahn]
couple das Paar [pahr]; das Ehepaar [eyə-pahr]
coupon der Abschnitt [ahp-Sniht]
course der Kurs [kuhrs]; (meal) der Gang [gahŋ]; **of course** selbstverständlich [zehlpst-fehr-Stehnt-lihç]; natürlich [nah-**tewr**-lihç]
cousin Cousin/e [koo-**zehn** / koo-**ziinə**]
cover (v) zudecken [tsoo-dehkən], bedecken [bə-**dehk**ən]
cow die Kuh [koo]
cozy gemütlich [gəmewt-lihç]
crash der Zusammenstoß [tsuh-**zahm**ən-Stos]
crazy verrückt [fehr-**rewkt**]
create (v) schaffen [Sahfən]
creative kreativ [krey-ah-**tiif**]
credit der Kredit [kreh-**diit**]
crew die Mannschaft [mahn-Sahft]
criticize (v) kritisieren [krih-tih-**ziir**ən]
cross (v) überqueren [ewbər-**kvehr**ən], überschreiten [ewbər-**Srayt**ən]; das Kreuz [kroyts]; (adj) ärgerlich [ehrgər-lihç]
crossing der Übergang [ewbər-gahŋ]
crossroads die (Straßen-)Kreuzung [(Strahsən-)kroyt-suhŋ]

A/Z

crowd die Menschenmenge [mehnSən-mehŋə]
crowded voll [fol]
cruise die Seereise [zey-rayzə]
cry *(v)* weinen [vaynən]
cube der Würfel [vewrfəl]
culture die Kultur [kuhl-**toor**]
cup der Becher [behçər]
curious neugierig [noy-gii-rohç]
current *(electricity)* der Strom [Strom], die Strömung [Strœ-muhŋ]
curtain der Vorhang [for-hahŋ]
curve die Kurve [kuhrvə]
cushion das Kissen [kihsən]
customer Kunde/Kundin [kuhndə / kuhn-dihn]
customs office das Zollamt [tsol-ahmt]
customs official der Zollbeamter [tsol-bɑahmtər]
cut *(v)* schneiden [Snaydən]
cute hübsch [hewpS]

D

damage die Beschädigung [bəSeh-dih-guhŋ], der Schaden [Sahdən]; *(v)* beschädigen [bəSeh-dihgən], schaden [Sahdən]
damages der Schadenersatz [Sahd(ə)nər-zahts]
damp feucht [foyçt]
dance der Tanz [tahnts]
danger die Gefahr [gəfahr]
dangerous gefährlich [gəfehr-lihç]
dare *(v)* wagen [vahgən]
dark dunkel [duhŋkəl], finster [fihnstər]
darling der Liebling [liip-lihŋ]
darn *(v)* flicken [flihkən]
date *(meeting)* die Verabredung [fehr-ahp-rey-duhŋ]; das Datum [dah-tuhm]; **up to date** modern [moh-**dehrn**]
daughter die Tochter [toxtər]
day der Tag [tahk]; **every day** alle Tage [ahlə tahgə], täglich [tehk-lihç]
dead tot [toht]
deadline der Termin [tehr-**miin**]
dear teuer [toyər]; **Dear George** Lieber Georg! [liibər gey-ork]
death der Tod [toht]
debt die Schuld [Suhlt]
deceitful betrügerisch [bətrew-gərihS]

decide *(v)* entscheiden [ehnt-**Say**dən], beschließen [bəSliisən]
decision der Entschluss [ehnt-**Sluhs**]
declare *(v)* erklären [ehr-**klehr**ən]
decline *(v)* ablehnen [ahp-leynən]
deep tief [tiif]
deer das Rotwild [roht-vihlt]
defective defekt [dey-**fehkt**]
defend *(v)* verteidigen [fehr-**tay**-dihgən]
definite(ly) endgültig [ehnt-gewl-tihç]
degree der Grad [graht]
delay der Aufschub [auf-Soop]; *(v)* verzögern [fehr-**tsœg**ərn]
delicate fein [fayn]
delighted entzückt [ehnt-**tsewk**t]
delightful entzückend [ehnt-**tsewk**ənt]
deliver *(v)* überbringen [ewbər-**brih**ŋən], liefern [liifərn]
demand die Forderung [fordə-ruhŋ]; *(v)* fordern [fordərn], verlangen [fehr-**lah**ŋən]
dense *(fog)* dicht [dihçt]
deny *(v)* leugnen [loygnən]
department *(government, etc.)* das Amt [ahmt]
department store das Kaufhaus [kauf-haus], das Warenhaus [vahrən-haus]
departure die Abreise [ahp-rayzə]
deposit das Pfand [pfahnt]; *(v)* hinter-legen [hihntər-**leyg**ən]
describe *(v)* beschreiben [bəSraybən]
description die Bezeichnung [bətsayç-nuhŋ], die Beschreibung [bəSray-buhŋ]
deserve *(v)* verdienen [fehr-**diin**ən]
desire die Lust [luhst]
desperate verzweifelt [fehr-tsvayfəlt]
destination das (Reise-)Ziel [(rayzə-)tsiil]
destroy *(v)* zerstören [tsehr-**Stœr**ən]
detail die Einzelheit [ayntsəl-hayt]
detailed ausführlich [aus-fewr-lihç]
details nähere Angaben [neyərə ahn-gahbən]
determined entschlossen [ehnt-**Slos**ən]
detour der Umweg [uhm-veyk]
develop *(v)* entwickeln [ehnt-**vihk**əln]
development die Entwicklung [ehnt-**vihk**-luhŋ]
diagnosis die Diagnose [dii-ahg-**noh**zə]
dial *(v)* wählen [vehlən]
dice (Spiel-)Würfel, *pl* (Spiil-)vewrfəl]
die der (Spiel-)Würfel [(Spiil-)vewrfəl]; *(v)* sterben (Stehrbən]

differ from (v) s. unterscheiden von [uhntər-**Say**dən fon]

difference der Unterschied [uhntər-Sayt]

different(ly) verschieden [fehr-**Sii**dən], anders [ahndərs]

difficult schwierig [Svii-rihç], schwer [Svehr]

difficulty die Schwierigkeit [Svii-rihç-kayt]

direct direkt [dih-**rehkt**]

direction die Richtung [rihç-tuhŋ]

director der Direktor [dih-**rehk**-tor]

directory das Verzeichnis [fehr-**tsayç**-nihs]

dirt der Schmutz [Smuhts]

dirty schmutzig [Smuht-sihç]; **dirty laundry** Wäsche [vehSə] (zum Waschen) (tsuhm vahSən]

disadvantage der Nachteil [nahx-tayl]

disappear (v) verschwinden [fehr-**Svihn**dən]

disappointed enttäuscht [ehnt-**toyst**]

discount der Rabatt [rah-**baht**]

discover (v) entdecken [ehnt-**deh**kən]

discovery die Entdeckung [ehnt-**deh**-kuhŋ]

dish die Platte [plahtə]; (meal) das Gericht [gə**rihçt**]

disorder die Unordnung [uhn-ord-nuhŋ]

dispatch (v) versenden [fehr-**zehn**dən]

dissatisfied unzufrieden [un-tsoo-friidən]

distance der Abstand [ahp-Stahnt], die Entfernung [ehnt-**fehr**-nuhŋ], die Strecke [Strehkə]

distant entfernt [ehnt-**fehrnt**]

distinct deutlich [doyt-lihç]

distinguish (v) unterscheiden [uhntər-**Say**dən]

distinguished fein [fayn], vornehm [for-neym]

distribute (v) verteilen [fehr-**tay**lən]

distribution die Verteilung [fehr-**tay**-luhŋ]

district die Gegend [geygənt], der Stadtteil [Staht-tayl]

distrust (v) misstrauen [mihs-**trau**ən]

disturb (v) stören [Stœrən]

disturbance die Störung [Stœ-ruhŋ]

divide (v) teilen [taylən], trennen [trehnən]

dizzy schwindlig [Svihnt-lihç]

do (v) tun [toon], machen [mahxən]

dock der (Landungs-)Steg [(lahn-duhŋs-)Stehk]

doctor der/die Arzt/Ärztin [ahrtst / ehrts-tihn]

document das Dokument [do-koo-**mehnt**]

dog der Hund [huhnt]

doll die Puppe [puhpə]

done erledigt [ehr-**ley**-dihkt], fertig [fehr-tihç]; (cooked) gar [gahr]

donkey der Esel [eyzəl]

door die Tür [tewr]; **front door** die Haustür [haus-tewr]

double doppelt [dopəlt]

doubt der Zweifel [tsvayfəl]; **without doubt** zweifellos [tsvayfəl-lohs]; **doubt s. th.** (v) zweifeln an etw [tsvayfəln ahn]

doubtful zweifelhaft [tsvayfəl-hahft]

doubtless zweifellos [tsvayfəl-lohs], ohne Zweifel [ohnə tsvayfəl]

down abwärts [ahp-vehrts]; **down there** dort unten [dort uhntən]; **downhill** bergab [behrk-**ahp**]; **down payment** die Kaution [kaut-**syohn**]

draft der Luftzug [luhft-tsuhk]; (beer) das Bier vom Fass [biir fom fahs]

draw (v) zeichnen [tsayçnən]

dreadful schrecklich [Srehk-lihç], fürchterlich [fewrçtər-lihç]

dream der Traum [traum]; (v) träumen [troymən]

dress die Kleidung [klay-duhŋ]; (v) s. anziehen [ahn-tsiiən]; (med.) verbinden [fehr-**bihn**dən]

dressing (med) der Verband [fehr-**bahnt**]; (salad) die Soße [zosə]

drink (v) trinken [trihŋkən]

drinkable trinkbar [trihŋk-bahr]

drip (v) tropfen [tropfən]

drive die Fahrt [fahrt]; (v) fahren [fahrən]; **drive a car** (v) Auto fahren [au-toh fahrən]

driver der Chauffeur [So-**fœr**], der/die Fahrer/in [fahrər / -ihn]

driveway die Einfahrt [ayn-fahrt]

drop der Tropfen [tropfən]

drunk betrunken [bə-**truhŋ**kən]; **get drunk** (v) s. betrinken [bətrihŋkən]

dry trocken [trokən]; (wine) herb [hehrp], trocken [trokən]

durable haltbar [hahlt-bahr]

A/Z

duration die Dauer [dauər]
during während [veh-rehnt]
dust der Staub [Staup]
duty die Pflicht [pflihçt]; *(customs)* der Zoll [tsol]; **pay duty on** *(v)* verzollen [fehr-**tsol**ən]

E

each jeder einzelne [yeydər ayntsəlnə]; **each other** einander [ayn-**ahn**dər]
earlier früher [frewər]
early früh [frew]
earn *(v)* verdienen [fehr-**diin**ən]
earnings der Verdienst [fehr-**diin**st]
earth die Erde [ehrdə]
earthenware die Tonwaren [tohn-vahrən] *f pl*
east der Osten [ohstən]
easy leicht [layçt]
eat *(v)* essen [ehsən]; **when eating** beim Essen [baym ehsən]
edge der Rand [rahnt]
edible essbar [ehs-bahr]
education die Erziehung [ehr-**tsii**-uhŋ], die Ausbildung [aus-bihl-duhŋ]
effect die Wirkung [vihr-kuhŋ]
effective wirksam [vihrk-zahm]
efficient tüchtig [tewç-tihç]
effort die Mühe [mewə], die Anstrengung [ahn-Strehŋ-uhŋ]
egg das Ei [ay]
either … or entweder … oder [ehnt-veydər ... ohdər]
election die Wahl [vahl]
electric elektrisch [ey-**lehk**-trihS]
elevator der Fahrstuhl [fahr-Stool]
elsewhere anderswo [ahndərs-voh]
emancipated emanzipiert [ey-mahnt-sih-**piirt**]
embassy die Botschaft [boht-Sahft]
embrace *(v)* umarmen [uhm-**ahr**mən]
emergency der Notfall [noht-fahl]; **in case of emergency** im Notfall [ihm noht-fahl]
employ *(v)* anwenden [ahn-vehndən], verwenden [fehr-**vehnd**ən]
empty leer [leyr]
enclosure *(letter)* die Anlage [ahn-lahgə]
end das Ende [ehndə], der Schluss [Sluhs]; **to end** *(v)* enden [ehndən]

engaged verlobt [fehr-lohpt]; **get engaged to** *(v)* s. verloben mit [zihç fehr-**lob**ən miht]
England England [ehŋ-lahnt]
English englisch [ehŋ-lihS]; **in English** auf Englisch [auf ehŋ-lihS]; **Englishman/-woman** der/die Engländer/in [ehŋ-lehndər / -ihn]
enjoy *(v)* genießen [gə**niis**ən]
enjoyment der Genuss [gə**nuhs**]
enormous gewaltig [gə**vahl**-tihç]
enough genug [gə**nook**]
enter *(v)* betreten [bə**treht**ən], hineingehen [hihn-**ayn**-geyən]; **enter (a country)** *(v)* einreisen [ayn-rayzən]; **enter (a room)** *(v)* eintreten [ayn-trehtən]
entertaining unterhaltend [uhntər-**hahlt**ənt]
entertainment die Unterhaltung [uhntər-**hahl**-tuhŋ]
enthusiastic (about) begeistert (von) [bə**gayst**ərt (fon)]
entire ganz [gahnts]
entitled berechtigt [bə**rehç**-tihkt]
entrance die Einfahrt [ayn-fahrt], der Eingang [ayn-gahŋ]; der Zugang [tsoo-gahŋ], *(fee)* der Eintritt [ayn-triht]; **main entrance** der Haupteingang [haupt-ayn-gahŋ]
environment die Umwelt [uhm-vehlt]
equipment die Ausrüstung [aus-rews-tuhŋ]
equivalent der Gegenwert [geygən-vehrt]; gleichwertig [glayç-vehr-tihç]
especially hauptsächlich [haupt-zehç-lihç], besonders [bə**zon**dərs]
estate das Landgut [lahnt-goot]
estimate *(v)* schätzen [Sehtsən]
Europe Europa [oy-**rohp**ə]
European der/die Europäer/in [oy-roh-**pey**ər / -ihn]; europäisch [oy-roh-**pey**-ihS]
even sogar [zoh-**gahr**]; **not even** nicht einmal [nihçt ayn-mahl]; **even if** sogar wenn [zoh-**gahr** vehn]
evening der Abend [ahbənt]; **in the evening** am Abend [ahm ahbənt]; **this evening** heute Abend [hoytə ahbənt]
event das Ereignis [ehr-**ayg**-nihs], die Veranstaltung [fehr-**ahn**-Stahl-tuhŋ]
ever je [yey], jemals [yey-mahls]
every jeder [yeydər]; **every time** jedes Mal [yeydəs mahl]

everybody jedermann [yeydər-mahn]

everything alles [ahləs]

everywhere überall [ewbər-**ahl**]

evil böse [ewbəl]

exact(ly) genau [gənau]

exaggerated übertrieben [ewbər-**triibən**]

exam(ination) die Prüfung [prew-fuhŋ]

examine (v) prüfen [prewfən], untersuchen [uhntər-**zooxən**]

example das Beispiel [bay-Spiil]; **for example** zum Beispiel [tsuhm bay-Spiil]

excellent ausgezeichnet [ausgətsayçnət]

except außer [ausər]

exception die Ausnahme [aus-nahmə]

exchange der Austausch [aus-tauS], der Wechsel [vehksəl]; (v) tauschen [tauSən], austauschen [aus-tauSən]

exchange rate der Wechselkurs [vehksəl-kuhrs]

excursion die Tour [toor]

excuse die Entschuldigung [ehnt-**Suhl**-dih-guhŋ]; (v) entschuldigen [ehnt-**Suhl**-dihgən]; **excuse me, please!** Entschuldigen Sie bitte! [ehnt-**Suhl**-dihgən zii bihtə!]

exempt frei [fray]

exercise die Übung [ew-buhŋ]

exercise book das (Schreib-)Heft [(Srayp-)hehft]

exhausted erschöpft [ehr-**Sœpft**]

exhibition die Ausstellung [aus-Steh-luhŋ], die Messe [mehsə]

exit der Ausgang [aus-gahŋ]; die (Autobahn-)Ausfahrt [(au-toh-bahn-)ausfahrt]

expect (v) erwarten [ehr-**vahr**tən]

expenses Spesen [Speyzən] pl, Unkosten [uhn-kostən] pl, die Ausgaben [aus-gahbən] f pl, Kosten [kostən] pl

expensive kostspielig [kost-Spii-lihç], teuer [toyər]

experience die Erfahrung [ehr-**fah**-ruhŋ]

experienced erfahren [ehr-**fah**rən]

experiment die Probe [prohbə]

expire (v) ablaufen [ahp-laufən]

explain (v) erklären [ehr-**kleh**rən]

explicit(ly) ausdrücklich [aus-drewk-lihç]

expression der Ausdruck [aus-druhk]

extend (v) verlängern [vehr-**lehŋ**ərn]

external äußerlich [oysər-lihç]

extinguish (v) löschen [lœSən]

extra extra [ehk-strah]

extraordinary außergewöhnlich [ausərgəvœn-lihç]

eye das Auge [augə]

F

fabric der Stoff [Stof]; das Gewebe [gəveybə]

fact die Tatsache [taht-zahxə]

factory die Fabrik [fah-**briik**]

faint (v) ohnmächtig werden [ohn-mehç-tihç vehrdən]

fair (exhibition) die Messe [mehsə]; gerecht [gərehçt], **fair** [fehr]; (weather) schön [Sœn]

fairly ziemlich [tsiim-lihç]

faith der Glaube [glaubə]

faithful treu [troy]

fall der Sturz [Stuhrts]; (v) stürzen [Stewrtsən], fallen [fahlən]

false unecht [uhn-ehçt]

family die Familie [fah-**mihl**yə]

famous berühmt [bərewmt]

fan der/die Anhänger/in [ahn-hehŋər / -ihn]

fancy vornehm [for-neym]

fantastic prima [priimə]

far weit [vayt]

farm der Bauernhof [bauərn-hohf]

farmer der Bauer [bauər]

fashion die Mode [mohdə]

fast schnell [Snehl]; **be fast** (clock) (v) vorgehen [for-geyən]

fasten (v) binden [bihndən]

fat fett [feht]; (person) dick [dihk]

father der Vater [fahtər]

fault der Fehler [feylər], der Mangel [mahŋəl]; **it's my fault** es ist meine Schuld [ehs ihst maynə Suhlt]

faulty defekt [dey-**fehkt**]

favor der Dienst [diinst], die Gefälligkeit [gəfeh-lihç-kayt]; **in favor of** zu Gunsten [tsoo guhnstən]

favorable günstig [gewns-tihç]

fear die Angst [ahŋst], die Furcht [fuhrxt]; (v) fürchten [fewrçtən], befürchten [bəfewrçtən]

feather die Feder [feydər]

fee das Honorar [hoh-noh-**rahr**]

feeble schwach [Svahx]

feed *(animal)* das (Tier-)Futter [(tiir-)fuhtər]
feel *(v)* fühlen [fewlən]
feeling das Gefühl [gəfewl]
fees die Gebühren [gəbewrən] *f pl*
female weiblich [vayp-lihç]
feminine weiblich [vayp-lihç]
festive feierlich [fayər-lihç]
fetch *(v)* holen [hohlən]
few wenig [vey-nihç]; **a few** ein paar [ayn pahr]
fiancé/fiancée der/die Verlobte [fehr-**lohptə**]
fib die Lüge [lewgə], der Schwindel [Svihndəl]; **tell fibs** *(v)* schwindeln (lügen) [Svihndəln (lewgən)]
field das Feld [fehlt]
figure die Nummer [nuhmər], die Zahl [tsahl]
fill *(v)* füllen [fewlən]; **fill up** *(v)* volltanken [fol-tahŋkən]
film der Film [fihlm]
filter der Filter [fihltər]
finally zuletzt [tsoo-**lehtst**], endlich [ehnt-lihç]
find *(v)* finden [fihndən]
fine *(punishment)* die Strafe [Strahfə], die Geldstrafe [gehlt-Strahfə]; *(thin)* fein [fayn]
finish *(v)* beenden [bə-**end**ən]
finished fertig [fehr-tihç]
fire das Feuer [foyər], der Brand [brahnt]
fire alarm der Feuermelder [foyər-mehldər]
fire department die Feuerwehr [foyər-vehr]
fire extinguisher der Feuerlöscher [foyər-lœSər]
firewood das Brennholz [brehn-holts]
fireworks das Feuerwerk [foyər-vehrk]
firm *(adj)* fest [fehst]; die Firma [fiirmə], das Unternehmen [uhntər-**neym**ən]
first erste(r, -s) [ehrstə(r,s)]; **first (of all)** zunächst [tsoo-**nehkst**]; **first(ly)** erstens [ehrstəns]; **(at) first** zuerst [tsoo-ehrst]; **first-class** erstklassig [ehrst-klah-sihç]
fish der Fisch [fihS]; *(v)* fischen [fihSən], angeln [ahŋəln]; **go fishing** *(v)* angeln gehen [ahŋəln geyən]

fish dealer der Fischhändler [fihS-hehndlər]
fit *(adj)* fit [fiht]; *(v)* passen [pahsən]
fix *(v)* festsetzen [fehst-zehtsən]
flame die Flamme [flahmə]
flammable feuergefährlich [foyər-gəfehr-lihç]
flash *(photo)* der Blitz [blihts]
flat eben; *(Reifen-)Panne [(rayfən-)pahnə]
flat rate die Pauschale [pau-**Sahl**ə]
fleece das (Schafs-)Fell [(Sahfs-)fehl]
flirt *(v)* flirten [flihrtən]
floor der Boden [bohdən]; *(story)* das Stockwerk [Stok-vehrk]; **on the third floor** im dritten Stock [ihm drihtən Stok]
flow *(v)* fließen [fliisən]; **flow into** (v) *(river)* münden [mewndən]
flower die Blume [bloomə]
fly die Fliege [fliigə]; *(v)* fliegen [fliigən]
foggy neblig [ney-blihç]
folder die Mappe [mahpə]
follow *(v)* folgen [folgən]
fond zärtlich [tsehrt-lihç]; **be fond of s. o.** *(v)* jdn lieb haben [liip hahbən]
food die Nahrung [nah-ruhŋ], die Verpflegung [fehr-**pfley**-guhŋ], das Lebensmittel [leybənz-mihtəl], das Essen [ehsən]; *(animal)* das (Tier-)Futter [(tiir-)fuhtər]; **food(stuff)** das Nahrungsmittel [nah-ruhŋz-mihtəl]
for für [fewr]; *(time)* seit [zayt]; *(reason)* denn [dehn]; **for this reason** aus diesem Grund [aus diizəm gruhnt]; **be for it** *(v)* dafür sein [dah-**fewr** zayn]
forbid *(v)* verbieten [fehr-**biit**ən]
forbidden verboten [fehr-**boht**ən]
force die Kraft [krahft]; *(v)* zwingen [tsvihŋən]
foreign fremd [frehmt], ausländisch [aus-lehn-dihS]
foreign countries das Ausland [aus-lahnt]
foreigner der/die Ausländer/in [aus-lehndər / -ihn]; der/die Fremde [frehmdə]
forget *(v)* vergessen [fehr-**gehs**ən]
forgive *(v)* verzeihen [fehr-**tsay**ən]
form das Formular [for-moo-**lahr**], die Form [form]; *(v)* bilden [bihldən]

format das Format [for-**maht**]
forward(s) vorwärts [for-vehrts]; **look forward to** (v) s. freuen auf [zihç froyən auf]
fountain der (Spring-)Brunnen [(Sprihŋ-)bruhnən]
fragile zerbrechlich [tsehr-**brehç**-lihç]
France Frankreich [frahŋk-rayç]
fraud der Betrug [bətrook]
free gratis [grah-tihs], frei [fray]; **free (of charge)** kostenlos [kostən-lohs], umsonst [uhm-**zonst**]
freeway die Autobahn [au-toh-bahn]
freeze (v) frieren [friirən]
freight die Fracht [frahxt]
French französisch [frahnt-**sœ**-zihS]
Frenchman/woman der Franzose/die Französin [frahnt-**sohz**ə / -**sœ**-zihn]
frequently häufig [hoy-fihç]
fresh frisch [frihS]
friend der/die Freund(in) [froynt, froyn-dihn], der/die Bekannte [bəkahntə]; **boy/girlfriend** der/die Freund/in [froynt, froyn-dihn]; **be friends** (v) befreundet sein [bə**froynd**ət]
friendly freundlich [froynt-lihç]
friendship die Freundschaft [froynt-Sahft]
frighten (v) erschrecken [ehr-**Srehk**ən]
from ab [ahp]; von [fon], aus [aus]
front die Vorderseite [fordər-zaytə]; **in front** vorn [forn]; **in front of** vor [for]
fry (v) braten [brahtən]
fuel oil das Heizöl [hayts-œl]
fulfill (v) verwirklichen [fehr-**vihrk**-lihçən]
full voll [fol], völlig [fœ-lihç], ganz [gahnts] (*but be careful with "voll" because it is also slang for "drunk"*)
fun der Spaß [Spahs]
funny lustig [luhs-tihç]
fur das Fell [fehl], der Pelz [pehlts]
furious wütend [vewtənt]
furnish (v) möblieren [mœb-**liir**ən]
furnishings die Ausstattung [aus-Stah-tuhŋ]
furniture Möbel [mœbəl] *n pl*
fuse (*electricity*) die Sicherung [zihçə-ruhŋ]
future die Zukunft [tsoo-kuhnft]; zukünftig [tsoo-kewnf-tihç]

G

gadget der Apparat [ah-pah-**raht**]
gain (v) gewinnen [gə**vihn**ən]; ~ **weight** (v) zunehmen [tsoo-neymən]
game das Spiel [Spiil]; das Wild [vihlt]
garage die Reparaturwerkstatt [rey-pah-rah-**toor**-vehrk-Staht], die Garage [gah-**rahZ**ə]
garbage der Müll [mewl]; **garbage can** die Mülltonne [mewl-tonə]
garden der Garten [gartən]
gas das Benzin [behn-**tsiin**]
gate das Tor [tohr]
gateway die Einfahrt [ayn-fahrt]
gear (*car*) der Gang [gahŋ]
general allgemein [ahl-gəmayn]; **in general** im Allgemeinen [ihm ahl-gəmaynən]
gentle zärtlich [tsehrt-lihç]
gentleman der Herr [hehr]
genuine echt [ehçt]
German der/die Deutsche [doytSə]; deutsch [doytS]
Germany Deutschland [doytS-lahnt]
get (v) bekommen [bəkomən], kriegen [kriigən]; (*obtain*) besorgen [bəzorgən]; **get on** (v) zusteigen [tsoo-Staygən]; **get up** (v) aufstehen [auf-Steyən]; **get hold of** (v) verschaffen [fehr-**Sahf**ən]; **get acclimated** (v) s. akklimatisieren [ahk-klii-mah-tih-ziirən]; **get sick** (v) krank werden [krahŋk vehrdən]
giddy schwindlig [Svihnd-lihç]
gift das Geschenk [gə**Sehŋk**]
girl das Mädchen [meytçən]
give (v) geben [geybən]; **give in** (v) nachgeben [nahx-geybən]; **give up** (v) aufgeben [auf-geybən]
glad froh [froh]; **glad (about)** erfreut (über) [ehr-**froyt** (ewbər)]
gladly gern [gehrn]
glass das Glas [glahs]
glasses die Brille [brihlə]
glorious herrlich [hehr-lihç], (fig) glänzend [glehntsənt]
gnat die Mücke [mewkə]
go (v) gehen [geyən], fahren [fahrən], reisen [rayzən]; **go in** (v) hineingehen [hin-**ayn**-geyən]; **go to** (v) reisen nach

A/Z

[rayzən nahx]; **go up** *(v)* hinaufgehen [hin-**auf**-geyən]; **go away** *(v)* verreisen [fehr-**rayz**ən]; **go back** *(v)* zurückgehen [tsuh-**rewk**-geyən]; **go down** *(v)* hinuntergehen [hihn-**uhn**tər-geyən]; **go out** *(v)* hinausgehen [hin-**aus**-geyən]; ausgehen [aus-geyən]; **go straight ahead** *(v)* geradeaus gehen [gərahdə-**aus** geyən]

God der Gott [got]

gone weg [vehk], vorüber [for-**ewb**ər]

good gut [goot]

goodbye auf Wiedersehen [auf viidər-zeyən]; **say goodbye** *(v)* Abschied nehmen [ahp-Siit neymən], s. verabschieden [zihç fehr-**ahp**-Siidən]

goodness die Güte [gewtə]; **thank goodness!** Gott sei Dank! [got zay dahŋk]

goods die Waren [vahrən] *f pl*

government die Regierung [reh-**gii**-ruhŋ]

grab *(v)* zugreifen [tsoo-grayfən]

grandfather der Großvater [grohs-fahtər]

grandmother die Großmutter [grohs-muhtər]

grant *(v)* gewähren [gəvehrən]

grass das Gras [grahs]; *(lawn)* der Rasen [rahzən]

great großartig [grohs-ahr-tihç], prima [priimə]; *(important)* groß [grohs]

greet *(v)* begrüßen [bəgrewsən], grüßen [grewsən]

grief der Kummer [kuhmər]

grill *(v)* braten [brahtən]

ground der Boden [bohdən], das Gelände [gəlehndə]

ground floor das Erdgeschoss [ehrt-gəSos]

group die Gruppe [gruhpə]

grow *(v)* wachsen [vahksən]

grumble *(v)* schimpfen [Sihmpfən]

guarantee die Garantie [gah-rahn-**tii**]

guard *(v)* bewachen [bəvahxən]

guess die Vermutung [fehr-**moo**-tuhŋ]; *(v)* raten [rahtən]

guest der Gast [gahst]

guide der Fremdenführer [frehmdən-fewrər], *(book)* der Reiseführer [rayzə-fewrər]

guilt die Schuld [Soolt]

guitar die Gitarre [gih-**tah**rə]

H

habit die Gewohnheit [gəvohn-hayt]

haggle *(v)* feilschen [faylSən]

half *(adj)* halb [hahlp]; die Hälfte [hehlftə]

hall die Halle [hahlə]; der Saal [zahl]

halt! halt! [hahlt!]

hammer der Hammer [hahmər]

hand die Hand [hahnt]; *(v)* reichen [rayçən]; **hand in** *(v)* abgeben [ahp-geybən]; **hand over** *(v)* übergeben [ewbər-**geyb**ən]

handbag die Handtasche [hahnt-tahSə]

handle der Griff [grihf]

handmade handgemacht [hahnt-gəmahxt]

hang *(v)* hängen [hehŋən], aufhängen [auf-hehŋən]

happen *(v)* s. ereignen [ehr-**aygn**ən], geschehen [gəSeyən], passieren [pah-**siir**ən]; **what has happened?** was ist geschehen? [vahs ihst gəSeyən]

happy froh [froh], glücklich [glewk-lihç]

hard hart [hahrt]

hard-working fleißig [flay-sihç]

hardly kaum [kaum]

harm *(v)* schaden [Sahdən]

harmful schädlich [Seht-lihç]

harvest die Ernte [ehrntə]

have *(v)* haben [hahbən]; **have to** *(v)* müssen [mewsən], sollen [zolən]; **I'll have to** ich werde müssen [ihç vehrdə mewsən]; **have a good time** *(v)* s. amüsieren [zihç ah-mew-**ziir**ən]

he er [ehr]

head der/die Leiter/in [laytər / -ihn], der Chef/die Chefin [Sehf, Seh-fihn]

headmaster der Rektor [rehk-tor], der Direktor [dih-**rehk**-tor]

headquarters der Sitz [zihts], das Hauptquartier [haupt-kvahr-tiir]

health die Gesundheit [gəzuhnt-hayt]; **good health** das Wohlbefinden [vohl-bəfihndən]

healthy gesund [gəzuhnt]

hear *(v)* erfahren [ehr-**fahr**ən], hören [hœrən]

heart das Herz [hehrts]

heat die Wärme [vehrmə], die Hitze [hihtsə]; *(v)* wärmen [vehrmən], heizen [haytsən]

heating oil das Heizöl [hayts-œl]

heaven *(rel)* der Himmel [hihmǝl]

heavy schwer [Svehr]

hectic hektisch [hehk-tihS]

heel der (Schuh-)Absatz [(Soo-)ahp-zahts]

height die Größe [grœsǝ], die Höhe [hœǝ]; *(career)* der Höhepunkt [hœǝ-puhŋkt]

hello hallo [hah-**loh**]

help die Hilfe [hihlfǝ]; **help s. o.** *(v)* jdm helfen [hehlfǝn], jdm behilflich [bǝhihlf-lihç]; **help yourself!** greifen Sie zu! [grayfǝn zii tsoo]

her ihr [iir]

here hier [hiir]

hesitate *(v)* zögern [tsœgǝrn]

hide das Fell [fehl], die Haut [haut]; *(v)* verstecken [fehr-**Stehk**ǝn], verbergen [fehr-**behrg**ǝn]

high hoch [hohx]

highlight der Höhepunkt [hœǝ-puhŋkt]

hike *(v)* wandern [vahndǝrn]

hill der Hügel [hewgǝl]

hinder *(v)* hindern [hihndǝrn]

his sein [zayn]

history die Geschichte [gǝ**Sihçt**ǝ]

hit *(v)* schlagen [Slahgǝn]

hobby das Hobby [ho-bii]

hole das Loch [lox]

holiday der Feiertag [fayǝr-tahk]

holy heilig [hay-lihç]

home die Heimat [hay-maht], das Inland [ihn-lahnt]; **at home** daheim [dah-**haym**]

honor die Ehre [ehrǝ]

hook der Haken [hahkǝn]

hope *(v)* hoffen [hofǝn]

horrible fürchterlich [fewrçtǝr-lihç]

hospitality die Gastfreundschaft [gahst-froynt-Sahft]

host/hostess Gastgeber/in [gahst-geybǝr / -ihn]

hot heiß [hays]; *(spicy)* scharf [Sahrf]

hotel das Hotel [hoh-**tehl**]

hour die Stunde [Stuhndǝ]; **a quarter of an hour** eine Viertelstunde[fiirtǝl-Stuhndǝ]; **half an hour** eine halbe Stunde [hahlbǝ Stuhndǝ]; **every two hours** alle zwei Stunden [ahlǝ tsvay Stuhndǝ]

hours of business die Öffnungszeiten [œf-nuhŋs-tsaytǝn] *f pl*

house das Haus [haus]

how wie [vii]

however jedoch [yey-**dox**], doch [dox]

hug *(v)* umarmen [uhm-**ahr**mǝn]

human menschlich [mehnS-lihç]

hundred hundert [huhndǝrt]

hunger der Hunger [huhŋǝr]

hungry hungrig [huhŋ-rihç]

hurry *(v)* s. beeilen [bǝ-aylǝn]; **be in a hurry** *(v)* es eilig haben [ehs ay-lihç hahbǝn]

hurt *(v)* schmerzen [Smehrtsǝn]

husband der Ehemann [eyǝ-mahn]

hut die Hütte [hewtǝ]

I

I ich [ihç]

ice das Eis [ays]

ice cream das (Speise-)eis [(Spayzǝ-)ays]

idea die Idee [ii-**dey**], die Ahnung [ah-nuhŋ]; die Vorstellung [for-Steh-luhŋ]; **no idea!** keine Ahnung! [kaynǝ ah-nuhŋ]

identity card der (Personal-)Ausweis [(pehr-zoh-**nahl**-)aus-vays]

if wenn [vehn], falls [fahls]

ill krank [krahŋk]; **be taken ill** *(v)* krank werden [krahŋk vehrdǝn]

illuminated beleuchtet [bǝ**loyçt**ǝt]

illustration das Bild [bihlt]

immediate(ly) unmittelbar [uhn-mihtǝl-bahr], sofort [zoh-**fort**], direkt [dih-**rehkt**]

impertinent unverschämt [uhn-fehr-Sehmt]

impolite unhöflich [uhn-hœf-lihç]

import die Einfuhr [ayn-fuhr]

importance die Bedeutung [bǝdoy-tuhŋ]

important bedeutend [bǝ**doyt**ǝnt], wichtig [vihç-tihç]

impossible ausgeschlossen [aus-gǝSlosǝn], unmöglich [uhn-mœg-lihç]

impression der Eindruck [ayn-druhk]

improbable unwahrscheinlich [uhn-vahr-Sayn-lihç]

improve *(v)* verbessern [vehr-**beh**sǝrn]

in in [ihn]

in case falls [fahls]

incident der Vorfall [for-fahl], der Zwischenfall [tsvihSǝn-fahl]

included inbegriffen [ihn-bəgrihfən]

incomplete unvollständig [uhn-fol-Stehn-dihç]

inconsiderate unüberlegt [uhn-ewbər-leykt], unbesonnen [uhn-bəzonən]; rücksichtslos [rewk-zihçts-lohs]

increase (v) erhöhen [ehr-**hœ**ən]; zunehmen [tsoo-neymən]

incredible unglaublich [un-glaup-lihç]

indeed in der Tat [ihn dehr taht]

indefinite unbestimmt [uhn-bəStihmt]

indicate (v) zeigen [tsaygən]; (car) blinken [blihŋkən]

indispensable unentbehrlich [uhn-ehnt-behr-lihç]

individual einzeln [ayntsəln]

indoors drinnen [drihnən], im Haus [ihm haus] ‹

industrious fleißig [flay-sihç]

inevitable unvermeidlich [uhn-fehr-mayt-lihç]

inexact ungenau [uhn-gənau]

inexperienced unerfahren [uhn-ehr-fahrən]

inflammable feuergefährlich [foyər-gəfahr-lihç]

inflate (v) aufpumpen [auf-puhmpən]

inform (v) benachrichtigen [bənahx-rihç-tihgən], informieren [ihn-for-**miir**ən], mitteilen [miht-taylən]; (report) melden [mehldən]; **inform s. o.** (v) jdn verständigen [fehr-**Stehn**-dihgən]

information die Auskunft [aus-kuhnft]; **information office** die Auskunftsstelle [aus-kuhnft-Stehlə]

inhabitant der Bewohner [bəvohnər], der Einwohner [ain-vohnər]

injured person der/die Verletzte [fehr-**leht**stə]

injury die Verletzung [fehr-**lehts**-uhŋ]

injustice die Ungerechtigkeit [uhn-gərehç-tihç-kayt], das Unrecht [uhn-rehçt]

inland das Inland [ihn-lahnt]

inn Gasthaus/Gasthof [gahst-haus / gahst-hohf]

innocent unschuldig [uhn-Suhl-dihç]

innovation die Neuheit [noy-hayt]

inquire (v) Auskunft einholen [aus-kuh-nft ayn-hohlən], s. erkundigen [ehr-**kuhn**-dihgən]

insect das Insekt [ihn-**zehkt**]

inside innen [ihnən], drin [drihn]; **the inside** das Innere [ihnərə]

insist (v) behaupten [bəhauptən]; **insist on** (v) bestehen auf [bəSteyən auf]

instead of statt [Staht], anstatt [ahn-Staht]

insufficient ungenügend [uhn-gənewgənt]

insult die Beleidigung [bəlay-dih-guhŋ]; (v) beleidigen [bə-**lay**-dihgən]

insurance die Versicherung [fehr-**zihç**ə-ruhŋ]

insure (v) versichern [fehr-**zihç**ərn]

intelligence der Verstand [fehr-**Staht**nt]

intelligent klug [kluhk]

intend (v) beabsichtigen [bə-**ahp**-sihç-tihgən]

intention die Absicht [ahp-zihçt]

interest das Interesse [ihn-teh-**reh**sə]; **be interested** (in) (v) s. interessieren (für) [ihn-teh-reh-**siir**ən (fewr)]

interesting interessant [ihn-teh-reh-**sahnt**]

international international [ihn-tehr-naht-syoh-**nahl**]

interrupt (v) unterbrechen [uhntər-**breh**çən]

interruption die Störung [Stœ-ruhŋ]

intersection die (Straßen-)Kreuzung [(Strahsən-)kroyt-suhŋ]

intolerable unerträglich [uhn-ehr-trehk-lihç]

introduce (v) vorstellen [for-Stehlən], bekannt machen [bəkahnt mahxən]

introduction die Vorstellung [for-Steh-luhŋ]

invalid ungültig [uhn-gewl-tihç]

invent (v) erfinden [ehr-**fihn**dən]

invitation die Einladung [ayn-lah-duhŋ]

invite (v) einladen [ayn-lahdən], auffordern [auf-fordərn]

Ireland Irland [iir-lahnt]; **Northern Ireland** Nordirland [nort-iir-lahnt]

Irish irisch [ii-rihS]

Irishman der Ire [iirə]

Irishwoman die Irin [ii-rihn]

iron das Eisen [ayzən]; (electric) das Bügeleisen [bewgəl-ayzən]; (v) bügeln [bewgəln]

irregular unregelmäßig [uhn-reygəl-meh-sihç]

island die Insel [ihnsəl]
isolated abgelegen [ahp-gəleygən]; einsam [ayn-zahm]
it es [ehs]
itch (v) jucken [yuhkən]
item der Gegenstand [geygən-Stahnt]
its sein [zayn]

J

jellyfish die Qualle [kvahlə]
jet (plane) das Düsenflugzeug [dewzən-fluhk-tsoyk]; (water) der Strahl [Strahl]
job die Arbeit [ahr-bayt]; (employment) die Stellung [Steh-luhng]
joke der Spaß [Spahs], der Scherz [Sehrts], der Witz [vihts]
journey die Fahrt [fahrt], die Reise [rayzə]; **go on a journey** (v) verreisen [fehr-rayzən]; **on a journey** auf der Reise [auf dehr rayzə]; **return journey** die Rückfahrt [rewk-fahrt], die Heimreise [haym-rayzə]; **journey home** die Heimreise [haym-rayzə]
joy die Lust [luhst], die Freude [froydə]
judge der/die Richter/in [rihçtər / -ihn]; (v) urteilen [oor-taylən], beurteilen [bə-oor-taylən]
judgment das Urteil [oor-tayl]
jump (v) springen [Sprihngən]
just (time) gerade [gərahdə[; gerecht [gəreçt]; **just as ... as** genauso ... wie [gənau-zoh ... vii]

K

keep (v) behalten [bəhahltən]; halten [hahltən]; (feed) unterhalten [uhntər-hahltən]
kind die Art [ahrt], die Sorte [zort]; freundlich [froynd-lihç], wohlwollend [vohl-volənd], liebenswürdig [liibəns-vewr-dihç]
kindness die Freundlichkeit [froynd-lihç-kayt], die Liebenswürdigkeit [liibəns-vewr-dihç-kayt]
kiss der Kuss [kuhs]; (v) küssen [kewsən]
kitchen die Küche [kewçə]

knock (v) anklopfen [ahn-klopfən]
knot der Knoten [knotən]
know (v) kennen [kehnən], wissen [vihsən], Bescheid wissen [bə**Sayt** vihsən]; **get to know s. o.** (v) jdn kennen lernen [kehnən lehrnən]; **well-known** bekannt [bə**kahnt**]; **knowledge** die Kenntnis [kehnt-nihs], das Wissen [vihsən]

L

lace (material) die Spitze [Spihtsə]; **shoelace** der Schnürsenkel [Snewrzən-ehnkəl]
lack der Mangel [mahnəl]
ladder die Leiter [laytər]
lady die Dame [dahmə]; **young lady** das Fräulein [froy-layn]
lake der See [zey]
lamp die Lampe [lahmpə]
land das Land [lahndə]
landing stage der (Landungs-)Steg [(lahn-duhngs-)Steyk]
landlady die Wirtin [vihr-tihn]
landlord der Wirt [vihrt]
language die Sprache [Sprahxə]
large groß [grohs]
last letzte(r, -s) [lehtstə(r,s)]; zuletzt [tsoo-**lehtst**]; (v) halten [hahltən], dauern [dauərn]; **last but one/second to the last** vorletzte(r, -s) [for-lehtstə(r,s)]
late spät [Speyt]; **be late** (v) s. verspäten [fehr-**Speytən**]
later später [Speytər]
laugh (v) lachen [lahxən]
lavatory die Toilette [toy-**leh**tə]
law and order Recht und Ordnung [reçt uhnt ord-nuhng]
lawn der Rasen [rahzən]
lazy faul [faul]
lead (v) führen [fewrən]
leaf das Blatt [blaht]
leaflet der Prospekt [proh-**spehkt**]
lean mager [mahgər]
learn (v) erfahren [ehr-**fahr**ən], lernen [lehrnən]
least das wenigste [vey-nihkstə]; **at least** mindestens [mihndəstəns], wenigstens [vey-nikstəns]

A/Z

leather das Leder [leydər]

leave (v) hinterlassen [hihntər-**lahs**ən], abfahren (von) [ahp-fahrən (fon)], verlassen [fehr-**lahs**ən], weggehen [vehk-geyən], hinausgehen [hihn-**aus**-geyən]; **leave (behind)** (v) zurücklassen [tsuh-**rewk**-lahsən]; **leave (for)** (v) abreisen (nach) [ahp-rayzən (nahx)]

left(-hand) linke(r, -s) [lihŋkə(r,s)]; **on the left, to the left** links [lihŋks]

left übrig [ewb-rihç]; **be left** (v) übrig bleiben [ewb-rihç blaybən]

lend (v) leihen [layən]

length die Länge [lehŋə]

less geringer [geh-**rihŋ**ər], weniger [vey-nihgər]

lesson die Unterrichtsstunde [uhntər-rihks-Stuhndə]

let (v) (permit) lassen [lahsən]; (apartment, etc.) vermieten [fehr-**miit**ən]

letter der Brief [briif]

level (adj) flach [flahx]

license (v) zulassen [tsoo-lahsən]

license plate das (Auto-)Kennzeichen [(au-toh-)kehn-tsayçən]

lie die Lüge [lewgə]; (v) lügen [lewgən]; (in horizontal position) liegen [liigən]; **lie down** (v) s. hinlegen [hihn-leygən]

life das Leben [leybən]

lift (v) heben [heybən]

light das Licht [lihçt]; (weight) leicht [layçt]; (v) anzünden [ahn-tsewndən]

lighter das Feuerzeug [foyər-tsoyk]

lighthouse der Leuchtturm [loyçt-tuhrm]

lightning der Blitz [blihts]

like (comparison) wie [vii]; (v) (person) schätzen [Sehtsən]; mögen [mœgən]

likewise gleichfalls [glayç-fahls]

line (railroad) die Strecke [Strehkə], die Linie [lih-niyə]; (telephone) die Leitung [lay-tuhŋ]

linen (bed) die Wäsche [vehSə]

lining (clothing) das Futter [fuhtər]

liquid flüssig [flew-sihç]

list das Verzeichnis [fehr-**tsayç**-nihs], die Liste [lihstə]

listen (v) zuhören [tsoo-hœrən]

lit up beleuchtet [bə-**loyçt**ət]

little wenig [vey-nihç], klein [klayn], gering [geh-**rihŋ**]; **a little** etwas [eht-vahs]

live (v) leben [laybən], wohnen [vohnən]

lively lebhaft [leyp-hahft]

load (v) aufladen [auf-lahdən]

local einheimisch [ayn-hay-mihS]

location die Lage [lahgə]

lock (door) das Schloss [Slos], der Verschluss [fehr-**Sluhs**]; (v) verschließen [fehr-**Sliis**ən], abschließen [ahp-Sliisən]; **lock (up)** (v) zuschließen [tsoo-Sliisən]; **lock in/up** (v) einschließen [ein-Sliisən]

logical logisch [loh-gihS]

lonely einsam [ayn-zahm]

long (way) weit [vayt], lang [lahŋ]; **before long** demnächst [dehm-**nehkst**]; **as long as** solange [zoh-lahŋə]

look der Blick [blihk]; (v) aussehen [aus-zeyən], schauen [Sauən]; **look at** (v) anschauen [ahn-Sauən], ansehen [ahn-zeyən], betrachten [bə-**traxt**ən]; **look for** (v) suchen [zooxən]; **have a look** (v) nachsehen [nahx-zeyən]; **look after** (v) aufpassen (auf) [auf-pahsən (auf)], sorgen für [zorgən (fewr)]; **look around** (v) s. umsehen [uhm-zeyən]; **look like** (v) gleichen [glayçən]; **look out (for)** (v) Acht geben (auf) [ahxt geybən (auf)]; **look out!** Achtung! [ahx-tuhŋ]

lose (v) verlieren [fehr-**liir**ən]; **lose one's way** (v) s. verirren [fehr-**ihr**ən]; **lose weight** (v) abnehmen [ahp-neymən]

loss der Verlust [fehr-**luhst**]; **get lost** (v) s. verirren [fehr-**ihr**ən]; **lost and found office** das Fundbüro [fuhnt-bew-roh]

lot das Los [lohs]; **the lot** alles [ahləs], der ganze Kram [gahntsə krahm]; **a lot of** viel [fiil], eine Menge [mehŋə]

loud laut [laut]

loudspeaker der Lautsprecher [laut-Sprehçər]

love die Liebe [liibə]; (v) lieben [liibən]

low tief [tiif], leise [layzə]

low season außerhalb der Saison [ausər-hahlp dehr zeh-**zohn**]

loyal treu [troy]

luck das Glück [glewk]; **good luck!** viel Glück! [fiil glewk]

lucky glücklich [glewk-lihç]; **be lucky** (v) Glück haben [glewk hahbən]

lunch das Mittagessen [mih-tahk-ehsən]

lust die Lust [luhst]

luxurious luxuriös [luhk-soor-**yœs**]
luxury der Luxus [luhk-suhs]

M

machine die Maschine [mah-**Siin**ə]
mad verrückt [fehr-**rewkt**]
magazine das Heft [hehft]
mail (v) aufgeben [auf-geybən]
maintain (v) behaupten [bə**haupt**ən]
make (v) (produce) machen [mahxən], schaffen [Sahfən]; (coffee, tea) kochen [koxən]; **make good** (Schaden) (v) ersetzen [ehr-**zehts**ən]; **make up one's mind** (v) beschließen [bə**Sliis**ən]; **put on make-up** (v) s. schminken [Smihŋkən]
male männlich [mehn-lihç]
man der Mann [mahn]; (mankind) der Mensch [mehnS]
management die Direktion [dih-rehk-**tsyohn**]
manager der Direktor [dih-**rehk**-tor], der Leiter [laytər]
manner die Weise [vayzə]; **manners** das Benehmen [bə-**neym**ən]
map die Landkarte [lahnt-kahrtə]
mark das Kennzeichen [kehn-tsayçən]
marriage die Heirat [hay-raht], die Ehe [eyə]
married couple das Ehepaar [eyə-paht]
marry (v) heiraten [hay-rah-ten]
marsh der Sumpf [zuhmpf]
marvelous wunderbar [vuhndər-bahr]
mass (rel) die Messe [mehsə]
match das Streichholz [Strayç-holts]
matchbox die Streichholzschachtel [Strayç-holts-Sahxtəl]
material das Material [mah-tehr-**yahl**], der Stoff [Stof]
matter die Angelegenheit [ahn-gəleygən-hayt], die Sache [zahxə]; **settle a matter** (v) eine Angelegenheit erledigen [ahn-gəleygən-hayt ehr-**ley**-dihgən]
mature reif [rayf]
maybe vielleicht [fih-**layçt**]
me mir [miir], mich [mihç]; **as for me** meinerseits [maynər-zayts]; **to me** mir [miir]
meadow die Wiese [viizə]

meal das Essen [ehsən], die Mahlzeit [mahl-tsayt]
mean gemein [gə**mayn**]; (v) bedeuten [bə**doyt**ən]
meaning die Bedeutung [bə**doy**-tuhŋ]
means das Mittel [mihtəl]
meanwhile inzwischen [ihn-**tsvihS**ən]
measure das Maß [mahs]; (v) messen [mehsən]
meat das Fleisch [flayS]
meet (v) treffen [trehfən], begegnen [bə**geyg**nən]; kennen lernen [kehnən lehrnən]; **arrange to meet** (v) s. verabreden [zihç fehr-**ahp**-reydən]; **meet again** (v) wieder sehen [viidər zeyən]
memo die (Haus-)Mitteilung [(haus-)miht-tay-luhŋ]
men die Männer [mehnər]
mend (v) flicken [flihkən]
menu die Speisekarte [Spayzə-kahrtə]
merit der Verdienst [fehr-**diinst**]
merry lustig [luhs-tihç], froh [froh]
message die Nachricht [nahx-rihçt]
middle die Mitte [mihtə]
midnight die Mitternacht [mihtər-nahxt]
mild mild [mihlt]
mile die Meile [maylə]
mind das Gedächtnis [gə**dehçt**-nihs] (memory), der Verstand [fehr-**Stahnt**], der Sinn [zihn]; (v) (be-)achten [(bə-)ahxtən]; **I don't mind** meinetwegen [mayn-eht-veygən]; **make up one's mind** (v) s. entschließen [zihç ehnt-**Sliis**ən]
minus minus [mii-nuhs]
minute die Minute [mih-**noot**ə]
miscalculate (v) s. verrechnen [fehr-**rehç**nən]
misfortune das Unglück [uhn-glewk]
Miss das Fräulein [froy-layn]
miss (v) verfehlen [fehr-**feyl**ən]; versäumen [fehr-zoymən]; **be missing** (v) fehlen [feylən]
mistake der Fehler [feylər], der Irrtum [ihr-tuhm]; **mistake for** (v) vertauschen [fehr-**tauS**ən], verwechseln [fehr-**vehks**əln]; **by mistake** aus Versehen [aus fehr-**zey**ən]; **make a mistake** (v) einen Fehler machen [aynən feylər mahxən], s. verrechnen [fehr-**rehç**nən]; **be mistaken** (v) s. täuschen [toyçən], s. irren [ihrən]

misty neblig [neyb-lihç]

misunderstand *(v)* missverstehen [mihs-fehr-Steyən]

misunderstanding das Missverständnis [mihs-fehr-Stehnt-nihs]

mix (v) *(drinks)* zubereiten [tsoo-bəraytən]; **mix up** *(v)* vertauschen [fehr-**tauS**ən]

mixed gemischt [gəmihSt]

model das Muster [muhstər]

moderate mäßig [meh-sihç]

modern modern [moh-**dehrn**]

moist nass [nahs], feucht [foyçt]

moment der Moment [moh-**mehnt**], der Augenblick [augən-blihk]

money das Geld [gehlt]

month der Monat [moh-naht]

monthly monatlich [moh-naht-lihç]

mood die Laune [launə]; **in a good mood** lustig [luhs-tihç]

moon der Mond [mont]

more mehr [mehr]; **more or less** mehr oder weniger [mehr ohdər vey-nihgər]; **more than** mehr als [mehr ahls]

morning der Morgen [morgən], der Vormittag [for-mih-tahk]; **in the morning** vormittags [for-mih-tahks]

mosquito die Mücke [mewkə]

most meist [mayst], am meisten [ahm maystən]; **at (the) most** höchstens [hœkstəns]

mother die Mutter [muhtər]

motive der Grund [gruhnt]

mountain der Berg [behrk]

mouth der Mund [muhnt]; *(river)* die Mündung [mewn-duhŋ]

move *(v)* bewegen [bəveygən]; *(to another house)* umziehen [uhm-tsiiən]

movement die Bewegung [bəvey-guhŋ]

movie der Film [fihlm]

Mr. Herr [hehr]

Mrs. Frau [frau]

Ms. Frau [frau]

much viel [fiil]

mud der Schlamm [Slahm]

mud flats das Watt [vaht]

mug der Becher [behçər]; *(v)* überfallen [ewbər-**fahl**ən]

music die Musik [moo-**ziik**]

must *(v)* müssen [mewsən]

my mein [mayn]; **I did it myself** ich habe es selbst gemacht [ihç hahbə ehs zehlpst gəmahxt]

N

nail der Nagel [nahgəl]

naked nackt [nahkt]

name der Name [nahmə]; *(v)* nennen [nehnən]; **what's your name?** wie heißen Sie? [vii haysən zii]

narrow schmal [Smahl], eng [ehŋ]

nation die Nation [naht-**syohn**]

native einheimisch [ayn-hay-mihS]; **native country** die Heimat [hay-maht]

natural natürlich [nah-tewr-lihç]

nature die Natur [nah-**toor**]

naughty böse [bœzə]

near nahe [nah-ə], in der Nähe von [ihn dehr neyə fon], bei [bay]; **near by** dicht dabei [dihçt dah-**bay**]

nearly beinahe [bay-nah-ə], fast [fahst]

neat ordentlich [ordənt-lihç]

necessary nötig [nœ-tihç], notwendig [noht-**veh**-dihç]

necessity die Notwendigkeit [noht-vehn-dihç-kayt]

necklace die Halskette [hals-kehtə]

need *(v)* brauchen [brauxən], benötigen [bənœ-tihgən]

needle die Nadel [nahdəl]

negative negativ [ney-gah-**tiif**]

neglect *(v)* vernachlässigen [fehr-**nahx**-leh-sihgən]

negligent nachlässig [nahx-leh-sihç]

negotiation die Verhandlung [fehr-**hahnd**-luhŋ]

neighbor der/die Nachbar/in [nahx-bahr / -ihn]

neither auch nicht [aux nihçt]; **neither … nor** weder … noch [veydər ... nohx]

nephew der Neffe [nehfə]

nervous nervös [nehr-**vœs**]

net das Netz [nehts]

never nie [nii]

nevertheless trotzdem [trots-dehm]

new neu [noy], frisch [frihS]

news die Nachrichten [nahx-rihçtən] *f pl*, die Neuigkeit [noy-ihç-kayt]

news dealer der Zeitungshändler [tsay-tuhŋs-hehndlər]

newspaper die Zeitung [tsay-tuhŋ]

newsstand der Zeitungskiosk [tsay-tuhŋs-kii-osk]

next nächste(r, s) [nehkstə(r,s)]; **next to** neben [neybən]

nice nett [neht], lieb [liip], sympathisch [zewm-**pah**-tihS]

niece die Nichte [nihçtə]

night die Nacht [nahxt]; der Abend [ahbənt]

no nein [nayn]; kein [kayn]; **in no way** keinesfalls [kaynəs-fahls]

nobody keine(r, s) [kaynə(r,s)], niemand [nii-mahnt]

noise das Geräusch [gəroyS], der Lärm [lehrm]

noisy laut [laut]

noon der Mittag [mih-tahk]; **at noon** mittags [mih-tahks]

nor auch nicht [aux nihçt]

normal normal [nor-**mahl**]

normally normalerweise [nor-**mahl**ər-vayzə]

north der Norden [nordən]

North Sea die Nordsee [nort-zey]

northern nördlich [**nœrd**-lihç]

not nicht [nihçt]; **not at all** gar nicht [duhrç nihçt], durchaus nicht [duhrç-**aus** nihçt]; **not yet** noch nicht [nox nihçt]

note die Aufzeichnung [auf-tsayç-nuhŋ]; der Geldschein [gehlt-Sayn]; **make a note of** (v) notieren [noh-**tiir**ən]

notebook das (Schreib-)Heft [(Srayp-)hehft]

nothing nichts [nihçts]; **nothing but** nichts als [nihçts ahls]; **nothing else** sonst nichts [zonst nihçts]

notice (v) bemerken [bə**mehrk**ən]

notion die Vorstellung [for-Steh-luhŋ]

nourishing nahrhaft [nahr-hahft]

now nun [nuhn], zur Zeit [tsuhr tsayt], jetzt [yehtst]; **just now** eben [eybən]; **till now** bis jetzt [bihs yehtst]

nowhere nirgends [nihrgənts]

nude nackt [nahkt]

number die Nummer [nuhmər]; (v) nummerieren [nuhmə-**riir**ən]

numerous zahlreich [tsahl-rayç]

nun die Nonne [nonə]

nurse die Krankenschwester [krahŋkən-Svehstər]

O

object der Gegenstand [geygən-Stahnt]

obligation die Verpflichtung [fehr-**pflihç**-tuhŋ], der Zwang [tsvahŋ]; **without**

obligation unverbindlich [uhn-fehr-bihnt-lihç]; **be obliged to** (v) verpflichtet sein [fehr-**pflihç**tət]

observe (v) beobachten [bey-**oh**-bahxtən]

obtain (v) beschaffen [bəSahfən], verschaffen [fehr-Sahfən], erlangen [ehr-lahŋən]

obtainable erhältlich [ehr-**hehlt**-lihç]

occasion die Gelegenheit [gə-**leyg**ən-hayt], der Anlass [ahn-lahs]

occasionally gelegentlich [gə**leyg**ənt-lihç]

occupied (seat) besetzt [bəzehtst]

occurrence der Vorfall [for-fahl]

ocean der Ozean [oht-sey-ahn]

of von [fon]; (material) aus [aus]; **of course!** natürlich [na-**tewr**-lihç], selbstverständlich! [zehlpst-fehr-Stehnd-lihç]

offend (v) beleidigen [bəlay-dihgən]

offer (v) anbieten [ahn-biitən], bieten [biitən]

office (position) das Amt [ahmt], das Büro [bew-**roh**]

official amtlich [ahmt-lihç], offiziell [o-fihts-**yehl**]

often oft [oft]

oil das Öl [œl]

old alt [ahlt]

old-fashioned altmodisch [ahlt-moh-dihS]

on an [ahn], auf [auf]; **on a journey/trip** auf der Reise [auf dehr rayzə]; **on Sunday** am Sonntag [ahm zon-tahk]; **on the Rhine** am Rhein [ahm rayn]; **on no account** keinesfalls [kaynəs-fahls]

once einmal [ayn-mahl]; **all at once** auf einmal [auf ayn-mahl]; **at once** sofort [zoh-**fort**], gleich [glayç]

one ein(e) [ayn(ə)], eins [ayns]; **one and a half** anderthalb [ahndərt-hahlp]; man [mahn]

only einzig [ayn-tsihç]; (not before) erst [ehrst]; nur [nuhr]

open offen [ofən], geöffnet [gə**œfn**ət]; (v) öffnen [œfnən], aufmachen [auf-mahxən]; **in the open air** im Freien [ihm frayən]

opening hours die Öffnungszeiten [œf-nuhŋs-tsaytən] f pl

operate (v) operieren [oh-peh-**riir**ən]

A/Z

opinion die Ansicht [ahn-zihçt], das Urteil [oor-tayl], die Meinung [may-nuhŋ]
opportunity (günstige) Gelegenheit [(gewns-tihgə) gəleygən-hayt]
opposite das Gegenteil [geygən-tayl]; entgegengesetzt [ehnt-**geyg**ən-gəzehtst]; gegenüber [geygən-**ewb**ər]; **in the opposite direction** in entgegengesetzter Richtung [ihn ehnt-**geyg**ən-gəzehtstər rihç-tuhŋ]
or oder [ohdər]
order die Ordnung [ord-nuhŋ]; *(rel)* der Orden [ordən]; die Bestellung [bəSteh-luhŋ]; *(v)* bestellen [bəStehlən]; **out of order** kaputt [kah-puht]; **order in advance** *(v)* vorbestellen [for-bəStehlən]
orderly ordentlich [ordənt-lihç]
ordinary gewöhnlich [gəvœn-lihç]
organize *(v)* veranstalten [fehr-**ahn**-Stahltən]
other der/die/das andere [ahndərə]; **the other day** neulich [noy-lihç]
otherwise sonst [zonst]
ought to *(v)* sollen [zolən]
our unser(e) [uhnzər(ə)]
out of order kaputt [kah-**puht**]
outdoors im Freien [ihm frayən]
outside außen [ausən], außerhalb [ausər-hahlp], draußen [drausən]
outskirts die Peripherie [peh-rih-feh-rii]; der Stadtrand [Staht-rahnt]
outward äußerlich [oysər-lihç]
over über [ewbər], vorüber [for-**ewb**ər], vorbei [for-**bay**]
over there drüben [drewbən]
overcrowded überfüllt [ewbər-**fewlt**]
overseas die Übersee [ewbər-zey]
owe *(v)* schulden [Suhldən]
own eigen [aygən]; *(v)* besitzen [bə**zihts**ən]
owner der/die Besitzer/in [bə**zihts**ər / -ihn], der/die Eigentümer/in [aygən-tewmər / -ihn]

P

pack die Packung [pah-kuhŋ]; *(v)* packen [pahkən], einpacken [ayn-pahkən], verpacken [fehr-**pahk**ən]
package das Päckchen [pehkçən]

packing die Verpackung [fehr-**pah**-kuhŋ]
page die Seite [zaytə]
painful schmerzhaft [Smehrts-hahft]
  take pains *(v)* s. Mühe geben [mewə geybən]
paint *(v)* malen [mahlən]; **painter** der/die Maler/in [mahlər / -ihn]
painting das Bild [bihlt]
pair das Paar [pahr]; **a pair of** ein Paar [pahr]
pale bleich [blayç]
pane *(window)* die Scheibe [Saybə]
panorama das Panorama [pah-no-**rahm**ə]
paragraph der Absatz [ahp-zahts]
parcel das Paket [pah-**keht**]
pardon die Verzeihung [fehr-**tsay**-uhŋ]; **I beg your pardon!** Ich bitte um Entschuldigung [ihç bihtə uhm ehnt-**Suhl**-dih-guhŋ]; **Pardon?** wie bitte? [vii bihtə]
parents die Eltern [ehltərn] *n pl*
park die Anlage [ahn-lahgə]; der Park [pahrk]; *(v) (car)* abstellen [ahp-Stehlən], parken [pahrkən]
part der Teil [tayl]
particularly besonders [bəzondərs]
particulars die Personalien [pehr-soh-**nahl**yən] *f pl*, nähere Angaben [neyərə ahn-gahbən]
party das Fest [fehst]
pass *(mountain)* der Pass [pahs]; *(v)* reichen [rayçən]; *(time)* vergehen [fehr-geyən], vorübergehen [for-**ewb**ər-geyən], vorbeigehen [for-**bay**-geyən]; überholen [ewbər-**hohl**ən]
passage der Durchgang [duhrç-gahŋ], der Gang [gahŋ], die Passage [pah-**sahZ**ə]
passenger der Fahrgast [fahr-gahst]
passing through auf der Durchreise [duhrç-rayzə]
passport der Pass [pahs]
past die Vergangenheit [fehr-**gahŋ**ən-hayt]; vorüber [for-**ewb**ər], vorbei [for-**bay**]
path der Weg [veyk], der Pfad [pfaht]
patience die Geduld [gəduhlt]
patient geduldig [gə**duhl**-dihç]
pawnshop die Pfandleihe [pfahnd-layə]
pay *(v)* zahlen [tsahlən], bezahlen [bə**tsahl**ən]

payment die Zahlung [tsah-luhŋ]
peace der Friede [friidə]
peak *(career)* der Höhepunkt [hœə-puhŋkt]
pear die Birne [bihrnə]
peculiar eigen [aygən]
pedestrian der/die Fußgänger/in [fuhs-gehŋər / -ihn]
peg der Kleiderhaken [klaydər-hahkən]
pen der Füller [fewlər]; der Kuli [koo-lii]
pencil der Bleistift [blay-Stihft]
people das Volk [folk], Leute [loytə] *pl*
per pro [proh]
percent das Prozent [proh-**tsehnt**]
percentage der Prozentsatz [proh-**tsehnt**-sahts]
perfect vollkommen [fol-**kom**ən]
performance *(theater)* die Vorstellung [for-Steh-luhŋ]
perhaps vielleicht [fih-**layçt**]; eventuell [ey-vehn-too-**ehl**]
period *(punct.)* der Punkt [puhŋkt]
permission die Erlaubnis [ehr-**laup**-nihs]; **grant permission** *(v)* genehmigen [gəney-mihgən]
permit *(v)* erlauben [ehr-**laub**ən], zulassen [tsoo-lahsən]
permitted zulässig [tsoo-leh-sihç]
person die Person [pehr-**zohn**]; der Mensch [mehnS]
personal persönlich [pehr-**zœn**-lihç]
personal data die Personalien [pehr-zoh-**nahly**ən] *f pl*
perspire *(v)* schwitzen [Svihtsən]
persuade *(v)* überreden [ewbər-**reyd**ən]
phone *(v)* telefonieren [teh-leh-foh-**niir**ən], anrufen [ahn-roofən]; **make a phone call** *(v)* telefonieren [teh-leh-foh-**niir**ən]
photo die Aufnahme [auf-nahmə], das Foto [foh-toh]; **take a photo** *(v)* fotografieren [foh-toh-grah-**fiir**ən]
pick *(v)* pflücken [pflewkən]
pick out *(v)* aussuchen [aus-zooxən]
pick up *(v)* abholen [ahp-hohlən]
picture das Bild [bihlt]; **take pictures** *(v)* fotografieren [foh-toh-grah-**fiir**ən]
piece das Stück [Stewk]
pier die Mole [mohlə]
pillow das Kopfkissen [kopf-kihsən]
pin die Stecknadel [Stehk-nahdəl]
pipe die Pfeife [pfayfə]; *(gas, water)* die Leitung [lay-tuhŋ]

pity das Mitleid [miht-layt]; **it's a pity** es ist schade [ehs ihst Sahdə]; **what a pity!** wie schade! [vii Sahdə]
place die Stelle [Stehlə], der Platz [plahts], der Ort [ort]
plain die Ebene [eybənə]
plan der Plan [plahn]
plant die Pflanze [pflahntsə]
plaster der Gips [gihps]
plastic das Plastik [plah-stihk]; der Kunststoff [kuhnst-Stof]
plate der Teller [tehlər]
play das Stück [Stewk]; *(v)* spielen [Spiilən]
pleasant sympathisch [zewm-**pah**-tihS], angenehm [ahn-gənaym]
please bitte [bihtə]; *(v)* gefallen [gəfahlən]; **be pleased (with/about)** *(v)* s. freuen (über) [froyən (ewbər)]
pleasure die Freude [froydə], das Gefallen [gəfahlən], die Lust [luhst], das Vergnügen [fehr-**gnew**gən]
plugged *(up)* verstopft [fehr-**Stopft**]
plus plus [pluhs]
pocket die Tasche [tahSə]
point die Spitze [Spihtsə], der Punkt [puhŋkt]
pointed spitz [Spihts]
pointless zwecklos [tsvehk-lohs]
poison das Gift [gihft]
poisonous giftig [gihf-tihç]
policy die Politik [po-lih-**tiik**]
polite höflich [hœf-lihç]
politeness die Höflichkeit [hœf-lihç-kayt]
politics die Politik [po-lih-**tiik**]
pool das Schwimmbad [Svihm-baht]
poor arm [ahrm]
posh vornehm [for-neym]
position *(profession)* die Stellung [Steh-luhŋ]; *(location)* die Lage [lahgə]
positive positiv [poh-zih-**tiif**]
possession der Besitz [bəzihts]
possibility die Möglichkeit [mœg-lihç-kayt]
possible möglich [mœg-lihç]; eventuell [ey-vehn-too-**ehl**]; **make possible** *(v)* ermöglichen [ehr-**mœg**-lihçən]
post office die Post [post]; **to/at the post office** auf die/der Post [auf dii/dehr post]
postcard die Postkarte [post-kahrtə]
poster das Plakat [plah-**kaht**]

A/Z

postpone *(v)* verschieben [fehr-**Siib**ən], aufschieben [auf-Siibən]

pot der Topf [topf]

pottery die Keramik [keh-**rah**-mihk]

powder das Pulver [puhlfər]

power of attorney die Vollmacht [fol-mahxt]

practical praktisch [prahk-tihS]

practice die Übung [ew-buhŋ]; *(v)* üben [ewbən]; *(profession)* ausüben [aus-ewbən]

praise *(v)* loben [lohbən]

pray *(v)* beten [beytən]

prayer das Gebet [gəbeyt]

prefer *(v)* etw. lieber haben [liibər hahbən], vorziehen [for-tsiiən]

preference der Vorzug [for-tsuhk]

pregnant schwanger [Svahŋər]

preparation die Vorbereitung [for-bə-ray-tuhŋ]

prepare *(v)* vorbereiten [for-bəraytən], zubereiten [tsoo-bəraytən]

present das Geschenk [gə**Sehŋk**]; anwesend [ahn-veyzənt]; **at present** zur Zeit [tsuhr tsayt]; **be present** *(v)* da sein [dah zayn]; **give as a present** *(v)* schenken [Sehŋkən]

press *(v) (button)* drücken [drewkən]

pretext der Vorwand [for-vahnt]

pretty *(adj)* hübsch [hewpS]; *(adv, fam)* ziemlich [tsiim-lihç]

prevent *(v)* verhindern [fehr-**hihnd**ərn], hindern [hihndərn]

price der Preis [prays]

priest der Priester [priistər]

principal der Rektor [rehk-tor], der Direktor [dih-**rehk**-tor]; *(adj)* hauptsächlich [haupt-zehç-lihç]

private privat [prii-**vaht**]

prize der Preis [prays]

probability die Wahrscheinlichkeit [vahr-**Sayn**-lihç-kayt]

probable wahrscheinlich [vahr-**Sayn**-lihç]

probably wahrscheinlich [vahr-**Sayn**-lihç]

problem das Problem [proh-**blehm**], die Frage [frahgə]

problems Ärger [ehrgər], der Kummer [kuhmər]

procession die Prozession [proh-tsehs-**yohn**]

produce *(v)* erzeugen [ehr-**tsoyg**ən]

product das Erzeugnis [ehr-**tsoyg**-nihs], das Produkt [proh-**duhkt**], die Ware [vahrə]

profession der Beruf [bə**roof**]

profit der Gewinn [gə**vihn**]

program das Programm [proh-**grahm**]; *(radio, tv)* die Sendung [zehn-duhŋ]

progress der Fortschritt [fort-Sriht]

prohibited verboten [fehr-**boht**ən]

promise das Versprechen [fehr-**Sprehç**ən]; *(v)* versprechen [fehr-**Sprehç**ən]

pronounce aussprechen [aus-Sprehçən]

pronunciation die Aussprache [aus-Sprahxə]

proof der Beweis [bə**vays**]

proper richtig [rihç-tihç]

property der Besitz [bə**zihts**]

prospectus der Prospekt [proh-**spehkt**]

protect *(v)* beschützen [bə**Sewt**sən]

protection der Schutz [Suhts]

protest *(v)* protestieren [proh-tehs-**tiir**ən]

prove *(v)* beweisen [bə**vayz**ən]

provide (with) *(v)* versorgen (mit) [fehr-**zorg**ən (miht)]

provisional provisorisch [proh-vii-**zoh**-rihS]

provisions der Vorrat [for-raht]

pub die Kneipe [knaypə], das Lokal [loh-**kahl**]

public das Publikum [puh-blih-kuhm]; öffentlich [œfənt-lihç]

pull *(v)* ziehen [tsiiən], reißen [raysən]

pump up *(v)* aufpumpen [auf-puhmpən]

punctual pünktlich [pewŋkt-lihç]

puncture das Loch [lox]

punishment die Strafe [Strahfə]

puppet die (Hand-)Puppe [(hahnt-)puhpə]

purchase die Besorgung [bə**zor**-guhŋ], der Kauf [kauf]

purpose der Zweck [tsvehk]; **on purpose** absichtlich [ahp-zihçt-lihç]

purse *(handbag)* die Handtasche [hahnt-tahS]

push der Stoß [Stohs]; *(v)* stoßen [Stohsən], drücken [drewkən], schieben [Siibən]

put *(v)* legen [leygən], stellen [Stehlən], setzen [zehtsən]; **put down** *(v)* hinlegen [hihn-leygən]; **put off** *(v)* verschieben [fehr-**Siib**ən], aufschieben [auf-Siibən]; **put on** *(v)* anziehen

A/Z

[ahn-tsiien]; **put up** *(v)* aufstellen [auf-Stehlən]; **put out** (v) *(fire, etc.)* ausmachen [aus-mahxən], löschen [lœSən]

Q

quality die Qualität [kvah-lih-**teyt**], die Eigenschaft [aygən-Sahft]
quantity die Menge [mehŋə]
quarrel der Streit [Strayt]; *(v)* streiten [Straytən], s. zanken [tsahŋkən]
a quarter ein Viertel [fiirtəl]
question die Frage [frahgə]
quick schnell [Snehl]; rasch [rahs]
quickly rasch [rahS]
quiet leise [layzə], ruhig [roo-ihç]; **keep quiet** *(v)* schweigen [Svaygən]
quite ganz [gahnts]

R

radiant glänzend [glehntsənd]
radio das Radio [rahd-yoh]
rage die Wut [voot]
railings das Gitter [gihtər]
rain *(v)* regnen [reygnən]
raise *(v)* *(price)* heraufsetzen [hehr-**auf**-zehtsən]
ramble *(v)* wandern [vahndərn]
rape *(v)* vergewaltigen [fehr-gəvahl-tihgən]
rare selten [zehltən]
rather lieber [liibər]; vielmehr [fiil-mehr], eher [eyər]; ziemlich [tsiim-lihç]
ray der Strahl [Strahl]
reach *(v)* erreichen [ehr-**ray**çən]
read *(v)* lesen [leyzən]
ready fertig [fehr-tihg], bereit [bərayt]
real wirklich [vihrk-lihç]
reality die Wirklichkeit [vihrk-lihç-kayt]
realize (v) *(understand)* erkennen [ehr-**kehn**ən], verwirklichen [fehr-**vihrk**-lihçən]
really unbedingt [uhn-bədihŋt]; wirklich [vihrk-lihç]
reason der Verstand [fehr-**Stahnt**]; der Anlass [ahn-lahs], der Grund [gruhnt], die Ursache [oor-zahxə]

reasonable vernünftig [fehr-**newnf**-tihç]
receipt die Quittung [kvih-tuhŋ]; **give a receipt** *(v)* quittieren [kvih-**tiir**ən]
receive *(v)* erhalten [ehr-hahltən], empfangen [ehmp-**fahŋ**ən]
reception der Empfang [ehmp-fahŋən], die Aufnahme [auf-nahmə]
recognize *(v)* erkennen [ehr-**kehn**ən]
recommend *(v)* empfehlen [ehmp-**fey**lən]
recommendation die Empfehlung [ehmp-**fey**-luhŋ]
record die Schallplatte [Sahl-plahtə]
recover *(v)* s. erholen [ehr-**hoh**lən]
recovery die Erholung [ehr-**hoh**-luhŋ]
reduce *(v)* *(price)* herabsetzen [hehr-**ahp**-zehtsən]
reduction die Ermäßigung [ehr-**meh**-sih-guhŋ]
reed(s) das Schilf [Sihlf]
refer to *(v)* s. beziehen auf [bətsiiən auf]
refreshment die Erfrischung [ehr-**frih**-Suhŋ]
refund *(v)* zurückzahlen [tsuh-**rewk**-tsahlən]
refuse *(v)* zurückweisen [tsuh-**rewk**-vayzən], s. weigern [veygərn], ablehnen [ahp-leynən]
region die Gegend [geygənt]
register *(v)* s. anmelden [zihç ahn-mehldən]; *(baggage)* aufgeben [auf-geybən]; *(car)* zulassen [tsoo-lahsən]
regret das Bedauern [bədauərn]; *(v)* bedauern [bədauərn]
regular regelmäßig [reygəl-mey-sihç]
reject *(v)* zurückweisen [tsuh-**rewk**-vayzən]
related verwandt [fehr-**vahnt**]
reliable zuverlässig [tsoo-fehr-leh-sihç]
reluctantly ungern [uhn-gehrn], nicht gern [nihçt gehrn]
remind s. o. of s. th. *(v)* jdn an etw. erinnern [ahn ... ehr-**ihn**ərn]
remain *(v)* bleiben [blaybən]
remark *(v)* *(to comment)* bemerken [bə**mehrk**ən]
remedy das Heilmittel [hayl-mihtəl]
remember *(v)* s. erinnern [ehr-**ihn**ərn]; **remember s. th.** *(v)* s. etw. merken [mehrkən]
remote abgelegen [ahp-gəleygən]

A/Z

renew *(v)* erneuern [ehr-**noy**ərn]

rent die Miete [miitə]; *(v)* mieten [miitən], vermieten [fehr-**miit**ən]

repair die Reparatur [reh-pah-rah-**toor**]; *(v)* reparieren [rey-pah-**riir**ən]

repeat *(v)* wiederholen [viidər-**hohl**ən]

replace *(v)* ersetzen [ehr-**zeht**sən]

replacement der Ersatz [ehr-**zahts**]

reply *(v)* erwidern [ehr-**vihd**ərn], antworten [ahnt-vortən], beantworten [bəahnt-vortən]

report der Bericht [bərihçt]

request der Wunsch [vuhnS], die Bitte [bihtə]

reserve *(v)* reservieren [rey-zehr-**viir**ən]; **reserve a seat** *(v)* einen Platz belegen [aynən plahts bəleygən]

residence *(place of)* der Wohnsitz [vohn-zihts], der Wohnort [vohn-ort]

responsible zuständig [tsoo-Stehn-dihç], verantwortlich [fehr-**ahnt**-vort-lihç]

rest *(remainder)* der Rest [rehst], die Ruhe [rooə], die Erholung [ehr-**hoh**-luhŋ]; *(v)* ruhen [rooən], s. ausruhen [aus-rooən]

rest room die Toilette [toy-**leht**ə]

restaurant das Lokal [loh-**kahl**], das Restaurant [reh-stau-**rahnt**]

restless unruhig [uhn-roo-ihç]

result das Ergebnis [ehr-**geyp**-nihs]

retire *(v)* s. zurückziehen [tsuh-**rewk**-tsiiən]

return die Rückkehr [rewk-kehr]; *(v)* wiederkommen [viidər-komən], zurückkehren [tsuh-**rewk**-kehrən]; wiedergeben [viidər-geybən]

reverse umgekehrt [uhm-gəkehrt]

reward die Belohnung [bəloh-nuhŋ]; *(v)* belohnen [bəlohnən]

ribbon das (Haar-)Band [(hahr-)bahnt]

rich reich [rayç]

ridiculous lächerlich [lehçər-lihç]

right das Recht [rehçt]; richtig [rihç-tihç]; **right(-hand)** rechts [rehçts], rechte(r, s) [rehçtə(r,s)]; **be right** *(v)* Recht haben [rehçt hahbən]; **on the right, to the right** rechts [rehçts]; **that's right!** das stimmt! [dahs Stihmt]

rigid fest [fehst]

ring der Ring [rihŋ]; *(v)* läuten [loytən], anrufen [ahn-roofən], klingeln [klihŋəln]

ripe reif [rayf]

risk das Risiko [rih-zii-koh]

river der Strom [Strom], der Fluss [fluhs]

road die Straße [Strahsə], der Weg [veyk]

roast der Braten [brahtən]; *(v)* braten [brahtən]

rock der Fels [fehls]

room der Saal [zahl]; *(space)* der Raum [raum]

rope das Seil [zayl]

rotten faul [faul], verdorben [fehr-**dorb**ən]

rough *(sea)* bewegt [bəveykt]

round rund [ruhnt]; *(boxing)* die Runde [ruhndə]; *(drinks)* die Runde [ruhndə]

route die Route [rootə]; (road) die Strecke [Stehkə]

row die Reihe [rayə]

rude unanständig [uhn-ahn-Stehn-dihç]

rule die Vorschrift [for-Srihft]

run *(v)* rennen [rehnən], laufen [laufən]; (nose) tropfen [tropfən]; *(bus, etc.)* verkehren [fehr-**kehr**ən]; **run into** *(v)* *(street)* münden [mewndən]

S

sack der Sack [zahk]

sad traurig [trau-rihç]

safe sicher [zihçər]

safety die Sicherheit [zihçər-hayt]; **safety pin** die Sicherheitsnadel [Sihçər-hayts-nahdəl]

sale der Verkauf [fehr-**kauf**]; **(clearance) sale** der Ausverkauf [aus-fehr-kauf]

same gleich [glayç]; **the same** dasselbe [dahs-**zehlb**ə], derselbe [dehr-**zehlb**ə]

sample das Muster [muhstər]

satisfied befriedigt [bəfrii-dihçt], zufrieden [tsoo-**frii**dən]

save *(v)* retten [rehtən]; sparen [Spahrən]

say *(v)* sagen [zahgən]

scales die Waage [vahgə]

scarcely kaum [kaum]

scarf das (Kopf-)Tuch [(kopf-)tuhx]; der Schal [Sahl]

school die Schule [Soolə]

scissors die Schere [Sehrə]

Scotland das Schottland [Sot-lahnt]

Scotsman der Schotte [Sotə]

Scotswoman die Schottin [So-tihn]
Scottish schottisch [So-tihS]
scream (v) schreien [Srayən]
sculpture die Skulptur [skuhlp-**toor**]
sea die See [zey], das Meer [meyr]
seagull die Möwe [mœvə]
seaside resort der Badeort [bahdə-ort]
season die Saison [zeh-**zohn**], die Jahreszeit [yahrəs-tsayt]; **in the off season** außerhalb der Saison [ausər-hahlp dehr zeh-**zohn**]
seat der Sitz [zihts], der Sitzplatz [zihts-plahts]
secluded einsam [ayn-zahm]
second zweite(r, s) [tsvaytə(r,s)], die Sekunde [zeh-**kuhndə**]; **second(ly)** zweitens [tsvaytəns]; **second to the last** vorletzte(r, -s) [for-lehtstə(r,s)]
secret heimlich [haym-lihç], geheim [gəhaym]; **keep secret** (v) verheimlichen [fehr-**haym**-lihçən]
security die Sicherheit [zihçər-hayt], der Schutz [Suhts]; die Kaution [kaut-**syohn**], die Bürgschaft [bewrk-Sahft]
see (v) sehen [zeyən]; **see again** (v) wieder sehen [viidər zeyən]; **see s. o.** (v) s. an jdn wenden [an ... vehndən]
seem (v) scheinen [Saynən]
seize (v) ergreifen [ehr-**grayf**ən]
seldom selten [zehltən]
self service die Selbstbedienung [zehlpst-bədii-nuhŋ]
sell (v) verkaufen [fehr-**kauf**ən]
send (v) senden [zehndən], schicken [Sihkən]; **send for** (v) abholen lassen [ahp-hohlən lahsən]
sense der Sinn [zihn]
sensible vernünftig [fehr-**newnf**-tihç]
sensitive zartfühlend [tsahrt-fewlənt], sensibel [zehn-**ziib**əl]
sentence der Satz [zahts]
separate getrennt [gə**trehnt**], einzeln [ayn-tsehln]; (v) trennen [trehnən]
serious ernst [ehrnst]; (illness) schwer [Svehr]
sermon die Predigt [prey-dihçt]
serve (v) servieren [zehr-**viir**ən], bedienen [bə**diin**ən], dienen [diinən]
service der Dienst [diinst], die Bedienung [bə**dii**-nuhŋ]
set (v) setzen [zehtsən], hin-, aufstellen [hihn-, auf-Stehlən]; (tv) der (Fernseh-) Apparat [(fehrn-zey-)ah-pah-raht]

settle (v) regeln [reygəln], erledigen [ehr-**ley**-dihgən]
severe (wound, accident) schwer [Svehr]; (judgment, winter) streng [Strehŋ]
sex der Sex [zehks]
shade die Schatten [Sahtən]; (color) der Ton [tohn]
shadow der Schatten [Sahtən]
shape die Form [form]
share (v) teilen [taylən]
sharp scharf [Sahrfə]; (pencil etc.) spitz [Spihts]
shave (v) rasieren [rah-**ziir**ən]
she sie [zii]
sheep das Schaf [Sahf]
shine (v) scheinen [Saynən], glänzen [glehntsən]; **shining** leuchtend [loyçtənt]
shoe der Schuh [Soo]; **shoelace** der Schnürsenkel [Snewrs-ehŋkəl]
shoot (v) schießen [Siisən]
shop das Geschäft [gə**Sehft**], der Laden [lahdən]; **shop window** das Schaufenster [Sau-fehnstər]; **go shopping** (v) einkaufen [ayn-kaufən]
shore (sea) das Ufer [oofər]
short kurz [kurts]; **at short notice** kurzfristig [kuhrts-frihs-tihç]
short cut die Abkürzung [ahp-kewrt-suhŋ]
shortage der Mangel [mahŋəl]
shot der Schuss [Suhs]
shout (v) schreien [Srayən]
shove der Stoß [Stos]
show die Ausstellung [aus-Steh-luhŋ]; die Revue [rey-voo]; (v) zeigen [tsaygən], vorzeigen [for-tsaygən]
shut zu [tsoo]; (v) schließen [Sliisən], zumachen [tsoo-mahxən]
shy schüchtern [Sewçtərn]
sick krank [krahŋk]; **I feel sick** mir ist übel [miir ihst ewbəl]
side die Seite [zaytə]
sign das Schild [Sihlt], das Zeichen [tsayçən]; (v) unterschreiben [uhntər-**Sray**bən]
signal das Signal [zihg-**nahl**]; (v) (car) blinken [blihŋkən]
signature die Unterschrift [uhntər-Sri-hft]
silence die Ruhe [rooə], das Schweigen [Svaygən]

A/Z

silent ruhig [roo-ihç]; **be silent** *(v)* schweigen [Svaygən]
silly blöd(e) [blœd(ə)]
similar ähnlich [ehn-lihç]
simple einfach [ayn-fahx]
simultaneously gleichzeitig [glayç-tsay-tihç]
since seit [zayt]; weil [vayl]; **since then** seitdem [zayt-dehm]; **since when?** seit wann? [zaht vahn]
sincere herzlich [hehrts-lihç]
sincerity die Herzlichkeit [herts-lihç-kayt]
sing *(v)* singen [zihŋən]; **singing** der Gesang [gəzahŋ]
single ledig [ley-dihç]
sip der Schluck [Sluhk]
sister die Schwester [Svehstər]
sister-in-law die Schwägerin [Sveygə-rihn]
sit *(v)* sitzen [zihtsən]; **sit down** *(v)* s. setzen, s. hinsetzen [hihn-zehtsən]
situation die Lage [lahgə]
size das Format [for-**maht**]; die Größe [grœsə]
skillful geschickt [gəSihkt]
sky der Himmel [hihməl]
skyscraper der Wolkenkratzer [volkən-krahtsər]
sleep der Schlaf [Slahf]; *(v)* schlafen [Slahfən]; **fall asleep** *(v)* einschlafen [ayn-Slahfən]
sleeper der Schlafwagen [Slahf-vahgən]
sleeping pill das Schlafmittel [Slahf-mihtəl]
slender schlank [Slahŋk], dünn [dewn]
slice *(bread)* die Scheibe [Saybə]
slide das Dia [dii-ah]
slight leicht [layçt]
slim dünn [dewn], schmal [Smahl], schlank [Slahŋk]
slippery glatt [glaht]
slope der Hang [hahŋ]
slow(ly) langsam [lahŋ-zahm]; **be slow** *(v)* *(clock)* nachgehen [nahx-geyən]
small gering [geh-**rihŋ**], klein [klayn]
smash *(v)* zerbrechen [tsehr-**brehçən**]
smell der Geruch [gərooх]; *(v)* riechen [riiçən], stinken [Stihŋkən]
smoke der Rauch [raux]; *(v)* rauchen [rauxən]

smooth glatt [glaht]
smuggle *(v)* schmuggeln [Smuhgəln]
snack der Imbiss [ihm-bihs]
snack bar der Schnellimbiss [Snehl-ihm-bihs]
snake die Schlange [Slahŋə]
snapshot die Aufnahme [auf-nahmə]; **take a snapshot** *(v)* knipsen [knihpsən]
sneeze *(v)* niesen [niizən]
snore *(v)* schnarchen [Snahrçən]
snow *(v)* schneien [Snayən]
so also [ahl-zoh]
soaked nass [nahs]
sober nüchtern [newçtərn]
society die Gesellschaft [gəzehl-Sahft]
soft weich [vayç]
solemn feierlich [fayər-lihç]
solid fest [fehst], hart [hahrt]
some einige [ay-nihgə]
somebody jemand [yey-mahnt]
somehow irgendwie [ihrgənt-vii]
someone irgendein(e, er, es) [ihrgənt-ayn(ə, ər, əs)]
someone else ein anderer [ayn ahndərər]
something etwas [eht-vahs]
somewhere irgendwohin [irgənt-voh-hihn], irgendwo [ihr-gənt-voh]
son der Sohn [zohn]
song das Lied [liit]
soon bald [bahlt]; **very soon** demnächst [dehm-**nehkst**]; **as soon as possible** so bald wie möglich [zoh bahlt vii mœg-lihç]
sort die Sorte [zortə], die Art [ahrt]
sound der Klang [klahŋ]
sour sauer [zauər]
source die Quelle [kvehlə]
south der Süden [zewdən]; **south of** südlich von [zewd-lihç]
southern südlich [zewd-lihç]
souvenir das Andenken [ahn-dehŋkən]
space der Raum [raum]; **outer space** der Weltraum [vehlt-raum]
spark der Funke [fuhŋkə]
speak *(v)* sprechen [Sprehçən]
special speziell [Speht-**syehl**], Sonder- [zondər-], extra [ehk-strah]
spectator der/die Zuschauer/in [tsoo-Sauər / -ihn]

speed die Geschwindigkeit [gə**Svihnd**-ihç-kayt]; **speed up** (v) beschleunigen [bə**Sloy**-nihgən]

spell (v) buchstabieren [buhx-Stah-**biirən**]

spend (v) ausgeben [aus-geybən]; (time) verbringen [fehr-**brihŋən**]; **spend the night** (v) übernachten [ewbər-**nahxtən**]

spicy scharf [Sahrf]

spirit die Seele [zeylə], das Temperament [tehm-peh-rah-**mehnt**], der Geist [gayst]

splendid herrlich [hehr-lihç]; (fig) glänzend [glehntsənd]

spoil (v) verderben [fehr-**dehrbən**]

spoiled verdorben [fehr-**dorbən**]

sport der Sport [Sport]

sports field der Sportplatz [Sport-plahts]

spot die Stelle [Stehlə]

spring die Feder [feydər]; (water) die Quelle [kvehlə]; (season) der Frühling [frew-lihŋ]; (v) springen [Sprihŋən]

square viereckig [fiir-eh-kihç]

staff das Personal [pehr-zoh-**nahl**]

stain Fleck(en) [flehk(ən)]; **stain remover** Fleck(en)mittel [flehk(ən)-mihtəl]

staircase die Treppe [trehpə]

stairs die Treppe [trehpə]

stamp der Stempel [Stehmpəl]; (postage) die (Brief-)Marke [(briif-)mahrkə]

stand (v) stehen [Steyən]; (endure) ertragen [ehr-**trahgən**]; **stand in line** (v) Schlange stehen [Slahŋə Steyən]

standard normal [nor-**mahl**]

star der Stern [Stehrn]

start der Beginn [bə**gihn**]; (v) beginnen [bə**gihnən**], starten [Stahrtən]; (motor) anspringen [ahn-Sprihŋən]; **start (from)** (v) abfahren (von) [ahp-fahrən (fon)]

startle (v) erschrecken [ehr-**Srehkən**]

state der Staat [Staht]; der Zustand [tsoo-Staht]; (v) feststellen [fehst-Stehlən], aussagen [aus-zahgən]

statement die Angabe [ahn-gahbə]; **make a statement** (v) eine Aussage machen [aynə aus-zahgə mahxən]

stay der Aufenthalt [auf-ehnt-hahlt]; (v) s. aufhalten [auf-hahltən], wohnen [vohnən], bleiben [blaybən], übernachten [ewbər-**nahxtən**]

steal (v) stehlen [Steylən]

steep steil [Stayl]

step der Schritt [Sriht]

steps die Treppe [trehpə]

stick der Stock [Stok]

still (quiet) still [Stihl]; (adv) noch [nox]

sting (v) stechen [Stehçən]

stink (v) stinken [Stihŋkən]

stock der Vorrat [for-raht]

stone der Stein [Stayn]

stony steinig [Stay-nihç]

stop (train) der Aufenthalt [auf-ehnt-hahlt]; (v) aufhören [auf-hœrən]; anhalten [ahn-hahltən], stehen bleiben [steyən blaybən], abbrechen [ahp-brehçən], halten [hahltən]; **stop! halt!** [hahlt!]

stop by (v) (visit) vorbeikommen [for-**bay**-komən]

store das Geschäft [gə**Sehft**], der Laden [lahdən]; der Vorrat [for-raht]

storm der Sturm [Stuhrm]

story das Stockwerk [Stok-vehrk]

story die Geschichte [gə**Sihçtə**]

stove der Ofen [ohfən]

straight gerade [gə**rahdə**]; **straight ahead** geradeaus [gərahdə-**aus**]; **straight across/through** quer durch [kvehr duhrç]

strange fremd [frehmt]

stranger der/die Fremde [frehmdə]

strap der Riemen [riimən]

street die Straße [Strahsə]; **in the street** auf der Straße [auf dehr Strahsə]

strength die Stärke [Stehrkə], die Kraft [krahft]

strenuous anstrengend [ahn-Strehŋənt]

strict streng [Stehŋ]

strike (v) (clock) schlagen [Slahgən]

string die Schnur [Snoor], der Bindfaden [bihnt-fahdən]

stroke der Schlaganfall [Slahk-ahn-fahl]

stroll der Bummel [buhməl], der Spaziergang [Spaht-siir-gahŋ]; (v) spazieren gehen [Spaht-siirən geyən]

strong stark [Stahrk], kräftig [krehf-tihç]

study (v) studieren [Stoo-**diirən**]

stupid dumm [duhm], blöd(e) [blœd(ə)]

A/Z

suburb die Vorstadt [for-Staht], der Vorort [for-ort]

subway die U-Bahn [oo-bahn]

success der Erfolg [ehr-**folk**]

such solch [zolç]

sudden(ly) plötzlich [plœts-lihç]

sufficient genug [gənook]; **be sufficient** (v) (aus-)reichen [(aus-)rayçən]

suggest (v) vorschlagen [for-Slahgən]

suggestion der Vorschlag [for-Slahk]

suit der Anzug [ahn-tsuhk]; (v) passen [pahsən]

suitable zweckmäßig [tsvehk-meh-sihç]

suitcase der Koffer [kofər]

sum die Summe [zuhmə]

summit der Gipfel [gihpfəl]

sun die Sonne [zonə]; **at sunrise** bei Sonnenaufgang [bay zonən-auf-gahŋ]; **at sunset** bei Sonnenuntergang [bay zonən-uhntər-gahŋ]

sunglasses die Sonnenbrille [zonən-brihlə]

sunny sonnig [zon-ihç]

superfluous überflüssig [ewbər-flew-sihç]

support die Unterstützung [uhntər-**Stewt**-suhŋ]

supporter der/die Anhänger/in [ahn-hehŋər / -ihn]

suppose (v) annehmen [ahn-neymən]

sure sicher [zihçər], gewiss [gəvihs]

surname der Familienname [fah-**mihl**-yən-nahmə]

surprised überrascht [ewbər-**rahSt**]; **be surprised (at)** (v) s. wundern (über) [vuhdərn (ewbər)]

suspicion der Verdacht [fehr-**dahxt**]

swamp der Sumpf [zuhmpf]

swap (v) tauschen [tauSən]

swear (v) schwören [Svœrən], fluchen [flooxən]

sweat (v) schwitzen [Svihtsən]

sweet süß [zews]

swim (v) baden [bahdən], schwimmen [Svihmən]

swimming pool der Swimmingpool [Svih-mihŋ-pool] ("pool" as in English)

swindle der Betrug [bətruhk]

swindler der/die Schwindler/in [Svihndlər / -ihn]

Swiss (man/woman) der/die Schweizer/in [Svaytsər / -ihn]

switch der Schalter [Sahltər]; **switch on/off the light** (v) Licht anmachen/ausmachen [lihçt ahn-mahxən / aus-mahxən]

Switzerland die Schweiz [Svayts]

T

table der Tisch [tihS]

take (v) nehmen [neymən]; (an-, ein-, weg-)nehmen [(ahn-, ayn-, vehk-) neymən]; (train, bus etc.) benutzen [bənootsən]; (time) brauchen [brauxən]; **take off** (v) (plane) starten [Startən], (clothing) abnehmen [ahp-neymən], ausziehen [aus-tsiiən]; **take over** (v) übernehmen [ewbər-**neym**ən]; **take part (in)** (v) teilnehmen (an) [tayl-neymən (ahn)]; **take place** (v) stattfinden [Staht-fihndən]; **take a picture** (v) fotografieren [foh-toh-grah-**fiir**ən], knipsen [knihpsən]

taken (seat) besetzt [bəzehtst]

talk das Gespräch [gə**Sprehç**]; (v) reden [reydən], s. unterhalten [uhntər-**hahlt**ən]

tall groß [grohs]

tap der Wasserhahn [vahsər-hahn]

tape das Tonband [tohn-bahnt]

taste der Geschmack [gə**Smahk**]; (v) (try food) versuchen [fehr-**zoox**ən]; **taste (like)** (v) schmecken (nach) [Smehkən (nahx)]

taxi das Taxi [tahk-sii]

teach (v) unterrichten [uhntər-**rihçt**ən], lehren [lehrən]

team (sports) die Mannschaft [mahn-Sahft]

tear (v) reißen [raysən], zerreißen [tsehr-**rays**ən]

tell (v) erzählen [ehr-**tsehl**ən], ausrichten [aus-rihçtən], sagen [zahgən]

temporary vorläufig [for-loy-fihç], vorübergehend [for-**ewbər**-geyənt], provisorisch [proh-vii-**zoh**-rihS]

tender zärtlich [tsehrt-lihç]; (soft) zart [tsahrt]

tent das Zelt [tsehlt]; **tent peg, tent stake** der Hering [heh-rihŋ]

terrible fürchterlich [fewrçtər-lihç], schrecklich [Srehk-lihç]

terrific herrlich [hehr-lihç]

than als [ahls]; **better than** besser als [behsər ahls]

thank (v) danken [dahŋkən]; **thankful** dankbar [dahŋk-bahr]; thanks der Dank [dahŋk]; **it's thanks to her** es ist ihr zu verdanken [ehs ihst iir tsoo fehr-**dahŋk**ən]

that diese(r, s) [diizə(r,s)]; jene(r, s) [yeynə(r,s)]; (conj) dass [dahs]

then (Zeit) dann [dahn], damals [dah-mahls]

there (Ort) da [dah], dort [dort], dorthin [dort-**hihn**]; **be there** (v) (anwesend) da sein [(ahn-veyzənt) dah zayn]; **there is/are** es gibt [ehs gihpt]

therefore daher [dah-hehr], deshalb [dehs-hahlp]

these diese [diizə]

they sie [zii]

thick dick [dihk]; (crowd, fog, etc.) dicht [dihçt]

thin dünn [dewn]; mager [mahgər], schmal [Smahl]; (sparse) spärlich [Spehr-lih], dürftig [dewrf-tihç]

thing das Ding [dihŋ], die Sache [zahxə]

think (v) meinen [maynən]; **think (of)** (v) denken (an) [dehŋkən (ahn)]

third dritte(r, s) [drihtə(r,s)]; **a third** ein Drittel [drihtəl]

third(ly) drittens [drihtəns]

thirst der Durst [duhrst]; **be thirsty** (v) durstig sein [duhrs-tihç]

this diese(r, s) [diizə(r,s)]

those diese [diizə]; jene [yeynə]

thought der Gedanke [gədahŋkə]

thread der Faden [fahdən]

through durch [duhrç]

throw der Wurf [vuhrf]; (v) werfen [vehrfən]

thunderstorm das Gewitter [gəvihtər]

thus so [zoh]; **also** [ahl-**zoh**]

ticket die Karte [kahrtə]; **admission ticket** die Eintrittskarte [ayn-trihts-kahrtə]; **ticket office** der (Fahrkarten-) Schalter [(fahr-kahrtən-)Sahltər], das Konzertbüro [kon-**tsehrt**-bew-roh]

tie up (v) binden [bihndən]

tight (clothes) eng [ehŋ]

till bis [bihs]

time die Zeit [tsayt]; das Mal [mahl]; **at that time** damals [dah-mahls]; **in time** (adv) rechtzeitig [rehçt-tsay-tihç]; **on**

time pünktlich [pewŋkt-lihç]; **for the time being** vorläufig [for-loy-fihç]; **from time to time** von Zeit zu Zeit [fon tsayt tsoo tsayt]; **a hundred times** hundertmal [huhndərt-mahl]

tip der Tipp [tihp]; (gratuity) das Trinkgeld [trihŋk-gehlt]

tired müde [mewdə]

to zu [tsoo]; (time) bis [bihs]; **to New York** nach New York [nahx New York]

tobacco der Tabak [tah-**bahk**]

today heute [hoytə]

together zusammen [tsoo-**zahm**ən]; gemeinsam [gə**mayn**-zahm]

toilet die Toilette [toy-**leht**ə]; **toilet paper** das Toilettenpapier [toy-**leht**ən-pah-piir]

tone der Ton [tohn]

tongs die Zange [tsahŋə]

tonight heute Nacht [hoytə nahxt]

too auch [aux]; (with adj) zu [tsoo]; **too many** zu viele [tsoo fiil]; **too much** zu viel [tsoo fiil]; zu sehr [tsoo zehr]

top (mountain) die Spitze [Spihtsə]

topic das (Gesprächs-)Thema [(gə**Sprehks**-)teymə]

touch (v) berühren [bə**rew**rən]

touched bewegt [bə**veykt**]

tour die Tour [toor]

tourist der/die Tourist/in [too-**rihst** / ihn]; der/die Reisende [rayzəndə]; **tourist information office** das Verkehrsbüro [fehr-**kehrs**-bew-roh]

towards gegen [geygən]

town die Ortschaft [ort-Sahft], die Stadt [Staht]

toy das Spielzeug [Spiil-tsoyk]

trace die Spur [Spuhr]

trademark die Handelsmarke [hahndəls-mahrkə]

traffic der Verkehr [fehr-**kehr**]

train der Zug [tsuhk]; **go by train** (v) (mit dem Zug) fahren [(miht deym tsuhk) fahrən]

training die Ausbildung [aus-bihl-duhŋ]

transfer (money) (v) überweisen [ewbər-**vayz**ən]

transferable übertragbar [ewbər-**trahk**-bahr]

transit visa das Durchreisevisum [duhrç-rayzə-vii-zuhm]

A/Z

translate (v) übersetzen [ewbər-**zehts**ən]

transport (v) transportieren [trahn-spor-**tiir**ən], befördern [bə**fœrd**ərn]

trash can die Mülltonne [mewl-tonə]

travel (v) reisen [rayzən]; **travel agency** das Reisebüro [rayzə-bew-roh]

traveler der/die Reisende [rayzəndə]

treat (v) behandeln [bə**hahnd**əln]

treatment die Behandlung [bə-**hahnd**-luhŋ]

tree der Baum [baum]

trial der Versuch [fehr-**zoox**], die Prüfung [prew-fuhŋ]; (court) die (Straf-)Verhandlung [Strahf-)fehr-hahnd-luhŋ]

trip die Tour [toor], die Fahrt [fahrt], die Reise [rayzə]; **trip back** die Rückfahrt [rewk-fahrt], **trip home** die Heimreise [haym-rayzə]

trouble die Umstände [uhm-Stehndə], die Mühe [mewə]

truck der Lastwagen [lahst-vahgən]

true wahr [vahr]; (real) wirklich [virk-lihç]

trust (v) vertrauen [fehr-**trau**ən]

truth die Wahrheit [vahr-hayt]

try (v) versuchen [fehr-**zoox**ən]; **try on** (v) anprobieren [ahn-proh-biirən]; **try hard** (v) s. bemühen [bə**mew**ən]

tube der Schlauch [Slaux], die Tube [toobə], das Rohr [rohr]

tunnel der Tunnel [tuhnəl]

turn (v) drehen [dreyən], wenden [vehndən]; einbiegen [ayn-biigən]; **turn off** (v) abstellen [ahp-Stehlən]; (light, etc.) ausmachen [aus-mahxən]; **turn back** (v) umkehren [uhm-kehrən]; **turn right/left** (v) einbiegen nach rechts/links [ayn-biigən nahx rehçts / lihŋks]

twice zweimal [tsvay-mahl]; doppelt [dopəlt]

typical(ly) typisch [tew-pihS]

U

ugly hässlich [hehs-lihç]

umbrella der Schirm [Sihrm]

unbearable unerträglich [uhn-ehr-treyk-lihç]

uncertain unsicher [uhn-zihçər], ungewiss [uhn-gəvihs]

uncle der Onkel [oŋkəl]

uncomfortable ungemütlich [uhn-gəmewt-lihç], unbequem [uhn-bəkvehm]

unconscious ohnmächtig [ohn-mehç-tihç]

undecided unentschlossen [uhn-ehnt-Slosən]

under unter [uhntər]

understand (v) verstehen [fehr-**Stey**ən]; **come to an understanding with** (v) s. verständigen mit [fehr-**Stehn**-dihgən miht]

underwear die Unterwäsche [uhntər-vehSə]

undo (v) lösen [lœzən]

undress (v) s. ausziehen [aus-tsiiən]

unemployed arbeitslos [ahr-bayts-lohs]

unexpected unerwartet [uhn-ehr-vahrtət]

unfair ungerecht [uhn-gərehçt]

unfavorable ungünstig [uhn-gewns-tihç]

unfit ungeeignet [uhn-gə-aygnət]

unfortunately unglücklicherweise [uhn-glewk-lihçər-vayzə], leider [laydər]

unfriendly unfreundlich [uhn-froynt-lihç]

ungrateful undankbar [uhn-dahŋk-bahr]

unhappy unglücklich [uhn-glewk-lihç]

unhealthy ungesund [uhn-gəzuhnt]

unimportant unwichtig [uhn-vihç-tihç]

unique einzigartig [ayn-tsihç-ahr-tihç]

unjust ungerecht [uhn-gərehçt]

unkind unfreundlich [uhn-froynt-lihç]

unknown unbekannt [uhn-bəkahnt], fremd [frehmt]

unlikely unwahrscheinlich [uhn-vahr-Sayn-lihç]

unload (v) abladen [ahp-lahdən]

unlucky unglücklich [uhn-glewk-lihç]

unnecessary unnötig [uhn-nœ-tihç]

unpack (v) auspacken [aus-pahkən]

unpleasant unerfreulich [uhn-ehr-froy-lihç], unangenehm [uhn-ahn-gəneym]

unpractical unpraktisch [uhn-prahk-tihS]

unsafe unsicher [uhn-zihçər]

unsuited ungeeignet [uhn-gə-aygnət]

untie (v) lösen [lœzən]

until bis [bihs]

unusual ungewöhnlich [uhn-gəvœn-lihç]

unwelcome unerwünscht [uhn-ehr-vewnSt]

unwell unwohl [uhn-vohl]

up aufwärts [auf-vehrts], nach oben [nahx ohbən], oben [ohbən]; **up there** dort oben [dort ohbən]

uphill (adv) bergauf [behrg-**auf**]

upstairs nach oben [nahx ohbən]

urgent dringend [drihŋənt], eilig [ay-lihç]

us uns [uhns]

use die Verwendung [fehr-**vehn**-duhŋ], der Gebrauch [gəbraux], die Anwendung [ahn-vehn-duhŋ]; (v) anwenden [ahn-vehndən], verwenden [fehr-**vehn**dən], gebrauchen [gəbrauxən], benutzen [bənootsən]; **get used to** (v) s. gewöhnen an [gəvœnən ahn]; **be used to s. th.** (v) etwas gewöhnt sein [gəvɛnt]

useful zweckmäßig [tsvehk-meh-sihç], nützlich [newts-lihç]

useless nutzlos [noots-lohs], unnütz [uhn-newts], zwecklos [tsvehk-lohs]

usual gewohnt [uhn-gəvohnt], gewöhnlich [gəvœn-lihç], üblich [ewb-lihç]; **as usual** wie gewöhnlich [vii gəvœn-lihç]

usually normalerweise [nor-**mahl**ər-vayzə]

V

vacation die Ferien [fehryən], der Urlaub [oor-laup]; **on vacation** in Ferien [ihn fehryən]

vain eitel [aytəl]; zwecklos [tsvehk-lohs]; **in vain** umsonst [uhm-**zonst**]

valid gültig [gewl-tihç]; **be valid** (v) gelten [gehltən]

validity die Gültigkeit [gewl-tihç-kayt]

valuables die Wertsachen [vehrt-zahxən]

value der Wert [vehrt]

varied bunt [buht]

variable (weather) unbeständig [uhn-bəStehn-dihç]

vending machine der Automat [au-toh-**maht**]

venison das Wild [vihlt]

versus gegen [geygən]

very sehr [zehr]; **very much** sehr [zehr]

view die Sicht [zihçt], die Aussicht [aus-zihçt], der Blick [blihk]; die Ansicht [ahn-zihçt], die Meinung [may-nuhŋ]; (tv) **viewer** der/die (Fernseh-)Zuschauer/in [(fehrn-zey-)tsoo-Sauər / -ihn]

village die Ortschaft [ort-Sahft], das Dorf [dorf]

vineyard der Weinberg [vayn-behrk]

visibility die Sicht [zihçt]

visible sichtbar [zihçt-bahr]

visit der Besuch [bəzoox]; (v) besichtigen [bəzihç-tihgən]; **visit s. o.** (v) jdn besuchen [bəzooxən]

voice die Stimme [Stihmə]

volume das Volumen [voh-**loom**ən]; (sound) die Lautstärke [laut-Stehrkə]; (book) der Band [bahnt]

vote die Stimme [Stihmə]; (v) wählen [veylən]

voucher der Gutschein [goot-Sayn]

voyage die Seereise [zey-rayzə], die Seefahrt [zey-fahrt]

vulgar ordinär [or-dih-**nehr**], gewöhnlich [gəvœn-lihç]

W

wages der Lohn [lohn]

wait (for) (v) warten (auf) [vahrtən (auf)], erwarten [ehr-**vahrt**ən]

wake (v) wecken [vehkən]; **wake up** (v) aufwachen [auf-vahxən]; **wake s. o. up** (v) jdn. aufwecken [auf-vehkən]

walk der Spaziergang [Spaht-**siir**-gahŋ]; (v) laufen [laufən], (zu Fuß) gehen [geyən]; **go for a walk** (v) spazieren gehen [Spaht-**siir**ən geyən], einen Spaziergang machen [aynən Spaht-**siir**-gahŋ mahxən]

wall die Wand [vahnt]

wallet die Brieftasche [briif-tahSə]

want (v) brauchen [brauxən]; wollen [volən]

war der Krieg [kriik]

warm herzlich [hehrts-lihç], **warm** [vahrm]; *(v)* wärmen [vehrmən]

warmth die Herzlichkeit [hehrts-lihç-kayt]

warn (of/about) *(v)* warnen (vor) [vahrnən (for)]

wash *(v)* waschen [vahSən]; **dirty laundry** Wäsche (zum Waschen) [vehSə (tsuhm vahSən)]

wasp die Wespe [vehspə]

watch die (Armband-)Uhr [(ahrm-bahnt-)oor]; *(v)* zuschauen [tsoo-Sauən], beobachten [bey-**oh**-bahxtən]

water das Wasser [vahsər]

wave *(v)* winken [vihŋkən]; die Welle [vehlə]

way die Weise [vayzə], der Weg [veyk]; **way back** der Rückweg [rewk-veyk], die Heimreise [haym-rayzə]; **way in** der Zugang [tsoo-gahŋ]; **by the way** übrigens [ewb-rigəns]; **on the way** unterwegs [uhntər-**vehks**]; **right of way** die Vorfahrt [for-fahrt]; **that way** dorthin [dort-hin]; **this way** hierher [hiir-hehr]

we wir [viir]

weak schwach [Svahx]

weakness die Schwäche [Svehçə]

wealth der Reichtum [rayç-tuhm]

wealthy wohlhabend [vohl-hahbənt]

wear *(v) (clothing)* tragen [trahgən]

weather das Wetter [vehtər]; **in weather like this** bei diesem Wetter [bay diizəm vehtər]

wedding die Hochzeit [hohx-tsayt]

week die Woche [voxə]; **once a week** wöchentlich [væçənt-lihç]; **in a week** in einer Woche [ihn aynər voxə]; **on weekdays** wochentags [voxən-tahks], werktags [vehrk-tahks]; **weekly** wöchentlich [væçənt-lihç]

weigh *(v)* wiegen [viigən]

weight das Gewicht [gəvihçt]; **put on weight** *(v)* zunehmen [tsoo-neymən]

weird seltsam [zehlt-zahm]

welcome willkommen [vihl-**kom**ən]; *(v)* empfangen [ehmp-**fah**ŋən], begrüßen [bəgrewsən]

well der Brunnen [bruhnən], die (Öl-)Quelle [(œl-)kvehlə]; *(comfortable)* wohl [vohl]; *(adv)* gut [goot]; **well-being** das Wohl [vohl]; **well-off** wohlhabend [vohl-hahbənt]

west der Westen [vehstən]

western westlich [vehst-lihç]

wet nass [nahs]

what was [vahs]; **what kind of … ?** was für ein/eine … ? [vahs fewr ayn/ə]

when wenn [vehn]; als [ahls]

when? wann? [vahn]

where? wo? [voh]

whether ob [op]

while *(conj)* während [vehrənt]; **for a while** eine Zeit lang [aynə tsayt lahŋ]

who? wer? [vehr]

whole ganz [gahnts]

why? warum? [vah-**ruhm**]

wide breit [brayt]; weit [vayt]

wife die Ehefrau [eyə-frau]

wild(ly) wild [vihlt]

win *(v)* gewinnen [gə**vih**nən]

windy windig [vihn-dihç]

wire der Draht [draht]; *(electricity)* die Leitung [lay-tuhŋ]

wireless das Radio [rahd-yoh]

wish der Wunsch [vuhnS]; *(v)* wollen [volən]; **wish for** *(v)* wünschen [vewnSən]

with mit [miht]

withdraw *(v)* s. zurückziehen [tsuh-**rewk**-tsiiən]

within *(time)* innerhalb [ihnər-hahlp]

without ohne [ohnə]

witness der Zeuge [tsoygə], die Zeugin [tsoy-gihn]

woman die Frau [frau]

wonderful wunderbar [vuhndər-bahr], toll [tol]

wood das Holz [hohlts]

word das Wort [vort]

work *(job)* die Tätigkeit [tey-tihç-kayt], die Arbeit [ahr-bayt]; *(v)* arbeiten [ahr-baytən], funktionieren [fuhŋk-tsyoh-niirən]; **work on** *(v)* bearbeiten [bə-ahr-baytən]

workshop die Reparaturwerkstatt [rey-pah-rah-**toor**-vehrk-Staht]

world die Welt [vehlt]

worm der Wurm [vuhrm]

worry die Sorge [zorgə]; *(v)* s. beunruhigen [bə-**uhn**-roo-ihgən]; **be worried about** *(v)* s. sorgen um [zorgən uhm]

worse schlimmer [Slihmər]

worst am schlimmsten [ahm Slihmstən]

worth der Wert [vehrt]; **be worth a lot**
(v) viel wert sein [fiil vehrt zayn]
worthless wertlos [vehrt-lohs]
wrap *(v)* einpacken [ayn-pahkən], verpacken [fehr-**pahk**ən]; **wrap up** *(v)*
einwickeln [ayn-vihkəln]
wrapping die Verpackung [fehr-**pah**-
kuhŋ]
write *(v)* schreiben [Sraybən]; **write
down** *(v)* aufschreiben [auf-Sraybən];
(hand)writing die (Hand-)Schrift
[(hahnt-)Srihft]; **in writing** schriftlich
[Srihft-lihç]
wrong falsch [fahlS]; **be wrong** *(v)* s.
täuschen [toySən], Unrecht haben
[uhn-rehçt hahbən]

Y

yard der Hof [hohf]; der Garten
[gahrtən]
yawn *(v)* gähnen [gehnən]
year das Jahr [yahr]
yet doch [dox]
you du [doo], ihr [iir], dich [dihç], euch
[oyç], Sie [zii]; *(to, for you)* dir [dihr],
euch [oyç], Ihnen [iinən]
young jung [yuhŋ]
your euer [oyər], dein [dayn], Ihr [iir]
youth die Jugend [yoogənt]

A/Z

Dictionary German-English

Unless otherwise indicated, the stress falls on the first syllable.

A

ab [ahp] from

abbestellen [ahp-bəStehlən] *(room, ticket)* to cancel

abbrechen [ahp-brehçən] to break off, to stop

Abend [ah-bənt] *m* evening, night

aber [ahbər] but

abfahren (von) [ahp-fahrən (fon)] to start (from), to leave

Abfall [ahp-fahl] *m* garbage

abgeben [ahp-geybən] to hand in; to check s. th.

abgelegen [ahp-gəleygən] remote, isolated

abholen [ahp-hohlən] to call for, to pick up; **abholen lassen** [ahp-hohlən lahsən] to send for, to have s. o. pick s. th. up

Abkürzung [ahp-kewrt-suhŋ] *f* abbreviation; shortcut

abladen [ahp-lahdən] to unload

ablaufen [ahp-laufən] to expire

ablehnen [ahp-leynən] to decline, to refuse

abnehmen [ahp-neymən] to take off; to lose weight

Abreise [ahp-rayzə] *f* departure

abreisen (nach) [ahp-rayzən (nahx)] to leave (for)

Absatz [ahp-zahts] *m* paragraph; *(shoe)* heel

Abschied nehmen [ahp-Siit neymən] to say goodbye

abschließen [ahp-Sliisən] to lock

Abschnitt [ahp-Sniht] *m* coupon, ticket, check

Absicht [ahp-zihçt] *f* intention

absichtlich [ahp-zihçt-lihç] on purpose

Abstand [ahp-Stahnt] *m* distance

abstellen [ahp-Stehlən] *(car)* to park; *(machine)* to turn off

abwärts [ahp-vehrts] down

abwesend [ahp-veyzənt] absent

Acht geben (auf) [ahxt geybən (aux)] to pay attention (to), to look out (for)

Achtung [ahx-tuhŋ] attention; look out!

Adresse [ah-**drehs**ə] *f* address

adressieren [ah-dreh-siirən] to address

Agentur [ah-gehn-toor] *f* agency

ähnlich [ehn-lihç] similar

Ahnung [ah-nuhŋ] *f* idea; **keine Ahnung!** [kaynə ah-nuhŋ] no idea!

akklimatisieren, s. [ah-klih-mah-tih-ziirən] to become acclimatized, to get acclimated

Algen [ahl-gehn] *f pl* algae

alle [ahlə] all; **auf alle Fälle** [auf ahlə fehlə] in any case; **alle Tage** [ahllə tahgə] every day; **alle zwei Stunden** [ahlə tsvay Stuhndən] every two hours

allein [ah-**layn**] alone

alles [ahləs] everything

allgemein [ahl-gəmayn] general; **im Allgemeinen** [ihm ahl-gəmaynən] in general

als [ahls] when; *(comparison)* than; **besser als** [behsər ahls] better than; **als ob** [ahls ohp] as if; **nichts als** [nihçts ahls] nothing but

also [ahl-zoh] so, thus

alt [ahlt] old

Alter [ahltər] *n* age

Amerika [ah-**meh**-rih-kah] America

Amerikaner/in [ah-meh-rih-**kah**nər / -ihn] American

Amt [ahmt] *n* office, department

amtlich [ahmt-lihç] official

amüsieren, s. [ah-moo-ziirən] to have a good time

an [ahn] on; **am Rhein** [ahm rayn] on the Rhine; **am Sonntag** [ahm zontahk] on Sunday; **am Abend** [ihm ah-bənt] in the evening

anbieten [ahn-biitən] to offer

Andenken [ahn-dehŋkən] *n* souvenir

andere, der [ahndərə] the other; **ein anderer** [ahndərər] someone else

andermal, ein [ahndər-mahl] another time

ändern [ehndərn] to change, to alter

anders [ahndərs] different(ly)

anderswo [ahndərs-voh] elsewhere

anderthalb [ahndərt-hahlp] one and a half

Anfang [ahn-fahŋ] *m* beginning

anfangen [ahn-fahŋən] to begin

Angabe [ahn-gahbə] *f* statement; **Angaben machen** [ahn-gahbən mahxən] to make a statement; **nähere Angaben** [ney-ərə ahn-gahbən] particulars, details

Angelegenheit [ahn-gəleygən-hayt] *f* matter; **eine Angelegenheit erledigen** [aynə ahn-gəleygən-haht ehr-ley-dihgən] to settle a matter

angeln [ahŋəln] to fish; **angeln gehen** [ahŋəln geyən] to go fishing

angenehm [ahn-gəneym] agreeable, pleasant

Angst [ahŋst] *f* fear

anhalten [ahn-hahltən] to stop

Anhänger/in [ahn-hehŋər / -ihn] supporter, fan; **Anhänger** [ahn-hehŋər] trailer

anklopfen [ahn-klopfən] to knock

Anlage [ahn-lahgə] *f (Park~)* park; *(letter)* enclosure

Anlass [ahn-lahs] *m* cause, reason; occasion

anmachen [ahn-mahxən] *(light)* to switch on, to turn on

anmelden [ahn-mehldən] to announce; **s. anmelden** to register

Annahme [ahn-nahmə] *f* acceptance; assumption

annehmen [ahn-neymən] to accept; to suppose

anprobieren [ahn-proh-biirən] *(clothes)* to try on

anrufen [ahn-roofən] to phone, to call

anschauen [ahn-Sauən] to look at

anscheinend [ahn-Saynənt] apparently

Anschrift [ahn-Srihft] *f* address

ansehen [ahn-zeyən] to look at

Ansicht [ahn-zihçt] *f* view; opinion

anspringen [ahn-Sprihŋən] *(motor)* to start

anstatt [ahn-Staht] instead of

anstrengend [ahn-Strehŋənt] strenuous

Anstrengung [ahn-Strehŋ-uhŋ] *f* effort

Antwort [ahnt-vort] *f* answer

antworten [ahn-vortən] to answer, to reply

anwenden [ahn-vehndən] to use, to employ

Anwendung [ahn-vehn-duhŋ] *f* use

anwesend [ahn-veyzənt] present

Anzeige [ahn-tsaygə] *f (newspaper, magazine)* advertisement

anziehen [ahn-tsiiən] to put on; **s. anziehen** to dress, to get dressed

anzünden [ahn-tsewndən] to light

Apparat [ah-pah-raht] *m* gadget; *(Foto~)* camera; *(Fernseh~)* television set

Appetit [ah-peh-tiit] *m* appetite

Arbeit [ahr-bayt] *f* work; job

arbeiten [ahr-baytən] to work

arbeitslos [ahr-bayts-lohs] unemployed

ärgern, s. (über) [ehr-gərn (ewbər)] to be angry (about/at)

arm [ahrm] poor

Ärmelkanal [ehrməl-kah-nahl] *m* the English Channel

Art [ahrt] *f* kind, sort

Artikel [ahr-tiikəl] *m* article

Atem [ahtəm] *m* breath; breathing

Atlantik [aht-lahn-tihk] *m* Atlantic

auch [aux] also; too; **auch nicht** [aux nihçt] nor, neither

auf [auf] on, **auf der Straße** [auf dehr Strahsə] in the street; **auf Englisch** [auf ehŋ-lihS] in English; **auf der Reise** [auf dehr rayzə] on a journey/trip; **auf die/der Post** [auf dii/dehr post] to/at the post office; **auf einmal** [auf ayn-mahl] all at once

aufbewahren [auf-bəvahrən] to keep *(in a safe place)*

aufbrechen [auf-brehçən] to break open

Aufenthalt [auf-ehnt-hahlt] *m* stay; *(train)* stop

auffordern [auf-fordərn] to ask, to invite

aufgeben [auf-geybən] *(baggage)* to check; *(post office)* to mail

aufhalten, s. [auf-hahltən] to stop, to stay

aufhängen [auf-hehŋən] to hang s. th. up

aufhören [auf-hœrən] to stop doing s. th.

aufladen [auf-lahdən] to put on, to load

aufmachen [auf-mahxən] to open

aufmerksam [auf-mehrk-sahm] attentive

Aufnahme [auf-nahmə] *f (video)* recording; photo, snapshot

aufnehmen [auf-neymən] to take pictures; to record

A/Z

aufpassen (auf) [auf-pahsən (auf)] to take care of, to look after

aufpumpen [auf-puhmpən] to pump up, to inflate

aufrufen [auf-roofən] to call *(out)*, to page

aufschieben [auf-Siibən] to put off, to postpone

aufschreiben [auf-Sraybən] to write down

Aufschub [auf-Soop] *m* delay

Aufseher/in [auf-zeyər / -ihn] *(guard)* attendant

aufstehen [auf-Steyən] to get up

aufstellen [auf-Stehlən] to put s. th. up

aufwachen [auf-vahxən] to wake up

aufwärts [auf-vehrts] up

aufwecken [auf-vehkən] to wake s. o. up

Aufzeichnung [auf-tsayç-nuhŋ] *f* note; *(audio, video)* recording

Auge [augə] *n* eye

Augenblick [augən-blihk] *m* moment

aus [aus] from; **aus New York** from New York; *(material)* of; *(reason)* for, **aus diesem Grund** [aus diizəm gruhnt] for this reason

Ausbildung [aus-bihl-duhŋ] *f* education, training

Ausdruck [aus-druhk] *m* expression

ausdrücklich [aus-drewk-lihç] explicit(ly)

Ausfahrt [aus-fahrt] *f (Autobahn~)* freeway exit

ausführen [aus-fewrən] *(work)* to carry out

ausführlich [aus-fewr-lihç] detailed

Ausgaben [aus-gahbən] *f pl* expenses

Ausgang [aus-gahŋ] *m* exit

ausgeben [aus-geybən] to spend

ausgehen [aus-geyən] to go out

ausgeschlossen [aus-gəSlosən] impossible

ausgezeichnet [aus-gətsayçnət] excellent

Auskunft [aus-kuhnft] *f* information; *(Telefon~)* telephone operator; **Auskunft einholen** [aus-kuhnft aynhohlən] to inquire

Ausland [aus-lahnt] *n* foreign countries; **im/ins Ausland** [ihm / ihns aus-lahnt] abroad

Ausländer [aus-lehndər] *m* foreigner

ausländisch [aus-lehn-dihS] foreign

ausmachen [aus-mahxən] *(light)* to turn off, *(fire)* to put out; *(agreement)* to agree

Ausnahme [aus-nahmə] *f* exception

auspacken [aus-pahkən] to unpack, to unwrap

ausreisen [aus-rayzən] to leave (a country)

ausrichten [aus-rihçtən] *(information)* to tell

ausruhen, s. [aus-rooən] to rest

aussehen [aus-zeyən] to look

außen [ausən] outside; **von außen** [fon ausən] from the outside

außer [ausər] except

außerdem [ausər-dehm] besides

außergewöhnlich [ausər-gəvœn-lihç] extraordinary

außerhalb [ausər-hahlp] outside

äußerlich [oysər-lihç] external, outward

Aussicht [aus-zihçt] *f* view

Aussprache [aus-Sprahxə] *f* pronunciation

aussprechen [aus-Sprehçən] to pronounce

Ausstattung [aus-Stah-tuhŋ] *f* equipment; *(house, room)* furnishings

aussuchen [aus-zooxən] to pick out

Austausch [aus-tauS] *m* exchange

austauschen [aus-tauSən] to exchange

ausüben [aus-ewbən] *(profession)* to practice

Ausverkauf [aus-fehr-kauf] *m* (clearance) sale

Auswahl [aus-vahl] *f* choice

Ausweis [aus-vays] *m* identity card

ausziehen [aus-tsiiən] to take off; **s. ausziehen** to undress, to get undressed

Auto [au-toh] *n* car; **Auto fahren** [au-toh fahrən] to drive a car

Automat [au-toh-maht] *m* vending machine

automatisch [au-toh-**mah**-tihS] automatic

B

Baby [bey-bii] *n* baby

Bad [baht] *n* bath; **Badeanstalt** [bahdə-ahn-Stahlt] *f* (public) baths; (public) swimming pool

baden [bahdən] to have a bath; to swim

Badeort [bahdǝ-ort] *m* seaside resort, beach resort

bald [bahlt] soon; **so bald wie möglich** [zoh bahlt vii mœg-lihç] as soon as possible

Ball [bahl] *m* ball; *(event)* ball, dance

Band [bahnt], das *(Haar~* [hahr-bahnt]*)* ribbon; **der Band** *(book)* volume; *(Ton~* [tohn-bahnt]*)* tape

Bank [bahŋk] *f* bank; *(Sitz~* [zihts-bahŋk]*)* bench

Batterie [bah-teh-rii] *f* battery

bauen [bauǝn] to build

Bauer [bauǝr] *m* farmer

Bauernhof [bauǝrn-hohf] *m* farm

Baum [baum] *m* tree

beabsichtigen [bǝahp-zihç-tihgǝn] to intend to

beachten [bǝahxtǝn] to pay attention to

Beanstandung [bǝahn-Stahn-duhŋ] *f* complaint

beantworten [bǝahnt-vortǝn] to reply, to answer

bearbeiten [bǝahr-baytǝn] to work on

Becher [behçǝr] *m* cup, mug

Bedauern [bǝdauǝrn] *n* regret

bedauern [bǝdauǝrn] to regret

bedecken [bǝdehkǝn] to cover

bedeuten [bǝdoytǝn] to mean

bedeutend [bǝdoytǝnt] important

Bedeutung [bǝdoy-tuhŋ] *f* meaning; importance

bedienen [bǝdiinǝn] to serve, to attend to

Bedienung [bǝdii-nuhŋ] *f* service; waitress

Bedingung [bǝdihŋ-uhŋ] *f* condition

beeilen, s. [bǝaylǝn] to hurry

beenden [bǝehndǝn] to finish

befinden, s. [bǝfihndǝn] to be (located at a place)

befolgen [bǝfolgǝn] to follow

befördern [bǝfœrdǝrn] to transport

befreundet sein mit [bǝfroyndǝt zayn miht] to be friends with

befriedigt [bǝfrii-dihkt] satisfied

befürchten [bǝfewrçtǝn] to fear, to be afraid (of)

begegnen [bǝgeygnǝn] to meet

begeistert (von) [bǝgaystǝrt (fon)] enthusiastic (about)

Beginn [bǝgihn] *m* beginning, start

beginnen [bǝgihnǝn] to begin, to start

begleiten [bǝglaytǝn] to accompany

begrüßen [bǝgrewsǝn] to greet, to welcome

behalten [bǝhahltǝn] to keep

Behälter [bǝhehltǝr] *m* container

behandeln [bǝhahndǝln] to treat

Behandlung [bǝhahnd-luhŋ] *f* treatment

behaupten [bǝhauptǝn] to maintain; to insist

behilflich, jdm ~ sein [bǝhihlf-lihç zayn] to help s. o.

Behörde [bǝhœrdǝ] *f* authorities

bei [bay] *(place)* near; **bei Tag/Nacht** [bay tahk/nahxt] by day/night; **bei Tisch** [bay tihS] at breakfast/lunch/dinner; **beim Essen** [baym ehsǝn] when eating; **bei diesem Wetter** [bay diizǝm vehtǝr] in weather like this

beide [baydǝ] both

Beifall [bay-fahl] *m* applause

Beileid [bay-layt] *n* condolence(s)

beinahe [bay-nah-ǝ] nearly, almost

Beispiel [bay-Spiil] *n* example; **zum Beispiel** [tsuhm bay-Spiil] for example

beißen [biisǝn] to bite

bekannt [bǝkahnt] well-known; **bekannt machen** [bǝkahnt mahxǝn] to introduce

Bekannte [bǝkahntǝ], **der/die** acquaintance, friend

Bekanntschaft [bǝkahnt-Sahft] *f* acquaintance

beklagen, s. (über) [bǝklahgǝn (ewbǝr)] to complain (of/about)

bekommen [bǝkomǝn] to get, to receive

belästigen [bǝlehs-tihgǝn] to bother, to harrass (sexually)

belegen: einen Platz ~ [aynǝn plahts bǝleygǝn] to reserve a seat

beleidigen [bǝlay-dihgǝn] to offend, to insult

Beleidigung [bǝlay-dih-guhŋ] *f* insult

beleuchtet [bǝ-loyçtǝt] lit up; illuminated

Belgien [behlg-yǝn] Belgium

Belgier/in [behlg-yǝr / -ihn] Belgian

belohnen [bǝlohnǝn] to reward

Belohnung [bǝloh-nuhŋ] *f* reward

bemerken [bǝmehrkǝn] to notice; *(say)* to remark

bemühen, s. [bǝmewǝn] to try hard

benachrichtigen [bǝnahx-rihç-tihgǝn] to inform

Benehmen [bəneymən] *n* behavior, manners

benötigen [bənœ-tihgən] to need

benutzen [bənootsən] to use; *(means of transport)* to take

Benzin [behn-tsiin] *n* gas

beobachten [bey-oh-bahxtən] to observe, to watch

bequem [bəkveym] comfortable

Bequemlichkeit [bəkveym-lihç-kayt] *f* comfort

berechnen [bərehçnən] to calculate

berechtigt [bərehç-tihkt] entitled

bereit [bərayt] ready

bereits [bərayts] already

Berg [behrk] *m* mountain

bergab [behrg-ahp] downhill

bergauf [behrg-auf] uphill

Bericht [bərihçt] *m* report

Beruf [bəroof] *m* job, profession

beruhigen, s. [bəroo-ihgən] to calm down

berühmt [bərewmt] famous

berühren [bərewrən] to touch

Berührung [bərew-ruhŋ] *f* contact, touch

beschädigen [bəSeh-dihgən] to damage

Beschädigung [bəSeh-dih-guhŋ] *f* damage

beschaffen [bəSahfən] to obtain

beschäftigt [bəSehf-tihçt] busy

Bescheid wissen [bəSayt vihsən] to know

bescheinigen [bəSay-nihgən] to certify

beschleunigen [bəSloy-nihgən] to accelerate, to speed up

beschließen [bəSliisən] to decide; to make up one's mind

beschreiben [bəSraybən] to describe

beschützen [bəSewtsən] to protect

Beschwerde [bəSvehrdə] *f* complaint

beschweren, s. (über) [bəSvehrən (ewbər)] to complain (about)

besetzt [bəzehtst] *(seat)* occupied, taken; full; *(telephone)* busy

besichtigen [bəzihç-tihgən] to visit

Besitz [bəzihts] *m* possession; property

besitzen [bəzitsən] to own

Besitzer/in [bəzitsər / -ihn] owner

besonders [bəzondərs] particularly, especially

besorgen [bəzorgən] to get

besorgt [bəzorkt] anxious, concerned

Besorgung [bəzor-guhŋ] *f* purchase

besser [behsər] better

bestätigen [bəSteh-tihgən] to confirm

beste (-r, -s) [behstə(r,s)] best

bestehen auf [bəsteyən auf] to insist on; **bestehen aus** [bəSteyən aus] to consist of

bestimmt [bəStihmt] certain(ly)

Besuch [bəzoox] *m* visit

besuchen: jdn ~ [bəzooxən] to visit s. o., to call on s. o.

beten [beytən] to pray

betrachten [bətrahxtən] to look at; to consider

beträchtlich [bətrehçt-lihç] considerable

Betrag [bətrahk] *m* amount

betragen [bətrahgən] *(sum of money)* to be, to come to

betreffend [bətrehfənt] concerning

betreten [bətreytən] to enter

betrinken, s. [bətrihŋkən] to get drunk

Betrug [bətrook] *m* swindle; fraud

betrügen [bətrewgən] to cheat

betrunken [bətruhŋkən] drunk

Bett [beht] *n* bed; **zu Bett gehen** [tsoo beht geyən] to go to bed

beunruhigen, s. [bəuhn-roo-ihgən] to worry

beurteilen [bəoor-taylən] to judge

Beutel [boytəl] *m* bag; *(Geld~)* purse

bevor [bəfor] before

bewachen [bəvahxən] to guard

bewegen [bəveygən] to move

bewegt [bəveykt] *(emotion)* touched; *(sea)* rough

Bewegung [bəvey-guhŋ] *f* movement

Beweis [bəvays] *m* proof

beweisen [bəvayzən] to prove

Bewohner [bəvohnər] *m* inhabitant

bewundern [bəvuhndərn] to admire

bewusst [bəvuhst] conscious, deliberate

bezahlen [bətsahlən] to pay

bezaubernd [bətsaubərnt] charming

Bezeichnung [bətsayç-nuhŋ] *f* description

beziehen: s. ~ auf [bətsiiən auf] to refer to

biegen [biigən] to bend

Biene [biinə] *f* bee

bieten [biitən] to offer

Bild [bihlt] *n* picture; illustration; painting

bilden [bihldən] to form
billig [bih-lihç] cheap
binden [bihndən] to tie up, to fasten
Bindfaden [bihnt-fahdən] *m* string
Birne [bihrnə] *f* pear; *(Glüh~)* [gly-bihrnə] light bulb
bis [bihs] to; *(time)* till, until; **bis jetzt** [bihs jetst] till now
bisschen, ein ~ [ayn bihsçən] a bit
bitte [bihtə] please; **wie bitte?** [vii bihtə] *(I beg your)* Pardon?
Bitte [bihtə] *f* request
bitten [bihtən], **jdn um etw** ~ to ask s. o. for s. th.
bitter [bihtər] bitter
Blatt [blaht] *n* leaf
bleiben [blaybən] to remain, to stay
bleich [blayç] pale
Blick [blihk] *m* look; view
blind [blihnt] blind
blinken [blihŋkən] *(car)* to indicate, to signal
Blitz [blihts] *m* lightning; *(photo)* flash
blöd(e) [blœd(ə)] silly, stupid
blühen [blewən] to blossom, to bloom
Blume [bloomə] *f* flower
Boden [bohdən] *m* ground; floor
Boot [boht] *n* boat
Bord, an ~ **gehen** [ahn bort geyən] to go on board
böse [bœzə] evil; naughty; angry
Botschaft [boht-Sahft] *f* embassy
Brand [brahnt] *m* fire
Braten [brahtən] *m* roast
braten [brahtən] to roast, to grill; to fry
brauchen [brauxən] to need, to want; *(time)* to take
braun [braun] brown
brechen [brehçən] to break
breit [brayt] broad, wide
brennen [brehnən] to burn
Brief [briif] *m* letter
Brieftasche [briif-tahSə] *f* wallet, billfold
Briefwechsel [briif-vehksəl] *m* correspondence
Brille [brihlə] *f* glasses
bringen [(hehr-/vehk-)brihŋən] *(her~)* to bring; *(weg~)* to take
Bruder [broodər] *m* brother
Brunnen [bruhnən] *m* fountain; well
Buch [buhx] *n* book
buchen [booxən] *(seat)* to book, to reserve

Büchse [bewksə] *f* box, case; *(food, etc.)* can; **Büchsenöffner** [bewksən-œfnər] *m* can opener
buchstabieren [boox-Stah-biirən] to spell
Bucht [buhxt] *f* bay
Bügeleisen [bewgəl-ayzən] *n* iron
Bummel [buhməl] *m* stroll
Bund [buhnt] *m (carrots, etc.)* bunch
bunt [buhnt] colorful; varied
Büro [bew-roh] *n* office
Bürste [bewrstə] *f* brush
bürsten [bewrstən] to brush
Busch [buhS] *m* bush

C

Café [kah-fey] *n* café
Chauffeur [So-fœr] *m* driver
Chef [Sehf] *m* head, boss
Chor [kohr] *m* choir
Cousin/e [koo-zeh / koo-zii-nə] cousin

D

da [dah] *(place)* there; *(time)* then; *(reason)* as, because
dafür sein [dah-fewr] to be for s. th.
dagegen sein [dah-geygən] to be against s. th.
daheim [dah-haym] at home
daher [dah-hehr] therefore
damals [dah-mahls] then, at that time
Dame [dahmə] *f* lady
danach [dah-nahx] afterwards
Dank [dahŋk] *m* thanks
dankbar [dahŋk-bahr] thankful
danken [dahŋkən] to thank
dann [dahn] then
da sein [dah] to be present, to be there
dass [dahs] that
dasselbe [dahs-zehlbə] the same
Datum [dah-tuhm] *n* date
Dauer [dauər] *f* duration
dauern [dauərn] to last
Decke [dehkə] *f* blanket; *(Bett~)* duvet; *(Zimmer~)* ceiling
defekt [dey-fehkt] faulty, broken
dein [dayn] your
demnächst [dehm-nekst] very soon, before long

denken (an) [dehŋkən (ahn)] to think (of)

denn [dehn] for

derselbe [dehr-**zehlbə**] the same

deshalb [dehs-hahlb] therefore

deutlich [doyt-lihç] distinct, clearly

deutsch [doytS] German

Deutsche, der/die [doytSə] German

Deutschland [doytS-lahnt] Germany

Dia [dii-ah] n slide

Diagnose [dii-ahg-**nohzə**] f diagnosis

dich [dihç] you

dicht [dihçt] (fog) dense; **dicht dabei** [dihçt dah-**bay**] near by

dick [dihk] thick, swollen; (person) stout, fat

dienen [diinən] to serve

Dienst [diinst] m service; favor

diese(r, s) [diizə(r,s)] this, these; that, those

Ding [dihŋ] n thing

dir [diir] to, for you

direkt [dih-**rehkt**] direct(ly); immediately

Direktion [dih-rehk-**tsyohn**] f management

Direktor [dih-**rehk**-tor] m director, manager; headmaster, principal

doch [dox] yet, however

Doktor/in [dok-tor / dok-**toh**-rihn] doctor

Dokument [do-kuh-**mehnt**] n document

doppelt [dopəlt] (adj) double; (adv) twice

Dorf [dorf] n village

dort [dort] there; **dorthin** [dort-**hihn**] that way; **dort oben/unten** [dort ohbən / uhntən] up/ down there

Dose [dohzə] f box; (food, etc.) can; **Dosenöffner** [dohzən-œfnər] m can opener

Draht [draht] m wire

draußen [drausən] outside

drehen [dreyən] to turn

drin, drinnen [drihn(ə)n] inside, indoors

dringend [drihŋənt] urgent

dritte(r,-s) [drihtə(r,s)] third

Drittel [drihtəl]: **ein ~** a third

drittens [drihtəns] thirdly

drüben [drewbən] over there

drücken [drewkən] to push; (button) to press

du [doo] you

dumm [duhm] stupid

dunkel [duhŋkəl] dark

dünn [dewn] thin; slim, slender

durch [duhrç] through; (quer ~) across; by (means of)

Durchgang [durç-gahŋ] m passage; gateway

Durchreise [duhrç-rayzə]: **auf der ~** passing through; **Durchreisevisum** [duhrç-rayzə-vii-zuhm] n transit visa

durchschnittlich [duhrç-Sniht-lihç] average; on (the) average

dürfen [dewrfən] to be allowed

Durst [duhrst] m thirst

durstig sein [duhrs-tihç] to be thirsty

E

eben [eybən] flat; smooth; (time) just now

Ebene [eybənə] f plain

echt [ehçt] genuine

Ecke [ehkə] f corner

Ehe [eyə] f marriage

Ehefrau [eyə-frau] f wife

Ehemann [eyə-mahn] m husband

Ehepaar [eyə-pahr] n married couple

eher [eyər] rather

Ehre [ehrə] f honor

Ei [ay] n egg

eigen [aygən] own; peculiar; strange, odd, weird

Eigenschaft [aygən-Sahft] f quality, characteristic

eigentlich [aygənt-lihç] actual(ly)

Eigentümer/in [aygən-tewmər / -ihn] owner

eilig [ay-lihç] urgent; **es eilig haben** to be in a hurry

ein(e) [ayn(ə)] one

einander [ayn-**ahn**dər] each other

einbiegen [ayn-biigən] to turn; **nach rechts/links einbiegen** [nahx rehçts/lihŋks ayn-biigən] to turn right/left

Eindruck [ayn-druhk] m impression

einfach [ayn-fahx] simple

Einfahrt [ayn-fahrt] f entrance, gateway, driveway

Einfuhr [ayn-fuhr] f import

Eingang [ayn-gahŋ] m entrance

einheimisch [ayn-hay-mihS] native, local

einig sein [ayn-ihç] to agree
einige [ayn-ihgə] some, any
einigen, s. [ayn-ihgən] to agree
einkaufen [ayn-kaufən] to buy, to go shopping
einladen [ayn-lahdən] to invite
Einladung [ayn-lah-duhŋ] *f* invitation
einmal [ayn-mahl] once
einpacken [ayn-pahkən] to wrap, to pack
einreisen [ayn-rayzən] to enter (a country)
eins [ayns] one
einsam [ayn-zahm] lonely; secluded, isolated
einschalten [ayn-Sahltən] to switch on
einschlafen [ayn-Slahfən] to fall asleep
einschließen [ayn-Sliisən] to lock in/up
eintreffen [ayn-trehfən] to arrive *(at)*
eintreten [ayn-trehtən] to enter *(a room)*
Eintritt [ayn-triht] *m* entrance; **Eintritt verboten!** [ayn-triht fehr-bohtən] no admittance!; **Eintrittskarte** [ayn-trihts-kahrtə] *f (admission)* ticket
Eintrittspreis [ayn-trihts-prays] *m* admission charge
Einverständnis [ayn-fehr-Stehnt-nihs] *n* agreement, consent
einwerfen [ayn-vehrfən] to mail
einwickeln [ayn-vihkəln] to wrap up
einwilligen [ayn-vih-lihgən] to consent to
Einwohner [ayn-vohnər] *m* inhabitant
Einzelheit [ayn-tsəlhayt] *f* detail
einzeln [ayn-tsəln] individual, separate
einzig [ayn-tsihç] only; **einzigartig** [ayn-tsihç-ahrtiç] unique
Eis [ays] *n* ice; ice cream
Eisen [ayzən] *n* iron
elektrisch [ey-lehk-trihS] electric
Eltern [ehltərn] *pl* parents
emanzipiert [ey-mahnt-sih-piirt] emancipated
Empfang [ehmp-fahŋ] *m* reception
empfangen [ehmp-fahŋən] to receive; to greet, to welcome
empfehlen [ehmp-feylən] to recommend
Empfehlung [ehmp-fey-luhŋ] *f* recommendation
Ende [ehndə] *n* end
enden [ehndən] to end
endgültig [ehnd-gewl-tihç] definite(ly)
endlich [ehnt-lihç] finally

eng [ehŋ] narrow; *(clothes)* tight
England [ehŋ-lahnt] England
Engländer/in [ehŋ-lehndər / -ihn] Englishman/-woman
englisch [ehŋ-lihS] English
Enkel/in [ehŋkəl / -ihn] grandson/granddaughter
entdecken [ehnt-dehkən] to discover
entfernt [ehnt-fehrnt] distant
Entfernung [ehnt-fehr-nuhŋ] *f* distance
entgegengesetzt [ehnt-geygən-gəzetst] opposite
enthalten [ehnt-hahltən] to contain
entlang [ehnt-lahŋ] along
entscheiden [ehnt-Saydən] to decide
entschließen, s. [ehnt-Sliisən] to make up one's mind
entschlossen sein [ehnt-Slosən] to be determined
Entschluss [ehnt-Sluhs] *m* decision
entschuldigen [ehnt-Suhl-dihgən] to excuse; **Entschuldigen Sie bitte!** [ehnt-Suhl-dihgən zii bihtə] excuse me, please!; **s. entschuldigen** to apologize
Entschuldigung [ehnt-Suhl-dih-guhŋ] *f* excuse; **Ich bitte um Entschuldigung!** [ihç bihtə oom ehnt-Suhl-dih-guhŋ] I beg your pardon!
enttäuscht [ehnt-toySt] disappointed
entweder ... oder [ehnt-veydər ... ohdər] either ... or
entwickeln [ehnt-vihkəln] to develop
Entwicklung [ehnt-vihk-luhŋ] *f* development
entzückend [ehnt-tsewkənt] charming, delightful
entzückt [ehnt-tsewkt] delighted
er [ehr] he
Erde [ehrdə] *f* earth
Erdgeschoss [ehrt-gəSos] *n* ground floor, first floor
ereignen, s. [ehr-ayknən] to happen
Ereignis [ehr-ayk-nihs] *n* event
erfahren [ehr-fahrən] to learn, to hear; *(adj)* experienced
Erfahrung [ehr-fah-ruhŋ] *f* experience
erfinden [ehr-fihndən] to invent
Erfolg [ehr-folk] *m* success
erfreut (über) [ehr-froyt (ewbər)] pleased (with), glad (of, about)
Erfrischung [ehr-frih-Suhŋ] *f* refreshment

Ergebnis [ehr-**geyp**-nihs] *n* result

ergreifen [ehr-**grayf**ən] to seize

erhalten [ehr-**hahlt**ən] to receive, to get

erhältlich [ehr-**hehlt**-lihç] obtainable, available

erhöhen [ehr-**hœ**ən] *(price)* to increase

erholen, s. [ehr-**hohl**ən] to recover

Erholung [ehr-**hoh**-luhŋ] *f* recovery; rest

erinnern [ehr-**ihn**ərn]: jdn an etw ~ to remind s. o. of s. th.; **s. erinnern** to remember

erkennen [ehr-**kehn**ən] to recognize; to realize

erklären [ehr-**klehr**ən] to declare; to explain

erkundigen, s. [ehr-**kuhn**-dihgən] to inquire

erlangen [ehr-**lahŋ**ən] to obtain, to get

erlauben [ehr-**laub**ən] to allow, to permit

Erlaubnis [ehr-**laup**-nihs] *f* permission

erledigen [ehr-**ley**-dihgən] to settle

Ermäßigung [ehr-**meh**-sih-guhŋ] *f* reduction

ermöglichen [ehr-**mœg**-lihçən] to make possible

erneuern [ehr-**noy**ərn] to renew

ernst [ehrnst] serious

Ernte [ehrntə] *f* harvest

erreichen [ehr-**rayç**ən] to reach

Ersatz [ehr-**zahts**] *m* replacement; compensation

erscheinen [ehr-**Sayn**ən] to appear; *(book)* to come out

erschöpft [ehr-**Sœpft**] exhausted

erschrecken [ehr-**Srehk**ən] to frighten, to startle; to be alarmed

ersetzen [ehr-**zets**ən] to replace

erst [ehrst] first of all; *(not later than)* only

erste(r,-s) [ehrstə(r,s)] first

erstens [ehrstəns] first(ly)

erstklassig [ehrst-**klah**-sihç] first-class

ertragen [ehr-**trahg**ən] to bear

Erwachsene(r) [ehr-**vahks**ənə(r)] adult

erwarten [ehr-**vahrt**ən] to expect, to wait for

erwidern [ehr-**vihd**ərn] to reply

erzählen [ehr-**tseyl**ən] to tell

erzeugen [ehr-**tsoyg**ən] to produce

Erzeugnis [ehr-**tsoyk**-nihs] *n* product

Erziehung [ehr-**tsii**-uhŋ] *f* education

es [ehs] it; **es gibt** [ehs gihpt] there is, there are

Esel [eyzəl] *m* donkey

essbar [ehs-**bahr**] edible

essen [ehsən] to eat **Essen** *n* meal; food

etwa [eht-vah] about

etwas [eht-vahs] something; anything; a little

euch [oyç] you

euer [oyər] your

Europa [oy-**roh**-pah] Europe

Europäer/in [oy-roh-**peyər** / -ihn] European

europäisch [oy-roh-**pey**-ihS] European

eventuell [ey-vehn-too-**ehl**] *(adj)* possible; *(adv)* perhaps

extra [ehks-trah] extra, special

F

Fabrik [fah-**briik**] *f* factory

Faden [fahdən] *m* thread

fähig [fey-ihç] capable of

fahren [fahrən] to go by train, car, etc.; to drive

Fahrer/in [fahrər / -ihn] driver

Fahrgast [fahr-gahst] *m* passenger

Fahrstuhl [fahr-Stool] *m* elevator

Fahrt [fahrt] *f* journey, trip, voyage; *(car)* drive

fair [feyr] fair

Fall [fahl] *m (incident)* case

fallen [fahlən] to fall

falls [fahls] in case, if

falsch [fahlS] wrong; deceitful

Familie [fah-**mihl**yə] *f* family; **Familienname** [fah-**mihl**yən-nahmə] *m* surname

fangen [fahŋən] to catch

Farbe [fahrbə] *f* color

farbig [fahr-bihç] colored

fast [fahst] almost, nearly

faul [faul] lazy; *(fruit)* rotten

Feder [feydər] *f* feather; pen; spring

fehlen [feylən] to be missing

Fehler [feylər] *m* mistake; fault

feierlich [fay(ə)r-lihç] solemn; festive

Feiertag [fay(ə)r-tahk] *m* holiday

feilschen [faylSən] to haggle

fein [fayn] fine; delicate; distinguished

Feld [fehlt] *n* field

Fell [fehl] *n* fur, fleece

Fels [fehls] *m* rock; cliff

Ferien [fehryən] *pl* holidays, vacation; **in Ferien** [ihn fehryən] on holiday, on vacation

Fernglas [fehrn-glahs] *n* binoculars

fertig [fehr-tihç] ready; finished

fest [fehst] firm, solid, rigid

Fest [fehst] *n* celebration, party

festsetzen [fehst-zehtsən] to fix

fett [feht] fat; greasy

feucht [foyçt] moist, damp

Feuer [foyər] *n* fire

feuergefährlich [foyər-gəfehr-lihç] inflammable

Feuerlöscher [foyər-lœSər] *m* fire extinguisher

Feuermelder [foyər-mehldər] *m* fire alarm

Feuerwehr [foyər-vehr] *f* fire department

Feuerwerk [foyər-vehrk] *n* fireworks

Feuerzeug [foyər-tsoyk] *n* lighter

Filiale [fihl-yahlə] *f* branch (office)

Film [fihlm] *m* film, movie; (roll of) film

Filter [fihltər] *m* filter

finden [fihndən] to find

finster [fihnstər] dark

Firma [fihrmə] *f* firm, company

Fisch [fihS] *m* fish; **Fischhändler** [fihS-hehndlər]] *m* fish dealer

fischen [fihSən] to fish

fit [fiht] fit

flach [flahx] flat; level

Flamme [flahmə] *f* flame

Flasche [flahSə] *f* bottle

Fleck(en) [flehk(ən)] stain; **Fleck(en)mittel** [flehk(ən)-mihtəl] *n* stain remover

Fleisch [flayS] *n* meat

fleißig [flay-sihç] industrious, hard-working

flicken [flihkən] to mend; to darn

Fliege [fliigə] *f* fly

fliegen [fliigən] to fly

fließen [fliisən] to flow

flirten [flihrtən] to flirt

Fluss [fluhs] *m* river

flüssig [flew-sihç] liquid

folgen [folgən] to follow

fordern [fordərn] to demand, to ask

Forderung [fordə-ruhŋ] *f* demand; claim

Form [form] *f* form, shape

Format [for-maht] *n* size, format

Formular [for-moo-lahr] *n* form

fort [fort] away

Fortschritt [fort-Sriht] *m* progress

fortsetzen [fort-zehtsən] to continue

Foto [foh-toh] *n* photo

Fotoapparat [foh-toh-ah-pah-raht] *m* camera

Fotograf [foh-toh-grahf] *m* photographer

fotografieren [foh-toh-grah-fiirən] to take a photo/picture

Fracht [frahxt] *f* freight

Frage [frahgə] *f* question; problem

fragen [frahgən] to ask

französisch [frahnt-sœ-zihS] French

Frau [frau] *f* woman; wife; Madam; Ms., Mrs.

Fräulein [froy-layn] *n* young lady; Miss

frei [fray] free; exempt; **im Freien** [ihm frayən] in the open air, outdoors

fremd [frehmt] strange; foreign; unknown

Fremde [frehmdə] *m/f* stranger; foreigner

Fremdenführer [frehmdən-fewrər] *m* guide

Freude [froydə] *f* joy, pleasure

freuen: s. ~ (über) [froyən (ewbər)] to be pleased (with/about); **s. freuen auf** [froyən auf] to look forward to

Freund/in [froynt / froyn-dihn] (boy)friend/(girl)friend

freundlich [froynt-lihç] friendly, kind

Freundlichkeit [froynt-lihç-kayt] *f* kindness

Freundschaft [froynt-Sahft] *f* friendship

Friede [friidə] *m* peace

frieren [friirən] to be cold, to freeze

frisch [frihS] fresh; cool; new; (clothing) clean

froh [froh] glad; happy; merry

früh [frew] early

früher [frewər] earlier

frühstücken [frew-Stewkən] to have breakfast

fühlen [fewlən] to feel

führen [fewrən] to lead

Führer [fewrər] *m* guide

füllen [fewlən] to fill

Fundbüro [fuhnt-bew-roh] *n* lost and found office

A/Z

Funke [fuhŋkə] *m* spark
funktionieren [fuhŋk-tsyoh-**niir**ən] to
work
für [fewr] for
Furcht [fuhrçt] *f* fear
fürchten [fewrçtən] to fear; **s. fürchten
vor** [fewrçtən for]] to be afraid of
fürchterlich [fewrçtər-lihç] terrible,
dreadful, horrible
Fußgänger/in [fuhs-gehŋər / -ihn]
pedestrian
Futter [fuhtər] *n (clothing)* lining;
(Tier~ [tiir-fuhtər]) animal food, feed

G

gähnen [gehnən] to yawn
Gang [gahŋ] *m* passage, corridor; *(car)*
gear; *(meal)* course
ganz [gahnts] *(adj)* whole; *(pl)* all; en-
tire, complete; *(adv)* quite
gar [gahr] cooked, done; **gar nicht**
[gahr nihçt] not at all
Garage [gah-**rah**Zə] *f* garage
Garantie [gah-rahn-**tii**] *f* guarantee
Garten [gahrtən] *m* garden, yard
Gast [gahst] *m* guest
Gastfreundschaft [gahst-froynt-Sahft] *f*
hospitality
Gastgeber/in [gahst-geybər / -ihn]
host/hostess
Gasthaus/Gasthof [gahst-haus / -hohf] *f*
hotel, inn
Gebäude [gəboydə] *n* building
geben [geybən] to give
Gebet [gəbeht] *n* prayer
geboren [gəbohrən] born
Gebrauch [gəbraux] *m* use
gebrauchen [gəbrauxən] to use
gebräuchlich [gəbroyç-lihç] common
Gebühren [gəbewrən] *f pl* fees
Geburt [gəboort] *f* birth; **Geburtsort**
[gəboorts-ort] *m* birthplace
Geburtstag [gəboorts-tahk] *m* birthday
Gedanke [gədahŋkə] *m* thought
Geduld [gəduhlt] *f* patience
geduldig [gəduhl-dihç] patient
Gefahr [gəfahr] *f* danger
gefährlich [gəfehr-lihç] dangerous
gefallen [gəfahlən] to please
Gefallen [gəfahlən] **, das** pleasure;
Gefallen, der favor

Gefälligkeit [gəfeh-lihç-kayt] *f* favor
Gefäß [gəfehs] *n* container
Gefühl [gəfewl] *n* feeling
gegen [geygən] against; *(sports)* versus;
towards; *(time)* about
Gegend [geygənt] *f* region, area, district
Gegenstand [geygən-Stahnt] *m* object,
item; *(discussion)* topic
Gegenteil [geygən-tayl] *n* opposite,
contrary; **im Gegenteil** [ihm geygən
tayl] on the contrary
gegenüber [geygən-**ewb**ər] opposite
geheim [gəhaym] secret
gehen [geyən] to go; to walk; **geradeaus gehen** [gərahdə-**aus**-geyən] to
go straight ahead; **vorwärts gehen**
[for-vehrts geyən] to go on; **zurückgehen** [tsuh-**rewk**-geyən] to go back
gehören [gəhœrən] to belong to
Gelände [gəlehndə] *n* ground
Geld [gehlt] *n* money; **Geldbeutel**
[gehlt-boytəl] *m* purse; **Geldstrafe**
[gehlt-Strahfə] *f* fine; **Geldstück**
[gehlt-Stewk] *n* coin
Geldwechsel [gehlt-vehksəl] *m (sign)*
bureau de change, exchange office
Gelegenheit [gəleygən-hayt] *f* occasion;
(günstige [gyn-stihgə] ~) opportunity
gelegentlich [gəleygənt-lihç] occa-
sional(ly)
gelten [gehltən] to be valid
gemein [gəmayn] mean; vulgar
gemeinsam [gəmayn-zahm] common;
together
gemischt [gəmihSt] mixed
gemütlich [gəmewt-lihç] comfortable,
cozy
genau [gənau] exact(ly); **genauso ...
wie** [gənau-zoh ... vii] just as ... as
Genauigkeit [gənau-ihç-kayt] *f* accuracy
genehmigen [gəney-mihgən] to grant
permission
genießen [gəniisən] to enjoy
genug [gənook] enough, sufficient
Genuss [gənuhs] *m* enjoyment
geöffnet [gəœfnət] open
gerade [gərahdə] straight; *(time)* just
geradeaus [gərahdə-aus] straight ahead
Geräusch [gəroyS] *n* noise
gerecht [gərehçt] just, fair
Gericht [gərihçt] *n (food)* dish; *(law)*
court

gering [geh-**rihŋ**] little, small; **geringer** less

gern [gehrn] gladly; **nicht gern** reluctantly

Geruch [gəruhx] *m* smell

Gesang [gəzahŋ] *m* singing

Geschäft [gəSehft] *n* shop, store; business

geschehen [gəSeyən] to happen; **was ist geschehen?** [vahs ihst gəSeyən] what (has) happened?

Geschenk [gəSehŋk] *n* present, gift

Geschichte [gəSihçtə] *f* history; story

geschickt [gəSihkt] skillful

geschlossen [gəSlosən] shut, closed

Geschmack [gəSmahk] *m* taste

Geschwindigkeit [gəSvihn-dihç-kayt] *f* speed

Gesellschaft [gəzehl-Sahft] *f* society; company

Gespräch [gəSprehç] *n* conversation, talk

gesund [gəzuhnt] healthy

Gesundheit [gəzuhnt-hayt] *f* health

getrennt [gətrehnt] separate

gewähren [gəvehrən] to grant

gewaltig [gəvahl-tihç] enormous

Gewebe [gəveybə] *n* fabric

Gewicht [gəvihçt] *n* weight

Gewinn [gəvihn] *m* profit

gewinnen [gəvihnən] to gain; to win

gewiss [gəvihs] certain(ly), sure(ly)

gewissenhaft [gəvihsən-hahft] conscientious(ly)

Gewitter [gəvihtər] *n* thunderstorm

gewöhnen: s. ~ an [gəvœhnən ahn] to get used to

Gewohnheit [gəvohn-hayt] *f* habit

gewöhnlich [gəvœn-lihç] usual, ordinary, ordinarily; vulgar; **wie gewöhnlich** [vii gəvœn-lihç] as usual

gewohnt [gəvohnt] usual; **etwas gewohnt sein** to be used to s. th.

gibt, es [ehs gihpt] there is, there are

Gift [gihft] *n* poison

giftig [gihf-tihç] poisonous

Gipfel [gihpfəl] *m* summit

Gips [gihps] *m* plaster, cast

Gitarre [gii-**tahr**ə] *f* guitar

Gitter [gihtər] *n* bars; railings

glänzen [glehntsən] to shine

glänzend [glehntsənt] radiant, brilliant; *(fig.)* splendid, glorious

Glas [glahs] *n* glass

glatt [glaht] smooth; slippery

Glaube [glaubə] *m* faith

glauben [glaubən] to believe

gleich [glayç] same; immediately, at once

gleichen [glayçən] to look like

gleichfalls [glayç-fahls] also, likewise

gleichwertig [glayç-vehr-tihç] equivalent

gleichzeitig [glayç-tsay-tihç] simultaneous(ly)

Glück [glewk] *n* luck; success; **viel Glück!** [fiil glewk] good luck!; **Glück haben** to be lucky

glücklich [glewk-lihç] happy; lucky

Glückwunsch [glewk-vuhnS] *m* congratulations

Glut [gloot] *f* heat

Gott [got] *m* God; **Gott sei Dank!** [got zay dahŋk] thank goodness!

Grad [graht] *n* degree

gratis [grah-tihs] free

gratulieren [grah-tuh-**liir**ən] to congratulate

Grenze [grehntsə] *f* border

Griff [grihf] *m (Hand~)* handle

groß [grohs] big, large; tall; great

großartig [grohs-ahr-tihç] great

Größe [grœsə] *f* size; height

Großmutter [grohs-muhtər] *f* grandmother

Großvater [grohs-fahtər] *m* grandfather

Grund [gruhnt] *m* reason, cause; *(Beweg~* [bəveyk-gruhnt]*)* motive

Gruppe [gruhpə] *f* group

grüßen [grewsən] to greet

gültig [gewl-tihç] valid

Gültigkeit [gewl-tihç-kayt] *f* validity

günstig [gewn-stihç] favorable

gut [goot] *(adj)* good; *(adv)* well

Gutschein [goot-Sayn] *m* voucher

H

haben [hahbən] to have

Hahn [hahn] *m* cock, rooster; *(Wasser~* [vahsər-hahn]*)* tap, faucet

Haken [hahkən] *m* hook; *(Kleider~* [klaydər-hahkən]*)* peg, clothes hook

halb [hahlp] half

Hälfte [hehlftə] *f* half

Halle [hahlə] *f* hall

hallo [hah-loh] hello
halt! [hahlt] halt!, stop!
haltbar [hahlt-bahr] durable; **haltbar sein** *(food)* to keep
halten [hahltən] to keep; to last; to stop
Hammer [hahmər] *m* hammer
Hand [hahnt] *f* hand
handgemacht [hahnt-gəmahxt] hand-made
Handtasche [hahnt-tahSə] *f* handbag, purse
Hang [hahŋ] *m (Ab~* [ahp-hahŋ]*)* slope
hängen [hehŋən] to hang
hart [hahrt] hard, solid
hässlich [hehs-lihç] ugly
häufig [hoy-fihç] frequent(ly)
Haupteingang [haupt-ayn-gahŋ] *m* main entrance
Hauptstadt [haupt-Staht] *f* capital
Haus [haus] *n* house
Haustür [haus-tewr] *f* front door
heben [heybən] to lift
Heft [hehft] *n (Schreib~* [Srayp-hehft]*)* notebook, exercise book; magazine
heilig [hay-lihç] holy
Heimat [hay-maht] *f* home, native country
heimlich [haym-lihç] secret
Heimreise [haym-rayzə] *f* return journey, trip home
Heirat [hay-rat] *f* marriage
heiraten [hai-rahtən] to marry
heiß [hays] hot
heißen [haysən] to be called; **wie heißen Sie?** [vii haysən zii] what's your name?
heiter [haytər] cheerful; *(weather)* bright, clear
heizen [haytsən] to heat
Heizöl [hayts-œl] *n* heating oil, fuel oil
hektisch [hehk-tihS] hectic
helfen [hehlfən]: **jdm ~** to help s. o.
hell [hehl] bright
herabsetzen [hehr-ahp-zehtsən] *(price)* to reduce
heraufsetzen [hehr-auf-zehtsən] *(price)* to raise
herausgeben [hehr-aus-geybən] *(money)* to give change for; to publish
herb [hehrp] *(wine)* dry
herein! [hehr-ayn] come in!
hereinkommen [hehr-ayn-komən] to come in

Hering [heh-rihŋ] *m* herring; tent peg, tent stake
Herr [hehr] *m* gentleman; Mr.
herrlich [hehr-lihç] glorious, splendid, terrific
Herz [hehrts] *n* heart
herzlich [hehrts-lihç] warm, sincere
Herzlichkeit [hehrts-lihç-kayt] *f* warmth, sincerity
heute [hoytə] today; **heute Abend** [hoytə ah-bənt] this evening; **heute Nacht** [hoytə nahxt] tonight
hier [hiir] here
hierher [hiir-hehr] this way
Hilfe [hihlfə] *f* help, aid; **erste Hilfe** [ehrstə hihlfə] first aid
Himmel [hihməl] *m* sky; heaven
hinaufgehen [hihn-auf-geyən] to go up
hinausgehen [hihn-aus-geyən] to go out, to leave
hindern [hihndərn] to prevent, to hinder
hineingehen [hihn-ayn-geyən] to go in, to enter
hinlegen [hihn-leygən] to put down; **s. hinlegen** to lie down
hinsetzen, s. [hihn-zetsən] to sit down
hinten [hihntən] at the back
hinter [hihntər] behind
hinterlassen [hihntər-lahsən] to leave
hinterlegen [hihntər-leygən] to deposit
hinuntergehen [hihn-uhntər-geyən] to go down
hinzufügen [hihn-tsoo-fewgən] to add
Hobby [ho-bii] *n* hobby
hoch [hohx] high
höchstens [hœkstəns] at the most, at best
Hochzeit [hohx-tsayt] *f* wedding
Hof [hohf] *m* (court)yard
hoffen [hofən] to hope
höflich [hœf-lihç] polite
Höflichkeit [hœf-lihç-kayt] *f* politeness
Höhe [hœə] *f* height
Höhepunkt [hœə-puhŋkt] *m* highlight; *(career)* peak, height; *(film, play)* climax
holen [hohlən] to fetch, to get
Holz [holts] *n* wood; *(Brenn~* [brehn-holts]*)* firewood
Honorar [hoh-noh-rahr] *n* fee
hören [hœrən] to hear; **zuhören** [tsoo-hœrən] to listen (to)
Hotel [hoh-tehl] *n* hotel

hübsch [hewpS] pretty, cute
Hügel [hewgəl] *m* hill
Hund [huhnt] *m* dog
hundert [huhndərt] a hundred; **hundertmal** [huhndərt-mahl] a hundred times
Hunger [huhŋər] *m* hunger
hungrig [huhŋ-rihç] hungry
husten [hoostən] to cough
Hütte [hewtə] *f* hut, cottage, cabin

I

ich [ihç] I
Idee [ii-**dey**] *f* idea
ihr [iir] her, their
Imbiss [ihm-bihs] *m* snack
immer [ihmər] always
im Stande sein [ihm Stahndə] to be able to
in [ihn] in
inbegriffen [ihn-bəgrihfən] included
informieren [ihn-for-**miirə**n] to inform
Inhalt [ihn-hahlt] *m* contents
Inland [ihn-lahnt] *n* home, homeland
innen [ihnən] inside
Innere [ihnərə]: **das** ~ the inside
innerhalb [ihnər-hahlp] (time) within
Insekt [ihn-**zehkt**] *n* insect
Insel [ihnzəl] *f* island
Inserat [ihn-zeh-**raht**] *n* advertisement
interessant [ihntər-reh-**sahnt**] interesting
Interesse [ihntə-**rehsə**] *n* interest
interessieren [ihntə-reh-**siirə**n (fewr)]: **s.** ~ **(für)** to be interested (in)
international [ihntər-naht-syoh-**nahl**] international
inzwischen [ihn-**tsvih**Sən] meanwhile
Ire [iirə] *m* Irishman
irgendein(e, er, es) [ihrgənt-ayn(ə,ər,əs] someone
irgendwie [ihrgənt-vii] somehow
irgendwo, irgendwohin [ihrgənt-voh(-hihn)] somewhere
Irin [ii-rihn] *f* Irishwoman
irisch [ii-rihS] Irish
Irland [iir-lahnt] Ireland, Eire
irren, s. [ihrən] to be mistaken
Irrtum [ihr-tuhm] *m* mistake

J

Jahr [yahr] *n* year
Jahreszeit [yahrəs-tsayt] *f* season
jährlich [yehr-lihç] annual(ly)
je [yey] ever; every
jeder [yeydər] every; **jeder Beliebige** [yeydər bəlii-bihgə] any; **jeder Einzelne** [yeydər ayn-tsehlnə] each; **jedermann** [yeydər-mahn] everybody
jedes Mal [yeydəs mahl] every time
jedoch [yey-**dox**] however
jemals [yey-mahls] ever
jemand [yey-mahnt] somebody; anybody
jene [yeynə] that, those
jenseits [yehn-zayts] beyond
jetzt [yehtst] now
jucken [yuhkən] to itch
Jugend [yoogənt] *f* youth
jung [yuhŋ] young
Junge [yuhŋə] *m* boy
Junggeselle [yuhŋ-gəzehlə] *m* bachelor

K

Kabine [kah-**biin**ə] *f* cabin
Kaffee [kah-fey] *m* coffee
Kahn [kahn] *m* boat
Kakerlake [kahkər-lahkə] *f* cockroach
kalt [kahlt] cold
Kanal [kah-**nahl**] *m* canal; channel
Kapelle [kah-**pehlə**] *f* chapel; *(Musik~* [moo-**zihk**-kah-pehlə]*)* band
kaputt [kah-**puht**] broken, out of order
Karte [kahrtə] *f* card; **Eintrittskarte** [ayn-trihts-kahrtə] *f* ticket ; **Landkarte** [lahnt-kahrtə] *f* map; **Postkarte** [post-kahrtə] *f* postcard; **Speisekarte** [Spayzə-kahrtə] *f* menu
Kasse [kahsə] *f* cashier's desk; box office, ticket office
Katze [kahtsə] *f* cat
Kauf [kauf] *m* purchase
kaufen [kaufən] to buy
Käufer [koyfər] *m* buyer; customer
Kaufhaus [kauf-haus] *n* department store
Kaugummi [kau-guh-mii] *m* chewing gum
kaum [kaum] hardly, scarcely, barely
Kaution [kaut-**syohn**] *f* security, down payment

kein [kayn] no
keine(r, s) [kaynə(r,s)] nobody
keinesfalls [kaynəs-fahls] on no account, no way
kennen [kehnən] to know; **kennen lernen** [kehnən lehrnən] to meet
kennen lernen [kehnən lehrnən]: **jdn ~** to get to know s. o.
Kenntnis [kehnt-nihs] f knowledge
Kennzeichen [kehn-tsayçən] n mark; (*Auto~* [au-toh-kehn-tsayçən]) license plate
Keramik [keh-**rah**-mihk] f pottery
Kerze [kehrtsə] f candle
Kette [kehtə] f chain; (*Hals~* [hahls-kehtə]) necklace
Kind [kihnt] n child
Kissen [kihsən] n cushion; (*Kopf~* [kopf-kihsən]) pillow
Kiste [kistə] f box, chest
Klang [klahŋ] m sound
klar [klahr] clear
Klasse [klahsə] f class
Kleidung [klay-duhŋ] f clothing
klein [klayn] little, small
Klima [kliimə] n climate
Klingel [klihŋəl] f bell
klingeln [klihŋəln] to ring
klug [klook] clever, intelligent
knipsen [knihpsən] (*photo*) to take a snapshot
Knopf [knopf] m button
Knoten [knohtən] m knot
kochen [koxən] to cook; (*coffee, tea*) to make; (*water*) to boil
Koffer [kofər] m suitcase
Kohle [kohlə] f coal
Kollege/Kollegin [koh-**leyg**ə / koh-**ley**-gihn] colleague
kommen [komən] to come
Kompass [kom-pahs] m compass
Kondom [kon-dohm] n condom
können [kœnən] to be able to
Konsulat [kon-zuh-**laht**] n consulate
konsultieren [kon-zul-**tiir**ən] to consult
Kontakt [kon-**tahkt**] m contact
kontrollieren [kon-troh-**liir**ən] to control; to check
Kopie [ko-**pii**] f copy
Korb [korp] m basket
Körper [kœrpər] m body
korrekt [ko-**rehkt**] correct
kosten [kostən] to cost

Kosten [kostən] pl costs, expenses
kostenlos [kostən-lohs] free (of charge)
kostspielig [kost-Spii-lihç] expensive
Kraft [krahft] f force, strength
kräftig [krehf-tihç] strong
krank [krahŋk] ill, sick; **krank werden** [krahŋk vehrdən]] to be taken ill, to get sick
Krankenwagen [krahŋkən-vahgən] m ambulance
kreativ [krey-ah-**tiif**] creative
Kredit [krey-**diit**] m credit
Kreuzung [kroyt-suhŋ] f (*Straßen~* [Strahsən-kroyt-suhŋ]) crossroads, intersection
Krieg [kriik] m war
kriegen [kriigən] to get
kritisieren [krih-tih-**ziir**ən] to criticize
Küche [kewçə] f kitchen
Kuh [koo] f cow
kühl [kewl] cool
Kultur [kuhl-**toor**] f culture
Kummer [kuhmər] m grief; problems
kümmern [kewmərn uhm]: **s. ~** um to look after s. o./s. th., to take care of s. o./s. th.
Kunde/Kundin [kuhndə / kuhn-dihn] customer
Kurs [kuhrs] m course; (*Wechsel~* [vehksəl-kuhrs]) exchange rate
Kurve [kuhrvə] f bend, curve
kurz [kuhrts] short
kurzfristig [kuhrts-frihs-tihç] at short notice
Kuss [kuhs] m kiss
küssen [kewsən] to kiss
Küste [kewstə] f coast

L

lachen [lahxən] to laugh
lächerlich [lehçər-lihç] ridiculous
Laden [lahdən] m shop, store
Lage [lahgə] f situation; position, location
Lampe [lahmpə] f lamp
Land [lahnt] n country; land
Landgut [lahnt-goot] n estate
Landhaus [lahnt-haus] n manor (house)
Landsmann [lahnts-mahn] m fellow countryman
lang [lahŋ] long

Länge [lehŋə] *f* length
langsam [lahŋ-zahm] slow(ly)
langweilig [lahŋ-vay-lihç] boring
Lärm [lehrm] *m* noise
lassen [lahsən] to let
lästig [leh-stihç] annoying
Lastwagen [lahst-vahgən] *m* truck
laufen [laufən] to run; to go; to walk
Laune [launə] *f* mood
laut [laut] loud; noisy
läuten [loytən] to ring
Lautsprecher [laut-Sprehçər] *m* loudspeaker
Leben [leybən] *n* life
leben [leybən] to live
lebend [leybənt] alive
Lebensmittel [leybəns-mihtəl] *n pl* food
lebhaft [leyp-hahft] lively
Leder [leydər] *n* leather
ledig [ley-dihç] single
leer [leyr] empty
legen [leygən] to put
lehren [lehrən] to teach
leicht [layçt] easy; slight; *(weight)* light
leider [laydər] unfortunately
leihen [layən] to lend; to borrow
leise [layzə] quiet
Leiter/in [laytər / -ihn], **der/die** ~ head,
boss, manager; **Leiter** *f* ladder
Leitung [lay-tuhŋ] *f (electricity)* wire;
(telephone) line; *(gas, water)* pipe
lernen [lehrnən] to learn
lesen [layzən] to read
letzte(r, -s) [letstə(r,s)] last
leuchtend [layçtət] shining, bright
Leuchtturm [loyçt-tuhrm] *m* lighthouse
leugnen [loygnən] to deny
Leute [loytə] *pl* people
Licht [lihçt] *n* light; **Licht
anmachen/ausmachen** [lihçt ahn/aus-
mahxən]) to switch on/off the light
lieb [liip] nice; **jdn lieb haben** to be
fond of s. o.; **Lieber Hans** Dear Hans
Liebe [liibə] *f* love
lieben [liibən] to love
liebenswürdig [liibəns-vewr-dihç] kind
Liebenswürdigkeit [liibəns-vewr-dihç-
kayt] *f* kindness
lieber [liibər] *(adv)* rather; **etw lieber
haben** to prefer
Liebling [liib-lihŋ] *m* darling;
(Lieblings-... [liib-lihŋs-]) favorite
Lied [Ilit] *n* song

liefern [liifərn] to deliver
liegen [liigən] to lie
liegen lassen [liigən lahsən]: **etw ~** to
forget s. th.
Linie [lihnyə] *f* line
linke(r, -s) [lihŋkə(r,s)] left(-hand)
links [lihŋks] on the left, to the left
Liste [lihstə] *f* list
loben [lohbən] to praise
Loch [lox] *n* hole; puncture
logisch [loh-gihS] logical; of course
Lohn [lohn] *m* wages; reward
Lokal [loh-**kahl**] *n* restaurant; pub,
saloon
löschen [lœSən] to extinguish, to put out
lösen [lœzən] to untie, to undo
Luft [luhft] *f* air
lüften [lewftən] to air
Luftzug [luhft-tsuhk] *m* draft
Lüge [lewgə] *f* lie
Lust [luhst] *f* pleasure, joy; desire; lust
lustig [luhs-tihç] merry, in a good
mood; funny
luxuriös [luhk-soor-**yœs**] luxurious
Luxus [luhk-suhs] *m* luxury

M

machen [mahxən] to do; to make;
machen lassen [mahxən lahsən] to
have s. th. made/done
Mädchen [mehtçən] *n* girl
mager [mahgər] thin; *(meat)* lean
Mahlzeit [mahl-tsayt] *f* meal
Mal [mahl] *n* time; **einmal** [ayn-mahl]
once; **zweimal** [tsvay-mahl] twice;
jedes Mal [yeydəs mahl] every time
malen [mahlən] to paint
man [mahn] one
Mangel [mahŋəl] *m* lack, shortage; fault
Mann [mahn] *m* man; *(Ehe~* [eyə-
mahn]*)* husband
männlich [mehn-lihç] male
Mannschaft [mahn-Sahft] *f* team; crew
Mappe [mahpə] *f* folder; briefcase
Marke [mahrkə] *f (Brief~* [briif-
mahrkə]*)* postage stamp; *(Handels~*
[hahndəls-mahrkə]*)* brand, trademark
Maschine [mah-**Siin**ə] *f* machine
Maß [mahs] *n* measure
mäßig [meh-sihç] moderate
Material [mah-tehr-**yahl**] *n* material

Meer [meyr] *n* sea
mehr [mehr] more; **mehr als** [mehr ahls] more than; **mehr oder weniger** [mehr ohdər vey-nihgər] more or less
Meile [maylə] *f* mile
mein [mayn] my; **meinerseits** [maynər-zayts] as for me ; **meinetwegen** [mayn-eht-veygən] I don't mind
meinen [maynən] to think
Meinung [may-nuhŋ] *f* opinion, view; **nach meiner Meinung** [nahx maynər may-nuhŋ] in my opinion
melden [mehldən] to announce; to inform
Menge [mehŋə] *f* quantity; *(Menschen~* [mehnSən-mehŋə]) crowd; **eine Menge** a lot of
Mensch [mehnS] *m* person, man/woman; *(der ~)* man
menschlich [mehnS-lihç] human
merken [mehrkən] to be aware of; **s. etw merken** to remember s. th.
Messe [mehsə] *f (rel.)* mass; fair, exhibition
messen [mehsən] to measure
mich [mihç] me
Miete [miitə] *f* rent
mieten [miitən] to rent, to hire
mild [mihlt] mild
mindestens [mihndəs-tehns] at least
minus [mii-noos] minus
Minute [mih-nootə] *f* minute
mir [miir] me, to me
misstrauen [mihs-trauən] to distrust
Missverständnis [mihs-fehr-Stehnd-nihs] *n* misunderstanding
missverstehen [mihs-fehr-Steyən] to misunderstand
mit [miht] with
mitbringen [miht-brihŋən] to bring
Mitleid [miht-layt] *n* pity
mitnehmen [miht-neymən] to take
Mittag [miht-tahk] *m* noon; **Mittagessen** [mih-tahk-ehsən] *n* lunch; **mittags** [mih-tahks] at noon
Mitte [mihtə] *f* middle
mitteilen [miht-taylən] to inform
Mitteilung [miht-tay-luhŋ] *f* announcement; memo
Mittel [mihtəl] *n* means; *(Heil~)* remedy
Mitternacht [mihtər-nahxt] *f* midnight; **um Mitternacht** [uhm mihtər-nahxt] at midnight

Möbel [mœbəl] *n* furniture
möblieren [mœb-liirən] to furnish
Mode [mohdə] *f* fashion
modern [moh-dehrn] modern, up to date
mögen [mœgən] to like; to want
möglich [mœg-lihç] possible
Möglichkeit [mœg-lihç-kayt] *f* possibility
Mole [mohlə] *f* pier
Moment [moh-mehnt] *m* moment
Monat [moh-naht] *m* month
monatlich [moh-naht-lihç] monthly
Mond [mohnt] *m* moon
Morgen [morgən] *m* morning
Möwe [mœvə] *f* seagull
Mücke [mewkə] *f* gnat, mosquito
müde [mewdə] tired
Mühe [mewə] *f* trouble, effort; **s. Mühe geben** [mewə geybən] to take pains
Müll [mewl] *m* garbage
Mülltonne [mewl-tonə] *f* trashcan
münden [mewndən] *(river)* to flow into; *(road)* to run into
Mündung [mewn-duhŋ] *f (river, road)* mouth
Münze [mewntsə] *f* coin
müssen [mewsən] to have to; **wir/sie müssen** [viir/zii mewsən] we/they must; **ich werde … müssen** [ihç vehrdə ... mewsən] I'll have to; **ich habe … müssen** [ihç hahbə ... mewsən] I have had to
Musik [moo-ziik] *f* music
Muster [muhstər] *n* model; sample
Mutter [muhtər] *f* mother

N

nach [nahx] after; **nach New York** to New York
Nachbar/in [nahx-bahr / -ihn] neighbor
nachgehen [nahx-geyən] to follow; *(clock)* to be slow
nachher [nahx-hehr] afterwards
nachlässig [nahx-leh-sihç] careless, negligent
Nachmittag [nahx-mih-tahk] *m* afternoon; **nachmittags** [nahx-mih-tahks] in the afternoon
nachprüfen [nahx-prewfən] to check
Nachricht [nahx-rihçt] *f* message

Nachrichten [nahx-rihçtən] *f pl* news

nachsehen [nahx-zeyən] to have a look, to check

nächste [nekstə] next

Nacht [nahxt] *f* night; **heute Nacht** [hoytə nahxt] tonight

Nachteil [nahx-tayl] *m* disadvantage

nackt [nahkt] naked, nude

Nadel [nahdəl] *f* needle

Nagel [nahgəl] *m* nail

nahe [nah-ə] near, close; **nahe bei** [nah-ə bay] close to

Nähe: in der ~ von [ihn dehr neyə fon] near

nähern [neyərn] *s.* to approach

nahrhaft [nahr-hahft] nourishing

Nahrung [nah-ruhŋ] *f* food; **Nahrungsmittel** [nah-ruhŋs-mihtəl] *n pl* food(stuffs)

Name [nahmə] *m* name

nass [nahs] wet, moist; soaked

Nation [naht-syohn] *f* nation

Natur [nah-toor] *f* nature

natürlich [nah-tewr-lihç] natural(ly); of course

neben [neybən] next to, beside

neblig [neyb-lihç] misty, foggy

Neffe [nehfə] *m* nephew

negativ [ney-gah-tiif] negative

nehmen [neymən] to take

nein [nayn] no

nennen [nehnən] to name, to call

nervös [nehr-vœs] nervous

nett [neht] nice

Netz [nehts] *n* net

neu [noy] new; recent

neugierig [noy-gii-rihç] curious

Neuheit [noy-hayt] *f* innovation

Neuigkeit [noy-ihç-kayt] *f* (piece of) news

neulich [noy-lihç] the other day

nicht [nihçt] not; **nicht einmal** [nihçt ayn-mahl] not even; **gar nicht** [gar nihçt] not at all; **noch nicht** [nox nihçt] not yet

Nichte [nihçtə] *f* niece

nichts [nihçts] nothing; **sonst nichts** [zonst nihçts] nothing else

nie [nii] never

nieder, niedrig [niidər, niid-rihç] low

niemand [nii-mahnt] nobody

niesen [niizən] to sneeze

nirgends [nihrgənts] nowhere

noch [nox] still; **noch nich** [nox nihçts] not yet

Nonne [nonə] *f* nun

Norden [nordən] *m* north

Nordirland [nort-iir-lahnt] Northern Ireland

nördlich [nœrt-lihç] northern; **nördlich von** [nœrt-lihç fon] (to the) north of

Nordsee [nort-zey] *f* North Sea

normal [nor-mahl] normal; standard

normalerweise [nor-mahlər-vayzə] normally, usually

Notfall: im ~ [ihm noht-fahl] in case of emergency

notieren [noh-tiirən] to make a note of

nötig [nœ-tihç] necessary

notwendig [noht-vehn-dihç] necessary

Notwendigkeit [noht-vehn-dihç-kayt] *f* necessity

nüchtern [newçtərn] sober

nummerieren [nuhmə-riirən] to number

Nummer [nuhmər] *f* number

nun [nuhn] now

nur [noor] only

nützlich [newts-lihç] useful

nutzlos [nuhts-lohs] useless

O

ob [op] whether

oben [obən] up; **dort oben** [dort obən] up there; **nach oben** [nahx obən] up; upstairs

obwohl [op-vohl] although

oder [ohdər] or

Ofen [ohfən] *m* stove

offen [ofən] open

öffentlich [œfənt-lihç] public

offiziell [oh-fiht-syehl] official

öffnen [œfnən] to open

Öffnungszeiten [œf-nuhŋs-tsaytən] *f pl* opening hours, hours of business

oft [oft] often

ohne [ohnə] without

ohnmächtig [ohn-mehç-tihç] unconscious; **~ werden** [ohn-mehç-tihç vehrdən] to faint

Öl [œl] *n* oil

Onkel [oŋkəl] *m* uncle

operieren [ohpə-riirən] to operate

Orden [ordən] *m* (rel.) order

ordentlich [ordənt-lihç] neat, orderly

A/Z

Ordnung [ord-nuhŋ] *f* order
Ort [ort] *m* place; spot
Ortschaft [ort-Sahft] *f* village, town
Osten [ohstən] *m* east
Österreich [œstər-rayç] Austria
Österreicher/in [œstər-rayçər / -ihn]
  Austrian
Ozean [oht-sey-ahn] *m* ocean

P

Paar [pahr] *m*: **ein ~** a pair of; **paar: ein ~**
  a few; *(Ehe~* [eyə-pahr]*)* couple
Päckchen [pehkçən] *n* package
packen [pahkən] to pack
Packung [pah-kuhŋ] *f* packet, pack; box
Paket [pah-keht] *n* parcel
Panorama [pah-noh-**rah**-mah] *n*
  panorama
Park [pahrk] *m* park
parken [pahrkən] to park
Party [pahr-tii] *f* party
Pass [pahs] *m* passport; *(mountain)* pass
Passage [pah-sah**Zə**] *f* passage;
  (Laden~ [lahdən-pah-sah**Zə**]*)* arcade
passen [pahsən] to fit; to suit
passieren [pah-siirən] to happen
Pauschale [pau-Sahlə] *f* flat rate
Pelz [pehlts] *m* fur
Peripherie [pey-rii-fey-**rii**] *f* outskirts
Person [pehr-**zohn**] *f* person
Personal [pehr-zoh-**nahl**] *n* staff
Personalien [pehr-zoh-**nahl**yən] *pl* par-
  ticulars, personal data
persönlich [pehr-**zœn**-lihç] personal
Pfad [pfaht] *m* path
Pfand [pfant] *n* deposit, security;
  Pfandleihe [pfahnt-layə] *f* pawnshop
Pfeife [pfayfə] *f* pipe
Pflanze [pflahntsə] *f* plant
Pflicht [pflihçt] *f* duty
pflücken [pflewkən] to pick
Plakat [plah-**kaht**] *n* poster
Plan [plahn] *m* plan; draft
Plastik [plah-stihk], *n* plastic; *f* sculp-
  ture
Platte [plahtə] *f* (meal) dish; *(Schall~*
  [Sahl-plahtə]*)* record
Plattenspieler [plahtən-Spiilər] *m*
  record player
Platz [plahts] *m* place; *(Sitz~* [zihts-
  plahts]*)* seat

platzen [plahtsən] to burst
plötzlich [plœts-lihç] suddenly
plus [ploos] plus
Politik [poh-lih-**tiik**] *f* politics; policy
positiv [poh-zih-**tiif**] positive
Post [post] *f* mail
praktisch [prahk-tihS] practical(ly)
Predigt [prey-dihçt] *f* sermon
Preis [prays] *m* price; prize
Priester [priistər] *m* priest
prima [priimə] fantastic, great
privat [prii-**vaht**] private
pro [proh] per
Probe [prohbə] *f* experiment, trial
Produkt [proh-**duhkt**] *n* product
Programm [proh-**grahm**] *n* program
Prospekt [proh-**Spehkt**] *m* prospectus,
  leaflet, brochure
protestieren [proh-tehs-tiirən] to
  protest
provisorisch [pro-vii-**zo**-rihS] provisional, temporary
Prozent [proh-**tsehnt**] *n* percent;
  Prozentsatz [proh-**tsehnt**-zahts] *m*
  percentage
Prozession [proh-tseh-**syohn**] *f* procession
prüfen [prewfən] to examine
Prüfung [prew-fuhŋ] *f* examination,
  exam
Publikum [poo-blih-kuhm] *n* public;
  audience
Pulver [puhlfər] *n* powder
Punkt [puhŋkt] *m* point; period
pünktlich [pewŋkt-lihç] punctual(ly);
  on time
Puppe [puhpə] *f* doll; *(Hand~* [hahnt-
  puhpə]*)* puppet
putzen [puhtsən] to clean

Q

Qualität [kvah-lih-**teyt**] *f* quality
Qualle [kvahlə] *f* jellyfish
Quelle [kvehlə] *f* source; spring
quer durch [kvehr duhrç] straight
  across/through
quittieren [kvih-**tiir**ən] to give a
  receipt
Quittung [kvih-tuhŋ] *f* receipt

R

Rabatt [rah-**baht**] *m* discount
Radio [rahd-yoh] *n* radio; **Radioapparat** *m* radio
Rand [rahnt] *m* edge, brink
rasch [rahS] quick; quickly
Rasen [rahzən] *m* lawn, grass
rasieren [rah-**ziir**ən] to shave
Rat [raht] *m* advice; **jdn um Rat fragen** [uhm raht frahgən] to ask s. o.'s advice
raten [rahtən] to advise; to guess
Rauch [raux] *m* smoke
rauchen [rauxən] to smoke
Raum [raum] *m* space; room
rechnen [rehçnən] to work out, to calculate
Rechnung [rehç-nuhŋ] *f* bill, invoice, check
Recht [rehçt] *n* right; **Recht und Ordnung** [rehçt uhnt ord-nuhŋ] law and order
Recht haben [rehçt hahbən] to be right
rechte(r, -s) [rehçtə(r,s)] right(-hand)
rechts [rehçts] on the right, to the right
rechtzeitig [rehçt-tsay-tihç] in time
reden [reydən] to talk
regelmäßig [reygəl-meh-sihç] regular
regeln [reygəln] to settle
Regierung [reh-**gii**-ruhŋ] *f* government
regnen [regnən] to rain
reich [rayç] rich
reichen [rayçən (aus)] *(aus~)* to be sufficient; **etw. (über)reichen** [(ewbər) rayçən] to hand s. th. over, to pass s. th. on
reichlich [rayç-lihç] ample, plenty of
Reichtum [rayç-tuhm] *m* wealth
reif [rayf] ripe; mature
Reihe [rayə] *f* row
reinigen [ray-nihgən] to clean
Reinigung [ray-nih-guhŋ] *f* (dry) cleaners
Reise [rayzə] *f* journey, trip; *(Schiffs~* [Sihfs-rayzə]*)* voyage
Reisebüro [rayzə-bew-roh] *n* travel agency
Reiseführer [rayzə-fewrər] *m* guide
Reisegesellschaft [rayzə-gəzehl-Sahft] *f* party, tour group
reisen [rayzən] to travel; **reisen nach** [rayzən nahx] to go to
Reisende [rayzəndə], **der/die** traveler, tourist

Reiseroute [rayzə-rootə] *f* route
reißen [raysən] to tear; to pull
Reklame [rey-**klahm**ə] *f* advertisement
reklamieren [rey-klah-**miir**ən] to complain
rennen [rehnən] to run
Reparatur [rey-pah-rah-**toor**] *f* repair; **Reparaturwerkstatt** [rey-pah-rah-**toor**-vehrk-Staht] *f* workshop, garage
reparieren [rey-pah-**riir**ən] to repair
reservieren [rey-zehr-**viir**ən] to reserve
Rest [rehst] *m* rest
Restaurant [rehs-tau-**rahnt**] *n* restaurant
retten [rehtən] to save
richtig [rihç-tihç] right; proper
richtig stellen [rihç-tihç Stehlən]: **etwas ~** to put s. th. right
Richtung [rihç-tuhŋ] *f* direction
riechen [riiçən] to smell
Riegel [riigəl] *m* bolt; *(chocolate)* bar
Riemen [riimən] *m* strap
Ring [rihŋ] *m* ring
Risiko [rii-zih-koh] *n* risk
Rohr [rohr] *n* pipe, tube
Route [rootə] *f* route
Rückfahrt [rewk-fahrt] *f* return journey, trip back
Rückkehr [rewk-kehr] *f* return
Rucksack [ruhk-zahk] *m* rucksack, backpack
Rücksicht [rewk-zihçt] *f* consideration
rücksichtslos [rewk-zihçt-lohs] inconsiderate, rude
rückwärts [rewk-vehrts] backwards
rufen [roofən] to call
Ruhe [rooə] *f* rest; calm; silence
ruhen [(aus-)rooən] *(aus~)* to rest
ruhig [roo-ihç] silent, quiet, calm
rund [ruhnt] round
Runde [ruhndə] *f* (drinks) round; *(athletics)* lap; *(boxing)* round

S

Saal [zahl] *m* room; hall
Sache [zahxə] *f* thing; matter, affair
Sack [zahk] *m* bag, sack
sagen [zahgən] to say; to tell
Saison [zeh-**zohn**] *f* season; **außerhalb der Saison** [ausər-hahlp dehr zeh-zohn] in the off season, low season

sammeln [zahməln] to collect
Sammlung [zahm-luhŋ] f collection
satt [zaht] full, not hungry
Satz [zahts] m sentence
sauber [zaubər] clean
sauer [zauər] sour
Schachtel [Sahxtəl] f box
schade: es ist ~ [ehs ihst Sahdə] it's a pity;
wie schade! [vii Sahdə] what a pity!
schaden [Sahdən] to harm, to damage
Schaden [Sahdən] m damage
Schadenersatz [Sahdənər-zahts] m
compensation, damages
schädlich [Seht-lihç] harmful
Schaf [Sahf] n sheep
schaffen [Sahfən] to make, to create
Schalter [Sahltər] m (bank) counter;
ticket office; (electric) switch
scharf [Sahrf] sharp; (food) hot, spicy
Schatten [Sahtən] m shadow
schätzen [Sehtsən] (person) to like; to
estimate (amount etc.)
schauen [Sauən] to look
Schaufenster [Sau-fehnstər] n
shop/store window
Scheibe [Saybə] f (window) pane; slice
(of bread, etc.)
Schein [Sayn] m light; (Geld~ [gehlt-
Sayn]) bank note; (An~ [ahn-Sayn])
appearance
scheinen [Saynən] to seem; to shine
schenken [Sehŋkən] to give as a
present
Schere [Seyrə] f scissors
Scherz [Sehrts] m joke
schicken [Sihkən] to send
schieben [Siibən] to push
schießen [Siisən] to shoot
Schild [Sihlt] n sign
Schilf [Sihlf] n reed(s)
schimpfen [Sihmpfən] to swear; to
grumble, to complain
Schirm [Sihrm] m umbrella
Schlaf [Slahf] m sleep
schlafen [Slahfən] to sleep
Schlafmittel [Slahf-mihtəl] n sleeping
pill
Schlafwagen [Slahf-vahgən] m sleeper,
sleeping car
Schlafzimmer [Slahf-tsihmər] n bed-
room
Schlag [Slahk] m blow; **Schlaganfall**
[Slahk-ahn-fahl] m stroke

schlagen [Slahgən] to hit, beat; (clock)
to strike
Schlamm [Slahm] m mud
Schlange [Slahŋə] f snake; **Schlange
stehen** [Slahŋə Steyən] to stand in line
schlank [Slahŋk] slim, slender
schlau [Slau] clever
Schlauch [Slaux] m tube
schlecht [Slehçt] bad(ly)
schließen [Sliisən] to shut, to close
schlimm [Slihm] bad; **schlimmer**
[Slihmər] worse; **am schlimmsten**
[ahm Slihmstən] worst
Schloss [Slos] n castle; (door) lock
Schluck [Sluhk] m sip
Schluss [Sluhs] m end; conclusion
schmal [Smahl] narrow; slim, thin
schmecken (nach) [Smehkən (nahx)] to
taste (of/like)
schmerzen [Smehrtsən] to hurt
schmerzhaft [Smehrts-hahft] painful
schminken, s. [Smihŋkən] to put on
make-up
schmuggeln [Smuhgəln] to smuggle
Schmutz [Smuhts] m dirt; mud
schmutzig [Smuht-sihç] dirty
schnarchen [Snahrçən] to snore
schneiden [Snaydən] to cut
schneien [Snayən] to snow
schnell [Snehl] quick(ly), fast
Schnellimbiss [Snehl-ihm-bihs] m
snack bar
Schnur [Snoor] f string; (electricity) cord
Schnürsenkel [Snewr-zehŋkəl] m
shoelace
schon [Sohn] already
schön [Sœn] beautiful(ly)
Schönheit [Sœn-hayt] f beauty
Schotte [Sotə] m Scotsman
Schottin [So-tihn] f Scotswoman
schottisch [So-tihS] Scottish
Schottland [Sot-lahnt] Scotland
schrecklich [Srehk-lihç] terrible, terri-
bly, awful(ly), dreadful(ly)
schreiben [Sraybən] to write
schreien [Srayən] to shout; to scream
Schrift [Srihft] f (Hand~) (hand)writing
schriftlich [Srihft-lihç] in writing
Schritt [Sriht] m step
schüchtern [Sewçtərn] shy
Schuh [Sooə] m shoe
Schuld [Suhlt] f guilt; **es ist meine ~**
[ehs ihst maynə Suhlt] it's my fault

schulden [Suhldən] to owe
Schulden [Suhldən] f pl debts
Schule [Soolə] f school
Schuss [Suhs] m shot
Schutz [Suhts] m protection
schwach [Svahx] weak, feeble
Schwäche [Svehçə] f weakness
Schwager [Svahgər] m brother-in-law
Schwägerin [Sveygə-rihn] f sister-in-law
schwanger [Svahŋər] pregnant
Schweigen [Svaygən] n silence
schweigen [Svaygən] to be silent, to keep quiet; **schweigend** [Svaygənt] silent(ly)
Schweiz [Svayts] f Switzerland
Schweizer/in [Svaytsər / -ihn] Swiss (man/woman)
schwer [Svehr] heavy; (illness) serious; difficult
Schwester [Svehstər] f sister; (Kranken~ [krahŋkən-Svehstər]) nurse; (Ordens~ [ordəns-Svehstər]) nun
schwierig [Svii-rihç] difficult
Schwierigkeit [Svii-rihç-kayt] f difficulty
schwimmen [Svihmən] to swim
schwindeln [Svihndəln] (lügen) to tell fibs; to cheat
Schwindler [Svihndlər] m swindler
schwindlig [Svihnt-lihç] dizzy, giddy
schwitzen [Svihtsən] to perspire, to sweat
See [zey] f sea; **See** [zey] m lake; **Seereise** [zey-rayzə] f voyage, cruise
Seeigel [zey-iigəl] m sea urchin
sehen [zeyən] to see
sehr [zehr] very; very much
Seil [zayl] n rope
sein [zayn] (v) to be (**bin** [bihn] **bist** [bihst] **ist** [ihst] **seid** [zayt] **sind** [zihnt])
sein [zayn] (poss pron) m his; n its
seit [zayt] since; for; **seitdem** [zayt-dehm] since then; **seit wann?** [zayt vahn] since when?
Seite [zaytə] f side; page
Sekunde [zeh-kuhndə] f second
selbst: ich habe es ~ gemacht [ihç hahbə ehs zehlpst gəmahxt] I did it myself; **~ wenn** [zehlpst vehn] even if
Selbstbedienung [zehlpst-bədii-nuhŋ] f self-service
selten [zehltən] rare; seldom

senden [zehndən] to send; to broadcast
Sendung [zehn-duhŋ] f (radio, television) program
servieren [zehr-viirən] to serve
setzen [zehtsən] to put; **s. setzen** to sit down
Sex [zehks] m sex
sicher [zihçər] safe; sure, certain(ly)
Sicherheit [zihçər-hayt] f safety; security; **Sicherheitsnadel** [zihçər-hayts-nahdəl] f safety pin
Sicherung [zihçə-ruhŋ] f (electricity) fuse
Sicht [zihçt] f visibility; (Aus~ [aus-zihçt]) view
sichtbar [sihçt-bahr] visible
sie [zii] she; **Sie** you; they
Signal [zihg-nahl] n signal
singen [zihŋən] to sing
Sinn [zihn] m sense
Sitz [zihts] m seat; (Wohn~ [vohn-zihts]) (place of) residence; headquarters
sitzen [zihtsən] to sit
so [zoh] so, thus
sofort [zoh-fort] at once, immediately
sogar [zoh-gahr] even
Sohn [zohn] m son
solange [zoh-lahŋə] as long as
solch [zolç] such
sollen [zolən] to have to; **Sie sollten** [zii zoltən] you ought to, you should
Sonder- [zondər-] special
sondern [zondərn] but
Sonne [zonə] f sun; **bei Sonnenaufgang** [bay zonən-auf-gahŋ] at sunrise; **bei Sonnenuntergang** [bay zonən-uhntər-gahŋ] at sunset
Sonnenbrille [zonən-brihlə] f sunglasses
sonnig [zo-nihç] sunny
sonst [zonst] else; otherwise
Sorge [zorgə] f care; worry
sorgen für [zorgən fewr] to look after; **s. sorgen um** [zorgən uhm] to be worried about
Sorgfalt [zork-fahlt] f care
sorgfältig [zork-fehl-tihç] careful
Sorte [zortə] f sort, kind; (cigarette) brand
sparen [Spahrən] to save
Spaß [Spahs] m joke; fun
spät [Speyt] late

später [Speytər] later
spazieren gehen [Spaht-siirən geyən] to go for a walk
Spaziergang [Spaht-siir-gahŋ] *m* walk, stroll; **einen Spaziergang machen** [aynən Spaht-siir-gahŋ mahxən] to go for a walk
Sperre [Spehrə] *f* barrier
Spesen [Speyzən] *pl* expenses
speziell [Speht-syehl] special
spielen [Spiilən] to play
Spielzeug [Spiil-tsoyk] *n* toy
Spiritus [Spii-rih-tuhs] *m (Brenn~* [brehn-Spii-rih-tuhs]*)* denatured alcohol; **Spirituskocher** [Spii-rih-tuhs-koxər] *m* spirit stove
spitz [Spihts] pointed; sharp
Spitze [Spihtsə] *f* point; summit, top; lace
Sport [Sport] *m* sport; **Sportplatz** [Sport-plahts] *m* sports field, athletic field
Sprache [Sprahxə] *f* language
sprechen [Sprehçə] to speak
springen [Sprihŋən] to jump
Spur [Spoor] *f* trace
Staat [Staht] *m* state
Stadt [Staht] *f* city, town; **Stadtplan** [Staht-plahn] *m* city map; **Stadtteil** [Staht-tayl] *m* district
stammen [Stahmən (aus, fon)] *(aus, von)* to come from
Stange [Stahŋə] *f* carton (of 200 cigarettes)
stark [Stahrk] strong; thick; *(pain)* severe
Stärke [Stehrkə] *f* strength
starten [Startən] to start; *(plane)* to take off
statt [Staht] instead of
stattfinden [Staht-fihndən] to take place
Staub [Staup] *m* dust
stechen [Stehçən] to sting
Stecknadel [Stehk-nahdəl] *f* pin
Steg [Steyk] *m (Landungs~* [lahn-duhŋs-Steyk]*)* landing stage, dock
stehen [Steyən] to stand
stehen bleiben [Steyən blaybən] to stop
stehlen [Steylən] to steal
steigen [Staygən] to climb
steil [Stayl] steep
Stein [Stayn] *m* stone
steinig [Stay-nihç] stony

Stelle [Stehlə] *f* spot, place; job
stellen [Stehlən] to put
Stellung [Steh-luhŋ] *f* position; job
Stempel [Stehmpəl] *m* stamp
sterben [Stehrbən] to die
Stern [Stehrn] *m* star
stets [Stehts] always
still [Stihl] quiet, silent; still, calm
Stimme [Stihmə] *f* voice; vote
stimmen [Stihmən] to be right/true; to vote
stinken [Stihŋkən] to smell, to stink
Stock [Stok] *m* stick; **im dritten ~** [ihm drihtən Stok] on the third floor
Stockwerk [Stok-vehrk] *n* floor, story
Stoff [Stof] *m* material
stören [Stœrən] to disturb, to bother
Störung [Stœ-ruhŋ] *f* disturbance; interruption
Stoß [Stohs] *m* push, shove
stoßen [Stohsən] to push
Strafe [Strahfə] *f* punishment; *(Geld~* [gehlt-Strahfə]*)* fine
Strahl [Strahl] *m* beam, ray; *(water)* jet
Strand [Strahnt] *m* beach
Straße [Strahsə] *f* street; *(Land~* [lahnt-Strahsə]*)* road
Strauß [Straus] *m* bunch of flowers
Strecke [Strehkə] *f* distance; *(railroad)* line; road, route
Streichholz [Strayç-hohlts] *n* match; **Streichholzschachtel** [Strayç-hohlts-Sahxtəl] *f* matchbox
Streit [Strayt] *m* quarrel, argument
streiten [Straytən] to argue, to quarrel
streng [Strehŋ] strict, severe
Strom [Strom] *m* (large) river; *(electricity)* current
Strömung [Strœ-muhŋ] *f* current
Stück [Stewk] *n* piece; *(Theater~* [tey-ahtər-Stewk]*)* play
studieren [Stoo-diirən] to study
Stuhl [Stool] *m* chair
Stunde [Stuhndə] *f* hour; **eine halbe Stunde** [aynə hahlbə Stuhndə] half an hour; **eine Viertelstunde** [aynə fiirtəl-Stuhndə] a quarter of an hour; *(Unterrichts~* [uhntər-rihçts-Stuhndə]*)* lesson
Sturm [Stuhrm] *m* storm
Sturz [Stuhrts] *m* fall
stürzen [Stewrtsən] to fall
suchen [zooxən] to look for

Süden [zewdən] *m* south

südlich [zewd-lihç] southern; **südlich von** south of

Summe [zuhmə] *f* sum; amount

Sumpf [zuhmpf] *m* marsh; swamp

süß [zews] sweet

Swimmingpool [Svih-mihŋ-pool] ("pool" as in English) *m* swimming pool

sympathisch [zewm-**pah**-tihS] nice, pleasant

T

Tabak [tah-**bahk**] *m* tobacco

Tag [tahk] *m* day

tanken [tahŋkən] to fill up

Tante [tahntə] *f* aunt

Tanz [tahnts] *m* dance

Tasche [tahSə] *f* pocket; bag; *(Hand~* [hahnt-tahSə]*)* handbag, purse

Tat [taht] *f* action, act; **in der Tat** indeed

Tätigkeit [tey-tihç-kayt] *f* activity; job, work

Tatsache [taht-zahxə] *f* fact

tauschen [tauSən] to exchange, to swap; *(money)* to change

täuschen, s. [toySən] to be mistaken, to be wrong

Taxi [tahk-sii] *n* taxi, cab

Teil [tayl] *m* part

teilen [taylən] to divide; to share

teilnehmen (an) [tayl-neymən (ahn)] to take part (in)

telefonieren [teh-leh-foh-**niir**ən] to make a phone call, to phone

Teller [tehlər] *m* plate

Termin [tehr-**miin**] *m* appointment; deadline

teuer [toyər] dear, expensive

tief [tiif] deep; low

Tier [tiir] *n* animal

Tipp [tihp] *m* tip

Tisch [tihS] *m* table

Tochter [toxtər] *f* daughter

Tod [toht] *m* death

Toilette [toy-**leht**ə] *f* toilet, rest room; **Toilettenpapier** [toy-**leht**ən-pah-piir] *n* toilet paper

toll [tol] wild, mad; ~! great!

Ton [tohn] *m* sound; tone; *(color)* shade

Tonwaren [tohn-vahrən] *f pl* earthenware

Topf [topf] *m* pot

Tor [tohr] *n* gate; *(soccer)* goal

tot [toht] dead

Tour [toor] *f* tour, excursion, trip

Tourist/in [too-**rihst** / -ihn] tourist

Tracht [trahxt] *f* dress, costume

tragen [trahgən] to carry; *(clothing)* to wear

transportieren [trahn-spor-**tiir**ən] to transport

Traum [traum] *m* dream

träumen [troymən] to dream

traurig [trau-rihç] sad

treffen [trehfən] to meet

trennen [trehnən] to separate; to divide

Treppe [trehpə] *f* stairs, staircase; steps

treu [troy] loyal, faithful

trinkbar [trihŋk-bahr] drinkable

trinken [trihŋkən] to drink

trocken [trokən] dry

trocknen [troknən] to dry

Tropfen [tropfən] *m* drop

tropfen [tropfən] to drip; *(nose)* to run

trotz [trots] in spite of

trotzdem [trots-dehm] nevertheless

trüb [trewp] *(liquid)* cloudy; *(weather)* overcast, cloudy

tschüs [tSews] bye-bye

Tube [toobə] *f* tube

Tuch [toox] *n* cloth; *(Kopf~)* scarf

tüchtig [tewç-tihç] capable, efficient

tun [toon] to do

Tunnel [tuhnəl] *m* tunnel

Tür [tewr] *f* door

Tüte [tewtə] *f* bag; *(ice cream)* cone

typisch [tew-pihS] typical

U

übel [ewbəl] bad; **mir ist übel** [miir ihst ewbəl] I feel sick

üben [ewbən] to practice

über [ewbər] over

überall [ewbər-ahl] everywhere

überbringen [ewbər-**brih**ŋən] to deliver

überfallen [ewbər-**fahl**ən] to attack, to assault, to mug

überflüssig [ewbər-flew-sihç] superfluous

überfüllt [ewbər-**fewlt**] overcrowded

Übergang [ewbər-gahŋ] *m* crossing; transition

übergeben [ewbər-geybən] to hand over

überholen [ewbər-hohlən] to pass

übernachten [ewbər-nahxtən] to stay, to spend the night

übernehmen [ewbər-neymən] to take on/over

überqueren [ewbər-kvehrən] to cross

überrascht [ewbər-rahSt] surprised

überreden [ewbər-reydən] to persuade

überschreiten [ewbər-Sraytən] to cross

Übersee [ewbər-zey] overseas

übersetzen [ewbər-zehtsən] to translate

übertragbar [ewbər-trahk-bahr] transferable

übertrieben [ewbər-triibən] exaggerated

überweisen [ewbər-vayzən] to transfer

überzeugen [ewbər-tsoygən] to convince

üblich [ewb-lihç] usual

übrig [ewb-rihç] left ~ **bleiben** [ewbrihç blaybən] to be left over

übrigens [ewb-rihgəns] by the way

Übung [ew-buhŋ] *f* practice; *(sports, textbook)* exercise

Ufer [oofər] *n (river)* bank; shore

Uhr [oor] *f (Armband~*[ahrm-bahnt-oor]) watch; *(Wand~*[vahnt-oor]) clock

um [uhm] around; *(time)* at, about

umarmen [uhm-ahrmən] to hug, to embrace

umgekehrt [uhm-gəkehrt] reverse; **in umgekehrter Richtung** [ihm uhm-gəkehrtər rihç-tuhŋ] in the opposite direction

umkehren [uhm-kehrən] to turn back

Umrechnung [uhm-rehç-nuhŋ] *f* conversion, **Umrechnungskurs** *m* exchange rate

umsehen, s. [uhm-zeyən] to look around

umsonst [uhm-zonst] free *(of charge)*; in vain

Umstände [uhm-Stehndə] *m pl* circumstances; trouble

umsteigen [uhm-Staygən] to change *(trains, buses etc.)*

umtauschen [uhm-tauSən] to change

Umweg [uhm-veyk] *m* detour

Umwelt [uhm-vehlt] *f* environment

umziehen [uhm-tsiiən] to move; **s. umziehen** to change *(clothes)*

unangenehm [uhn-ahn-gəneym] unpleasant

unanständig [uhn-ahn-Stehn-dihç] rude

unbedingt [uhn-bədihŋt] really; ~ **!** certainly!, of course!

unbekannt [uhn-bəkahnt] unknown

unbequem [uhn-bəkvehm] uncomfortable

unbeständig [uhn-bəStehn-dihç] *(weather)* changeable, variable

unbestimmt [uhn-bəStihmt] indefinite

und [uhnt] and; **und so weiter** [uhnt zoh vaytər] and so forth

undankbar [uhn-dahŋk-bahr] ungrateful

unecht [uhn-ehçt] false

unentbehrlich [uhn-ehnt-behr-lihç] indispensable

unentschlossen [uhn-ehnt-Slosən] undecided

unerfahren [uhn-ehr-fahrən] inexperienced

unerfreulich [uhn-ehr-froy-lihç] unpleasant

unerträglich [uhn-ehr-trehk-lihç] intolerable, unbearable

unerwartet [uhn-ehr-vahrtət] unexpected

unerwünscht [uhn-ehr-vewnSt] unwelcome

unfähig [uhn-fey-ihç] incapable (of); incompetent

Unfall [uhn-fahl] *m* accident

unfreundlich [uhn-froynt-lihç] unkind, unfriendly

ungeeignet [uhn-gəaygnət] unsuited, unfit

ungefähr [uhn-gəfehr] about

ungemütlich [uhn-gəmewt-lihç] uncomfortable

ungenau [uhn-gənau] inexact

ungenügend [uhn-gənewgənt] insufficient

ungerecht [uhn-gərehçt] unfair, unjust

Ungerechtigkeit [uhn-gərehç-tihç-kayt] *f* injustice

ungern [uhn-gehrn] reluctantly

ungesund [uhn-gəzuhnt] unhealthy

ungewiss [uhn-gəvihs] uncertain

ungewöhnlich [uhn-gəvœn-lihç] unusual

unglaublich [uhn-glaup-lihç] incredible

Unglück [uhn-glewk] n accident; misfortune

unglücklich [uhn-glewk-lihç] unhappy; unlucky

unglücklicherweise [uhn-glewk-lihçər-vayzə] unfortunately

ungültig [uhn-gewl-tihç] invalid

ungünstig [uhn-gewns-tihç] unfavorable

unhöflich [uhn-hœf-lihç] impolite

Unkosten [uhn-kostən] pl expenses

unmittelbar [uhn-mihtəl-bahr] immediate(ly)

unmodern [uhn-moh-dehrn] old-fashioned

unmöglich [uhn-mœg-lihç] impossible

unnötig [uhn-nœ-tihç] unnecessary

unnütz [uhn-newts] useless

Unordnung [uhn-ord-nuhŋ] f disorder

unpraktisch [uhn-prahk-tihS] unpractical

Unrecht [uhn-rehçt] n injustice

Unrecht haben [uhn-rehçt hahbən] to be wrong

unregelmäßig [uhn-reygəl-meh-sihç] irregular

unruhig [uhn-roo-ihç] restless

uns [uhns] us

unschuldig [uhn-Suhl-dihç] innocent

unser, unsere [uhnzər(ə)] our

unsicher [uhn-zihçər] unsafe; uncertain

unten [uhntən] below; **dort unten** [dort uhntən] down there

unter [uhnter] under; among; **unter anderem** [uhnter ahndərəm] among other things; **unterhalb** [uhntər-hahlp] below

unterbrechen [uhntər-brehçən] to interrupt

Unterführung [uhntər-few-ruhŋ] f underpass

unterhalten, s. [uhntər-hahltən] to talk; to amuse oneself

unterhaltend [uhntər-hahltənt] amusing, entertaining

Unterhaltung [uhntər-hahl-tuhŋ] f conversation; entertainment

Unterkunft [uhntər-kuhnft] f accommodations

Unternehmen [uhntər-neymən] n firm, company, corporation

unterrichten [uhntər-rihçtən] to inform; to teach

unterscheiden [uhntər-Saydən] to distinguish; **s. unterscheiden von** [uhntər-Saydən fon] to differ from

Unterschied [uhntər-Siit] m difference

unterschreiben [uhntər-Sraybən] to sign

Unterschrift [uhntər-Srihft] f signature

Unterstützung [uhntər-Stewt-suhŋ] f support

untersuchen [uhntər-zooxən] to examine

unterwegs [uhntər-vehks] on the way

unverbindlich [uhn-fehr-bihnd-lihç] without obligation

unvermeidlich [uhn-fehr-mayd-lihç] inevitable

unverschämt [uhn-fehr-Sehmt] impertinent, cheeky, rude

unvollständig [uhn-fol-Stehn-dihç] incomplete

unvorsichtig [uhn-for-zihç-tihç] careless

unwahrscheinlich [uhn-vahr-Sayn-lihç] unlikely, improbable

unwichtig [uhn-vihç-tihç] unimportant

unwohl [uhn-vohl] unwell

unzufrieden [uhn-tsoo-friidən] dissatisfied

Urlaub [oor-laup] m holidays, vacation

Ursache [oor-zahxə] f cause; reason

Urteil [oor-tayl] n judgment; opinion

urteilen [oor-taylən] to judge

V

Vater [fahtər] m father

Vaterland [fahtər-lahnt] n native country

verabreden, s. [fehr-ahp-reydən] to arrange to meet

Verabredung [fehr-ahp-rey-duhŋ] f appointment; date

verabschieden, s. [fehr-ahp-Siidən] to say goodbye

verändern [fehr-ehndərn] to change

Veränderung [fehr-ehndə-ruhŋ] f change

veranstalten [fehr-ahn-Stahltən] to organize, to arrange

Veranstaltung [fehr-ahn-Stahl-tuhŋ] f event

verantwortlich [fehr-ahnt-vort-lihç] responsible

Verband [fehr-**bahnt**] *m (med.)* dressing, bandage

verbessern [fehr-**behs**ərn] to improve; to correct

verbieten [fehr-**biit**ən] to forbid

verbinden [fehr-**bihnd**ən] *(med.)* to dress, to bandage; *(telephone)* to connect

Verbindung [fehr-**bihn**-duhŋ] *f* connection

Verbot [fehr-**boht**] *n* ban

verboten! [fehr-**boht**ən] forbidden!, prohibited!

Verbrauch [fehr-**braux**] *m* consumption

verbrennen [fehr-**brehn**ən] to burn

verbringen [fehr-**brih**ŋən] *(time)* to spend

Verdacht [fehr-**dahxt**] *m* suspicion

verderben [fehr-**dehr**bən] to spoil; to go bad

verdienen [fehr-**diin**ən] to earn; to deserve

Verdienst [fehr-**diinst**], *m* earnings; *n* merit, **es ist ihr ~** [ehs ihst iir fehr-**diinst**] it's thanks to her

verdorben [fehr-**dorb**ən] spoiled; rotten; corrupt

Verein [fehr-**ayn**] *m* association, club

vereinbaren [fehr-**ayn**-bahrən] to agree on

Verfassung [fehr-**fah**-suhŋ] *f (Staats~* [Stahts-fehr-fah-suhŋ]*)* constitution; *(condition)* state

verfehlen [fehr-**feyl**ən] to miss

Vergangenheit [fehr-**gahŋ**ən-hayt] *f* past

vergehen [fehr-**gey**ən] (time) to pass

vergessen [fehr-**gehs**ən] to forget

vergewaltigen [fehr-gə-**vahl**-tihgən] to rape

Vergleich [fehr-**glayç**] *m* comparison

vergleichen [fehr-**glayç**ən] to compare

Vergnügen [fehr-**gnew**gən] *n* pleasure

Verhandlung [fehr-**hahnt**-luhŋ] *f* negotiations; *(Straf~* [Strahf-fehr-hahnt-luhŋ]*)* trial

verheimlichen [fehr-**haym**-lihçən] to conceal, to keep secret

verheiratet (mit) [fehr-**hay**-rahtət (miht)] married (to)

verhindern [fehr-**hihnd**ərn] to prevent

Verhütungsmittel [fehr-**hew**-tuhŋs-mihtəl] *n* contraceptive

verirren, s. [fehr-**iir**ən] to lose one's way, to get lost

Verkauf [fehr-**kauf**] *m* sale

verkaufen [fehr-**kauf**ən] to sell

Verkehr [fehr-**kehr**] *m* traffic

verkehren [fehr-**kehr**ən] *(bus, train, etc.)* to run

Verkehrsbüro [fehr-**kehrs**-bew-roh] *n* tourist information office

verlangen [fehr-**lahŋ**ən] to ask for; to demand

verlängern [fehr-**lehŋ**ərn] to extend

verlassen [fehr-**lahs**ən] to leave

Verletzte [fehr-**lehts**tə] *m/f* injured person

verlieren [fehr-**liir**ən] to lose

verloben: s. ~ mit [fehr-**lohb**ən miht] to get engaged to

Verlobte [fehr-**lohp**tə] *m/f* fiancé/fiancée

Verlust [fehr-**luhst**] *m* loss

vermeiden [fehr-**mayd**ən] to avoid

vermieten [fehr-**miit**ən] to rent

Vermittler [fehr-**miht**lər] *m* agent

vermuten [fehr-**moot**ən] to suppose, to assume

Vermutung [fehr-**moo**-tuhŋ] *f* guess, assumption

vernachlässigen [fehr-**nahx**-leh-sihgən] to neglect

vernünftig [fehr-**newnf**-tihç] reasonable, sensible

verpacken [fehr-**pahk**ən] to wrap, to pack

Verpackung [fehr-**pah**-kuhŋ] *f* wrapping, packing

Verpflegung [fehr-**pfley**-guhŋ] *f* food

verpflichtet sein [fehr-**pflihç**tət] to be obliged to

Verpflichtung [fehr-**pflihç**-tuhŋ] *f* obligation

verrechnen, s. [fehr-**rehç**nən] to miscalculate, to make a mistake

verreisen [fehr-**rayz**ən] to go on a journey/trip

verrückt [fehr-**rewkt**] mad, crazy

versäumen [fehr-**zoym**ən] to miss *(deadline, etc.)*

verschaffen [fehr-**Sahf**ən] to get hold of, to obtain

verschieben [fehr-**Siib**ən] to put off, to postpone

verschieden [fehr-**Siid**ən] different

verschließen [fehr-**Slii**sən] to lock
Verschluss [fehr-**Sluhs**] *m* lock
verschwinden [fehr-**Svihn**dən] to disappear
Versehen, aus ~ [aus fehr-**zey**ən] by mistake
versenden [fehr-**zehn**dən] to dispatch
versichern [fehr-**zih**çərn] to assure; to insure
Versicherung [fehr-**zih**çə-ruhŋ] *f* insurance
versorgen mit [fehr-**zorg**ən miht] to provide with
verspäten, s. [fehr-**Spey**tən] to be late
Versprechen [fehr-**Spreh**çən] *n* promise
versprechen [fehr-**Spreh**çən] to promise
Verstand [fehr-**Staht**] *m* brains, intelligence; reason
verständigen [fehr-**Stehn**-dihgən]: **jdn ~** to inform s. o.; **s. verständigen** to come to an understanding
verstecken [fehr-**Stehk**ən] to hide
verstehen [fehr-**Stey**ən] to understand
verstopft [fehr-**Stopft**] stopped (up), plugged (up)
Versuch [fehr-**zoox**] *m* attempt
versuchen [fehr-**zoox**ən] to try; to taste
vertauschen [fehr-**tau**Sən] to mistake for; to mix up
verteidigen [fehr-**tay**-dihgən] to defend
verteilen [fehr-**tay**lən] to distribute
Verteilung [fehr-**tay**-luhŋ] *f* distribution
Vertrag [fehr-**trahk**] *m* contract
vertragen [fehr-**trahg**ən] to tolerate; to endure
Vertrauen [fehr-**trau**ən] *n* confidence
vertrauen [fehr-**trau**ən] to trust
vertrauensvoll [fehr-**trau**əns-fol] confident
verunglücken [fehr-**uhn**-glewkən] to have an accident
verursachen [fehr-**oor**-zahxən] to cause
Verwaltung [fehr-**vahl**-tuhŋ] *f* administration
verwandt [fehr-**vahnt**] related
verwechseln [fehr-**vehk**səln] to mistake for
verwenden [fehr-**vehn**dən] to employ, to use
Verwendung [fehr-**vehn**-duhŋ] *f* use
verwirklichen [fehr-**vihrk**-lihçən] to realize, to fulfill

Verzeichnis [fehr-**tsayç**-nihs] *n* list, directory
verzeihen [fehr-**tsay**ən] to forgive
verzögern [fehr-**zœg**ərn] to delay
verzollen [fehr-**tsol**ən] to pay duty on
verzweifelt [fehr-**tsvay**fəlt] desperate
viel [fiil] a lot of; much
vielleicht [fih-**layçt**] perhaps, maybe
vielmehr [fiil-**mehr**] rather
viereckig [fiir-eh-kihç] square
Viertel, ein [ayn fiirtəl] a quarter
Vogel [fohgəl] *m* bird
Volk [folk] *n* people
voll [fol] full; crowded
vollenden [fol-**ehn**dən] to complete
vollkommen [fol-**kom**ən] perfect
Vollmacht [fol-mahxt] *f* power of attorney
vollständig [fol-Stehn-dihç] complete
von [fon] from; of; by
vor [for] in front of; before; **vor allem** [for ahləm]] above all
Voraus, im ~ [ihm for-aus] in advance
vorbei [for-**bay**] past, over
vorbeigehen [for-**bay**-geyən] to pass
vorbeikommen [for-**bay**-komən] to call in, to visit, to stop by
vorbereiten [for-bəraytən] to prepare
vorbestellen [for-bəStehlən] to order in advance, to reserve
Vorfahrt [for-fahrt] *f* right of way
Vorfall [for-fahl] *m* occurrence; incident
vorgehen [for-geyən] to happen; *(clock)* to be fast
Vorhang [for-hahŋ] *m* curtain
vorher [for-hehr] before
vorläufig [for-loy-fihç] temporary; for the time being
vorletzte(r, -s) [for-lehtstə(r,s)] last but one, next to the last
Vormittag [for-mih-tahk] *m* morning; **vormittags** [for-mih-tahks] in the morning
vorn [forn] in front
vornehm [for-neym] distinguished, noble
Vorort [for-ort], **Vorstadt** [for-Staht] suburb
Vorrat [for-raht] *m* stock, store, provisions
Vorschlag [for-Slahk] *m* suggestion
vorschlagen [for-Slahgən] to suggest
Vorschrift [for-Srihft] *f* rule

A/Z

Vorsicht [for-zihçt] *f* caution; ~! look out!
vorsichtig [for-zihç-tihç] careful, cautious
vorstellen [for-Stehlən] to introduce; **sich etw. vorstellen** to imagine s. th.
Vorstellung [for-Steh-luhŋ] *f* introduction; notion, idea; *(theater)* performance
Vorteil [for-tayl] *m* advantage
vorteilhaft [for-tayl-hahft] advantageous
vorüber [for-**ewbər**] past, over; gone
vorübergehen [for-**ewbər**-geyən] to pass
vorübergehend [for-**ewbər**-geyənt] temporary
Vorwand [for-vahnt] *m* pretext
vorwärts [for-vehrts] forward(s)
vorzeigen [for-tsaygən] to show
vorziehen [for-tsiiən] to prefer
Vorzug [for-tsuhk] *m* preference; advantage

W

Waage [vahgə] *f* scales
wach [vahx] awake
wachsen [vahksən] to grow
wagen [vahgən] to dare
Wagen [vahgən] *m* car; carriage, coach
Wahl [vahl] *f* choice; election
wählen [veylən] to choose; to vote; *(telephone)* to dial
wahr [vahr] true
während [vehrənt] during; while
Wahrheit [vahr-hayt] *f* truth
wahrscheinlich [vahr-**Sayn**-lihç] probable; probably
Wahrscheinlichkeit [vahr-**Sayn**-lihç-kayt] *f* probability
Wales [vahləs] Wales
Waliser/in [vah-**liiz**ər / -ihn] Welshman/Welshwoman
walisisch [vah-**lii**-zihS] Welsh
Wand [vahnt] *f* wall
wann? [vahn] when?
wandern [vahndərn] to hike
Ware [vahrə] *f* product **Waren** [vahrən] *f pl* goods; **Warenhaus** [vahrən-haus] *n* department store
warm [vahrm] warm
Wärme [vehrmə] *f* heat

wärmen [vehrmən] to warm, to heat
warnen (vor) [vahrnən (for)] to warn (of/about)
warten (auf) [vahrtən (auf)] to wait (for)
warum? [vah-**ruhm**] why?
was [vahs] what; **was für ein/eine …?** [vahs fewr ayn(ə)] what kind of …?
Wäsche [vehSə] *f (Bett~* [beht-vehSə]*)* linen, bedclothes; *(Unter~* [uhntər-vehSə]*)* underwear; (dirty) laundry
waschen [vahSən] to wash
Wasser [vahsər] *n* water
Watt [vaht] *n (electricity)* watt; mud flats
Wechsel [vehksəl] *m* change; exchange
Wechselgeld [vehksəl-gehlt] *n (money)* change
wechseln [veksəln] *(money)* to change
wecken [vehkən] to wake
Wecker [vehkər] *m* alarm clock
weder … noch [veydər … nox] neither … nor
weg [vehk] away; gone
Weg [veyk] *m* way; path; road
wegen [veygən] because of
weggehen [vehk-geyən] to go away, to leave
wegnehmen [vehk-neymən] to take away
wegschicken [vehk-Sihkən] to send off/away
weiblich [vayp-lihç] female; feminine
weich [vayç] soft
weigern, s. [vaygərn] to refuse
weil [vayl] because, since
Weinberg [vayn-behrk] *m* vineyard
weinen [vaynən] to cry
Weise [vayzə] *f* manner, way
weit [vayt] wide; (distance) long; far
Welt [vehlt] *f* world
wenden [vehndən] to turn; **s. an jdn wenden** to see s. o.
wenig [vey-nihç] little, few; **ein wenig** a little; **ein wenig von …** a bit of …; **weniger** [vey-nihgər] less, fewer; **das wenigste** [dahs vey-nihkstə] the least, the fewest
wenigstens [vey-nihkstəns] at least
wenn [vehn] if; when
wer? [vehr] who?
werden [vehrdən] to become
werfen [vehrfən] to throw

werktags [vehrk-tahks] on weekdays
Wert [vehrt] *m* value
wert: viel ~ sein [fiil vehrt] to be worth a lot
wertlos [vehrt-lohs] worthless
Wertsachen [vehrt-zahxən] *f pl* valuables
Wespe [vehspə] *f* wasp
westlich [vehst-lihç] western
Wettbewerb [veht-bəvehrp] *m* competition
Wette [vehtə] *f* bet
wetten [vehtən] to bet
Wetter [vehtər] *n* weather
wichtig [vihç-tihç] important
wie [vii] how?; *(comparison)* like
wieder [viidər] again
wiederbekommen [viidər-bəkomən] to get back
wiedergeben [viidər-geybən] to give back, to return
wiederholen [viidər-**hohl**ən] to repeat
wiederkommen [viidər-komən] to come back, to return
wieder sehen [viidər zeyən] to see again; to meet again
wiegen [viigən] to weigh
Wiese [vayzə] *f* meadow
Wild [vihlt] *n* game; *(Rot~* [roht-vihlt]*)* deer; venison
wild [vihlt] wild(ly)
willkommen [vihl-**kom**ən] welcome
windig [vihn-dihç] windy
Winkel [vihŋkəl] *m* corner
winken [vihŋkən] to wave
wir [viir] we
wirklich [vihrk-lihç] real; true; really
Wirklichkeit [vihrk-lihç-kayt] *f* reality
wirksam [vihrk-zahm] effective
Wirkung [vihr-kuhŋ] *f* effect
Wirt [vihrt] *m* landlord
Wirtin [vihr-tihn] *f* landlady
Wissen [vihsən] *n* knowledge, **wissen** to know
Witz [vihts] *m* joke
wo? [voh] where?
Woche [voxə] *f* week; **in einer Woche** [ihn aynər voxə] in a week
wochentags [voxən-tahks] on weekdays
wöchentlich [vœçənt-lihç] weekly; once a week
wohl [vohl] (adv) well
Wohl [vohl] *n* well-being; **Wohlbefinden** [vohl-bəfihndən] *n* good health

wohlhabend [vohl-hahbənt] wealthy, well-off
wohlwollend [vohl-volənt] kind
wohnen [vohnən] to live, to stay
Wohnort [vohn-ort], **Wohnsitz** [vohn-zihts] (place of) residence
Wohnung [voh-nuhŋ] *f* apartment; **möblierte Wohnung** [mœb-liirtə voh-nuhŋ] furnished apartment
Wolkenkratzer [volkən-krahtsər] *m* skyscraper
wollen [volən] to want, to wish
Wort [vort] *n* word
wunderbar [vuhndər-bahr] wonderful, marvelous
wundern [vuhndərn (ewbər)]: **s. ~ (über)** to be surprised (at/about)
Wunsch [vuhnS] *m* wish; request
wünschen [vewnSən] to want; to wish for
Wurf [vuhrf] *m* throw
Würfel [vewrfəl] *m* cube; *(Spiel~)* dice
Wurm [vuhrm] *m* worm
Wut [voot] *f* rage
wütend [vewtənt] furious

Z

Zahl [tsahl] *f* number, figure
zahlen [tsahlən] to pay
zählen [tseylən] to count
zahlreich [tsahl-rayç] numerous
Zahlung [tsah-luhŋ] *f* payment
Zange [tsahŋə] *f* tongs
zanken, s. [tsahŋkən] to quarrel
zart [tsahrt] tender; sensitive
zärtlich [tsehrt-lihç] tender, gentle
Zeichen [tsayçən] *n* sign
zeichnen [tsayçnən] to draw
zeigen [tsaygən] to show
Zeit [tsayt] *f* time; **von Zeit zu Zeit** [fon tsayt tsoo tsayt] from time to time; **zur Zeit** [tsuhr tsayt] now, at present
Zeit lang: eine ~ [aynə lahŋə tsayt] for a while
Zeitung [tsay-tuhŋ] *f* newspaper; **Zeitungshändler** [tsay-tuhŋs-hehndlər] *m* news dealer; **Zeitungskiosk** [tsay-tuhŋs-kii-osk] *m* newsstand
zentral [tsehn-**trahl**] central
Zentrum [tsehn-truhm] *n* center; downtown

zerbrechen [tsehr-**brehç**ən] to break, to smash

zerbrechlich [tsehr-**brehç**-lihç] fragile

zerreißen [tsehr-**rays**ən] to tear

zerstören [tsehr-**Stœr**ən] to destroy

Zeuge [tsoygə] *m* witness

Zeugnis [tsoyg-nihs] *n* reference; *(school)* report card; certificate

ziehen [tsiiən] to pull

Ziel [tsiil] *n* aim; *(Reise~* [rayzə-tsiil]*)* destination

ziemlich [tsiim-lihç] fairly, rather, pretty

Zigarette [tsih-gah-**reht**ə] *f* cigarette

Zigarillo [tsih-gah-**rih**-loh] *m/n* cigarillo

Zigarre [tsih-**gah**rə] *f* cigar

zögern [tsœgərn] to hesitate

Zoll [tsol] *m* duty; **Zollamt** [tsol-ahmt] *n* customs office; **Zollbeamter** [tsol-bəahmtər] *m* customs official

zornig [tsor-nihç] angry

zu [tsoo] to; shut, closed; **zu sehr** [tsoo zehr], **zu viel** [tsoo fiil] too much

zubereiten [tsoo-bəraytən] to prepare; *(drinks)* to mix; *(food)* to cook

zudecken [tsoo-dehkən] to cover

zuerst [tsoo-**ehrst**] (at) first

Zufall [tsoo-fahl] *m* chance, coincidence

zufällig [tsoo-feh-lihç] by chance

zufrieden [tsoo-**friid**ən] satisfied

Zugang [tsoo-gahŋ] *m* entrance

zugreifen [tsoo-grayfən] to grab; **greifen Sie zu!** [grayfən zii tsoo] help yourself!

zu Gunsten [tsoo guhnstən] in favor of

zuhören [tsoo-hœrən] to listen

Zukunft [tsoo-kuhnft] *f* future

zukünftig [tsoo-kewnf-tihç] *(adj)* future

zulassen [tsoo-lahsən] to permit; *(car)* to license, to register

zulässig [tsoo-leh-sihç] permitted, allowed

zuletzt [tsoo-**lehtst**] finally; last

zumachen [tsoo-mahxən] to close, to shut

zunächst [tsoo-**nehkst**] first (of all)

zunehmen [tsoo-neymən] to increase; to gain weight

zurück [tsuh-**rewk**] back

zurückbringen [tsuh-**rewk**-briŋən] to bring back

zurückfahren [tsuh-**rewk**-fahrən] to return; to drive back

zurückgeben [tsuh-**rewk**-geybən] to give back

zurückkehren [tsuh-**rewk**-kehrən] to come back

zurücklassen [tsuh-**rewk**-lahsən] to leave (behind)

zurückweisen [tsuh-**rewk**-vayzən] to reject; to refuse

zurückzahlen [tsuh-**rewk**-tsahlən] to pay back, to refund

zurückziehen, s. [tsuh-**rewk**-tsiiən] to retire, to withdraw

zusagen [tsoo-zahgən] *(invitation)* to accept

zusammen [tsuh-**zahm**ən] together

zusammenrechnen [tsuh-**zahm**-rehçnən] to add up

Zusammenstoß [tsuh-**zahm**-ən-Stos] *m* collision, crash

zusätzlich [tsoo-zehts-lihç] additional; in addition

zuschauen [tsoo-Sauən] to watch

Zuschauer [tsoo-Sauər] *m* spectator; *(Fernseh~* [fehrn-zey-tsoo-Sauər]*)* television viewer

zuschließen [tsoo-Sliisən] to lock (up)

Zustand [tsoo-Stahnt] *m* state, condition

zuständig [tsoo-Stehn-dihç] responsible

zusteigen [tsoo-Staygən] to get on

zustimmen [tsoo-Stihmən] to agree (to)

zuverlässig [tsoo-fehr-leh-sihç] reliable

zu viel [tsoo fiil] too much; **zu viele** [tsoo fiilə] too many

Zwang [tsvahŋ] *m* compulsion, obligation

Zweck [tsvehk] *m* purpose

zwecklos [tsvehk-lohs] useless, pointless

zweckmäßig [tsvehk-meh-sihç] suitable; useful

Zweifel [tsvayfəl] *m* doubt; **ohne Zweifel** [ohnə tsvayfəl] doubtless

zweifelhaft [tsvayfəl-hahft] doubtful

zweifellos [tsvayfəl-lohs] without doubt, doubtless

zweifeln an etw [tsvayfəln ahn] to doubt s. th.

zweite(r, -s) [tsvaytə(r,s)] second

zweitens [tsvaytəns] second(ly)

zwingen [tsviŋən] to force, to compel

zwischen [tsvihSən] between; among

Zwischenfall [tsvihSən-fahl] *m* incident